THE **COMPLETE WORKS** OF **SWAMI VIVEKANANDA**

VOLUME V

Discovery Publisher

2019, Discovery Publisher

No part of this book may be reproduced in any form or by any electronic or mechanical means including information storage and retrieval systems, without permission in writing from the publisher.

Author: Swami Vivekananda

616 Corporate Way, Suite 2-4933
Valley Cottage, New York, 10989
www.discoverypublisher.com
edition@discoverypublisher.com
facebook.com/discoverypublisher
twitter.com/discoverypb

New York • Paris • Dublin • Tokyo • Hong Kong

TABLE OF CONTENTS

Epistles - First Series   3

1 — FAKIR	4
2 — PANDITJI MAHARAJ	4
3 — ALASINGA	5
4 — ALASINGA	7
5 — ALASINGA	11
6 — HARIPADA	13
7 — FRIENDS	14
8 — ALASINGA	15
9 — SHARAT	16
10 — ALASINGA	17
11 — ALASINGA	18
12 — SISTER	19
13 — ALASINGA	20
14 — ALASINGA	21
15 — KIDI	22
16 — SISTER	22
17 — ALASINGA	22
18 — ALASINGA	23
19 — VEHEMIA	23
20 — SISTER	23
21 — BLESSED AND BELOVED	24
22 — ALASINGA	25
23 — KIDI	26
24 — BLESSED AND BELOVED	26
25 — ALASINGA	27
26 — DHARMAPALA	28
27 — ALASINGA	28
28 — MRS. BULL	29
29 — G. G.	30
30 — ALASINGA	31
31 — MRS. OLE BULL	32
32 — SISTER	33
33 — ALASINGA	34
34 — SISTER	35
35 — ALASINGA	35
36 — SISTER	35
37 — ALASINGA	36
38 — S___	36
39 — ALASINGA	37
40 — ALASINGA	39

41 — FRIEND	39	66 — NANJUNDA RAO	52
42 — KIDI	39	67 — ALASINGA	52
43 — ALASINGA	39	68 — ALASINGA	53
44 — MRS. WILLIAM STURGES	40	69 — ALASINGA	54
45 — MOTHER	41	70 — INDIAN MIRROR	55
46 — FRIEND	41	71 — ALASINGA	55
47 — MAHARAJA OF KHETRI	42	72 — ALASINGA	56
48 — FRIEND	42	73 — MADAM	56
49 — ALASINGA	42	74 — HONOURED MADAM	57
50 — MRS. BULL	43	75 — DOCTOR SHASHI	58
51 — FRIEND	43	76 — MR. ——	59
52 — ALASINGA	44	77 — SARAT CHANDRA	59
53 — ALASINGA	44	78 — SISTER	60
54 — ALASINGA	44	79 — MOTHER	62
55 — ALASINGA	45	80 — JOE	63
56 — SISTER	45	81 — JAGMOHANLAL	63
57 — BLESSED AND BELOVED	46	82 — M.	63
58 — ALASINGA	48	83 — YOUR HIGHNESS	63
59 — ALASINGA	48	84 — YOUR HIGHNESS	64
60 — ALASINGA	49	85 — YOUR HIGHNESS	64
61 — DR. NANJUNDA RAO	49	86 — YOUR HIGHNESS	64
62 — DR. NANJUNDA RAO	49	87 — YOUR HIGHNESS	65
63 — ALASINGA	50	88 — YOUR HIGHNESS	65
64 — ALASINGA	50	89 — MOTHER	65
65 — BLESSED AND BELOVED	51	90 — JOE	67

91 — FRIEND	67	116 — SISTER NIVEDITA	79
92 — ——	68	117 — RAKHAL	79
93 — SHASHI	68	118 — RAKHAL	79
94 — MOTHER	68	119 — RAKHAL	80
95 — STURDY	69	120 — BRAHMANANDA	80
96 — MOTHER	69	121 — JOE	81
97 — SHASHI	70	122 — JOE	81
98 — MOTHER	70	123 — DHIRA MATA	81
99 — JOE	70		
100 — JOE	71		
101 — MOTHER	71		
102 — SWARUP	72		
103 — MARY	72		
104 — SHASHI	72		
105 — JOE	73		
106 — JOE	74		
107 — JOE	74		
108 — MARY	74		
109 — CHRISTINE	75		
110 — MARY	75		
111 — BLESSED AND BELOVED	76		
112 — BLESSED AND BELOVED	76		
113 — JOE	77		
114 — SWARUP	77		
115 — MRS. OLE BULL	78		

Interviews — 83

MIRACLES — 84
The Memphis Commercial, 15th January, 1894

AN INDIAN YOGI IN LONDON — 85
The Westminster Gazette, 23rd October, 1895

INDIA'S MISSION — 86
Sunday Times, London, 1896

INDIA AND ENGLAND — 89
India, London, 1896

INDIAN MISSIONARY'S MISSION TO ENGLAND — 92
The Echo, London, 1896

WITH THE SWAMI VIVEKANANDA AT MADURA — 93
The Hindu, Madras, February, 1897

THE ABROAD AND THE PROBLEMS AT HOME — 95
The Hindu, Madras, February, 1897

THE MISSIONARY WORK OF THE FIRST HINDU SANNYASIN TO THE WEST AND HIS PLAN OF REGENERATION OF INDIA — 99
Madras Times, February, 1897

REAWAKENING OF HINDUISM ON A NATIONAL BASIS — 102
Prabuddha Bharata, September, 1898

ON INDIAN WOMEN — THEIR PAST, PRESENT AND FUTURE — 103
Prabuddha Bharata, December, 1898

ON THE BOUNDS OF HINDUISM — 105
Prabuddha Bharata, April, 1899

Notes from Lectures and Discourses — 107

- ON KARMA-YOGA — 108
- ON FANATICISM — 109
- WORK IS WORSHIP — 110
- WORK WITHOUT MOTIVE — 111
- SADHANAS OR PREPARATIONS FOR HIGHER LIFE — 112
- THE COSMOS AND THE SELF — 114
- WHO IS A REAL GURU? — 115
- ON ART — 116
- ON LANGUAGE — 116
- THE SANNYASIN — 116
- THE SANNYASIN AND THE HOUSEHOLDER — 117
- THE EVILS OF ADHIKARIVADA — 118
- ON BHAKTI-YOGA — 119
- ISHVARA AND BRAHMAN — 120
- ON JNANA-YOGA — 121
- THE CAUSE OF ILLUSION — 123
- EVOLUTION — 124
- BUDDHISM AND VEDANTA — 125
- ON THE VEDANTA PHILOSOPHY — 125
- LAW AND FREEDOM — 128
- THE GOAL AND METHODS OF REALISATION — 130
- WORLD-WIDE UNITY — 130
- THE AIM OF RAJA-YOGA — 131

Questions and Answers — 133

    I — DISCUSSION AT THE GRADUATE PHILOSOPHICAL SOCIETY OF HARVARD UNIVERSITY — 134

    II — AT THE TWENTIETH CENTURY CLUB OF BOSTON — 140

    III — AT THE BROOKLYN ETHICAL SOCIETY, BROOKLYN — 140

    IV — SELECTIONS FROM THE MATH DIARY — 141

    V — YOGA, VAIRAGYA, TAPASYA, LOVE — 144

    VI — IN ANSWER TO NIVEDITA — 144

    VII — GURU, AVATARA, YOGA, JAPA, SEVA — 145

Conversations and Dialogues — 149

    I — SHRI SURENDRA NATH DAS GUPTA — 150

    I — Think of Death Always and New Life Will Come within—Work for Others—God the Last Refuge — 150
Shri Suredra Nath Das Gupta

    II — V SHRI SURENDRA NATH SEN — 151

    II — The Loss of Shraddha in India and Need of Its Revival—Men We Want—Real Social Reform — 151
Shri Surendra Nath Sen—from private dairy

    III — Reconciliation of Jnana-Yoga and Bhakti-Yoga—God in Good and in Evil Too—Use Makes a Thing Good or Evil—Karma—Creation—God—Maya — 152
Shri Surendra Nath Sen—from private dairy

    IV — Intermarriage Among Subdivisions of a Varna—Against Early Marriage—The Education that Indians Need—Brahmacharya — 154
Shri Surendra Nath Sen —from private dairy

V — Madhura-Bhava—Prema—Namakirtana—Its Danger—Bhakti Tempered With Jnana—A Curious Dream ... 156

Shri Surendra Nath Sen —from private dairy

VI — X SHRI PRIYA NATH SINHA ... 158

VI — Reminiscences—The Problem of Famines in India and Self-Sacrificing Workers—East and West—Is it Sattva or Tamas—A Nation of Mendicants—The "Give and Take" Policy—Tell a Man his Defects Directly but Praise his Virtues Before Others—Vivekananda Everyone may Become—Unbroken Brahmacharya is the Secret of Power—Samadhi and Work ... 158

Shri Priya Nath Sinha

VII — Reminiscences—Pranayama—Thought-Reading—Knowledge of Previous Births ... 163

VIII — The Art and Science of Music, Eastern and Western ... 163

IX — The Old Institution of Living with the Guru—The Present University System—Lack of Shraddha—We have a National History—Western Science Coupled with Vedanta—The So-called Higher Education—The Need of Technical Education and Education on National Lines—The Story of Satyakama—Mere Book-Learning and Education under Tyagis—Shri Ramakrishna and the Pandits—Establishment of Maths with Sadhus in Charge of Colleges—Text-Books for Boys to be Compiled—Stop Early Marriage!—Plan of Sending Unmarried Graduates to Japan—The Secret of Japan's Greatness—Art, Asian and European—Art and Utility—Styles of Dress—The Food Question and Poverty ... 165

X — The Discrimination of the Four Castes According to Jati and Guna—Brahmanas and Kshatriyas in the West—The Kula-Guru System in Bengal ... 170

XI — XV FROM THE DIARY OF A DISCIPLE, SHRI SARAT CHANDRA CHAKRAVARTY ... 171

XII — Reconciliation of Jnana and Bhakti—Sat-Chit-Ananda—How Sectarianism Originates—Bring in Shraddha and the Worship of Shakti and avataras—The Ideal of the Hero We Want Now, not the

	Madhura-Bhava—Shri Ramakrishna—Avataras	173
XIII —	Brahman and Differentiation—Personal Realisation of Oneness—Supreme Bliss is the Goal of All—Think Always, I am Brahman—Discrimination and Renunciation are the Means—Be Fearless	176
XIV —	Renunciation of Kama-kanchana—God's Mercy Falls on Those Who Struggle for Realisation—Unconditional Mercy and Brahman Are One	178
XV —	Doctrine of Ahimsa and Meat-Eating—Sattva, Rajas, Tamas in Man—Food And Spirituality—'Âhâra'—Three Defects in Food—Don't-Touchism and Caste-Prejudices—Restoring the Old Chaturvarnya and the Laws of the Rishis	180

Sayings and Utterances — 185

Writings: Prose and Poems — 193

REASON, FAITH AND LOVE	194
SIX SANSKRIT MOTTOES	196
THE MESSAGE OF DIVINE WISDOM	197
BONDAGE	197
THE LAW	197
THE ABSOLUTE AND THE ATTAINMENT OF FREEDOM	199
THE BELUR MATH: AN APPEAL	199
THE ADVAITA ASHRAMA, HIMALAYAS	200
THE RAMAKRISHNA HOME OF SERVICE VARANASI: AN APPEAL	200
WHO KNOWS HOW MOTHER PLAYS!	201
TO THE FOURTH OF JULY	202

The East and the West — 203

- I — INTRODUCTION — 204
- II. CUSTOMS: EASTERN AND WESTERN — 213
- III. FOOD AND COOKING — 219
- IV. CIVILISATION IN DRESS — 228
- V. ETIQUETTE AND MANNERS — 230
- VI. FRANCE — PARIS — 231
- VII. PROGRESS OF CIVILISATION — 236

THE **COMPLETE WORKS** OF SWAMI VIVEKANANDA

VOLUME V

EPISTLES - FIRST SERIES

Note: Before leaving for the U.S.A. Swamiji used to change his name very often. In earlier years, he signed as Narendra or Naren; then for some time as Vividishananda or Sachchidananda. But for the convenience of the readers, these volumes use the more familiar name of Vivekananda.

1 — FAKIR

(Translated from Bengali)

Allahabad
5th January, 1890.

My Dear Fakir[1],

... A word for you. Remember always, I may not see you again. Be moral. Be brave. Be a heart-whole man. Strictly moral, brave unto desperation. Don't bother your head with religious theories. Cowards only sin, brave men never, no, not even in mind. Try to love anybody and everybody. Be a man and try to make those immediately under your care, namely Ram, Krishnamayi, and Indu, brave, moral, and sympathising. No religion for you, my children, but morality and bravery. No cowardice, no sin, no crime, no weakness — the rest will come of itself... And don't take Ram with you ever or ever allow him to visit a theatre or any enervating entertainment whatever.

Yours affectionately,
Vivekananda.

My Dear Ram, Krishnamayi, and Indu,

Bear in mind, my children, that only cowards and those who are weak commit sin and tell lies. The brave are always moral. Try to be moral, try to be brave, try to be sympathising.

Yours,

Vivekananda.

---

1. Shri Yajneshwar Bhattacharya.

2 — PANDITJI MAHARAJ

Bombay,
20th September, 1892.

Dear Panditji Mahârâj[2],

Your letter has reached me duly. I do not know why I should be undeservingly praised. "None is good, save One, that is, God", as the Lord Jesus bath said. The rest are only tools in His hands. "Gloria in Excelsis", "Glory unto God in the highest", and unto men that deserve, but not to such an undeserving one like me. Here "the servant is not worthy of the hire"; and a Fakir, especially, has no right to any praise whatsoever, for would you praise your servant for simply doing his duty?

... My unbounded gratitude to Pandit Sundarlalji, and to my Professor[3] for this kind remembrance of me.

Now I would tell you something else. The Hindu mind was ever deductive and never synthetic or inductive. In all our philosophies, we always find hair-splitting arguments, taking for granted some general proposition, but the proposition itself may be as childish as possible. Nobody ever asked or searched the truth of these general propositions. Therefore independent thought we have almost none to speak of, and hence the dearth of those sciences which are the results of observation and generalization. And why was it thus? — From two causes: The tremendous heat of the climate forcing us to love rest and contemplation better than activity, and the Brâhmins as priests never undertaking journeys or voyages to distant lands. There were voyagers and people who travelled far; but they were almost always traders, i.e. people from whom priestcraft and their own sole love for gain had taken away all capacity for intellectual development. So their observations, instead of adding to the store of human knowledge, rather degenerated it; for their observations were bad and their accounts exaggerated and tortured into fantastical shapes, until

---

2. Pandit Shankarlal of Khetri.

3. With whom he read the Mahâ-Bhâshya on Pânini.

they passed all recognition.

So you see, we must travel, we must go to foreign parts. We must see how the engine of society works in other countries, and keep free and open communication with what is going on in the minds of other nations, if we really want to be a nation again. And over and above all, we must cease to tyrannise. To what a ludicrous state are we brought! If a Bhângi comes to anybody as a Bhangi, he would be shunned as the plague; but no sooner does he get a cupful of water poured upon his head with some mutterings of prayers by a Pâdri, and get a coat on his back, no matter how threadbare, and come into the room of the most orthodox Hindu — I don't see the man who then dare refuse him a chair and a hearty shake of the hands! Irony can go no further. And come and see what they, the Pâdris, are doing here in the Dakshin (south). They are converting the lower classes by lakhs; and in Travancore, the most priestridden country in India — where every bit of land is owned by the Brahmins ... nearly one-fourth has become Christian! And I cannot blame them; what part have they in David and what in Jesse? When, when, O Lords shall man be brother to man?

Yours,

Vivekananda.

3 — ALASINGA

Oriental Hotel
Yokohama.
10th July, 1893.

Dear Alasinga, Balaji, G. G., Banking Corporation, and All My Madras Friends,

Excuse my not keeping you constantly informed of my movements. One is so busy every day, and especially myself who am quite new to the life of possessing things and taking care of them. That consumes so much of my energy. It is really an awful botheration.

From Bombay we reached Colombo. Our steamer remained in port for nearly the whole day, and we took the opportunity of getting off to have a look at the town. We drove through the streets, and the only thing I remember was a temple in which was a very gigantic Murti (image) of the Lord Buddha in a reclining posture, entering Nirvâna...

The next station was Penang, which is only a strip of land along the sea in the body of the Malaya Peninsula. The Malayas are all Mohammedans and in old days were noted pirates and quite a dread to merchantmen. But now the leviathan guns of modern turreted battleships have forced the Malayas to look about for more peaceful pursuits. On our way from Penang to Singapore, we had glimpses of Sumatra with its high mountains, and the Captain pointed out to me several places as the favourite haunts of pirates in days gone by. Singapore is the capital of the Straits Settlements. It has a fine botanical garden with the most splendid collection of palms. The beautiful fan-like palm, called the traveller's palm, grows here in abundance, and the bread-fruit tree everywhere. The celebrated mangosteen is as plentiful here as mangoes in Madras, but mango is nonpareil. The people here are not half so dark as the people of Madras, although so near the line. Singapore possesses a fine museum too.

Hong Kong next. You feel that you have reached China, the Chinese element predominates so much. All labour, all trade seems to be in their hands. And Hong Kong is real China. As soon as the steamer casts anchor, you are besieged with hundreds of Chinese boats to carry you to the land. These boats with two helms are rather peculiar. The boatman lives in the boat with his family. Almost always, the wife is at the helms, managing one with her hands and the other with one of her feet. And in ninety per cent of cases, you find a baby tied to her back, with the hands and feet of the little Chin left free. It is a quaint sight to see the little John Chinaman dangling very quietly from his mother's back, whilst she is now setting with might and main, now pushing heavy loads, or jumping with wonderful agility from boat to boat. And there is such a rush of boats and steamlaunches coming in and going out. Baby John is every moment put into the risk of having his little head pulverised, pigtail and all; but he does not care a fig. This busy life seems to have no charm for him, and he is quite content to learn the anatomy of a bit of rice-cake given to him from time to time by the madly busy mother. The Chinese child is quite a philosopher and calmly goes to work at an age when your Indian boy can hardly crawl on all fours. He has learnt the philosophy of necessity too well. Their extreme poverty is one of the causes why the Chinese and the Indians have remained in a state of mummified civilisation. To an ordinary Hindu or Chinese, everyday necessity is too hideous to allow him to think of anything else.

Hong Kong is a very beautiful town. It is built on the slopes of hills and on the tops too, which are much cooler than the city. There is an almost perpendicular tramway going to the top of the hill, dragged by wire-rope and steam-power.

We remained three days at Hong Kong and went to see Canton, which is eighty miles up a river. The river is broad enough to allow the biggest steamers to pass through. A number of Chinese steamers ply between Hong Kong and Canton. We took passage on one of these in the evening and reached Canton early in the morning. What a scene of bustle and life! What an immense number of boats almost covering the waters! And not only those that are carrying on the trade, but hundreds of others which serve as houses to live in. And quite a lot of them so nice and big! In fact, they are big houses two or three storeys high, with verandahs running round and streets between, and all floating!

We landed on a strip of ground given by the Chinese Government to foreigners to live in. Around us on both sides of the river for miles and miles is the big city — a wilderness of human beings, pushing, struggling, surging, roaring. But with all its population, all its activity, it is the dirtiest town I saw, not in the sense in which a town is called dirty in India, for as to that not a speck of filth is allowed by the Chinese to go waste; but because of the Chinaman, who has, it seems, taken a vow never to bathe! Every house is a shop, people living only on the top floor. The streets are very very narrow, so that you almost touch the shops on both sides as you pass. At every ten paces you find meat-stalls, and there are shops which sell cat's and dog's meat. Of course, only the poorest classes of Chinamen eat dog or cat.

The Chinese ladies can never be seen. They have got as strict a zenana as the Hindus of Northern India; only the women of the labouring classes can be seen. Even amongst these, one sees now and then a woman with feet smaller than those of your youngest child, and of course they cannot be said to walk, but hobble.

I went to see several Chinese temples. The biggest in Canton is dedicated to the memory of the first Buddhistic Emperor and the five hundred first disciples of Buddhism. The central figure is of course Buddha, and next beneath Him is seated the Emperor, and ranging on both sides are the statues of the disciples, all beautifully carved out of wood.

From Canton I returned back to Hong Kong, and from thence to Japan. The first port we touched was Nagasaki. We landed for a few hours and drove through the town. What a contrast! The Japanese are one of the cleanliest peoples on earth. Everything is neat and tidy. Their streets are nearly all broad, straight, and regularly paved. Their little houses are cage-like, and their pine-covered evergreen little hills form the background of almost every town and village. The short-statured, fair-skinned, quaintly-dressed Japs, their movements, attitudes, gestures, everything is picturesque. Japan is the land of the picturesque! Almost every house has a garden at the back, very nicely laid out according to Japanese fashion with small shrubs, grass-plots, small artificial waters, and small stone bridges.

From Nagasaki to Kobe. Here I gave up the steamer and took the land-route to Yokohama, with a view to see the interior of Japan.

I have seen three big cities in the interior — Osaka, a great manufacturing town, Kyoto, the former capital, and Tokyo, the present capital. Tokyo is nearly twice the size of Calcutta with nearly double the population.

No foreigner is allowed to travel in the interior without a passport.

The Japanese seem now to have fully awakened themselves to the necessity of the present times. They have now a thoroughly organised army equipped with guns which one of their own officers has invented and which is said to be second to none. Then, they are continually increasing their navy. I have seen a tunnel nearly a mile long, bored by a Japanese engineer.

The match factories are simply a sight to see, and they are bent upon making everything they want in their own country. There is a Japanese line of steamers plying between China and Japan, which shortly intends running between Bombay and Yokohama.

I saw quite a lot of temples. In every temple there are some Sanskrit Mantras written in Old Bengali characters. Only a few of the priests know Sanskrit. But they are an intelligent sect. The modern rage for progress has penetrated even the priesthood. I cannot write what I have in my mind about the Japs in one short letter. Only I want that numbers of our young men should pay a visit to Japan and China every year. Especially to the Japanese, India is still the dreamland of everything high and good. And you, what are you? … talking twaddle all your lives, vain talkers, what are you? Come, see these people, and then go and hide your faces in shame. A race of dotards, you lose your caste if you come out! Sitting down these hundreds of years with an ever-increasing load of crystallised superstition on your heads, for hundreds of years spending all your energy upon discussing the touchableness or untouchableness of this food or that, with all humanity crushed out of you by the continuous social tyranny of ages — what are you? And what are you doing now? … promenading the sea-shores with books in your hands — repeating undigested stray bits of European brainwork, and the whole soul bent upon getting a thirty-rupee clerkship, or at best becoming a lawyer — the height of young India's ambition — and every student with a whole brood of hungry children cackling at his heels and asking for bread! Is there not water enough in the sea to drown you, books, gowns, university diplomas, and all?

Come, be men! Kick out the priests who are always against progress, because they would never mend, their hearts would never become big. They are the offspring of centuries of superstition and tyranny. Root out priest craft first. Come, be men! Come out of your narrow holes and have a look abroad. See how nations are on the march! Do you love man? Do you love your country? Then come, let us struggle for higher and better things; look not back, no, not even if you see the dearest and nearest cry. Look not back, but forward!

India wants the sacrifice of at least a thousand or her young men — men, mind, and not brutes. The English Government has been the instrument, brought over here by the Lord, to break your crystallised civilisation, and Madras supplied the first men who helped in giving the English a footing. How many men, unselfish, thorough-going men, is Madras ready now to supply, to struggle unto life and death to bring about a new state of things sympathy for the poor, and bread to their hungry mouths, enlightenment to the people at large — and struggle unto death to make men of them who have been brought to the level of beasts, by the tyranny of your forefathers?

Yours etc.,
Vivekananda.

PS. Calm and silent and steady work, and no newspaper humbug, no name-making, you must always remember.

4 — ALASINGA

Breezy Meadows,
Metcalf, Mass.,
20th August, 1893.

Dear Alasinga,

Received your letter yesterday. Perhaps you have by this time got my letter from Japan. From Japan I reached Vancouver. The way was by the Northern Pacific. It was very cold and I suffered much for want of warm clothing. However, I reached Vancouver anyhow, and thence went through Canada to Chicago. I remained about twelve days in Chicago. And almost every day I used to go to the Fair. It is a tremendous affair. One must take at least ten days to go through it. The lady to whom Varada Rao introduced me and her husband belong to the highest Chicago society, and they were so very kind to me. I took my departure from Chicago and came to Boston. Mr. Lâlubhâi was with me up to Boston. He was very kind to me...

The expense I am bound to run into here is awful. You remember, you gave me £170 in notes and £9 in cash. It has come down to £130 in all!! On an average it costs me £1 every day; a cigar costs eight annas of our money. The Americans are so rich that they spend money like water, and by forced legislation keep up the price of everything so high that no other nation on earth can approach it. Every common coolie earns nine or ten rupees a day and spends as much. All those rosy ideas we had before starting have melted, and I have now to fight against impossibilities. A hundred times I had a mind to go out of the country and go back to India. But I am determined, and I have a call from Above; I see no way, but His eyes see. And I must stick to my guns, life or death...

Just now I am living as the guest of an old lady in a village near Boston. I accidentally made her acquaintance in the railway train, and she invited me to come over and live with her. I have an advantage in living with her, in saving for some time my expenditure of £1 per day, and she has the advantage of inviting her friends over here and showing them a curio from India! And all this must be borne. Starvation, cold, hooting in the streets on account of my quaint dress, these are what I have to fight against. But, my dear boy, no great things were ever done without great labour.

... Know, then, that this is the land of Christians, and any other influence than that is almost zero. Nor do I care a bit for the enmity of any — ists in the world. I am here amongst the children of the Son of Mary and the Lord Jesus will help me. They like much the broad views of Hinduism and my love for the Prophet of Nazareth. I tell them that I preach nothing against the Great One of Galilee. I only ask the Christians to take in the Great Ones of Ind along with the Lord Jesus, and they appreciate it.

Winter is approaching and I shall have to get all sorts of warm clothing, and we require more warm clothing than the natives... Look sharp, my boy, take courage. We are destined by the Lord to do great things in India. Have faith. We will do. We, the poor and the despised, who really feel, and not those...

In Chicago, the other day, a funny thing happened The Raja of Kapurthala was here, and he was being lionised by some portion of Chicago society. I once met the Raja in the Fair grounds, but he was too big to speak with a poor Fakir. There was an eccentric Mahratta Brâhmin selling nail-made pictures in the Fair, dressed in a dhoti. This fellow told the reporters all sorts of things against the Raja —, that he was a man of low caste, that those Rajas were nothing but slaves, and that they generally led immoral lives, etc., etc. And these truthful (?) editors, for which America is famous, wanted to give to the boy's stories some weight; and so the next day they wrote huge columns in their papers about the description of a man of wisdom from India, meaning me — extolling me to the skies, and putting all sorts of words in my mouth, which I never even dreamt of, and ascribing to me all those remarks made by the Mahratta Brahmin about the Raja of Kapurthala. And it was such a good brushing that Chicago society gave up the Raja in hot haste... These newspaper editors made capital out of me to give my countryman a brushing. That shows, however, that in this country intellect carries more weight than all the pomp of money and title.

Yesterday Mrs. Johnson, the lady superintendent of the women's prison, was here. They don't call it prison but reformatory here. It is the grandest thing I have seen in America. How the inmates are benevolently treated, how they are reformed and sent back as useful members of society; how grand, how beautiful, You must see to believe! And, oh, how my heart ached to think of what we think of the poor, the low, in India. They have no chance, no escape, no way to climb up. The poor, the low, the sinner in India have no friends, no help — they cannot rise, try however they may. They sink lower and lower every day, they feel the blows showered upon them by a cruel society, and they do not know whence the blow comes. They have forgotten that they too are men. And the result is slavery. Thoughtful people within the last few years have seen it, but unfortunately laid it at the door of the Hindu religion, and to them, the only way of bettering is by crushing this grandest religion of the world. Hear me, my friend, I have discovered the secret through the grace of the Lord. Religion is not in fault. On the other hand, your religion teaches you that every being is only your own self multiplied. But it was the want of practical application, the want of sympathy — the want of heart. The Lord once more came to you as Buddha and taught you how to feel, how to sympathise with the poor, the miserable, the sinner, but you heard Him not. Your priests invented the horrible story that the Lord was here for deluding demons with false doctrines! True indeed, but we are the demons, not those that believed. And just as the Jews denied the Lord Jesus and are since that day wandering over the world as homeless beggars, tyrannised over by everybody, so you are bond-slaves to any nation that thinks it worth while to rule over you. Ah, tyrants! you do not know that the obverse is tyranny, and the reverse slavery. The slave and the tyrant are synonymous.

Balaji and G. G. may remember one evening at Pondicherry — we were discussing the matter of sea-voyage with a Pandit, and I shall always remember his brutal gestures and his Kadâpi Na (never)! They do not know that India is a very small part of the world, and the whole world looks down with contempt upon the three hundred millions of earthworms crawling upon the fair soil of India and trying to oppress each other. This state of things must be removed, not by destroying religion but by following the great teachings of the Hindu faith, and joining with it the wonderful sympathy of that logical development of Hinduism — Buddhism.

A hundred thousand men and women, fired with the zeal of holiness, fortified with eternal faith in the Lord, and nerved to lion's courage by their sympathy for the poor and the fallen and the downtrodden, will go over the length and breadth of the land, preaching the gospel of salvation, the gospel of help, the gospel of social raising-up — the gospel of equality.

No religion on earth preaches the dignity of humanity in such a lofty strain as Hinduism, and no religion on earth treads upon the necks of the poor and the low in such a fashion as Hinduism. The Lord has shown me that religion is not in fault, but it is the Pharisees and Sadducees in Hinduism, hypocrites, who invent all sorts of engines of tyranny in the shape of doctrines of Pâramârthika and Vyâvahârika.

Despair not; remember the Lord says in the Gita, "To work you have the right, but not to the result." Gird up your loins, my boy. I am called by the Lord for this. I have been dragged through a whole life full of crosses and tortures, I have seen the nearest and dearest die, almost of starvation; I have been ridiculed, distrusted, and have suffered for my sympathy for the very men who scoff and scorn. Well, my boy, this is the school of misery, which is also the school for great souls and prophets for the cultivation of sympathy, of patience, and, above all, of an indomitable iron will which quakes not even if the universe be pulverised at our feet. I pity them. It is not their fault. They are children, yea, veritable children, though they be great and high in society. Their eyes see nothing beyond their little horizon of a few yards — the routine-work, eating, drinking, earning, and begetting, following each other in mathematical precision. They know nothing beyond — happy little souls! Their sleep is never disturbed, their nice little brown studies of lives never rudely shocked by the wail of woe, of misery, of degradation, and poverty, that has filled the Indian atmosphere — the result of centuries of oppression. They little dream of the ages of tyranny, mental, moral, and physical, that has reduced the image of God to a mere beast of burden; the emblem of the Divine Mother, to a slave to bear children; and life itself, a curse. But there are others who see, feel, and shed tears of blood in their hearts, who think that there is a remedy for it, and who are ready to apply this remedy at any cost, even to the giving up of life. And "of such is the kingdom of Heaven". Is it not then natural, my friends, that they have no time to look down from their heights to the vagariese of these contemptible little insects, ready every moment to spit their little venoms?

Trust not to the so-called rich, they are more dead than alive. The hope lies in you — in the meek, the lowly, but the faithful. Have faith in the Lord; no policy, it is nothing. Feel for the miserable and look up for help — it shall come. I have travelled twelve years with this load in my heart and this idea in my head. I have gone from door to door of the so-called rich and great. With a bleeding heart I have crossed half the world to this strange land, seeking for help. The

Lord is great. I know He will help me. I may perish of cold or hunger in this land, but I bequeath to you, young men, this sympathy, this struggle for the poor, the ignorant, the oppressed. Go now this minute to the temple of Pârthasârathi[1], and before Him who was friend to the poor and lowly cowherds of Gokula, who never shrank to embrace the Pariah Guhaka, who accepted the invitation of a prostitute in preference to that of the nobles and saved her in His incarnation as Buddha — yea, down on your faces before Him, and make a great sacrifice, the sacrifice of a whole life for them, for whom He comes from time to time, whom He loves above all, the poor, the lowly, the oppressed. Vow, then, to devote your whole lives to the cause of the redemption of these three hundred millions, going down and down every day.

It is not the work of a day, and the path is full of the most deadly thorns. But Parthasarathi is ready to be our Sârathi — we know that. And in His name and with eternal faith in Him, set fire to the mountain of misery that has been heaped upon India for ages — and it shall be burned down. Come then, look it in the face, brethren, it is a grand task, and we are so low. But we are the sons of Light and children of God. Glory unto the Lord, we will succeed. Hundreds will fall in the struggle, hundreds will be ready to take it up. I may die here unsuccessful, another will take up the task. You know the disease, you know the remedy, only have faith. Do not look up to the so-called rich and great; do not care for the heartless intellectual writers, and their cold-blooded newspaper articles. Faith, sympathy — fiery faith and fiery sympathy! Life is nothing, death is nothing, hunger nothing, cold nothing. Glory unto the Lord — march on, the Lord is our General. Do not look back to see who falls — forward — onward! Thus and thus we shall go on, brethren. One falls, and another takes up the work.

From this village I am going to Boston tomorrow. I am going to speak at a big Ladies' Club here, which is helping Ramâbâi. I must first go and buy some clothing in Boston. If I am to live longer here, my quaint dress will not do. People gather by hundreds in the streets to see me. So what I want is to dress myself in a long black coat, and keep a red robe and turban to wear when I lecture. This is what the ladies advise me to do, and they are the rulers here, and I must have their sympathy. Before you get this letter my money would come down to somewhat about £70 of £60. So try your best to send some money. It is necessary to remain here for some time to have any influence here. I could not see the phonograph for Mr. Bhattacharya as I got his letter here. If I go to Chicago again, I will look for them. I do not know whether I shall go back to Chicago or not. My friends there write me to represent India. And the gentleman, to whom Varada Rao introduced me, is one of the directors of the Fair; but then I refused as I would have to spend all any little stock of money in remaining more than a month in Chicago.

In America, there are no classes in the railway except in Canada. So I have to travel first-class, as that is the only class; but I do not venture in the Pullmans. They are very comfortable — you sleep, eat, drink, even bathe in them, just as if you were in a hotel — but they are too expensive.

It is very hard work getting into society and making yourself heard. Now nobody is in the towns, they are all away in summer places. They will all come back in winter. Therefore I must wait. After such a struggle, I am not going to give up easily. Only try your best to help me as much as you can; and even if you cannot, I must try to the end. And even if I die of cold or disease or hunger here, you take up the task. Holiness sincerity, and faith. I have left instructions with Cooks to forward any letter or money to me wherever I am. Rome was not built in a day. If you can keep me here for six months at least, I hope everything will come right. In the meantime I am trying my best to find any plank I can float upon. And if I find out any means to support myself, I shall wire to you immediately.

First I will try in America; and if I fail, try in England; if I fail, go back to India and wait for further commands from High. Ramdas's father has gone to England. He is in a hurry to gone home. He is a very good man at heart, only the Baniya roughness on the surface. It would take more than twenty days for the letter to reach. Even now it is so cold in New England that every day we have fires night and morning.

---

1. Shri Krishna as Sârathi, charioteer, of Pârtha or Arjuna.

Canada is still colder. I never saw snow on such low hills as there.

Gradually I can make my way; but that means a longer residence in this horribly expensive country. Just now the raising of the Rupee in India has created a panic in this country, and lots of mills have been stopped. So I cannot hope for anything just now, but I must wait.

Just now I have been to the tailor and ordered some winter clothings, and that would cost at least Rs. 300 and up. And still it would not be good clothes, only decent. Ladies here are very particular about a man's dress, and they are the power in this country. They... never fail the missionaries. They are helping our Ramabai every year. If you fail in keeping me here, send some money to get me out of the country. In the meantime if anything turns out in my favour, I will write or wire. A word costs Rs. 4 in cable!!

Yours,
Vivekananda.

5 — ALASINGA

Chicago,
2nd November, 1893.

Dear Alasinga,

I am so sorry that a moment's weakness on my part should cause you so much trouble; I was out of pocket at that time. Since then the Lord sent me friends. At a village near Boston I made the acquaintance of Dr. Wright, Professor of Greek in the Harvard University. He sympathised with me very much and urged upon me the necessity of going to the Parliament of Religions, which he thought would give me an introduction to the nation. As I was not acquainted with anybody, the Professor undertook to arrange everything for me, and eventually I came back to Chicago. Here I, together with the oriental and occidental delegates to the Parliament of Religions, were all lodged in the house of a gentleman.

On the morning of the opening of the Parliament, we all assembled in a building called the Art Palace, where one huge and other smaller temporary halls were erected for the sittings of the Parliament. Men from all nations were there. From India were Mazoomdar of the Brâhmo Samâj, and Nagarkar of Bombay, Mr. Gandhi representing the Jains, and Mr. Chakravarti representing Theosophy with Mrs. Annie Besant. Of these, Mazoomdar and I were, of course, old friends, and Chakravarti knew me by name. There was a grand procession, and we were all marshalled on to the platform. Imagine a hall below and a huge gallery above, packed with six or seven thousand men and women representing the best culture of the country, and on the platform learned men of all the nations of the earth. And I, who never spoke in public in my life, to address this august assemblage!! It was opened in great form with music and ceremony and speeches; then the delegates were introduced one by one, and they stepped up and spoke. Of course my heart was fluttering, and my tongue nearly dried up; I was so nervous and could not venture to speak in the morning. Mazoomdar made a nice speech, Chakravarti a nicer one, and they were much applauded. They were all prepared and came with ready-made speeches. I was a fool and had none, but bowed down to Devi Sarasvati and stepped up, and Dr. Barrows introduced me. I made a short speech. I addressed the assembly as "Sisters and Brothers of America", a deafening applause of two minutes followed, and then I proceeded; and when it was finished, I sat down, almost exhausted with emotion. The next day all the papers announced that my speech was the hit of the day, and I became known to the whole of America. Truly has it been said by the great commentator Shridhara— "मूकं करोति वाचालं—Who maketh the dumb a fluent speaker."

His name be praised! From that day I became a celebrity, and the day I read my paper on Hinduism, the hall was packed as it had never been before. I quote to you from one of the papers: "Ladies, ladies, ladies packing every place — filling every corner, they patiently waited and waited while the papers that separated them from Vivekananda were read", etc. You would be astonished if I sent over to you the newspaper cuttings, but you already know that I am a hater of celebrity. Suffice it to say, that whenever I went on the platform, a deafening applause would be raised for me. Nearly all the papers paid high tributes to me, and even the most bigoted had to admit that "This man with his handsome face and magnetic presence and wonderful oratory is the most prominent figure in the Parliament", etc., etc. Sufficient for you to know that never before did an Oriental make such an impression on American society.

And how to speak of their kindness? I have no more wants now, I am well off, and all the money that I require to visit Europe I shall get from here... A boy called Narasimhâchârya has cropped up in our midst. He has been loafing about the city for the last three years. Loafing or no loafing, I like him; but please write to me all about him if you know anything. He knows you. He came in the year of the Paris Exhibition to Europe...

I am now out of want. Many of the handsomest houses in this city are open to me. All the time I am living as a guest of somebody or other. There is a curiosity in this nation, such as you meet with nowhere else. They want to know everything, and their women — they are the most advanced in the world. The average American woman is far more cultivated than the average American man. The men slave all their life for money, and the women snatch every opportunity to improve themselves. And they are a very kind-hearted, frank people. Everybody who has a fad to preach comes here, and I am sorry to say that most of these are not sound. The Americans have their faults too, and what nation has not? But this is my summing up: Asia laid the germs of civilization, Europe developed man, and America is developing the woman and the masses. It is the paradise of the woman and the labourer. Now contrast the American masses and women with ours, and you get the idea at once. The Americans are fast becoming liberal. Judge them not by the specimens of hard-shelled Christians (it is their own phrase) that you see in India. There are those here too, but their number is decreasing rapidly, and this great nation is progressing fast towards that spirituality which is the standard boast of the Hindu.

The Hindu must not give up his religion, but must keep religion within its proper limits end give freedom to society to grow. All the reformers in India made the serious mistake of holding religion accountable for all the horrors of priestcraft and degeneration and went forth with to pull down the indestructible structure, and what was the result? Failure! Beginning from Buddha down to Ram Mohan Roy, everyone made the mistake of holding caste to be a religious institution and tried to pull down religion and caste all together, and failed. But in spite of all the ravings of the priests, caste is simply a crystallised social institution, which after doing its service is now filling the atmosphere of India with its stench, and it can only be removed by giving back to the people their lost social individuality. Every man born here knows that he is a man. Every man born in India knows that he is a slave of society. Now, freedom is the only condition of growth; take that off, the result is degeneration. With the introduction of modern competition, see how caste is disappearing fast! No religion is now necessary to kill it. The Brâhmana shopkeeper, shoemaker, and wine-distiller are common in Northern India. And why? Because of competition. No man is prohibited from doing anything he pleases for his livelihood under the present Government, and the result is neck and neck competition, and thus thousands are seeking and finding the highest level they were born for, instead of vegetating at the bottom.

I must remain in this country at least through the winter, and then go to Europe. The Lord will provide everything for me. You need not disturb yourself about it. I cannot express my gratitude for your love.

Day by day I am feeling that the Lord is with me, and I am trying to follow His direction. His will be done... We will do great things for the world, and that for the sake of doing good and not for name and fame.

"Ours not to reason why, ours but to do and die." Be of good cheer and believe that we are selected by the Lord to do great things, and we will do them. Hold yourself in readiness, i.e. be pure and holy, and love for love's sake. Love the poor, the miserable, the downtrodden, and the Lord will bless you.

See the Raja of Ramnad and others from time to time and urge them to sympathise with the masses of

India. Tell them how they are standing on the neck of the poor, and that they are not fit to be called men if they do not try to raise them up. Be fearless, the Lord is with you, and He will yet raise the starving and ignorant millions of India. A railway porter here is better educated than many of your young men and most of your princes. Every American woman has far better education than can be conceived of by the majority of Hindu women. Why cannot we have the same education? We must.

Think not that you are poor; money is not power, but goodness, holiness. Come and see how it is so all over the world.

Yours with blessings,
Vivekananda.

PS. By the bye, your uncle's paper was the most curious phenomenon I ever saw. It was like a tradesman's catalogue, and it was not thought fit to be read in the Parliament. So Narasimhacharya read a few extracts from it in a side hall, and nobody understood a word of it. Do not tell him of it. It is a great art to press the largest amount of thought into the smallest number of words. Even Manilal Dvivedi's paper had to be cut very short. More than a thousand papers were read, and there was no time to give to such wild perorations. I had a good long time given to me over the ordinary half hour, ... because the most popular speakers were always put down last, to hold the audience. And Lord bless them, what sympathy they have, and what patience! They would sit from ten o'clock in the morning to ten o'clock at night — only a recess of half an hour for a meal, and paper after paper read, most of them very trivial, but they would wait and wait to hear their favourites.

Dharmapâla of Ceylon was one of the favourites But unfortunately he was not a good speaker. He had only quotations from Max Müller and Rhys Davids to give them. He is a very sweet man, and we became very intimate during the Parliament.

A Christian lady from Poona, Miss Sorabji, and the Jain representative, Mr. Gandhi, are going to remain longer in the country end make lecture tours. I hope they will succeed. Lecturing is a very profitable occupation in this country and sometimes pays well.

Mr. Ingersoll gets five to six hundred dollars a lecture. He is the most celebrated lecturer in this country. Do not publish this letter. After reading, send it to the Maharaja (of Khetri). I have sent him my photograph in America.

6 — HARIPADA

(Translated from Bengali)

C/O George W. Hale Esq.,
541 Dearborn Avenue, Chicago,
28th December, 1893.

Dear Haripada[1],

It is very strange that news of my Chicago lectures has appeared in the Indian papers; for whatever I do, I try my best to avoid publicity. Many things strike me here. It may be fairly said that there is no poverty in this country. I have never seen women elsewhere as cultured and educated as they are here. Well-educated men there are in our country, but you will scarcely find anywhere women like those here. It is indeed true, that "the Goddess Herself lives in the houses of virtuous men as Lakshmi". I have seen thousands of women here whose hearts are as pure and stainless as snow. Oh, how free they are! It is they who control social and civic duties Schools and colleges are full of women, and in our country women cannot be safely allowed to walk in the streets! Their kindness to me is immeasurable. Since I came here, I have been welcomed by them to their houses. They are providing me with food, arranging for my lectures, taking me to market, and doing everything for my comfort and convenience. I shall never be able to repay in the least the deep debt of gratitude I owe to them.

Do you know who is the real "Shakti-worshipper"? It is he who knows that God is the omnipresent force in the universe and sees in women the manifestation of that Force. Many men here look upon their wom-

---

1. Haripada Mitra.

en in this light. Manu, again, has said that gods bless those families where women are happy and well treated. Here men treat their women as well as can be desired, and hence they are so prosperous, so learned, so free, and so energetic. But why is it that we are slavish, miserable, and dead? The answer is obvious.

And how pure and chaste are they here! Few women are married before twenty or twenty-five, and they are as free as the birds in the air. They go to market, school, and college, earn money, and do all kinds of work. Those who are well-to-do devote themselves to doing good to the poor. And what are we doing? We are very regular in marrying our girls at eleven years of age lest they should become corrupt and immoral. What does our Manu enjoin? "Daughters should be supported and educated with as much care and attention as the sons." As sons should be married after observing Brahmacharya up to the thirtieth year, so daughters also must observe Brahmacharya and be educated by their parents. But what are we actually doing? Can you better the condition of your women? Then there will be hope for your well-being. Otherwise you will remain as backward as you are now.

If anybody is born of a low caste in our country, he is gone for ever, there is no hope for him. Why? What a tyranny it is! There are possibilities, opportunities, and hope for every individual in this country. Today he is poor, tomorrow he may become rich and learned and respected. Here everyone is anxious to help the poor. In India there is a howling cry that we are very poor, but how many charitable associations are there for the well-being of the poor? How many people really weep for the sorrows and sufferings of the millions of poor in India? Are we men? What are we doing for their livelihood, for their improvement? We do not touch them, we avoid their company! Are we men? Those thousands of Brâhmanas — what are they doing for the low, downtrodden masses of India? "Don't touch", "Don't touch", is the only phrase that plays upon their lips! How mean and degraded has our eternal religion become at their hands! Wherein does our religion lie now? In "Don't-touchism" alone, and nowhere else!

I came to this country not to satisfy my curiosity, nor for name or fame, but to see if I could find any means for the support of the poor in India. If God helps me, you will know gradually what those means are.

As regards spirituality, the Americans are far inferior to us, but their society is far superior to ours. We will teach them our spirituality and assimilate what is best in their society.

With love and best wishes,

Yours,
Vivekananda.

7 — FRIENDS

C/O George W. Hale Esq.,
541 Dearborn Avenue, Chicago,
24th January, 1894.

Dear Friends[2],

Your letters have reached me. I am surprised that so much about me has reached you. The criticism you mention of the Interior is not to be taken as the attitude of the American people. That paper is almost unknown here, and belongs to what they call a "blue-nose Presbyterian paper", very bigoted. Still all the "blue-noses" are not ungentlemanly. The American people, and many of the clergy, are very hospitable to me. That paper wanted a little notoriety by attacking a man who was being lionised by society. That trick is well known here, and they do not think anything of it. Of course, our Indian missionaries may try to make capital out of it. If they do, tell them, "Mark, Jew, a judgment has come upon you!" Their old building is tottering to its foundation and must come down in spite of their hysterical shrieks. I pity them — if their means of living fine lives in India is cut down by the influx of oriental religions here. But not one of their leading clergy is ever against me. Well, when I am in the pond, I must bathe thoroughly.

I send you a newspaper cutting of the short sketch of our religion which I read before them. Most of

---
2. His disciples in Madras.

my speeches are extempore. I hope to put them in book form before I leave the country. I do not require any help from India, I have plenty here. Employ the money you have in printing and publishing this short speech; and translating it into the vernaculars, throw it broadcast; that will keep us before the national mind. In the meantime do not forget our plan of a central college, and the starting from it to all directions in India. Work hard...

About the women of America, I cannot express my gratitude for their kindness. Lord bless them. In this country, women are the life of every movement, and represent all the culture of the nation, for men are too busy to educate themselves.

I have received Kidi's letters. With the question whether caste shall go or come I have nothing to do. My idea is to bring to the door of the meanest, the poorest, the noble ideas that the human race has developed both in and out of India, and let them think for themselves. Whether there should be caste or not, whether women should be perfectly free or not, does not concern me. "Liberty of thought and action is the only condition of life, of growth and well-being." Where it does not exist, the man, the race, the nation must go down.

Caste or no caste, creed or no creed, any man, or class, or caste, or nation, or institution which bars the power of free thought and action of an individual — even so long as that power does not injure others — is devilish and must go down.

My whole ambition in life is to set in motion a machinery which will bring noble ideas to the door of everybody, and then let men and women settle their own fate. Let them know what our forefathers as well as other nations have thought on the most momentous questions of life. Let them see specially what others are doing now, and then decide. We are to put the chemicals together, the crystallization will be done by nature according to her laws. Work hard, be steady, and have faith in the Lord. Set to work, I am coming sooner or later. Keep the motto before you — "Elevation of the masses without injuring their religion".

Remember that the nation lives in the cottage. But, alas! nobody ever did anything for them. Our modern reformers are very busy about widow remarriage. Of course, I am a sympathiser in every reform, but the fate of a nation does not depend upon the number of husbands their widows get, but upon the condition of the masses. Can you raise them? Can you give them back their lost individuality without making them lose their innate spiritual nature? Can you become an occidental of occidentals in your spirit of equality, freedom, work, and energy, and at the same time a Hindu to the very backbone in religious culture and instincts? This is to be done and we will do it. You are all born to do it. Have faith in yourselves, great convictions are the mothers of great deeds. Onward for ever! Sympathy for the poor, the downtrodden, even unto death — this is our motto. Onward, brave lads!

Yours affectionately,
Vivekananda.

PS. Do not publish this letter; but there is no harm in preaching the idea of elevating the masses by means of a central college, and bringing education as well as religion to the door of the poor by means of missionaries trained in this college. Try to interest everybody.

I send you a few newspaper cuttings — only from the very best and highest. The one by Dr. Thomas is very valuable as written by one of the, if not the leading clergymen of America. The Interior with all its fanaticism and thirst for notoriety was bound to say that I was the public favourite. I cut a few lines from that magazine also.

8 — ALASINGA

New York,
9th April, 1894.

Dear Alasinga,

I got your last letter a few days ago. You see I am so very busy here, and have to write so many letters every day, that you cannot expect frequent communications from me. But I try my best to keep you in touch with whatever is going on here. I will write to

Chicago for one of the books on the Parliament of Religions to be sent over to you. But by this time you have got two of my short speeches.

Secretary Saheb writes me that I must come back to India, because that is my field. No doubt of that. But my brother, we are to light a torch which will shed a lustre over all India. So let us not be in a hurry; everything will come by the grace of the Lord. I have lectured in many of the big towns of America, and have got enough to pay my passage back after paying the awful expenses here. I have made a good many friends here, some of them very influential. Of course, the orthodox clergymen are against me; and seeing that it is not easy to grapple with me, they try to hinder, abuse, and vilify me in every way; and Mazoomdar has come to their help. He must have gone mad with jealousy. He has told them that I was a big fraud, and a rogue! And again in Calcutta he is telling them that I am leading a most sinful life in America, specially unchaste! Lord bless him! My brother, no good thing can be done without obstruction. It is only those who persevere to the end that succeed... I believe that the Satya Yuga (Golden Age) will come when there will be one caste, one Veda, and peace and harmony. This idea of Satya Yuga is what would revivify India. Believe it. One thing is to be done if you can do it. Can you convene a big meeting in Madras, getting Ramnad or any such big fellow as the President, and pass a resolution of your entire satisfaction at my representation of Hinduism here, and send it to the Chicago Herald, Inter-Ocean, and the New York Sun, and the Commercial Advertiser of Detroit (Michigan). Chicago is in Illinois. New York Sun requires no particulars. Detroit is in the State of Michigan. Send copies to Dr. Barrows, Chairman of the Parliament of Religions, Chicago. I have forgotten his number, but the street is Indiana Avenue. One copy to Mrs. J. J. Bagley of Detroit, Washington Ave.

Try to make this meeting as big as possible. Get hold of all the big bugs who must join it for their religion and country. Try to get a letter from the Mysore Maharaja and the Dewan approving the meeting and its purpose — so of Khetri — in fact, as big and noisy a crowd as you can.

The resolution would be of such a nature that the Hindu community of Madras, who sent me over, expressing its entire satisfaction in my work here etc.

Now try if it is possible. This is not much work. Get also letters of sympathy from all parts you can and print them and send copies to the American papers — as quickly as you can. That will go a long way, my brethren. The B—— S—— fellows here are trying to talk all sorts of nonsense. We must stop their mouths as fast as we can.

Up boys, and put yourselves to the task! If you can do that, I am sure we will be able to do much in future. Old Hinduism for ever! Down with all liars and rogues! Up, up, my boys, we are sure to win!

As to publishing my letters, such parts as ought to be published may be published for our friends till I come. When once we begin to work, we shall have a tremendous "boom", but I do not want to talk without working. I do not know, but G. C. Ghosh and Mr. Mitra of Calcutta can get up all the sympathisers of my late Gurudeva to do the same in Calcutta. If they can, so much the better. Ask them, if they can, to pass the same resolutions in Calcutta. There are thousands in Calcutta who sympathise with our movement. However I have more faith in you than in them.

Nothing more to write.

Convey my greetings to all our friends — for whom I am always praying.

Yours with blessings,
Vivekananda.

9 — SHARAT

U. S. A.,
20th May, 1894.

My Dear Sharat (Saradananda),

I am in receipt of your letter and am glad to learn that Shashi (Ramakrishnananda) is all right. Now I tell you a curious fact. Whenever anyone of you is sick, let him himself or anyone of you visualise him in your mind, and mentally say and strongly imagine that he is all right. That will cure him quickly. You can do it even without his knowledge, and even with thousands of miles between you. Remember it and do not be ill any more. You have received the money by this time. If you all like, you can give to Gopal Rs. 300/- from the amount I sent for the Math. I have no more to send now. I have to look after Madras now.

I cannot understand why Sanyal is so miserable on account of his daughters' marriage. After all, he is going to drag his daughters through the dirty Samsâra (world) which he himself wants to escape! I can have but one opinion of that — condemnation! I hate the very name of marriage, in regard to a boy or a girl. Do you mean to say that I have to help in putting someone into bondage, you fool! If my brother Mohin marries, I will throw him off. I am very decided about that...

Yours in love,
Vivekananda.

10 — ALASINGA

Chicago,
28th May, 1894.

Dear Alasinga,

I could not reply to your note earlier, because I was whirling to and fro from New York to Boston, and also I awaited Narasimha's letter. I do not know when I am going back to India. It is better to leave everything in the hands of Him who is at my back directing me. Try to work without me, as if I never existed. Do not wait for anybody or anything. Do whatever you can. Build your hope on none. Before writing about myself, I will tell you about Narasimha. He has proved a complete failure... However he wrote to me for help in the last stage, and I will try to help him as much as is in my power. Meanwhile you tell his people to send money as soon as they can for him to go over... He is in distress. Of course I will see that he does not starve.

I have done a good deal of lecturing here... The expenses here are terrible; money has to fly, although I have been almost always taken care of everywhere by the nicest and the highest families.

I do not know whether I shall go away this summer or not. Most probably not. In the meantime try to organise and push on our plans. Believe you can do everything. Know that the Lord is with us, and so, onward, brave souls!

I have had enough appreciation in my own country. Appreciation or no appreciation, sleep not, slacken not. You must remember that not a bit even of our plans has been as yet carried out.

Act on the educated young men, bring them together, and organise them. Great things can be done by great sacrifices only. No selfishness, no name, no fame, yours or mine, nor my Master's even! Work, work the idea, the plan, my boys, my brave, noble, good souls — to the wheel, to the wheel put your shoulders! Stop not to look back for name, or fame, or any such nonsense. Throw self overboard and work. Remember, "The grass when made into a rope by being joined together can even chain a mad elephant." The Lord's blessings on you all! His power be in you all— as I believe it is already. "Wake up, stop not until the goal is reached", say the Vedas. Up, up, the long night is passing, the day is approaching, the wave has risen, nothing will be able to resist its tidal fury. The spirit, my boys, the spirit; the love, my children, the love; the faith, the belief; and fear not! The greatest sin is fear.

My blessings on all. Tell all the noble souls in Madras who have helped our cause that I send them my eternal love and gratitude, but I beg of them not to slacken. Throw the idea broadcast. Do not be proud; do not insist upon anything dogmatic; do not go against anything — ours is to put chemicals together, the Lord knows how and when the crystal will form. Above all, be not inflated with my success or yours. Great works are to be done; what is this small success in comparison with what is to come? Believe, believe, the decree has gone forth, the fiat of the Lord has gone forth — India must rise, the masses and the poor are to be made happy. Rejoice that you are the chosen instruments in His hands. The flood of spirituality has risen. I see it is rolling over the land resistless, boundless, all-absorbing. Every man to the fore, every good will be added to its forces, every hand will smooth its way, and glory be unto the Lord! . . .

I do not require any help. Try to get up a fund, buy some magic-lanterns, maps, globes, etc., and some chemicals. Get every evening a crowd of the poor and low, even the Pariahs, and lecture to them about religion first, and then teach them through the magic-lantern and other things, astronomy, geography, etc., in the dialect of the people. Train up a band of fiery young men. Put your fire in them and gradually increase the organization, letting it widen and widen its circle. Do the best you can, do not wait to cross the river when the water has all run down. Printing magazines, papers, etc., are good, no doubt, but actual work, my boys even if infinitesimal, is better than eternal scribbling and talking. Call a meeting at Bhattacharya's. Get a little money and buy those things I have just now stated, hire a hut, and go to work. Magazines are secondary, but this is primary. You must have a hold on the masses. Do not be afraid of a small beginning, great things come afterwards. Be courageous. Do not try to lead your brethren, but serve them. The brutal mania for leading has sunk many a great ship in the waters of life. Take care especially of that, i.e. be unselfish even unto death, and work. I could not write all I was going to say, but the Lord will give you all understanding, my brave boys. At it, my boys! Glory unto the Lord! . . .

Yours affectionately,
Vivekananda.

11 — ALASINGA

U. S. A.,
11th July, 1894.

Dear Alasinga,

You must never write to me anywhere else but 541 Dearborn Ave., Chicago. Your last letter has travelled the whole country to come to me, and this was only because I am so well known. Some of the resolutions are to be sent to Dr. Barrows with a letter thanking him for his kindness to me and asking him to publish the letter in some American newspapers — as that would be the best refutation of the false charges of the missionaries that I do not represent anybody. Learn business, my boy. We will do great things yet! Last year I only sowed the seeds; this year I mean to reap. In the meanwhile, keep up as much enthusiasm as possible in India. Let Kidi go his own way. He will come out all right in time. I have taken his responsibility. He has a perfect right to his own opinion. Make him write for the paper; that will keep him in good temper! My blessings on him.

Start the journal and I will send you articles from time to time. You must send a paper and a letter to Professor J. H. Wright of Harvard University, Boston, thanking him as having been the first man who stood as my friend and asking him to publish it in the papers, thus giving the lie to the missionaries.

In the Detroit lecture I got $900, i.e. Rs. 2,700. In other lectures, I earned in one, $2,500, i.e. Rs. 7,500 in one hour, but got only 200 dollars! I was cheated by a roguish Lecture Bureau. I have given them up. I spent a good deal here; only about $3,000 remains.

I shall have to print much matter next year. I am going regularly to work... The sheer power of the will will do everything... You must organise a society which should regularly meet, and write to me about it as often as you can. In fact, get up as much enthusiasm as you can. Only, beware of falsehood. Go to work, my boys, the fire will come to you! The faculty of organisation is entirely absent in our nature, but this has to be infused. The great secret is — absence of jealousy. Be always ready to concede to the opinions of your brethren, and try always to conciliate. That is the whole secret. Fight on bravely! Life is short! Give it up to a great cause. Why do you not write anything about Narasimha? He is almost starving. I gave him something. Then he went over to somewhere, I do not know where, and does not write. Akshaya is a good boy. I like him very much. No use quarrelling with the Theosophists. Do not go and tell them all I write to you... Theosophists are our pioneers, do you know? Now Judge is a Hindu and Col. a Buddhist, and Judge is the ablest man here. Now tell the Hindu Theosophists to support Judge. Even if you can write Judge a letter, thanking him as a co-religionist and for his labours in presenting Hinduism before Americans; that will do his heart much good. We must not join any sect, but we must sympathise and work with each... Work, work — conquer all by your love! ...

Try to expand. Remember the only sign of life is motion and growth. You must send the passed resolution to Dr. J. H. Barrows. . ., Dr. Paul Carus. . ., Senator Palmer. . ., Mrs. J. J. Bagley. . ., it must come officially... I write this because I do not think you know the ways of foreign nations... Keep on steadily. So far we have done wonderful things. Onward, brave souls, we will gain! Organise and found societies and go to work, that is the only way.

At this time of the year there is not much lecturing to be done here; so I will devote myself to my pen and write. I shall be hard at work all the time, and then, when the cold weather comes and people return to their homes, I shall begin lecturing again and at the same time organise societies.

My love and blessings to you all. I never forget anybody, though I do not write often. Then again, I am now, continuously travelling, and letters have to be redirected from one place to another.

Work hard. Be holy and pure and the fire will come.

Yours affectionately,
Vivekananda.

12 — SISTER

Annisquam,
20th August, 1894.

Dear Sister[1],

Your very kind letter duly reached me at Annisquam. I am with the Bagleys once more. They are kind as usual. Professor Wright was not here. But he came day before yesterday and we have very nice time

1. Isabelle McKindley.

together. Mr. Bradley of Evanston, whom you have met at Evanston, was here. His sister-in-law had me sit for a picture several days and had painted me. I had some very fine boating and one evening overturned the boat and had a good drenching — clothes and all.

I had very very nice time at Greenacre. They were all so earnest and kind people. Fanny Hartley and Mrs. Mills have by this time gone back home I suppose.

From here I think I will go back to New York. Or I may go to Boston to Mrs. Ole Bull. Perhaps you have heard of Mr. Ole Bull, the great violinist of this country. She is his widow. She is a very spiritual lady. She lives in Cambridge and has a fine big parlour made of woodwork brought all the way from India. She wants me to come over to her any time and use her parlour to lecture. Boston of course is the great field for everything, but the Boston people as quickly take hold of anything as give it up; while the New Yorkers are slow, but when they get hold of anything they do it with a mortal grip.

I have kept pretty good health all the time and hope to do in the future. I had no occasion yet to draw on my reserve, yet I am rolling on pretty fair. And I have given up all money-making schemes and will be quite satisfied with a bite and a shed and work on.

I believe you are enjoying your summer retreat. Kindly convey my best regards and love to Miss Howe and Mr. Frank Howe.

Perhaps I did not tell you in my last how I slept and lived and preached under the trees and for a few days at least found myself once more in the atmosphere of heaven.

Most probably I will make New York my centre for the next winter; and as soon as I fix on that, I will write to you. I am not yet settled in my ideas of remaining in this country any more. I cannot settle anything of that sort. I must bide my time. May the Lord bless you all for ever and ever is the constant prayer of your ever affectionate brother,

Vivekananda.

13 — ALASINGA

U. S. A.,
31st August, 1894.

Dear Alasinga,

I just now saw an editorial on me about the circular from Madras in the Boston Transcript. Nothing has reached me yet. They will reach me soon if you have sent them already. So far you have done wonderfully, my boy. Do not mind what I write in some moments of nervousness. One gets nervous sometimes alone in a country 15,000 miles from home, having to fight every inch of ground with orthodox inimical Christians. You must take those into consideration, my brave boy, and work right along.

Perhaps you have heard from Bhattacharya that I received a beautiful letter from G. G. His address was scrawled in such a fashion as to become perfectly illegible to me. So I could not reply to him direct. But I have done all that he desired. I have sent over my photograph and written to the Raja of Mysore. Now I have sent a phonograph to Khetri Raja...

Now send always Indian newspapers about me to me over here. I want to read them in the papers themselves — do you know? Now lastly, you must write to me all about Mr. Charu Chandra who has been so kind to me. Give him my heartfelt thanks; but (between you and me) I unfortunately do not remember him. Would you give me particulars?

The Theosophists here now like me, but they are 650 in all!! There are the Christian Scientists. All of them like me. They are about a million. I work with both, but join none, and will with the Lord's grace would them both after the true fashion; for they are after all mumbling half realised truth. Narasimha, perhaps, by the time this reaches you, will get the money etc.

I have received a letter from Cat, but it requires a book to answer all his queries. So I send him my blessings through you and ask you to remind him that we agree to differ — and see the harmony of contrary points. So it does not matter what he believes in; he must act. Give my love to Balaji, G. G., Kidi, Doctor, and to all our friends and all the great and patriotic souls, who were brave and noble enough to sink their differences for their country's cause.

With a magazine or journal or organ — you become the Secretary thereof. You calculate the cost of starting the magazine and the work, how much the least is necessary to start it, and then write to me giving name and address of the Society, and I will send you money myself, and not only that, I will get others in America to subscribe annually to it liberally. So ask them of Calcutta to do the same. Give me Dharmapala's address. He is a great and good man. He will work wonderfully with us. Now organise a little society. You will have to take charge of the whole movement, not as a leader, but as a servant. Do you know, the least show of leading destroys everything by rousing jealousy?

Accede to everything. Only try to retain all of my friends together. Do you see? And work slowly up. Let G. G. and others, who have no immediate necessity for earning something, do as they are doing, i.e. casting the idea broadcast. G. G. is doing well at Mysore. That is the way. Mysore will be in time a great stronghold.

I am now going to write my mems in a book and next winter will go about this country organising societies here. This is a great field of work, and everything done here prepares England. So far you have done very well indeed, my brave boy — all strength shall be given to you.

I have now Rs. 9,000 with me, part of which I will send over to you for the organisation; and I will get many people to send money to you in Madras yearly, half-yearly, or monthly. You now start a Society and a journal and the necessary apparatus. This must be a secret amongst only a few — but at the same time try to collect funds from Mysore and elsewhere to build a temple in Madras which should have a library and some rooms for the office and the preachers who should be Sannyâsins, and for Vairâgis (men of renunciation) who may chance to come. Thus we shall progress inch by inch. This is a great field for my work, and everything done here prepares the way for my coming work in England...

You know the greatest difficulty with me is to keep or even to touch money. It is disgusting and debasing. So you must organise a Society to take charge of the practical and pecuniary part of it. I have friends here who take care of all my monetary concerns. Do you see? It will be a wonderful relief to me to get rid of horrid money affairs. So the sooner you organise yourselves and you be ready as secretary and treasurer to enter into direct communication with my friends and sympathisers here, the better for you and me. Do that quickly, and write to me. Give the society a non-sectarian name... Do you write to my brethren at the Math to organise in a similar fashion... Great things are in store for you Alasinga. Or if you think proper, you get some of the big folks to be named as office-bearers of the Society, while you work in the real sense. Their name will be a great thing. If your duties are too severe and do not let you have any time, let G. G. do the business part, and by and by I hope to make you independent of your college work so that you may, without starving yourself and family, devote your whole soul to the work. So work, my boys, work! The rough part of the work has been smoothened and rounded; now it will roll on better and better every year. And if you can simply keep it going well until I come to India, the work will progress by leaps and bounds. Rejoice that you have done so much. When you feel gloomy, think what has been done within the last year. How, rising from nothing, we have the eyes of the world fixed upon us now. Not only India, but the world outside, is expecting great things of us. Missionaries or M — or foolish officials — none will be able to resist truth and love and sincerity. Are you sincere? unselfish even unto death? and loving? Then fear not, not even death. Onward, my lads! The whole world requires Light. It is expectant! India alone has that Light, not in magic, mummery, and charlatanism, but in the teaching of the glories of the spirit of real religion — of the highest spiritual truth. That is why the Lord has preserved the race through all its vicissitudes unto the present day. Now the time has come. Have faith that you are all, my brave lads, born to do great things! Let not the barks of puppies frighten you — no, not even the thunderbolts of heaven — but stand up and work!

Ever yours affectionately,
Vivekananda.

14 — ALASINGA

U. S. A,
21st September, 1894.

Dear Alasinga,

... I have been continuously travelling from place to place and working incessantly, giving lectures, holding classes, etc.

I have not been able to write yet for my proposed book. Perhaps I may be able to take it in hand later on. I have made some nice friends here amongst the liberal people, and a few amongst the orthodox. I hope to return soon to India — I have had enough of this country and especially as too much work is making me nervous. The giving of too many public lectures and constant hurry have brought on this nervousness. I do not care for this busy, meaningless, money-making life. So you see, I will soon return. Of course, there is a growing section with whom I am very popular, and who will like to have me here all the time. But I think I have had enough of newspaper blazoning and humbugging of a public life. I do not care the least for it...

There is no hope for money for our project here. It is useless to hope. No large number of men in any country do good out of mere sympathy. The few who really give money in the Christian lands often do so through priestcraft and fear of hell. So it is as in our Bengali proverb, "Kill a cow and make a pair of shoes out of the leather and give them in charity to a Brahmana". So it is here, and so everywhere; and then, the Westerners are miserly in comparison to our race. I sincerely believe that the Asians are the most charitable race in the world, only they are very poor.

I am going to live for a few months in New York. That city is the head, hand, and purse of the country. Of course, Boston is called the Brahmanical city, and here in America there are hundreds of thousands that sympathise with me... The New York people are very open. I will see what can be done there, as I have some very influential friends. After all, I am getting disgusted with this lecturing business. It will take a long time for the Westerners to understand the higher spirituality, Everything is £. s. d. to them. If a religion brings them money or health or beauty or long life, they will all flock to it, otherwise not...

Give to Balaji, G. G., and all of our friends my best love.

Yours with everlasting love,
Vivekananda.

15 — KIDI

U. S. A.,
21st September, 1894.

Dear Kidi,

I am very sorry to hear your determination of giving up the world so soon. The fruit falls from the tree when it gets ripe. So wait for the time to come. Do not hurry. Moreover, no one has the right to make others miserable by his foolish acts. Wait, have patience, everything will come right in time.

Yours with blessings,
Vivekananda.

16 — SISTER

Boston,
26th Sept, 1894.

Dear Sister[1],

Your letter with the India mail just to hand. A quantity of newspaper clippings were sent over to me from India. I send them back for your perusal and safe keeping.

I am busy writing letters to India last few days. I will remain a few days more in Boston.

With my love and blessings,

Yours ever affly.,
Vivekananda.

---

1. Isabelle Mckindley.

17 — ALASINGA

U. S. A.
27th September, 1894.

Dear Alasinga,

... One thing I find in the books of my speeches and sayings published in Calcutta. Some of them are printed in such a way as to savour of political views; whereas I am no politician or political agitator. I care only for the Spirit — when that is right everything will be righted by itself... So you must warn the Calcutta people that no political significance be ever attached falsely to any of my writings or sayings. What nonsense I ... I heard that Rev. Kali Charan Banerji in a lecture to Christian missionaries said that I was a political delegate. If it was said publicly, then publicly ask the Babu for me to write to any of the Calcutta papers and prove it, or else take back his foolish assertion. This is their trick! I have said a few harsh words in honest criticism of Christian governments in general, but that does not mean that I care for, or have any connection with politics or that sort of thing. Those who think it very grand to print extracts from those lectures and want to prove that I am a political preacher, to them I say, "Save me from my friends." . . .

... Tell my friends that a uniform silence is all my answer to my detractors. If I give them tit for tat, it would bring us down to a level with them. Tell them that truth will take care of itself, and that they are not to fight anybody for me. They have much to learn yet, and they are only children. They are still full of foolish golden dreams — mere boys!

. . .This nonsense of public life and newspaper blazoning has disgusted me thoroughly. I long to go back to the Himalayan quiet.

Ever yours affectionately,
Vivekananda.

18 — ALASINGA

U. S. A.,
29th September, 1894.

Dear Alasinga,

You all have done well, my brave unselfish children. I am so proud of you... Hope and do not despair. After such a start, if you despair you are a fool...

Our field is India, and the value of foreign appreciation is in rousing India up. That is all... We must have a strong base from which to spread... Do not for a moment quail. Everything will come all right. It is will that moves the world.

You need not be sorry, my son, on account of the young men becoming Christians. What else can they be under the existing social bandages, especially in Madras? Liberty is the first condition of growth. Your ancestors gave every liberty to the soul, and religion grew. They put the body under every bondage, and society did not grow. The opposite is the case in the West — every liberty to society, none to religion. Now are falling off the shackles from the feet of Eastern society as from those of Western religion.

Each again will have its type; the religious or introspective in India, the scientific or out-seeing in the West. The West wants every bit of spirituality through social improvement. The East wants every bit of social power through spirituality. Thus it was that the modern reformers saw no way to reform but by first crushing out the religion of India. They tried, and they failed. Why? Because few of them ever studied their own religion, and not one ever underwent the training necessary to understand the Mother of all religions. I claim that no destruction of religion is necessary to improve the Hindu society, and that this state of society exists not on account of religion, but because religion has not been applied to society as it should have been. This I am ready to prove from our old books, every word of it. This is what I teach, and this is what we must struggle all our lives to carry out. But it will take time, a long time to study. Have patience and work. उध्दरेदात्मनात्मानम् — Save yourself by yourself.

Yours etc.,
Vivekananda.

PS. The present Hindu society is organised only for spiritual men, and hopelessly crushes out everybody else. Why? Where shall they go who want to enjoy the world a little with its frivolities? Just as our religion takes in all, so should our society. This is to be worked out by first understanding the true principles of our religion and then applying them to society. This is the slow but sure work to be done.

19 — VEHEMIA

Washington,
23rd October, 1894.

Dear Vehemia Chand Limbdi,

I am going on very well in this country. By this time I have become one of their own teachers. They all like me and my teachings... I travel all over the country from one place to another, as was my habit in India, preaching and teaching. Thousands and thousands have listened to me and taken my ideas in a very kindly spirit. It is the most expensive country, but the Lord provides for me everywhere I go.

With my love to you and all my friends there (Limbdi, Rajputana).

Yours,
Vivekananda.

20 — SISTER

Washington,
C/O Mrs. T. Totten.
1708 W I Street,
26th (?) October, 1894.

Dear Sister[1],

Excuse my long silence; but I have been regularly writing to Mother Church. I am sure you are all enjoying this nice cool weather. I am enjoying Bal-

---
1. Isabelle Mckindley.

timore and Washington very much. I will go hence to Philadelphia. I thought Miss Mary was in Philadelphia, and so I wanted her address. But as she is in some other place near Philadelphia, I do not want to give her the trouble to come up to see me, as Mother Church says.

The lady with whom I am staying is Mrs. Totten, a niece of Miss Howe. I will be her guest more than a week yet; so you may write to me to her care.

I intend going over to England this winter somewhere in January or February. A lady from London with whom one of my friends is staying has sent an invitation to me to go over as her guest; and from India they are urging me every day to come back.

How did you like Pitoo in the cartoon? Do not show it to anybody. It is too bad of our people to caricature Pitoo that way.

I long ever so much to hear from you, but take a little more care to make your letter just a bit more distinct. Do not be angry for the suggestion.

Your ever loving brother,
Vivekananda.

21 — BLESSED AND BELOVED

Washington,
27th October, 1894.

Blessed And Beloved[2],

By this time you must have received my other letters. You must excuse me for certain harshness of tone sometimes, and you know full well how I love you. You have asked me often to send over to you all about my movements in this country and all my lecture reports. I am doing exactly here what I used to do in India. Always depending on the Lord and making no plans ahead... Moreover you must remember that I have to work incessantly in this country, and that I have no time to put together my thoughts in the form of a book, so much so, that this constant rush has worn my nerves, and I am feeling it. I cannot express my obligation to you, G. G., and all my friends in Madras, for the most unselfish and heroic work you did for me. But it was not at all meant to blazon me, but to make you conscious of your own strength. I am not an organiser, my nature tends towards scholarship and meditation. I think I have worked enough, now I want rest and to teach a little to those that have come to me from my Gurudeva (venerable Guru). You have known now what you can do, for it is really you, young men of Madras, that have done all; I am only the figurehead. I am a Tyâgi (detached) monk. I only want one thing. I do not believe in a God or religion which cannot wipe the widow's tears or bring a piece of bread to the orphan's mouth. However sublime be the theories, however well-spun may be the philosophy — I do not call it religion so long as it is confined to books and dogmas. The eye is in the forehead and not in the back. Move onward and carry into practice that which you are very proud to call your religion, and God bless you!

Look not at me, look to yourselves. I am happy to have been the occasion of rousing an enthusiasm. Take advantage of it, float along with it, and everything will come right. Love never fails, my son; today or tomorrow or ages after, truth will conquer. Love shall win the victory. Do you love your fellow men? Where should you go to seek for God — are not all the poor, the miserable, the weak, Gods? Why not worship them first? Why go to dig a well on the shores of the Gangâ? Believe in the omnipotent power of love. Who cares for these tinsel puffs of name? I never keep watch of what the newspapers are saying. Have you love? — You are omnipotent. Are you perfectly unselfish? If so, you are irresistible. It is character that pays everywhere. It is the Lord who protects His children in the depths of the sea. Your country requires heroes; be heroes! God bless you!

Everybody wants me to come over to India. They think we shall be able to do more if I come over. They are mistaken, my friend. The present enthusiasm is only a little patriotism, it means nothing. If it is true and genuine, you will find in a short time hundreds of heroes coming forward and carrying on the work.

---

2. Alasinga Perumal.

Therefore know that you have really done all, and go on. Look not for me. Akshoy Kumar Ghosh is in London. He sent a beautiful invitation from London to come to Miss Müller's. And I hope I am going in January or February next. Bhattacharya writes me to come over. Here is a grand field. What have I to do with this "ism" or that "ism"? I am the servant of the Lord, and where on earth is there a better field than here for propagating all high ideas? Here, where if one man is against me, a hundred hands are ready to help me; here, where man feels for man, weeps for his fellow-men and women are goddesses! Even idiots may stand up to hear themselves praised, and cowards assume the attitude of the brave when everything is sure to turn out well, but the true hero works in silence. How many Buddhas die before one finds expression! My son, I believe in God, and I believe in man. I believe in helping the miserable. I believe in going even to hell to save others. Talk of the Westerners? They have given me food, shelter, friendship, protection — even the most orthodox Christians! What do our people do when any of their priests go to India? You do not touch them even, they are Mlechchhas! No man, no nation, my son, can hate others and live; India's doom was sealed the very day they invented the word Mlechchha and stopped from communion with others. Take care how you foster that idea. It is good to talk glibly about the Vedanta, but how hard to carry out even its least precepts!

Ever yours with blessings,
Vivekananda.

PS. Take care of these two things — love of power and jealousy. Cultivate always "faith in yourself".

22 — ALASINGA

U. S. A.,
30th November, 1894.

Dear Alasinga,

I am glad to leant that the phonograph and the letter have reached you safely. You need not send any more newspaper cuttings. I have been deluged with them. Enough of that. Now go to work for the organisation. I have started one already in New York and the Vice-President will soon write to you. Keep correspondence with them. Soon I hope to get up a few in other places. We must organise our forces not to make a sect — not on religious matters, but on the secular business part of it. A stirring propaganda must be launched out. Put your heads together and organise.

What nonsense about the miracle of Ramakrishna! . . .Miracles I do not know nor understand. Had Ramakrishna nothing to do in the world but turning wine into the Gupta's medicine? Lord save me from such Calcutta people! What materials to work with! If they can write a real life of Shri Ramakrishna with the idea of showing what he came to do and teach, let them do it, otherwise let them not distort his life and sayings. These people want to know God who see in Shri Ramakrishna nothing but jugglery! ... Now let Kidi translate his love, his knowledge, his teachings, his eclecticism, etc. This is the theme. The life of Shri Ramakrishna was an extraordinary searchlight under whose illumination one is able to really understand the whole scope of Hindu religion. He was the object-lesson of all the theoretical knowledge given in the Shâstras (scriptures). He showed by his life what the Rishis and Avatâras really wanted to teach. The books were theories, he was the realisation. This man had in fifty-one years lived the five thousand years of national spiritual life and so raised himself to be an object-lesson for future generations. The Vedas can only be explained and the Shastras reconciled by his theory calf Avasthâ or stages — that we must not only tolerate others, but positively embrace them, and that truth is the basis of all religions. Now on these lines a most impressive and beautiful life can be written. Well, everything in good time. Avoid all irregular indecent expressions about sex etc. . ., because other nations think it the height of indecency to mention such things, and his life in English is going to be read by the whole world. I read a Bengali life sent over. It is full of such words... So take care. Carefully avoid such words and expressions. The Calcutta friends have not a cent worth of ability; but they have their assertions of individuality. They are too high to listen to advice. I do not know what to do with these wonderful gentlemen. I have not got much hope in that quarter. His will be done. I am simply ashamed of the Bengali book. The writer perhaps thought he was a frank recorder of truth and keeping the very language of Paramahamsa. But he does not remember that Ramakrishna would never use that language before ladies. And this man expects his work to be read by men and women alike! Lord, save me from fools! They, again, have their own freaks; they all knew him! Bosh and rot... Beggars taking upon themselves the air of kings! Fools thinking they are all wise! Puny slaves thinking that they are masters! That is their condition. I do not know what to do. Lord save me. I have all hope in Madras. Push on with your work; do not be governed by the Calcutta people. Keep them in good humour in the hope that some one of them may turn good. But push on with your work independently. "Many come to sit at dinner when it is cooked." Take care and work on.

Yours ever with blessings,
Vivekananda.

23 — KIDI

U. S. A.
30th November, 1894.

Dear Kidi,

... As to the wonderful stories published about Shri Ramakrishna, I advise you to keep clear of them and the fools who write them. They are true, but the fools will make a mess of the whole thing, I am sure. He had a whole world of knowledge to teach, why insist upon unnecessary things as miracles really are! They do not prove anything. Matter does not prove Spirit. What connection is there between the existence of God, Soul, or immortality, and the working of miracles?... Preach Shri Ramakrishna. Pass the Cup that has satisfied your thirst... Preach Bhakti. Do not disturb your head with metaphysical nonsense, and do not disturb others by your bigotry...

Yours ever with blessings,
Vivekananda.

24 — BLESSED AND BELOVED

U. S. A.,
26th December, 1894.

Blessed And Beloved[1],

... In reference to me every now and then attacks are made in missionary papers (so I hear), but I never care to see them. If you send any of those made in India, I should throw them into the waste-paper basket. A little agitation was necessary for our work. We have had enough. Pay no more attention to what people say about me, whether good or bad. You go on with your work and remember that "Never one meets with evil who tries to do good" (Gita, VI. 40).

Every day the people here are appreciating me. And between you and me, I am more of an influence here than you dream of. Everything must proceed slowly ... I have written to you before, and I write again, that I shall not pay heed to any criticism or praise in the newspapers. They are consigned to the fire. Do you do the same. Pay no attention whatsoever to newspaper nonsense or criticism. Be sincere and do your duty. Everything will come all right Truth must triumph. . .

Missionary misrepresentations should be beneath your notice... Perfect silence is the best refutation to them and I wish you to maintain the same... Make Mr. Subrahmanya Iyer the President of your Society. He is one of the sincerest and noblest men I know; and in him intellect and emotion are beautifully blended. Push on in your work, without counting much on me; work on your own account... As for me, I do not know when I shall go back; I am working here and in India as well...

With my love to you all,

---

1. Alasinga Perumal.

Yours ever with blessings,
Vivekananda.

25 — ALASINGA

541 Dearborn Avenue,
Chicago, 1894.

Dear Alasinga,

Your letter just to hand... I was mistaken in asking you to publish the scraps I sent you. It was one of my awful mistakes. It shows a moment's weakness. Money can be raised in this country by lecturing for two or three years. But I have tried a little, and although there is much public appreciation of my work, it is thoroughly uncongenial and demoralising to me...

I have read what you say about the Indian papers and their criticisms, which are natural. Jealousy is the central vice of every enslaved race. And it is jealousy and want of combination which cause and perpetuate slavery. You cannot feel the truth of this remark until you come out of India. The secret of Westerners' success is this power of combination, the basis of which is mutual trust and appreciation. The weaker and more cowardly a nation is, so much the more is this sin visible... But, my son, you ought not to expect anything from a slavish race. The case is almost desperate no doubt, but let me put the case before you all. Can you put life into this dead mass — dead to almost all moral aspiration, dead to all future possibilities — and always ready to spring upon those that would try to do good to them? Can you take the position of a physician who tries to pour medicine down the throat of a kicking and refractory child? ... An American or a European always supports his countrymen in a foreign country... Let me remind you again, "Thou hast the right to work but not to the fruits thereof." Stand firm like a rock. Truth always triumphs. Let the children of Shri Ramakrishna be true to themselves and everything will be all right. We may not live to see the outcome, but as sure as we live, it will come sooner or later. What India wants is a new electric fire to stir up a fresh vigour in the national veins. This was ever, and always will be, slow work. Be content to work, and, above all, be true to yourself. Be pure, staunch, and sincere to the very backbone, and everything will be all right. If you have marked anything in the disciples of Shri Ramakrishna, it is this — they are sincere to the backbone. My task will be done, and I shall be quite content to die, if I can bring up and launch one hundred such men over India. He, the Lord, knows best. Let ignorant men talk nonsense. We neither seek aid nor avoid it — we are the servants of the Most High. The petty attempts of small men should be beneath our notice. Onward! Upon ages of struggle a character is built. Be not discouraged. One word of truth can never be lost; for ages it may be hidden under rubbish, but it will show itself sooner or later. Truth is indestructible, virtue is indestructible, purity is indestructible. Give me a genuine man; I do not want masses of converts. My son, hold fast! Do not care for anybody to help you. Is not the Lord infinitely greater than all human help? Be holy — trust in the Lord, depend on Him always, and you are on the right track; nothing can prevail against you...

Let us pray, "Lead, Kindly Light" — a beam will come through the dark, and a hand will be stretched forth to lead us. I always pray for you: you must pray for me. Let each one of us pray day and night for the downtrodden millions in India who are held fast by poverty, priestcraft, and tyranny — pray day and night for them. I care more to preach religion to them than to the high and the rich. I am no metaphysician, no philosopher, nay, no saint. But I am poor, I love the poor. I see what they call the poor of this country, and how many there are who feel for them! What an immense difference in India! Who feels there for the two hundred millions of men and women sunken for ever in poverty and ignorance? Where is the way out? Who feels for them? They cannot find light or education. Who will bring the light to them — who will travel from door to door bringing education to them? Let these people be your God — think of them, work for them, pray for them incessantly — the Lord will show you the way. Him I call a Mahâtman (great soul) whose heart bleeds for the poor, otherwise he is a Durâtman (wicked soul). Let us unite our wills in continued prayer for their good. We may die unknown, unpitied, unbewailed, without accomplishing anything — but not one thought will be lost. It will take effect, sooner or later. My heart is too full to express my feeling; you know it, you can imagine it. So long as the millions live in hunger and ignorance, I hold every man a traitor who, having been educated at their expense, pays not the least heed to them! I call those men who strut about in their finery, having got all their money by grinding the poor, wretches, so long as they do not do anything for those two hundred millions who are now no better than hungry savages! We are poor, my brothers, we are nobodies, but such have been always the instruments of the Most High. The Lord bless you all.

With all love,
Vivekananda.

26 — DHARMAPALA

U. S. A.,
1894. Dear Dharmapala,

I have forgotten your address in Calcutta; so I direct this to the Math. I heard about your speeches in Calcutta and how wonderful was the effect produced by them. A certain retired missionary here wrote me a letter addressing me as brother and then hastily went to publish my short answer and make a show. But you know what people here think of such gentlemen. Moreover, the same missionary went privately to some of my friends to ask them not to befriend me. Of course he met with universal contempt. I am quite astonished at this man's behaviour — a preacher of religion to take to such underhand dealings! Unfortunately too much of that in every country and in every religion. Last winter I travelled a good deal in this country although the weather was very severe. I thought it would be dreadful, but I did not find it so after all. You remember Col. Neggenson, President of the Free Religious Society. He makes very kind inquiries about you. I met Dr. Carpenter of Oxford (England) the other day. He delivered an address on the ethics of Buddhism at Plymouth. It was very sympathetic and scholarly. He made inquiries about you and your paper. Hope, your noble work will succeed. You are a worthy servant of Him who came Bahujana Hitâya Bahujana Sukhâya (for the good of the many, for the happiness of the many).

... The Christianity that is preached in India is quite different from what one sees here; you will be astonished to hear, Dharmapala, that I have friends in this country amongst the clergy of the Episcopal and even Presbyterian churches, who are as broad, as liberal, and as sincere as you are in your own religion. The real spiritual man is broad everywhere. His love forces him to be so. Those to whom religion is a trade are forced to become narrow and mischievous by their introduction into religion of the competitive, fighting, and selfish methods of the world.

Yours ever in brotherly love,
Vivekananda.

27 — ALASINGA

U. S. A.,
1894.

Dear Alasinga,

Listen to an old story. A lazy tramp sauntering along the road saw an old man sitting at the door of his house and stopped to inquire of him the whereabouts of a certain place. "How far is such and such a village?" he asked. The old man remained silent. The man repeated his query several times. Still there was no answer. Disgusted at this, the traveller turned to go away. The old man then stood up and said, "The village of — is only a mile from here." "What!" said the tramp, "Why did you not speak when I asked you before?" "Because then", said the old man, "you seemed so halting and careless about proceeding, but now you are starting off in good earnest, and you have a right to an answer."

Will you remember this story, my son? Go to work, the rest will come: "Whosoever not trusting in anything else but Me, rests on Me, I supply him with everything he needs" (Gitâ, IX. 22). This is no dream.

... The work should be in the line of preaching and serving, at the present time. Choose a place of meeting where you can assemble every week holding a service and reading the Upanishads with the commentaries, and so slowly go on learning and working. Every thing will come to you if you put your shoulders to the wheel. . .

Now, go to work! G. G.'s nature is of the emotional type, you have a level head; so work together; plunge in; this is only the beginning. Every nation must save itself; we must not depend upon funds from America for the revival of Hinduism, for that is a delusion. To have a centre is a great thing; try to secure such a place in a large town like Madras, end go on radiating a living force in all directions. Begin slowly. Start with a few lay missionaries; gradually others will come who will devote their whole lives to the work. Do not try to be a ruler. He is the best ruler who can serve well. Be true unto death. The work we want — we do not seek wealth, name or fame... Be brave... Endeavour to interest the people of Madras in collecting funds for the purpose, and then make a beginning... Be perfectly unselfish and you will be sure to succeed... Without losing the independence in work, show all regards to your superiors. Work in harmony... My children must be ready to jump into fire, if needed, to accomplish their work. Now work, work, work! We will stop and compare notes later on. Have patience, perseverance, and purity.

I am writing no book on Hinduism just now. I am simply jotting down my thoughts. I do not know if I shall publish them. What is in books? The world is too full of foolish things already. If you could start a magazine on Vedantic lines, it would further our object. Be positive; do not criticise others. Give your message, teach what you have to teach, and there stop. The Lord knows the rest...

Do not send me any more newspapers, as I do not notice the missionary criticisms on myself; and here the public estimation of me is better for that reason.

... If you are really my children, you will fear nothing, stop at nothing. You will be like lions. We must rouse India and the whole world. No cowardice. I will take no nay. Do you understand? Be true unto death!
... The secret of this is Guru-Bhakti — faith in the Guru unto death! Have you that? I believe with all my heart that you have, and you know that I have confidence in you — so go to work. You must succeed. My prayers and benedictions follow every step you take. Work in harmony. Be patient with everybody. Every one has my love. I am watching you. Onward! Onward! This is just the beginning. My little work here makes a big echo in India, do you know? So I shall not return there in a hurry. My intention is to do something permanent here, and with that object I am working day by day. I am every day gaining the confidence of the American people... Expand your hearts and hopes, as wide as the world. Study Sanskrit, especially the three Bhâshyas (commentaries) on the Vedanta. Be ready, for I have many plans for the future. Try to be a magnetic speaker. Electrify the people. Everything will come to you if you have faith. So tell Kidi, in fact, tell all my children there. In time they will do great things at which the world will wonder. Take heart and work. Show me something you have done. Show me a temple, a press, a paper, a home for me. Where shall I come to if you cannot make a home for me in Madras? Electrify people. Raise funds and preach. Be true to your mission. Thus far you promise well, so go on and do better and better still.

. . .Do not fight with people; do not antagonise anyone. Why should we mind if Jack and John become Christians? Let them follow whatever religion suits them. Why should you mix in controversies? Bear with the various opinions of everybody. Patience, purity, and perseverance will prevail.

Yours etc.,
Vivekananda.

28 — MRS. BULL

541 Dearborn Avenue,
Chicago,
3rd January, 1895.

Dear Mrs. Bull,

I lectured at Brooklyn last Sunday, Mrs. Higgins gave a little reception the evening I arrived, and some of the prominent members of the Ethical Society including Dr. Jain [Janes] were there. Some of them thought that such Oriental religious subjects will not interest the Brooklyn public.

But the lecture, through the blessings of the Lord, proved a tremendous success. About 800 of the élite of Brooklyn were present, and the very gentlemen who thought it would not prove a success are trying for organising a series in Brooklyn. The New York course for me is nearly ready, but I do not wish to fix the dates until Miss Thursby comes to New York. As such Miss Phillips who is a friend of Miss Thursby's and who is arranging the New York course for me will act with Miss Thursby in case she wants to get up something in New York.

I owe much to the Hale family and I thought to give them a little surprise by dropping in on New Year's day. I am trying to get a new gown here. The old gown is here, but it is so shrunken by constant washings that it is unfit to wear in public. I am almost confident of finding the exact thing in Chicago.

I hope your father is all right by this time.

With my love to Miss Farmer, Mr. and Mrs. Gibbons and the rest of the holy family, I am ever yours,

Affectionately,
Vivekananda.

PS. I saw Miss Couring at Brooklyn. She was as kind as ever. Give her my love if you write her soon.

29 — G. G.

Chicago,
11th January, 1895.

Dear G. G, (G. G. Narasimhachariar)

Your letter just to hand... The Parliament of Religions was organised with the intention of proving the superiority of the Christian religion over other forms of faith, but the philosophic religion of Hinduism was able to maintain its position notwithstanding. Dr. Barrows and the men of that ilk are very orthodox, and I do not look to them for help... The Lord has sent me many friends in this country, and they are always on the increase. The Lord bless those who have tried to injure me... I have been running all the time between Boston and New York, two great centres of this country, of which Boston may be called the brain and New York, the purse. In both, my success is more than ordinary. I am indifferent to the newspaper reports, and you must not expect me to send any of them to you. A little boom was necessary to begin work. We have had more than enough of that.

I have written to Mani Iyer, and I have given you my directions already. Now show me what you can do. No foolish talk now, but actual work; the Hindus must back their talk with real work; if they cannot they do not deserve anything; that is all. America is not going to give you money for your fads. And why should they? As for me, I want to teach the truth; I do not care whether here or elsewhere.

In future do not pay any heed to what people say either for or against you or me. Work on, be lions; and the Lord will bless you. I shall work incessantly until I die, and even after death I shall work for the good of the world. Truth is infinitely more weighty than untruth; so is goodness. If you possess these, they will make their way by sheer gravity.

I have no connection with the Theosophists. And Judge will help me — pooh! ... Thousands of the best men do care for me; you know this, and have faith in the Lord. I am slowly exercising an influence in this land greater than all the newspaper blazoning of me can do. The orthodox feel it, but they cannot help it. It is the force of character, of purity, and of truth — of personality. So long as I have these things, you can feel easy; no one will be able to injure a hair of my head. If they try, they will fail, saith the Lord... Enough of books and theories. It is the life that is the highest and the only way to stir the hearts of people; it carries the personal magnetism... The Lord is giving me a deeper and deeper insight every day. Work, work, work... Truce to foolish talk; talk of the Lord. Life is too short to be spent in talking about frauds and cranks

You must always remember that every nation must save itself; so must every man; do not look to others for help. Through hard work here, I shall be able now and then to send you a little money for your work; but that is all. If you have to look forward to that, better stop work. Know also that this is a grand field for my ideas, and that I do not care whether they are Hindus or Mohammedans or Christians, but those that love the Lord will always command my service.

... I like to work on calmly and silently, and the Lord is always with me. Follow me, if you will, by being intensely sincere, perfectly unselfish, and, above all, by being perfectly pure. My blessings go with you. In this short life there is no time for the exchange of compliments. We can compare notes and compliment each other to our hearts' content after the battle is finished. Now, do not talk; work, work! work! I do not see anything permanent you have done in India — I do not see any centre you have made — I do not see any temple or hall you have erected — I do not see anybody joining hands with you. There is too much talk, talk, talk! We are great, we are great! Nonsense! We are imbeciles; that is what we are! This hankering after name and fame and all other humbugs — what are they to me? What do I care about them? I should like to see hundreds coming to the Lord! Where are they? I want them, I want to see them. You must seek them out. You only give me name and fame. Have done with name and fame; to work, my brave men, to work! You have not caught my fire yet — you do not understand me! You run in the old ruts of sloth and enjoyments. Down with all sloth, down with all enjoyments here or hereafter. Plunge into the fire and bring the people towards the Lord.

That you may catch my fire, that you may be intensely sincere, that you may die the heroes' death on the field of battle — is the constant prayer of Vivekananda.

PS. Tell Alasinga, Kidi, Dr. Balaji, and all the others not to pin their faith on what Tom, Dick, and Harry say for or against us, but to concentrate all their energy on work.

30 — ALASINGA

U.S.A.,
12th January, 1895.

Dear Alasinga,

I am sorry you still continue to send me pamphlets and newspapers, which I have written you several times not to do. I have no time to peruse them and take notice of them. Please send them no more. I do not care a fig for what the missionaries or the Theosophists say about me. Let them do as they please. The very taking notice of them will be to give them importance. Besides, you know, the missionaries only abuse and never argue.

Now know once and for all that I do not care for name or fame, or any humbug of that type. I want to preach my ideas for the good of the world. You have done a great work; but so far as it goes, it has only given me name and fame. My life is more precious than spending it in getting the admiration of the world. I have no time for such foolery. What work have you done in the way of advancing the ideas and organising in India? None, none, none!

An organisation that will teach the Hindus mutual help and appreciation is absolutely necessary. Five thousand people attended that meeting that was held in Calcutta, and hundreds did the same in other places, to express an appreciation of my work here — well and good! But if you asked them each to give an anna, would they do it? The whole national character is one of childish dependence. They are all ready to enjoy food if it is brought to their mouth, and even some want it pushed down… You do not deserve to live if you cannot help yourselves.

I have given up at present my plan for the education of the masses. It will come by degrees. What I now want is a band of fiery missionaries. We must have a College in Madras to teach comparative religions, Sanskrit, the different schools of Vedanta, and some European languages; we must have a press, and papers printed in English and in the Vernaculars. When this is done, then I shall know that you have accomplished something. Let the nation show that they are ready to do. If you cannot do anything of the kind in India, then let me alone. I have a message to give, let me give it to the people who appreciate it and who will work it out. What care I who takes it? "He who doeth the will of my Father," is my own…

My name should not be made prominent; it is my ideas that I want to see realised. The disciples of all the prophets have always inextricably mixed up the ideas of the Master with the person, and at last killed the ideas for the person. The disciples of Shri Ramakrishna must guard against doing the same thing. Work for the idea, not the person. The Lord bless you.

Yours ever with blessings,
Vivekananda.

31 — MRS. OLE BULL

Brooklyn,
20th January, 1895.

(Written to Mrs. Ole Bull whom Swamiji called "Dhirâ Mâtâ", the "Steady Mother" on the occasion of the loss of her father.)

… I had a premonition of your father's giving up the old body and it is not my custom to write to anyone when a wave of would-be inharmonious Mâyâ strikes him. But these are the great turning points in life, and I know that you are unmoved. The surface of the sea rises and sinks alternately, but to the observant soul — the child of light — each sinking reveals more and more of the depth and of the beds of pearls and coral at the bottom. Coming and going is all pure delusion. The soul never comes nor goes. Where is the place to which it shall go when all space is in the soul? When shall be the time for entering and departing when all time is *in the soul*?

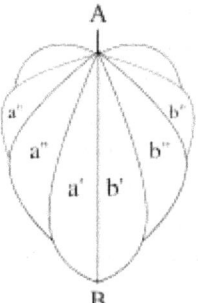

The earth moves, causing the illusion of the movement of the sun; but the sun does not move. So Prakriti, or Maya, or Nature, is moving, changing, unfolding veil after veil, turning over leaf after leaf of this grand book — while the witnessing soul drinks in knowledge, unmoved, unchanged. All souls that ever have been, are, or shall be, are all in the present tense and — to use a material simile — are all standing at one geometrical point. Because the idea of space does occur in the soul, therefore all that were ours, are ours, and will be ours, are always with us, were always with us, and will be always with us. We are in them. They are in us. Take these cells. Though each separate, they are all nevertheless inseparably joined at A B. There they are one. Each is an individual, yet all are one at the axis A B. None can escape from that axis, and however broken or torn the circumference, yet by standing at the axis, we may enter any one of the chambers. This axis is the Lord. There we are one with Him, all in all, and all in God.

The cloud moves across the face of the moon, creating the illusion that the moon is moving. So nature, body, matter moves on, creating the illusion that the soul is moving. Thus we find at last that, that instinct (or inspiration?) which men of every race, whether high or low, have had to feel, viz the presence of the departed about them, is true intellectually also.

Each soul is a star, and all stars are set in that infinite azure, that eternal sky, the Lord. There is the root, the reality, the real individuality of each and all. Religion began with the search after some of these stars that had passed beyond our horizon, and ended in finding them all in God, and ourselves in the same place. The whole secret is, then, that your father has given up the old garment he was wearing and is standing where he was through all eternity. Will he manifest another such garment in this or any other world? I sincerely pray that he may not, until he does so in full consciousness. I pray that none may be dragged anywhither by the unseen power of his own past actions. I pray that all may be free, that is to say, may know that they are free. And if they are to dream again, let us pray that their dreams be all of peace and bliss...

Yours etc.,
Vivekananda.

32 — SISTER

54 W. 33rd Street, N.Y.,
1st February, 1895.

Dear Sister[1],

I just received your beautiful note... Well, sometimes it is a good discipline to be forced to work for work's sake, even to the length of not being allowed to enjoy the fruits of one's labour... I am very glad of your criticisms and am not sorry at all. The other day at Miss Thursby's I had an excited argument with a Presbyterian gentleman, who, as usual, got very hot, angry, and abusive. However, I was afterwards severely reprimanded by Mrs. Bull for this, as such things hinder my work. So, it seems, is your opinion.

I am glad you write about it just now, because I have been giving a good deal of thought to it. In the first place, I am not at all sorry for these things — perhaps that may disgust you — it may. I know full well how good it is for one's worldly prospects to be sweet. I do everything to be sweet, but when it comes to a horrible compromise with the truth within, then I stop. I do not believe in humility. I believe in Samadarshitva — same state of mind with regard to all.

---

1. Miss Mary Hale.

The duty of the ordinary man is to obey the commands of his "God", society; but the children of light never do so. This is an eternal law. One accommodates himself to surroundings and social opinion and gets all good things from society, the giver of all good to such. The other stands alone and draws society up towards him. The accommodating man finds a path of roses; the non-accommodating, one of thorns. But the worshippers of "Vox populi" go to annihilation in a moment; the children of truth live for ever.

I will compare truth to a corrosive substance of infinite power. It burns its way in wherever it falls — in soft substance at once, hard granite slowly, but it must. What is writ is writ. I am so, so sorry, Sister, that I cannot make myself sweet and accommodating to every black falsehood. But I cannot. I have suffered for it all my life. But I cannot. I have essayed and essayed. But I cannot. At last I have given it up. The Lord is great. He will not allow me to become a hypocrite. Now let what is in come out. I have not found a way that will please all, and I cannot but be what I am, true to my own self. "Youth and beauty vanish, life and wealth vanish, name and fame vanish, even the mountains crumble into dust. Friendship and love vanish. Truth alone abides." God of Truth, be Thou alone my guide! I am too old to change now into milk and honey. Allow me to remain as I am. "Without fear — without shopkeeping, caring neither for friend nor foe, do thou hold on to Truth, Sannyâsin, and from this moment give up this world and the next and all that are to come — their enjoyments and their vanities. Truth, be thou alone my guide." I have no desire for wealth or name or fame or enjoyments, Sister — they are dust unto me. I wanted to help my brethren. I have not the tact to earn money, bless the Lord. What reason is there for me to conform to the vagaries of the world around me and not obey the voice of Truth within? The mind is still weak, Sister, it sometimes mechanically clutches at earthly help. But I am not afraid. Fear is the greatest sin my religion teaches.

The last fight with the Presbyterian priest and the long fight afterwards with Mrs. Bull showed me in a clear light what Manu says to the Sannyasin, "Live alone, walk alone." All friendship, all love, is only limitation. There never was a friendship, especially of women, which was not exacting. O great sages! You were right. One cannot serve the God of Truth who leans upon somebody. Be still, my soul! Be alone! and the Lord is with you. Life is nothing! Death is a delusion! All this is not, God alone is! Fear not, my soul! Be alone. Sister, the way is long, the time is short, evening is approaching. I have to go home soon. I have no time to give my manners a finish. I cannot find time to deliver my message. You are good, you are so kind, I will do anything for you; and do not be angry, I see you all are mere children.

Dream no more! Oh, dream no more, my soul! In one word, I have a message to give, I have no time to be sweet to the world, and every attempt at sweetness makes me a hypocrite. I will die a thousand deaths rather than lead a jelly-fish existence and yield to every requirement of this foolish world, no matter whether it be my own country or a foreign country. You are mistaken, utterly mistaken, if you think I have a work, as Mrs. Bull thinks; I have no work under or beyond the sun. I have a message, and I will give it after my own fashion. I will neither Hinduise my message, nor Christianise it, nor make it any "ise" in the world. I will only my-ise it and that is all. Liberty, Mukti, is all my religion, and everything that tries to curb it, I will avoid by fight or flight. Pooh! I try to pacify the priests!! Sister, do not take this amiss. But you are babies and babies must submit to be taught. You have not yet drunk of that fountain which makes "reason unreason, mortal immortal, this world a zero, and of man a God". Come out if you can of this network of foolishness they call this world. Then I will call you indeed brave and free. If you cannot, cheer those that dare dash this false God, society, to the ground and trample on its unmitigated hypocrisy; if you cannot cheer them, pray, be silent, but do not try to drag them down again into the mire with such false nonsense as compromise and becoming nice and sweet.

I hate this world, this dream, this horrible nightmare with its churches and chicaneries, its books and blackguardisms, its fair faces and false hearts, its howling righteousness on the surface and utter hollowness beneath, and, above all, its sanctified shopkeeping. What! measure my soul according to what the bond-slaves of the world say? — Pooh! Sister, you do not know the Sannyasin. "He stands on the heads of the Vedas!" say the Vedas, because he is free from churches and sects and religions and prophets and books and all of that ilk! Missionary or no missionary, let them howl and attack me with all they can, I take them as Bhartrihari says, "Go thou thy ways, Sannyasin! Some will say, 'Who is this mad man?' Others, 'Who is this Chandâla?' Others will know thee to be a sage. Be glad at the prattle of the worldlings." But when they attack, know that, "The elephant passing through the market-place is always beset by curs, but he cares not. He goes straight on his own way. So it is always, when a great soul appears there will be numbers to bark after him."[2]

I am living with Landsberg at 54 W. 33rd Street. He is a brave and noble soul, Lord bless him. Sometimes I go to the Guernseys' to sleep.

Lord bless you all ever and ever — and may He lead you quickly out of this big humbug, the world! May you never be enchanted by this old witch, the world! May Shankara help you! May Umâ open the door of truth for you and take away all your delusions!

Yours with love and blessings,
Vivekananda.

33 — ALASINGA

19 W., 38 St.,
New York, 1895.

Dear Alasinga,

... Meddle not with so-called social reform, for there cannot be any reform without spiritual reform first. Who told you that I want social reform? Not I. Preach the Lord — say neither good nor bad about the superstitions and diets. Do not lose heart, do not lose faith in your Guru, do not lose faith in God. So long as you possess these three, nothing can harm you, my child. I am growing stronger every day. Work

---
2. Tulasidasa.

on, my brave boys.

Ever yours with blessings,
Vivekananda.

34 — SISTER

54 West, 33 New York,
25th February, 1895.

Dear Sister[1],

I am sorry you had an attack of illness. I will give you an absent treatment though your confession takes half the strength out of my mind.

That you have rolled put of it is all right. All's well that ends well.

The books have arrived in good condition and many thanks for them.

Your ever affectionate bro.,
Vivekananda.

35 — ALASINGA

U. S. A.,
6th March, 1895.

Dear Alasinga,

... Do not for a moment think the "Yankees" are practical in religion. In that the Hindu alone is practical, the Yankee in money-making, so that as soon as I depart, the whole thing will disappear. Therefore I want to have a solid ground under my feet before I depart. Every work should be made thorough... You need not insist upon preaching Shri Ramakrishna. Propagate his ideas first, though I know the world always wants the Man first, then the idea... Do not figure out big plans at first, but begin slowly, feel your ground, and proceed up and up.

... Work on, my brave boys. We shall see the light some day.

Harmony and peace! ... Let things slowly grow. Rome was not built in a day. The Maharaja of Mysore is dead — one of our greatest hopes. Well! the Lord is great. He will send others to help the cause.

Send some Kushâsanas (small sitting-mats) if you can.

Yours ever with blessings,
Vivekananda.

36 — SISTER

54 W., 33 New York,
27th March, 1895.

Dear Sister, (Isabelle McKindley)

Your kind note gave me pleasure inexpressible. I was also able to read it through very easily. I have at last hit upon the orange and have got a coat, but could not as yet get any in summer material. If you get any, kindly inform me. I will have it made here in New York. Your wonderful Dearborn Ave misfit tailor is too much even for a monk.

Sister Locke writes me a long letter and perhaps wondering at my delay in reply. She is apt to be carried away by enthusiasm; so I am waiting, and again I do not know what to answer. Kindly tell her from me that it is impossible for me to fix any place just now. Mrs. Peake though noble, grand, and very spiritual, is as much clever in worldly matter as I, yet I am getting cleverer every day. Mrs. Peake has been offered, by some one whom she knows only hazily in Washington, a place for summer.

Who knows that she will not be played upon? This is a wonderful country for cheating, and 99.9 per cent have some motive in the background to take advantage of others. If any one just but closes his eyes for a moment, he is gone!! Sister Josephine is fiery. Mrs.

---

1. Isabelle McKindley. Swamiji took delight in gently teasing the Hale sisters (of whom Isabelle was one) about their study and practice of Christian Science. He wrote this short note from New York, and in this he slyly poked fun at the "'Scientists'" practice of never confessing to sickness.

Peake is a simple good woman. I have been so well handled by the people here that I look round me for hours before I take a step. Everything will come to right. Ask Sister Josephine to have a little patience.

You are every day finding kindergarten better than running an old man's home I am sure. You saw Mrs. Bull, and I am sure you were quite surprised to find her so tame and gentle. Do you see Mrs. Adams now and then? Mrs. Bull has been greatly benefited by her lessons. I also took a few, but no use; the ever increasing load in front does not allow me to bend forward as Mrs. Adams wants it. If I try to bend forward in walking, the centre of gravity comes to the surface of the stomach, and so I go cutting front somersaults.

No millionaire coming? Not even a few hundred thousands? Sorry, very sorry!!! I am trying my best; what I can do? My classes are full of women. You of course cannot marry a woman. Well, have patience. I will keep my eyes open and never let go an opportunity. If you do not get one, it would not be owing to any laziness at least on my part.

Life goes on the same old ruts. Sometimes I get disgusted with eternal lecturings and talkings, want to be silent for days and days.

Hoping you the best dreams (for that is the only way to be happy).

I remain ever your loving bro.,
Vivekananda.

37 — ALASINGA

U. S. A.,
4th April, 1895.

Dear Alasinga,

Your letter just to hand. You need not be afraid of anybody's attempting to hurt me. So long as the Lord protects me I shall be impregnable. Your ideas of America are very hazy... This is a huge country, the majority do not care much about religion... Christianity holds its ground as a mere patriotism, and nothing more.

... Now my son, do not lose courage... Send me the Vedanta-Sutras and the Bhâshyas (commentaries) of all the sects... I am in His hands. What is the use of going back to India? India cannot further my ideas. This country takes kindly to my ideas. I will go back when I get the Command. In the meanwhile, do you all gently and patiently work. If anybody attacks me, simply ignore his existence... My idea is for you to start a Society where people could be taught the Vedas and the Vedanta, with the commentaries. Work on this line at present... Know that every time you feel weak, you not only hurt yourself but also the Cause. Infinite faith and strength are the only conditions of success.

Be cheerful... Hold on to your own ideal... Above all, never attempt to guide or rule others, or, as the Yankees say, "boss" others. Be the servant of all.

Ever yours with blessings,
Vivekananda.

38 — S___

U. S. A.,
2nd May, 1895.

Dear S— ,

So you have made up your mind to renounce the world. I have sympathy with your desire. There is nothing so high as renunciation of self. But you must not forget that to forgo your own favourite desire for the welfare of those that depend upon you is no small sacrifice. Follow the spotless life and teachings of Shri Ramakrishna and look after the comforts of your family. You do your own duty, and leave the rest to Him.

Love makes no distinction between man and man, between an Aryan and a Mlechchha, between a Brâhmana and a Pariah, nor even between a man and a woman. Love makes the whole universe as one's own home. True progress is slow but sure. Work among those young men who can devote heart and soul to this one duty — the duty of raising the masses of India. Awake them, unite them, and inspire them with this spirit of renunciation; it depends wholly on the young people of India.

Cultivate the virtue of obedience, but you must not sacrifice your own faith. No centralization is possible unless there is obedience to superiors. No great work can be done without this centralization of individual forces. The Calcutta Math is the main centre; the members of all other branches must act in unity and conformity with the rules of that centre.

Give up jealousy and conceit. Learn to work unitedly for others. This is the great need of our country.

Yours with blessings,
Vivekananda.

39 — ALASINGA

U. S. A.,
6th May, 1895.

Dear Alasinga,

This morning I received your last letter and that first volume of the Bhâshya of Râmânujâcharya. A few days ago I received another letter from you. Also I received a letter from Mr. Mani Iyer. I am doing well and going on in the same old rate. You mention about the lectures of Mr. Lund. I do not know who he is or where he is. He may be some one lecturing in Churches; for had he big platforms, we would have heard of him. Maybe, he gets them reported in some newspapers and sends them to India; and the missionaries may be making trade out of it. Well, so far I guess from the tone of your letters. It is no public affair here to call forth any defence from us; for in that case I will have to fight hundreds of them here every day. For India is now in the air, and the orthodox, including Dr. Barrows and all the rest, are struggling hard to put out the fire. In the second place, every one of these orthodox lectures against India must have a good deal of abuse hurled against me. If you hear some of the filthy stories the orthodox men and women invent against me, you will be astonished. Now, do you mean to say that a Sannyâsin should go about defending himself against the brutal and cowardly attacks of these self-seeking men and women? I have some very influential friends here who, now and then, give them their quietus. Again, why should I waste my energies defending Hinduism if the Hindus all go to sleep? What are you three hundred millions of people doing there, especially those that are so proud of their learning etc.? Why do you not take up the fighting and leave me to teach and preach? Here am I struggling day and night in the midst of strangers... What help does India send? Did the world ever see a nation with less patriotism than the Indian? If you could send and maintain for a few years a dozen well-educated strong men to preach in Europe and America, you would do immense service to India, both morally and politically. Every man who morally sympathises with India becomes a political friend. Many of the Western people think of you as a nation of half-naked savages, and therefore only fit to be whipped into civilization. If you three hundred millions become cowed by the missionaries — you cowards — and dare not say a word, what can one man do in a far distant land? Even what I have done, you do not deserve.

Why do you not send your defences to the American magazines? What prevents you? You race of cowards — physical, moral, and spiritual! You animals fit to be treated as you are with two ideas before you — lust and money — you want to prod a Sannyasin to a life of constant fighting, and you are afraid of the "Saheb logs", even missionaries! And you will do great things, pish! Why not some of you write a beautiful defence and send it to the Arena Publishing Company of Boston? The Arena is a magazine which will gladly publish it and perhaps pay you hard money. So far it ends. Think of this when you will be tempted to be a fool. Think that up to date every blackguard of a Hindu that had hitherto come to western lands had too often criticised his own faith and country in order to get praise or money. You know that I did not come to seek name and fame; it was forced upon me. Why shall I go back to India? Who will help me? ... You are children, you prattle you do not know what. Where are the men in Madras who will give up the world to preach religion? Worldliness and realization of God cannot go together. I am the one man who dared defend his country, and I have given them such ideas as they never expected from a Hindu. There are many who are against me, but I will never be a coward like you. There are also thousands in the country who are my friends, and hundreds who would follow me unto death; every year they will increase, and if I live and work with them, my ideals of life and religion will be fulfilled. Do you see?

I do not hear much now about the Temple Universal that was to be built in America; yet I have a firm footing in New York, the very centre of American life, and so my work will go on. I am taking several of my disciples to a summer retreat to finish their training in Yoga and Bhakti and Jnâna, and then they will be able to help carry the work on. Now my boys, go to work.

Within a month I shall be in a position to send some money for the paper. Do not go about begging from the Hindu beggars. I will do it all myself with my own brain and strong right hand. I do not want the help of any man here or in India... Do not press too much the Ramakrishna Avatâra.

Now I will tell you my discovery. All of religion is contained in the Vedanta, that is, in the three stages of the Vedanta philosophy, the Dvaita, Vishishtâdvaita and Advaita; one comes after the other. These are the three stages of spiritual growth in man. Each one is necessary. This is the essential of religion: the Vedanta, applied to the various ethnic customs and creeds of India, is Hinduism. The first stage, i.e. Dvaita, applied to the ideas of the ethnic groups of Europe, is Christianity; as applied to the Semitic groups, Mohammedanism. The Advaita, as applied in its Yoga-perception form, is Buddhism etc. Now by religion is meant the Vedanta; the applications must vary according to the different needs, surroundings, and other circumstances of different nations. You will find that although the philosophy is the same, the Shâktas, Shaivas, etc. apply it each to their own special cult and forms. Now, in your journal write article after article on these three systems, showing their harmony as one following after the other, and at the same time keeping off the ceremonial forms altogether. That is, preach the philosophy, the spiritual part, and let people suit it to their own forms. I wish to write a book on this subject, therefore I wanted the three Bhashyas; but only one volume of the Ramanuja (Bhashya) has reached me as yet.

The American Theosophists have seceded from the others, and now they hate India. Poor things! And Sturdy of England who has lately been in India and met my brother Shivananda wrote me a letter wanting to know when I go over to England. I wrote him a nice letter. What about Babu Akshay Kumar Ghosh? I do not hear anything from him more. Give the missionaries and others their dues. Get up some of our very strong men and write a nice, strong, but good-toned article on the present religious revival in India and send it to some American magazine. I am acquainted with only one or two of them. You know I am not much of a writer. I am not in the habit of going from door to door begging. I sit quiet and let things come to me... Now, my children, I could have made a grand success in the way of organising here, if I were a worldly hypocrite. Alas! That is all of religion here; money and name = priest, money and lust = layman. I am to create a new order of humanity here who are sincere believers in God and care nothing for the world. This must be slow, very slow. In the meantime you go on with your work, and I shall steer my boat straight ahead. The journal must not be flippant but steady, calm, and high-toned... Get hold of a band of fine, steady writers... Be perfectly unselfish, be steady and work on. We will do great things; do not fear... One thing more. Be the servant of all, and do not try in the least to govern others. That will excite jealousy and destroy everything... Go on. You have worked wonderfully well. We do not wait for help, we will work it out, my boy, be self-reliant, faithful and patient. Do not antagonise my other friends, live in harmony with all. My eternal love to all.

Ever yours with blessings,
Vivekananda.

PS. Nobody will come to help you if you put yourself forward as a leader... Kill self first if you want to succeed.

40 — ALASINGA

New York,
14th May, 1895.

Dear Alasinga,

... Now I have got a hold on New York, and I hope to get a permanent body of workers who will carry on the work when I leave the country. Do you see, my boy, all this newspaper blazoning is nothing? I ought to be able to leave a permanent effect behind me when I go; and with the blessings of the Lord it is going to be very soon... Men are more valuable than all the wealth of the world.

You need not worry about me. The Lord is always protecting me. My coming to this country and all my labours must not be in vain.

The Lord is merciful, and although there are many who try to injure me any way they can, there are many also who will befriend me to the last. Infinite patience, infinite purity, and infinite perseverance are the secret of success in a good cause.

Ever yours with blessings,
Vivekananda.

41 — FRIEND

C/O Miss Dutcher,
Thousand Island Park, N.Y.,
18th June, 1895.

Dear Friend, (Mr. F. Leggett)

A letter reached me from Mrs. Sturges the day before she left, including a cheque for $50. It was impossible to make the acknowledgement reach her the next day; so I take this opportunity to ask you the favour of sending her my thanks and acknowledgement in your next to her.

We are having a nice time here except, as an old Hindu proverb says, that "a pestle must pound even if it goes to heaven". I have to work hard all the same. I am going to Chicago in the beginning of August. When are you starting?

All our friends here send their respects to you. Hoping you all bliss and joy and health, and ever praying for the same.

I remain, yours affectionately,
Vivekananda.

42 — KIDI

19 W 38th St., New York
22nd June, 1895.

Dear Kidi,

I will write you a whole letter instead of a line. I am glad you are progressing. You are mistaken in thinking that I am not going to return to India; I am coming soon. I am not giving to failures, and here I have planted a seed, and it is going to become a tree, and it must. Only I am afraid it will hurt its growth if I give it up too soon...

Work on, my boy. Rome was not built in a day. I am guided by the Lord, so everything will come all right in the end.

With my love ever and ever to you,

Yours sincerely,
Vivekananda.

43 — ALASINGA

U. S. A.,
1st July, 1895.

Dear Alasinga,

I received your missionary book and the Ramnad photos. I have written to the Raja as well as the Dewan at Mysore. The missionary pamphlet must have reached here long ago, as the Ramabai circle controversy with Dr. Janes savoured of it, it seems. Now you need not be afraid of anything. There is one misstatement in that pamphlet. I never went to a big hotel in this country, and very few times to any other. At Baltimore, the small hotels, being ignorant, would not take in a black man, thinking him a negro. So my host, Dr. Vrooman, had to take me to a larger one, because they knew the difference between a negro and a foreigner. Let me tell you, Alasinga, that you have to defend yourselves. Why do you behave like babies? If anybody attacks your religion, why cannot, you defend it? As for me, you need not be afraid, I have more friends than enemies here, and in this country one-third are Christians, and only a small number of the educated care about the missionaries. Again, the very fact of the missionaries being against anything makes the educated like it. They are less of a power here now, and are becoming less so every day. If their attacks pain you, why do you behave like a petulant child and refer to me? ... Cowardice is no virtue.

Here I have already got a respectable following. Next year I will organise it on a working basis, and then the work will be carried on. And when I am off to India, I have friends who will back me here and help me in India too; so you need not fear. So long as you shriek at the missionary attempts and jump without being able to do anything, I laugh at you; you are little dollies, that is what you are... What can Swami do for old babies!!

I know, my son, I shall have to come and manufacture men out of you. I know that India is only inhabited by women and eunuchs. So do not fret. I will have to get means to work there. I do not put myself in the hands of imbeciles. You need not worry, do what little you can. I have to work alone from top to bottom... "This Âtman (Self) is not to be reached by cowards." You need not be afraid for me. The Lord is with me, you defend yourselves only and show me you can do that; and I will be satisfied. Don't bother me any more with what any one says about me. I am not waiting to hear any fool's judgment of me. You babies, great results are attained only by great patience, great courage, and great attempts... Kidi's mind is taking periodic somersaults, I am afraid...

The brave alone do great things, not the cowards.

Know once for all, you faithless ones, that I am in the hands of the Lord. So long as I am pure and His servant, not a hair of my head will be touched... Do something for the nation, then they will help you, then the nation will be with you. Be brave, be brave! Man dies but once. My disciples must not be cowards.

Ever yours with love,
Vivekananda.

44 — MRS. WILLIAM STURGES

Thousand Island Park,
29th (July?), 1895.

A glorious time to you, dear Mother[1] and I am sure this letter will find you in all health. Many thanks for the $50 you sent; it went a long way.

We have had such a nice time here. Two ladies came up all the way from Detroit to be with us here. They are so pure and good. I am going from the Thousand Island to Detroit and thence to Chicago.

Our class in New York is going on, and they have carried it bravely on, although I was not there.

By the by, the two ladies who have come from Detroit were in the class, and unfortunately were mighty frightened with imps and other persons of that ilk. They have been taught to put a little salt, just a little, in burning alcohol, and if there is a black precipitate, that must be the impurities showing the presence of the imps. However, these two ladies had too much fright from the imps. It is said that these imps are everywhere filling the whole universe. Father Leggett must be awfully downcast at your absence, as I did not hear from him up to date. Well, it is better to let grief have its way. So I do not bother him any more.

Aunt Joe Joe must have had a terrible time at sea. All is well that ends well.

The babies[2] must be enjoying their stay in Germany very much. My shiploads of love to them.

1. Mrs. William Sturges.

2. Hollister and Alberta — then at school in Germany.

We all here send you love, and I wish you a life that will be like a torch to generations to come.

Your son,
Vivekananda.

45 — MOTHER

C/O Miss Dutcher,
Thousand Island Park,
July, 1895.

Dear Mother[1],

I am sure you are in New York by this time, and that it is not very hot there now.

We are having great times here. Marie Louise arrived yesterday. So we are exactly seven now including all that have come yet.

All the sleep of the world has come upon me. I sleep at least two hours during the day and sleep through the whole night as a piece of log. This is a reaction, I think, from the sleeplessness of New York. I am also writing and reading a little, and have a class every morning after breakfast. The meals are being conducted on the strictest vegetarian principles, and I am fasting a good deal.

I am determined that several pounds of my fat shall be off before I leave. This is a Methodist place, and they will have their camp meeting in August. It is a very beautiful spot, but I am afraid it becomes too crowded during the season.

Miss Joe Joe's fly-bite has been cured completely by this time, I am sure Where is ... Mother? Kindly give her my best regards when you write her next.

I will always look back upon the delightful time I had at Percy, and always thank Mr. Leggett for that treat I shall be able to go to Europe with him. When you meet him next, kindly give him my eternal love and gratitude The world is always bettered by the love of the likes of him.

Are you with your friend, Mrs. Dora (long German name). She is a noble soul, a genuine Mahâtmâ (great soul). Kindly give her my love and regards.

I am in a sort of sleepy, lazy, happy state now and do not seem to dislike it. Marie Louise brought a little tortoise from New York, her pet. Now, arriving here, the pet found himself surrounded with his natural element. So by dint of persistent tumbling and crawling, he has left the love and fondlings of Marie Louise far, far behind. She was a little sorry at first, but we preached liberty with such a vigour that she had to come round quick

May the Lord bless you and yours for ever and ever is the constant prayer of Vivekananda

PS. Joe Joe did not send the birch bark book. Mrs. Bull was very glad to have the one I had sent her.

I had a large number of very beautiful letters from India Everything is all right there. Send my love to the babies on the other side — the real "innocents abroad".

46 — FRIEND

C/O Miss Dutcher,
Thousand Island Park, N. Y.
7th July, 1895.

Dear Friend[2],

I see you are enjoying New York very much, so excuse my breaking into your reverie with a letter.

I had two beautiful letters from Miss MacLeod and Mrs. Sturges. Also they sent over two pretty birch bark books. I have filled them with Sanskrit texts and translations, and they go by today's post.

Mrs. Dora[3] is giving, I hear, some startling performances in the Mahatma line.

Since leaving Percy[4] I have invitations to come over to London from unexpected quarters, and that I look

---

1. Mrs. Betty Sturges.

2. Mr. F. Leggett.

3. Mrs. Dora Rosthlesberger, an occultist who had introduced Miss MacLeod and Mrs. Sturges to Swami Vivekananda.

4. Mr. Leggett's camp in New Hampshire. From here Swami Vivekananda went to Thousand Island Park.

forward to with great expectations.

I do not want to lose this opportunity of working in London. And so your invitation, coupled with the London one, is, I know, a divine call for further work.

I shall be here all this month and only have to go to Chicago for a few days sometime in August.

Don't fret, Father Leggett, this is the best time for expectation — when sure in love.

Lord bless you ever and ever, and may all happiness be yours for ever, as you richly deserve it.

Ever yours in love and affection,
Vivekananda.

47 — MAHARAJA OF KHETRI

U. S. A.,
9th July, 1895.

... About my coming to India, the matter stands thus I am, as your Highness[5] well knows, a man of dogged perseverance. I have planted a seed in this country; it is already a plant, and I expect it to be a tree very soon. I have got a few hundred followers. I shall make several Sannyâsins, and then I go to India leaving the work to them. The more the Christian priests oppose me, the more I am determined to leave a permanent mark on their country... I have already some friends in London. I am going there by the end of August... This winter anyway has to be spent partly in London and partly in New York, and then I shall be free to go to India. There will be enough men to carry on the work here after this winter if the Lord is kind. Each work has to pass through these stages — ridicule, opposition, and then acceptance. Each man who thinks ahead of his time is sure to be misunderstood. So opposition and persecution are welcome, only I have to be steady and pure and must have immense faith in God, and all these will vanish...

Vivekananda.

---

5. The Maharaja of Khetri.

48 — FRIEND

C/O Miss Dutcher,
Thousand Island Park, N. Y.
31st July, 1895.

Dear Friend[6],

I wrote you before this a letter, but as I am afraid it was not posted carefully, I write another.

I shall be in time before the 14th. I shall have to come to New York before the 11th anyway. So there will be time enough to get ready.

I shall go with you to Paris, for my principal object in going with you is to see you married. When you go away for a trip, I go to London. That is all.

It is unnecessary to repeat my everlasting love and blessings for you and yours.

Ever your son,
Vivekananda.

49 — ALASINGA

U. S. A.,
August 1895.

By the time this reaches you, dear Alasinga, I shall be in Paris... I have done a good deal of work this year and hope to do a good deal more in the next. Don't bother about the missionaries. It is quite natural that they should cry. Who does not when his bread is dwindling away? The missionary funds have got a big gap the last two years, and it is on the increase. However, I wish the missionaries all success. So long as you have love for God and Guru and faith in truth, nothing can hurt you, my son. But the loss of any of these is dangerous. You have remarked well; my ideas are going to work in the West better than in India... I have done more for India than India ever did for me... I believe in truth, the Lord sends me workers by the scores wherever I go — and they are not like the

---

6. Francis Leggett.

... disciples either — they are ready to give up their lives for their Guru. Truth is my God, the universe my country I do not believe in duty. Duty is the curse of the Samsâri (householder), not for the Sannyâsin. Duty is humbug. I am free, my bonds are cut; what care I where this body goes or does not go. You have helped me well right along. The Lord will reward you. I sought praise neither from India nor from America, nor do I seek such bubbles. I have a truth to teach, I, the child of God And He that gave me the truth will send me fellow workers from the earth's bravest and best. You Hindus will see in a few years what the Lord does in the West. You are like the Jews of old — dogs in the manger, who neither eat nor allow others to eat. You have no religion your God is the kitchen, your Bible the cooking-pots... You are a few brave lads... Hold on, boys, no cowards among my children... Are great things ever done smoothly? Time, patience, and indomitable will must show. I could have told you many things that would have made your heart leap, but I will not. I want iron wills and hearts that do not know how to quake. Hold on. The Lord bless you.

Ever yours with blessings,
Vivekananda.

50 — MRS. BULL

Thousand Island Park,
August, 1895.

Dear Mrs. Bull,

... Now here is another letter from Mr. Sturdy I send it over to you. See how things are being prepared ahead. Don't you think this coupled with Mr. Leggett's invitation as a divine call? I think so and am following it. I am going by the end of August with Mr. Leggett to Paris, and then I go to London.

What little can be done for my brethren and my work is all the help I want from you now. I have done my duty to my people fairly well. Now for the world that gave me this body — the country that gave me the ideas, the humanity which allows me to be one of them!

The older I grow, the more I see behind the idea of the Hindus that man is the greatest of all beings. So say the Mohammedans too. The angels were asked by Allah to bow down to Adam. Iblis did not, and therefore he became Satan. This earth is higher than all heavens; this is the greatest school in the universe; and the Mars or Jupiter people cannot be higher than we, because they cannot communicate with us. The only so-called higher beings are the departed, and these are nothing but men who have taken another body. This is finer, it is true, but still a man-body, with hands and feet, and so on. And they live on this earth in another Âkâsha, without being absolutely invisible. They also think, and have consciousness, and everything else like us. So they also are men, so are the Devas, the angels. But man alone becomes God; and they all have to become men again in order to become God...

Yours etc.,
Vivekananda.

51 — FRIEND

Hotel Continental,
3 Rue Castiglione, Paris,
26th August, 1895.

Aum tat sat

Dear Friend[1],

I arrived here day before yesterday. I came over to this country as the guest of an American friend who is going to be married here next week.

I shall have to stop here with him till that time; and after that I shall be free to come to London.Eagerly anticipating the joy of meeting you,Ever yours in Sat,

Vivekananda.

---
1. Mr. E. T. Sturdy.

52 — ALASINGA

Paris,
9th September, 1895.

Dear Alasinga,

... I am surprised you take so seriously the missionaries' nonsense... If the people in India want me to keep strictly to my Hindu diet, please tell them to send me a cook and money enough to keep him. This silly bossism without a mite of real help makes me laugh. On the other hand, if the missionaries tell you that I have ever broken the two great vows of the Sannyâsin — chastity and poverty — tell them that they are big liars. Please write to the missionary Hume asking him categorically to write you what misdemeanour he saw in me, or give you the names of his informants, and whether the information was first-hand or not; that will settle the question and expose the whole thing...

As for me, mind you, I stand at nobody's dictation. I know my mission in life, and no chauvinism about me; I belong as much to India as to the world, no humbug about that. I have helped you all I could. You must now help yourselves. What country has any special claim on me? Am I any nation's slave? Don't talk any more silly nonsense, you faithless atheists.

I have worked hard and sent all the money I got to Calcutta and Madras, and then after doing all this, stand their silly dictation! Are you not ashamed? What do I owe to them? Do I care a fig for their praise or fear their blame? I am a singular man, my son, not even you can understand me yet. Do your work; if you cannot, stop; but do not try to "boss" me with your nonsense. I see a greater Power than man, or God, or devil at my back. I require nobody's help. I have been all my life helping others... They cannot raise a few rupees to help the work of the greatest man their country ever produced — Ramakrishna Paramahamsa; and they talk nonsense and want to dictate to the man for whom they did nothing, find who did everything he could for them! Such is the ungrateful world!

Do you mean to say I am born to live and die one of those caste-ridden, superstitious, merciless, hypocritical, atheistic cowards that you find only amongst the educated Hindus? I hate cowardice; I will have nothing to do with cowards or political nonsense. I do not believe in any politics. God and truth are the only politics in the world, everything else is trash.

I am going to London tomorrow...

Yours with blessings,
Vivekananda.

53 — ALASINGA

London,
24th October, 1895.

Dear Alasinga,

... I have already delivered my first address, and you may see how well it has been received by the notice in the Standard. The Standard is one of the most influential conservative papers. I am going to be in London for a month, then I go off to America and shall come back again next summer. So far you see the seed is well sown in England...

Take courage and work on. Patience and steady work — this is the only way. Go on; remember — patience and purity and courage and steady work... So long as you are pure, and true to your principles, you will never fail — Mother will never leave you, and all blessings will be yours.

Yours with love,
Vivekananda.

54 — ALASINGA

London,
18th November, 1895.

Dear Alasinga,

... In England my work is really splendid, I am astonished myself at it. The English people do not talk much in the newspapers, but they work silently. I am sure of more work in England than in America. Bands and bands come, and I have no room for so many; so they squat on the floor, ladies and all. I tell them to imagine that they are under the sky of India, under a spreading banyan, and they like the idea. I shall have to go away next week, and they are so sorry. Some think my work here will be hurt a little if I go away so soon. I do not think so. I do not depend on men or things. The Lord alone I depend upon — and He works through me.

... Please everybody without becoming a hypocrite and without being a coward. Hold on to your own ideas with strength and purity, and whatever obstructions may now be in your way, the world is bound to listen to you in the long run...

I have no time even to die, as the Bengalis say. I work, work, work, and earn my own bread and help my country, and this all alone, and then get only criticism from friends and foes for all that! Well, you are but children, I shall have to bear everything. I have sent for a Sannyâsin from Calcutta and shall leave him to work in London. I want one more for America — I want my own man. Guru-Bhakti is the foundation of all spiritual development.

... I am really tired from incessant work. Any other Hindu would have died if he had to work as hard as I have to... I want to go to India for a long rest...

Ever yours with love and blessings,
Vivekananda.

55 — ALASINGA

228 W. 39th St., New York,
20th December, 1895.

Dear Alasinga,

... Have patience and be faithful unto death. Do not fight among yourselves. Be perfectly pure in money dealings... We will do great things yet... So long as you have faith and honesty and devotion, everything will prosper.

... In translating the Suktas, pay particular attention to the Bhâshyakâras (commentators), and pay no attention whatever to the orientalists. They do not understand a single thing about our Shâstras (scriptures). It is not given to dry philologists to understand philosophy or religion... For instance the word Ânidavâtam in the Rig-Veda was translated — "He lived without breathing". Now, here the reference is really to the chief Prâna, and Avâtam has the root-meaning for unmoved, that is, without vibration. It describes the state in which the universal cosmic energy, or Prana, remains before the Kalpa (cycle of creation) begins: vide — the Bhashyakaras. Explain according to our sages and not according to the so-called European scholars. What do they know?

... Be bold and fearless, and the road will be clear... Mind, you have nothing whatsoever to do with the Theosophists. If you all stand by me and do not lose patience, I assure you, we shall do great work yet. The great work will be in England, my boy, by and by. I feel you sometimes get disheartened, and I am afraid you get temptations to play in the hands of the Theosophists. Mind you, the Guru-Bhakta will conquer the world — this is the one evidence of history... It is faith that makes a lion of a man. You must always remember how much work I have to do. Sometimes I have to deliver two or three lectures a day — and thus I make my way against all odds — hard work; any weaker man would die.

... Hold on with faith and strength; be true, be honest, be pure, and don't quarrel among yourselves. Jealousy is the bane of our race.

With love to you and all our friends there,

Yours,
Vivekananda.

56 — SISTER

228 W. 39th Street,
New York,
10th February, 1896.

Dear Sister[1],

I was astonished at learning that you have not received my letter yet. I wrote immediately after the receipt of yours and also sent you some booklets of three lectures I delivered in New York. These Sunday public lectures are now taken down in shorthand and printed. Three of them made two little pamphlets, several copies of which I have forwarded to you. I shall be in New York two weeks more, and then I go to Detroit to come back to Boston felt a week or two.

My health is very much broken down this year by constant work. I am very nervous. I have not slept a single night soundly this winter. I am sure I am working too much, yet a big work awaits me in England.

I will have to go through it, and then I hope to reach India and have a rest all the rest of my life. I hale tried at least to do my best for the world, leaving the result to the Lord. Now I am longing for rest. Hope I will get some, and the Indian people will give me up. How I would like to become dumb for some years and not talk at all! I was not made for these struggles and fights of the world. I am naturally dreamy and restful. I am a born idealist, can only live in a world of dreams; the very touch of fact disturbs my visions arid makes me unhappy. They, will be done!

I am ever ever grateful to you four sisters; to you I owe everything I have in this country. May you be ever blessed and happy. Wherever I be, you will always be remembered with the deepest gratitude and sincerest love. The whole life is a succession of dreams. My ambition is to be a conscious dreamer, that is all. My love to all — to Sister Josephine.

Ever your affectionate brother,
Vivekananda.

---

1. Miss Mary Hale.

57 — BLESSED AND BELOVED

228 W. 39th Street, New York,
13th February, 1896.

Blessed And Beloved[2],

About the Sannyâsin coming over from India, I am sure he will help you in the translation work, also in other work. Later on, when I come, I may send him over to America. Today another Sannyasin has been added to the list. This time it is a man who is a genuine American and a religious teacher of some standing in the country. He was Dr. Street. He is now Yogananda, as his leaning is all towards Yoga.

I have been sending regular reports to the Brahmavâdin from here. They will be published soon. It takes such a long time for things to reach India! Things are growing nobly in India. As there was no hocus-pocus from the beginning, the Vedanta is drawing the attention of the highest classes in American society. Sarah Bernhardt, the French actress, has been playing "Iziel" here. It is a sort of Frenchified life of Buddha, where a courtesan "Iziel" wants to seduce the Buddha, under the banyan - and the Buddha preaches to her the vanity of the world, whilst she is sitting all the time in Buddha's lap. However, all is well that ends well — the courtesan fails. Madame Bernhardt acts the courtesan. I went to see the Buddha business — and Madame spying me in the audience wanted to have an interview with me. A swell family of my acquaintance arranged the affair. There were besides Madame M. Morrel, the celebrated singer, also the great electrician Tesla. Madame is a very scholarly lady and has studied up the metaphysics a good deal. M. Morrel was being interested, but Mr. Tesla was charmed to hear about the Vedantic Prâna and Âkâsha and the Kalpas, which according to him are the only theories modern science can entertain. Now both Akasha and Prana again are produced from the cosmic Mahat, the Universal Mind, the Brahmâ or Ishvara. Mr. Tesla thinks he can demonstrate mathematically that force and matter are reducible to potential energy. I am to go and see him next week, to get this new mathematical demonstration.

---

2. E. T. Sturdy.

In that case, the Vedantic cosmology will be placed on the surest of foundations. I am working a good deal now upon the cosmology and eschatology[1] of the Vedanta. I clearly see their perfect unison with modern science, and the elucidation of the one will be followed by that of the other. I intend to write a book later on in the form of questions and answers[2]. The first chapter will be on cosmology, showing the harmony between Vedantic theories and modern science.

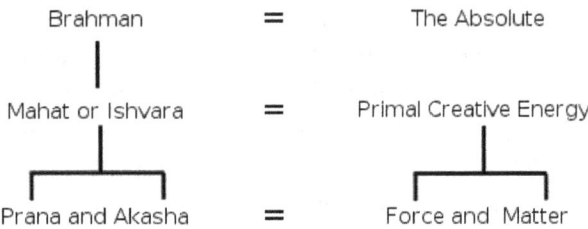

The eschatology will be explained from the Advaitic standpoint only. That is to say, the dualist claims that the soul after death passes on to the Solar sphere, thence to the Lunar sphere, thence to the Electric sphere. Thence he is accompanied by a Purusha to Brahmaloka. (Thence, says the Advaitist, he goes to Nirvâna.)

Now on the Advaitic side, it is held that the soul neither comes nor goes, and that all these spheres or layers of the universe are only so many varying products of Akasha and Prana. That is to say, the lowest or most condensed is the Solar sphere, consisting of the visible universe, in which Prana appears as physical force, and Akasha as sensible matter. The next is called the Lunar sphere, which surrounds the Solar sphere. This is not the moon at all, but the habitation of the gods, that is to say, Prana appears in it as psychic forces, and Akasha as Tanmâtras or fine particles. Beyond this is the Electric sphere, that is to say, a condition in which the Prana is almost inseparable from Akasha, and you can hardly tell whether Electricity is force or matter. Next is the Brahmaloka, where there is neither Prana nor Akasha, but both are merged in the mind stuff, the primal energy. And here — there big neither Prana nor Akasha — the Jiva contemplates the whole universe as Samashti or the sum total of Mahat or mind. This appears as a Purusha, an abstract universal soul, yet not the Absolute, for still there is multiplicity. From this the Jiva finds at last that Unity which is the end. Advaitism says that these are the visions which rise in succession before the Jiva, who himself neither goes nor comes, and that in the same way this present vision has been projected. The projection (Srishti) and dissolution must take place in the same order, only one means going backward, and the other coming out.

Now as each individual can only see his own universe, that universe is created with his bondage and goes away with his liberation, although it remains for others who are in bondage. Now name and form constitute the universe. A wave in the ocean is a wave, only in so far as it is bound by name and form. If the wave subsides, it is the ocean, but those name and form have immediately vanished for ever. So though the name and form of wave could never be without water that was fashioned into the wave by them, yet the name and form themselves were not the wave. They die as soon as ever it returns to water. But other names and forms live in relation to other waves. This name-and-form is called Mâyâ, and the water is Brahman. The wave was nothing but water all the time, yet as a wave it had the name and form. Again this name and form cannot remain for one moment separated from the wave, although the wave as water can remain eternally separate from name and form. But because the name and form can never he separated, they can never be said to exist. Yet they are not zero. This is called Maya.

I want to work; all this out carefully, but you will see at a glance that I am on the right track. It will take more study in physiology, on the relations between the higher and lower centres, to fill out the psychology of mind Chitta (mind-stuff), and Buddhi (intellect), and so on. But I have clear light now, free of all hocus-pocus. I want to give them dry, hard reason, softened in tile sweetest syrup of love and made spicy with intense work, and cooked in the kitchen of Yoga, so that even a baby can easily digest it.

Yours etc.,
Vivekananda.

---

1. That is, doctrine of the last things — death, judgement, etc.

2. This was never done. But from his lectures in London in 1896, it is easy to see that his mind was still working on these ideas. (See also Vol. VIII Sayings and Utterances).

58 — ALASINGA

U. S. A.,
17th February, 1896.

Dear Alasinga,

... I have used some very harsh words in my letters, which you ought to excuse, as you know, I get nervous at times. The work is terribly hard; and the more it is growing, the harder it is becoming. I need a long rest very badly. Yet a great work is before me in England.

Have patience, my son — it will grow beyond all your expectations... Every work has got to pass through hundreds of difficulties before succeeding. Those that persevere will see the light, sooner or later.

I have succeeded now in rousing the very heart of the American civilisation, New York, but it has been a terrific struggle... I have spent nearly, all I had on this New York work and in England. Now things are in such a shape that they will go on. Just as I am writing to you, every one of my bones is paining after last afternoon's long Sunday public lecture. Then you see, to put the Hindu ideas into English and then make out of dry philosophy and intricate mythology and queer startling psychology, a religion which shall be easy, simple, popular, and at the same time meet the requirements of the highest minds — is a task only those can understand who have attempted it. The dry, abstract Advaita must become living — poetic — in everyday life; out of hopelessly intricate mythology must come concrete moral forms; and out of bewildering Yogi-ism must come the most scientific and practical psychology — and all this must be put in a form so that a child may grasp it. That is my life's work. The Lord only knows how far I shall succeed. "To work we have the right, not to the fruits thereof." It is hard work, my boy, hard work! To keep one's self steady in the midst of this whirl of Kâma-Kânchana (lust and gold) and hold on to one's own ideals, until disciples are moulded to conceive of the ideas of realisation and perfect renunciation, is indeed difficult work, my boy. Thank God, already there is great success. I cannot blame the missionaries and others for not understanding me — they hardly ever saw a man who did not care in the least about women and money. At first they could not believe it to be possible; how could they? You must not think that the Western nations have the same ideas of chastity and purity as the Indians. Their equivalents are virtue and courage... People are now flocking to me. Hundreds have now become convinced that there are men who can really control their bodily desires; and reverence and respect for these principles are growing. All things come to him who waits. May you be blessed for ever and ever!

Yours with love,
Vivekananda.

59 — ALASINGA

Boston,
23rd March, 1896.

Dear Alasinga,

... One of my new Sannyâsins is indeed a woman... The others are men. I am going to make some more in England and take them over to India with me. These "white" faces will have more influence in India than the Hindus; moreover, they are vigorous, the Hindus are dead. The only hope of India is from the masses. The upper classes are physically and morally dead...

My success is due to my popular style — the greatness of a teacher consists in the simplicity of his language.

... I am going to England next month. I am afraid I have worked too much; my nerves are almost shattered by this long-continued work. I don't want you to sympathise, but only I write this so that you may not expect much from me now. Work on, the best way you can. I have very little hope of being able to do great things now. I am glad, however, that a good deal of literature has been created by taking down stenographic notes of my lectures. Four books are ready... Well, I am satisfied that I have tried my best to do good, and shall have a clear conscience when I retire from work and sit down in a cave.

With love and blessings to all,
Vivekananda.

60 — ALASINGA

U. S. A.,
March, 1896.

Dear Alasinga,

... Push on with the work. I will do all I can... If it pleases the Lord, yellow-garbed Sannyâsins will be common here and in England. Work on, my children.

Mind, so long as you have faith in your Guru, nothing will be able to obstruct your way. That translation of the three Bhâshyas (commentaries) will be a great thing in the eyes of the Westerners.

... Wait, my child, wait and work on. Patience, patience... I will burst on the public again in good time...

Yours with love,
Vivekananda.

61 — DR. NANJUNDA RAO

New York,
14th April, 1896.

Dear Dr. Nanjunda Rao,

I received your note this morning. As I am sailing for England tomorrow, I can only write a few hearty lines. I have every sympathy with your proposed magazine for boys, and will do my best to help it on. You ought to make it independent, following the same lines as the Brahmavâdin, only making the style and matter much more popular. As for example, there is a great chance, much more than you ever dream of, for those wonderful stories scattered all over the Sanskrit literature, to be re-written and made popular. That should be the one great feature of your journal. I will write stories, as many as I can, when time permits. Avoid all attempts to make the journal scholarly — the Brahmavadin stands for that — and it will slowly make its way all over the world, I am sure. Use the simplest language possible, and you will succeed. The main feature should be the teaching of principles through stories. Don't make it metaphysical at all. As to the business part, keep it wholly in your hands. "Too many cooks spoil the broth." In India the one thing we lack is the power of combination, organisation, the first secret of which is obedience.

I have also promised to help starting a magazine in Bengali in Calcutta. Only the first year I used to charge for my lectures The last two years, my work was entirely free of all charges. As such, I have almost no money to send you or the Calcutta people. But I will get people to help you with funds very soon. Go on bravely. Do not expect success in a day or a year. Always hold on to the highest. Be steady. Avoid jealousy and selfishness. Be obedient and eternally faithful to the cause of truth, humanity, and your country, and you will move the world. Remember it is the person, the life, which is the secret of power — nothing else. Keep this letter and read the last lines whenever you feel worried or jealous. Jealousy is the bane of all slaves. It is the bane of our nation. Avoid that always. All blessings attend you and all success.

Yours affectionately,
Vivekananda.

62 — DR. NANJUNDA RAO

England,
14th July, 1896.

Dear Dr. Nanjunda Rao,

The numbers of *Prabuddha Bharata* have been received and distributed too to the class. It is very satisfactory. It will have a great sale, no doubt, in India. In America I may get also a number of subscribers. I have already arranged for advertising it in America and Goodyear has done it already. But here in England the progress will be slower indeed. The great drawback here is — they all want to start papers of their own; and it is right that it should be so, seeing that, after all, no foreigner will ever write the English language as well as the native Englishman, end the ideas, when put in good English, will spread farther than in Hindu English. Then again it is much more difficult to write a story in a foreign language than an essay. I am trying my best to get you subscribers here. But you must not depend on any foreign help. Nations, like individuals, must help themselves. This is real patriotism. If a nation cannot do that, its time has not yet come. It must wait. It is from Madras that the new light must spread all over India. With this end you must stork. One point I will remark however. The cover is simply barbarous. It is awful and hideous. If it is possible, change it. Make it symbolical and simple, without human figures at all. The banyan tree does not mean awakening, nor does the hill, nor the saint, nor the European couple. The lotus is a symbol of regeneration.

We are awfully behindhand in art especially in that of painting. For instance, make a small scene of spring re-awakening in a forest, showing how the leaves and buds are coming again. Slowly go on, there are hundreds of ideas to be put forward. You see the symbol I made for the Raja-Yoga, printed by Longman Green and Co. You can get it at Bombay. It consists of my lectures on Raja-Yoga in New York.

I am going to Switzerland next Sunday, and shall return to London in the autumn, and take up the work again... I want rest very badly, you know.

Yours with all blessings etc.,
Vivekananda.

63 — ALASINGA

Switzerland,
6th August, 1896.

Dear Alasinga,

I learnt from your letter the bad financial state the Brahmavâdin is in. I will try to help you when I go back to London. You must not lower the tone. Keep up the paper. Very soon I will be able to help you in such a manner as to make you free of this nonsense teacher business. Do not be afraid. Great things are going to be done, my child. Take heart. The Brahmavadin is a jewel — it must not perish. Of course, such a paper has to be kept up by private help always, and we will do it. Hold on a few months more.

Max Müller's article on Shri Ramakrishna has been published in the Nineteenth Century. I will send you a copy as soon as I get it. He writes me very nice letters and wants material for a big work on Ramakrishna's life. Write to Calcutta to send all the material they can to Max Müller.

I have received the communication to the American paper before. You must not publish it in India. Enough of this newspaper blazoning, I am tired of it anyhow. Let us go our own way, and let fools talk. Nothing can resist truth.

I am, as you see, now in Switzerland and am always on the move. I cannot and must not do anything in the way of writing, nor much reading either. There is a big London work waiting for me from next month. In winter I am going back to India and will try to set things on their feet there.

My love to all. Work on, brave hearts, fail not — no saying nay; work on — the Lord is behind the work. Mahâshakti is with you.

Yours with love and blessings,
Vivekananda.

64 — ALASINGA

Switzerland,
8th August, 1896.

Dear Alasinga,

Since writing to you a few days ago I have found my way to let you know that I am in a position to do this for the Brahmavadin. I will give you Rs. 100 a month for a year or two, i.e. £60 or £70 a year, i.e. as much as would cover Rs. 100 a month. That will set you free to work for the Brahmavadin and make it a better success. Mr. Mani Iyer and a few friends can help in raising fund that would cover the printing etc. What is the income from subscription? Can these be employed to pay the contributors and get a fine series of articles? It is not necessary that everybody should understand all that is written in the Brahmavadin, but that they must subscribe from patriotism and good Karma — the Hindus I mean.

Several things are necessary. First there should be strict integrity. Not that I even hint that any of you would digress from it, but the Hindus have a peculiar slovenliness in business matters, not being sufficiently methodical and strict in keeping accounts etc.

Secondly, entire devotion to the cause, knowing that your salvation depends upon making the Brahmavadin a success. Let this paper be your Ishtadevata, and then you will see how success comes. I have already sent for Abhedânanda from India. I hope there will be no delay with him as it was with the other Swami. On receipt of this letter you send me a clear account of all the income and the expenses of the Brahmavadin so that I may judge from it what best can be done. Remember that perfect purity, disinterestedness, and obedience to the Guru are the secret of all success...

A big foreign circulation of a religious paper is impossible. It must be supported by the Hindus if they have any sense of virtue or gratitude left to them.

By the by, Mrs. Annie Besant invited me to speak at her Lodge, on Bhakti. I lectured there one night. Col. Olcott also was there. I did it to show my sympathy for all sects... Our countrymen must remember that in things of the Spirit we are the teachers, and not foreigners — but in things of the world we ought to learn from them.

I have read Max Müller's article, which is a good one, considering that when he wrote it, six months ago, he had no material except Mazoomdar's leaflet. Now he writes me a long and nice letter offering to write a book on Shri Ramakrishna. I have already supplied him with much material, but a good deal more is needed from India.

Work on! Hold on! Be brave! Dare anything and everything!

... It is all misery, this Samsâra, don't you see!

Yours with blessings and love,
Vivekananda.

65 — BLESSED AND BELOVED

Lucerne,
23rd August, 1896.

Blessed And Beloved[1],

Today I received a letter from India written by Abhedânanda that in all probability he had started on the 11th August by the B.I.S.N., "S.S.Mombassa". He could not get an earlier steamer; else he would have started earlier. In all probability he would be able to secure a passage on the Mombassa. The Mombassa will reach London about the 15th of September. As you already know, Miss Müller changed the date of my visiting Deussen to the 19th September. I shall not be in London to receive Abhedananda. He is also coming without any warm clothing; but I am afraid by that time it will begin to cool in England, and he will require at least some underwear and an overcoat. You know all about these things much better than I. So kindly keep a look out for this Mombassa. I expect also another letter from him.

I am suffering from a very bad cold indeed. I hope by this time Mohin's money from the Raja has arrived

---
1. E. T. Sturdy.

to your care. If so, I do not want the money I gave him back. You may give him the whole of it.

I had some letters from Goodwin and Sâradânanda. They are doing well. Also one from Mrs. Bull regretting that you and I could not be corresponding members of some Society, she is founding at Cambridge. I do remember to have written to her about your and my non-acquiescence in this membership. I have not yet been able to write even a line. I had not a moment's time even to read, climbing up hill and going down dale all the time. We will have to begin the march again in a few days. Kindly give my love to Mohin and Fox when you see them next.

With love to all our friends, Yours ever,
Vivekananda.

66 — NANJUNDA RAO

Switzerland,
26th August, 1896.

Dear Nanjunda Rao,

I have just now got your letter. I am on the move. I have been doing a great deal of mountain-climbing and glacier-crossing in the Alps. Now I am going to Germany. I have an invitation from Prof. Deussen to visit him at Kiel. From thence I go back to England. Possibly I will return to India this winter.

What I objected to in the design for the *Prabuddha Bhârata* was not only its tawdriness, but the crowding in of a number of figures without any purpose. A design should be simple, symbolical, and condensed. I will try to make a design for Prabuddha Bharata in London and send it over to you...

The work is going on beautifully, I am very glad to say... I will give you one advice however. All combined efforts in India sink under the weight of one iniquity — we have not yet developed strict business principles. Business is business, in the highest sense, and no friendship — or as the Hindu proverb says "eye-shame" — should be there. One should keep the clearest account of everything in one's charge — and never, never apply the funds intended for one thing to any other use whatsoever — even if one starves the next moment. This is business integrity. Next, energy unfailing. Whatever you do let that be your worship for the time. Let this paper be your God for the time, and you will succeed.

When you have succeeded in this paper, start vernacular ones on the same lines in Tamil, Telugu, Canarese, etc. We must reach the masses. The Madrasis are good, energetic, and all that, but the land of Shankarâchârya has lost the spirit of renunciation, it seems.

My children must plunge into the breach, must renounce the world — then the firm foundation will be laid.

Go on bravely — never mind about designs and other details at present — "With the horse will come the reins". Work unto death — I am with you, and when I am gone, my spirit will work with you. This life comes and goes — wealth, fame, enjoyments are only of a few days. It is better, far better to die on the field of duty, preaching the truth, than to die like a worldly worm. Advance!

Yours with all love and blessings,
Vivekananda.

67 — ALASINGA

C/O Miss H. Müller,
Airlie Lodge, Ridgeway Gardens,
Wimbledon, England,
22nd September, 1896.

Dear Alasinga,

I am sure you have got the article on Ramakrishna, I sent you, by Max Müller. Do not be sorry, he does not mention me there at all, as it was written six months before he knew me. And then who cares whom he mentions, if he is right in the main point. I had a beautiful time with Prof. Deussen in Germany. Later, he and I came together to London, and we have already become great friends.

I am soon sending you an article on him. Only pray do not put that old-fashioned "Dear Sir" before my articles. Have you seen the Râja-Yoga book yet? I will try to send you a design for the coming year. I send you a Daily News article on a book of travel written by the Czar of Russia. The paragraph in which he speaks of India as the land of spirituality and wisdom, you ought to quote in your paper and send the article to the Indian Mirror.

You are very welcome to publish the Jnâna-Yoga lectures, as well as Dr. (Nanjunda Rao) in his Awakened India — only the simpler ones. They have to be very carefully gone through and all repetitions and contradictions taken out. I am sure I will now have more time to write. Work on with energy.

With love to all.

Yours,
Vivekananda.

PS. I have marked the passage to be quoted, the rest of course is useless for a paper.

I do not think it would be good just now to make the paper a monthly one yet, unless you are sure of giving a good bulk. As it is now, the bulk and the matter are all very poor. There is yet a vast untrodden field, namely — the writing of the lives and works of Tulasidâsa, Kabir, Nânak, and of the saints of Southern India. They should be written in a thorough-going, scholarly style, and not in a slipshod, slovenly way. In fact, the ideal of the paper, apart from the preaching of Vedanta, should be to make it a magazine of Indian research and scholarship, of course, bearing on religion. You must approach the best writers and get carefully-written articles from their pen. Work on with all energy.

Yours with love,
Vivekananda.

68 — ALASINGA

14 Grey Coat Gardens,
Westminster, London.
1896

Dear Alasinga,

I have returned about three weeks from Switzerland but could not write you further before. I have sent you by last mail a paper on Paul Deussen of Kiel. Sturdy's plan about the magazine is still hanging fire. As you see, I halve left the St. George's Road place. We have a lecture hall at 39 Victoria Street. C/o E. T. Sturdy will always reach me for a year to come. The rooms at Grey Coat Gardens are only lodgings for self and the other Swami taken for three mouths only. The work in London is growing apace, the classes are becoming bigger as they go on. I have no doubt this will go on increasing at this rate and the English people are steady and loyal. Of course, as soon as I leave, most of this fabric will tumble down. Something will happen. Some strong man will arise to take it up. The Lord knows what is good. In America there is room for twenty preachers on the Vedanta and Yoga. Where to get these preachers and where also the money to bring them? Half the United States can be conquered in ten years, given a number of strong and genuine men. Where are they? We are all boobies over there! Selfish cowards, with our nonsense of lip-patriotism, orthodoxy, and boasted religious feeling! The Madrasis have more of go and steadiness, but every fool is married. Marriage! Marriage! Marriage! ... Then the way our boys are married nowadays! ... It is very good to aspire to be a nonattached householder; but what we want in Madras is not that just now — but non-marriage...

My child, what I want is muscles of iron and nerves of steel, inside which dwells a mind of the same material as that of which the thunderbolt is made. Strength, manhood, Kshatra-Virya + Brahma-Teja. Our beautiful hopeful boys — they have everything, only if they are not slaughtered by the millions at the altar of this brutality they call marriage. O Lord, hear my wails! Madras will then awake when at least one hundred of its very heart's blood, in the form of its educated young men, will stand aside from the world, gird their loins, and be ready to fight the battle of truth, marching on from country to country. One blow struck outside of India is equal to a hundred thousand struck within. Well, all will come if the Lord wills it.

Miss Müller was the person who offered that money I promised. I have told her about your new proposal. She is thinking about it. In the meanwhile I think it is better to give her some work. She has consented to be the agent for the Brahmavadin and Awakened India. Will you write to her about it? Her address is Airlie Lodge, Ridgeway Gardens, Wimbledon, England. I was living with her over there for the last few weeks. But the London work cannot go on without my living in London. As such I have changed quarters. I am sorry it has chagrined Miss Müller a bit. Cannot help. Her full name is Miss Henrietta Müller. Max Müller is getting very friendly. I am soon going to deliver two lectures at Oxford.

I am busy writing something big on the Vedanta philosophy. I am busy collecting passages from the various Vedas bearing on the Vedanta in its threefold aspect. You can help me by getting someone to collect passages bearing on, first the Advaitic idea, then the Vishishtâdvaitic, and the Dvaitic from the Samhitâs, the Brâhmanas, the Upanishads, and the Purânas. They should be classified and very legibly written with the name and chapter of the book, in each case. It would be a pity to leave the West without leaving something of the philosophy in book form.

There was a book published in Mysore in Tamil characters, comprising all the one hundred and eight Upanishads; I saw it in Professor Deussen's library. Is there a reprint of the same in Devanâgari? If so, send me a copy. If not, send me the Tamil edition, and also write on a sheet the Tamil letters and compounds, and all juxtaposed with its Nagari equivalents, so that I may learn the Tamil letters.

Mr. Satyanathan, whom I met in London the other day, said that there has been a friendly review of my Râja-Yoga book in the *Madras Mail*, the chief Anglo-Indian paper in Madras. The leading physiologist in America, I hear, has been charmed with my speculations. At the same time, there have been some in England, who ridiculed my ideas. Good! My speculations of course are awfully bold; a good deal of them will ever remain meaningless; but there are hints in it which the physiologists had better taken up earlier. Nevertheless, I am quite satisfied with the result. "Let them talk badly of me if they please, but let them talk", is my motto.

In England, of course, they are gentlemen and never talk the rot I had in America. Then again the English missionaries you see over there are nearly all of them from the dissenters. They are not from the gentleman class in England. The gentlemen here, who are religious; all belong to the English Church. The dissenters have very little voice in England and no education. I never hear of those people here against whom you time to time warn me. They are unknown here and dare not talk nonsense. I hope Ram K. Naidu is already in Madras, and you are enjoying good health.

Persevere on, my brave lads. We have only just begun. Never despond! Never say enough! ... As soon as a man comes over to the West and sees different nations, his eyes open. This way I get strong workers — not by talking, but by practically showing what we have in India and what we have not. I wish at least that a million Hindus had travelled all over the world!

Yours ever with love,
Vivekananda.

69 — ALASINGA

C/O E. T. Sturdy, Esq.,
39 Victoria Street, London,
28th October, 1896.

Dear Alasinga,

… I am not yet sure what month I shall reach India. I will write later about it. The new Swami[1] delivered his maiden speech yesterday at a friendly society's meeting. It was good and I liked it; he has the making of a good speaker in him, I am sure.

... You have not yet brought out the — . . Again, books must be cheap for India to have a large sale; the types must be bigger to satisfy the public... You can very well get out a cheap edition of — if you like. I have not reserved any copyright on it purposely. You have missed a good opportunity by not getting out the — book earlier, but we Hindus are so slow that when we have done a work, the opportunity has already passed away, and thus we are the losers. Your — book came out after a year's talk! Did you think the Western people would wait for it till Doomsday? You have lost three-fourths of the sale by this delay... That Haramohan is a fool, slower than you, and his printing is diabolical. There is no use in publishing books that way; it is cheating the public, and should not be done. I shall most probably return to India accompanied by Mr. and Mrs. Sevier, Miss Müller, and Mr. Goodwin. Mr. and Mrs. Sevier are probably going to settle in Almora at least for some time, and Goodwin is going to become a Sannyâsin. He of course will travel with me. It is he to whom we owe all our books. He took shorthand notes of my lectures, which enabled the books to be published... All these lectures were delivered on the spur of the moment, without the least preparation, and as such, they should be carefully revised and edited... Goodwin will have to live with me... He is a strict vegetarian.

Yours with love,
Vivekananda.

PS. I have sent a little note to the Indian Mirror today about Dr. Barrows and how he should be welcomed. You also write some good words of welcome for him in the *Brahmavadin*. All here send love.

70 — INDIAN MIRROR

London,
28th October, 1896.

(On the eve of the lecture-tour of Dr. Barrows in India at the end of 1896, Swami Vivekananda in a letter to the Indian Mirror, Calcutta, introduced the distinguished visitor to his countrymen and advised them to give him a fitting reception. He wrote among other things as follows:)

Dr. Barrows was the ablest lieutenant Mr. C. Boney could have selected to carry out successfully his great plan of the Congresses at the World's Fair, and it is now a matter of history how one of these Congresses scored a unique distinction under the leadership of Dr. Barrows.

It was the great courage, untiring industry, unruffled patience, and never-failing courtesy of Dr. Barrows that made the Parliament a grand success.

India, its people, and their thoughts have been brought more prominently before the world than ever before by that wonderful gathering at Chicago, and that national benefit we certainly owe to Dr. Barrows more than to any other man at that meeting.

Moreover, he comes to us in the sacred name of religion, in the name of one of the great teachers of mankind, and I am sure, his exposition of the system of the Prophet of Nazareth would be extremely liberal and elevating. The Christ-power this man intends to bring to India is not that of the intolerant, dominant superior, with heart full of contempt for everything else but its own self, but that of a brother who craves for a brother's place as a co-worker of the various powers already working in India. Above all, we must remember that gratitude and hospitality are the peculiar characteristics of Indian humanity; and as such, I would beg my countrymen to behave in such a manner that this stranger from the other side of the globe may find that in the midst of all our misery, our poverty, and degradation, the heart beats as warm as of yore, when the "wealth of Ind" was the proverb of nations and India was the land of the "Aryas".

71 — ALASINGA

14 Grey Coat Gardens,
Westminster, S. W.,
11th November, 1896.

Dear Alasinga,

I shall most probably start on the 16th of December, or may be a day or two later. I go from here to Italy, and after seeing a few places there, join the steamer at Naples. Miss Müller, Mr. and Mrs. Sevier, and a young man called Goodwin are accompanying me. The Seviers are going to settle at Almora. So is Miss Müller. Sevier was an officer in the Indian army for 5 years. So he knows India a good deal. Miss Müller was a Theosophist who adopted Akshay. Goodwin is an Englishman, through whose shorthand notes it has been possible for the pamphlets to be published.

I arrive at Madras first from Colombo. The other people go their way to Almora. I go from thence direct to Calcutta. I will write you the exact information when I start.

Yours affly.,
Vivekananda.

PS. The first edition of Râja-Yoga is sold out, and a second is in the press. India and America are the biggest buyers.

72 — ALASINGA

39 Victoria Street,
London, S. W.,
20th November, 1896.

Dear Alasinga,

I am leaving England on the 16th of December for Italy, and shall catch the North German Lloyd S. S. Prinz Regent Luitpold at Naples. The steamer is due at Colombo on the 14th of January next.

I intend to see a little of Ceylon, and shall then go to Madras. I am being accompanied by three English friends — Capt. and Mrs. Sevier and Mr. Goodwin. Mr. Sever and his wife are going to start a place near Almora in the Himalayas which I intend to make my Himalayan Centre, as well as a place for Western disciples to live as Brahmachârins and Sannyâsins. Goodwin is an unmarried young man who is going to travel and live with me, he is like a Sannyasin.

I am very desirous to reach Calcutta before the birthday festival of Shri Ramakrishna... My present plan of work is to start two centres, one in Calcutta and the other in Madras, in which to train up young preachers. I have funds enough to start the one in Calcutta, which being the scene of Shri Ramakrishna's life-work, demands my first attention. As for the Madras one, I expect to get funds in India.

We will begin work with these three centres; and later on, we will get to Bombay and Allahabad. And from these points, if the Lord is pleased, we will invade not only India, but send over bands of preachers to every country in the world. That should be our first duty. Work on with a heart. 39 Victoria will be the London headquarters for some time to come, as the work will be carried on there. Sturdy had a big box of Brahmavâdin I did not know before. He is now canvassing subscribers for it.

Now we have got one Indian magazine in English fixed. We can start some in the vernaculars also. Miss M. Noble of Wimbledon is a great worker. She will also canvass for both the Madras papers. She will write you. These things will grow slowly but surely. Papers of this kind are supported by a small circle of followers. Now they cannot be expected to do too many things at a time — they have to buy the books, find the money for the work in England, subscribers for the paper here, and then subscribe to Indian papers. It is too much. It is more like trading than teaching. Therefore you must wait, and yet I am sure there will be a few subscribers here. Again, there must be work for the people here to do when I am gone, else the whole thing will go to pieces. Therefore there must be a paper here, so also in America by and by. The Indian papers are to be supported by the Indians. To make a paper equally acceptable to all nationalities means a staff of writers from all nations; and that means at least a hundred thousand rupees a year.

You must not forget that my interests are international and not Indian alone. I am in good health; so is Abhedananda.

With all love and blessings,
Vivekananda.

73 — MADAM

London,
13th December, 1896.

Dear Madam,[1]

We have only to grasp the idea of gradation of morality and everything becomes clear.

Renunciation — non-resistance — non-destructiveness — are the ideals to be attained through less and less worldliness, less and less resistance, less and less destructiveness. Keep the ideal in view and work towards it. None can live in the world without resistance, without destruction, without desire. The world has not come to that state yet when the ideal can be realised in society.

The progress of the world through all its evils making it fit for the ideals, slowly but surely. The majority will have to go on with this slow growth — the exceptional ones will have to get out to realise the idea in the present state of things.

Doing the duty of the time is the best way, and if it is done only as a duty, it does not make us attached.

Music is the highest art and, to those who understand is the highest worship.

We must try our best to destroy ignorance and evil. Only we have to learn that evil is destroyed by the growth of good.

Yours faithfully,
Vivekananda.

---

1. An American Lady.

74 — HONOURED MADAM

ॐ तत् सत्

Rose Bank,
The Maharaja Of Burdwan'S House,
Darjeeling,
6th April, 1897.

Honoured Madam[2],

I feel much obliged for the Bhârati sent by you, and consider myself fortunate that the cause, to which my humble life has been dedicated, has been able to win the approbation off highly talented ladies like you.

In this battle of life, men are rare who encourage the initiator off new thought, not to speak of women who would offer him encouragement, particularly in our unfortunate land. It is therefore that the approbation of an educated Bengali lady is more valuable than the loud applause of all the men of India.

May the Lord grant that many women like you be born in this country, and devote their lives to the betterment of their motherland!

I have something to say in regard to the article you have written about me in the *Bharati*. It is this. It has been for the good of India that religious preaching in the West has been and will be done. It has ever been my conviction that we shall not be able to rise unless the Western people come to our help. In this country no appreciation of merit can yet be found, no financial strength, and what is most lamentable of all, there is not a bit of practicality.

There are many things to be done, but means are wanting in this country. We have brains, but no hands. We have the doctrine of Vedanta, but we have not the power to reduce it into practice. In our books there is the doctrine of universal equality, but in work we make great distinctions. It was in India that unselfish and disinterested work of the most exalted type was preached but in practice we are awfully cruel, awfully heartless — unable to think of anything besides our own mass-of-flesh bodies.

Yet it is only through the present state of things that

---

2. Shrimati Sarala Ghoshal — Editor, **Bharati**

it is possible to proceed to work. There is no other way. Every one has the power to judge of good end evil, but he is the hero who undaunted by the waves of Samsâra — which is full of errors, delusions, and miseries — with one hand wipes the tears, and with the other, unshaken, shows the path of deliverance. On the one hand there is the conservative society, like a mass of inert matter; on the other the restless, impatient, fire-darting reformer; the way to good lies between the two. I heard in Japan that it was the belief of the girls of that country that their dolls would be animated if they were loved with all their heart. The Japanese girl never breaks her doll. O you of great fortune! I too believe that India will awake again if anyone could love with all his heart the people of the country — bereft of the grace of affluence, of blasted fortune, their discretion totally lost, downtrodden, ever-starved, quarrelsome, and envious. Then only will India awake, when hundreds of large-hearted men and women, giving up all desires of enjoying the luxuries of life, will long and exert themselves to their utmost for the well-being of the millions of their countrymen who are gradually sinking lower and lower in the vortex of destitution and ignorance. I have experienced even in my insignificant life that good motives, sincerity, and infinite love can conquer the world. One single soul possessed of these virtues can destroy the dark designs of millions of hypocrites and brutes.

My going to the West again is yet uncertain; if I go, know that too will be for India. Where is the strength of men in this country? Where is the strength of money? Many men and women of the West are ready to do good to India by serving even the lowest Chandâlas, in the Indian way, and through the Indian religion. How many such are there in this country? And financial strength! To meet the expenses or my reception, the people of Calcutta made me deliver a lecture and sold tickets! ... I do not blame nor censure anybody for this, I only want to show that our well-being is impossible without men and money coming from the West.

Ever grateful and ever praying to the Lord for your welfare,

Vivekananda.

75 — DOCTOR SHASHI

Almora,
29th May, 1897.

My dear Doctor Shashi (Bhushan Ghosh),

Your letter and the two bottles containing the medicines were duly received. I have begun from last evening a trial of your medicines. Hope the combination will have a better effect than the one alone.

I began to take a lot of exercise on horseback, both morning and evening. Since that I am very much better indeed. I was so much better the first week of my gymnastics that I have scarcely felt so well since I was a boy and used to have kusti (wrestling) exercises. I really began to feel that it was a pleasure to have a body. Every movement made me conscious of strength — every movement of the muscles was pleasurable. That exhilarating feeling has subsided somewhat, yet I feel very strong. In a trial of strength I could make both G. G. and Niranjan go down before me in a minute. In Darjeeling I always felt that I was not the same man. Here I feel that I have no disease whatsoever, but there is one marked change. I never in my life could sleep as soon as I got into bed. I must toss for at least two hours. Only from Madras to Darjeeling (during the first month) I would sleep as soon as my head touched the pillow. That ready disposition to sleep is gone now entirely, and my old tossing habit and feeling hot after the evening meal have come back. I do not feel any heat after the day meal. There being an orchard here, I began to take more fruit than usual as soon as I came. But the only fruit to be got here now is the apricot. I am trying to get more varieties from Naini Tâl. There has not been any thirst even though the days are fearfully hot... On the whole my own feeling is one of revival of great strength and cheerfulness, and a feeling of exuberant health, only I am afraid I am getting fat on a too much milk diet. Don't you listen to what Yogen writes. He is a hypochondriac himself and wants to make everybody so. I ate one-sixteenth of a barphi (sweetmeat) in Lucknow, and that according to Yogen was what put me out of sorts in Almora! Yogen is expected here in a few days.

I am going to take him in hand. By the by, I am very susceptible to malarious influences. The first week's indisposition at Almora might have been caused to a certain extent by my passage through the Terai. Anyhow I feel very, very strong now. You ought to see me, Doctor, when I sit meditating in front of the beautiful snow-peaks and repeat from the Upanishads:

"न तस्य रोगो न जरा न मृत्युः प्राप्तस्य योगाग्निमयं शरीरम् — He has neither disease, nor decay, nor death; for, verily, he has obtained a body full of the fire of Yoga."

I am very glad to learn of the success of the meetings of the Ramakrishna Mission at Calcutta. All blessings attend those that help in the great work…

With all love, Yours in the Lord,
Vivekananda.

76 — MR. ——

Almora,
1st June, 1897.

Dear Mr. ——,

The objections you show about the Vedas would be valid if the word Vedas meant Samhitâs. The word Vedas includes the three parts, the Samhitas, the Brâhmanas, and the Upanishads, according to the universally received opinion in India. Of these, the first two portions, as being the ceremonial parts, have been nearly put out of sight; the Upanishads have alone been taken up by all our philosophers and founders of sects.

The idea that the Samhitas are the only Vedas is very recent and has been started by the late Swâmi Dayânanda. This opinion has not got any hold on the orthodox population.

The reason of this opinion was that Swami Dayananda thought he could find a consistent theory of the whole, based on a new interpretation of the Samhitas, but the difficulties remained the same, only they fell back on the Brahmanas. And in spite of the theories of interpretation and interpolation a good deal still remains.

Now if it is possible to build a consistent religion on the Samhitas, it is a thousand times more sure that a very consistent and harmonious faith can be based upon the Upanishads, and moreover, here one has not to go against the already received national opinion. Here all the Âchâryas (Teachers) of the past would side with you, and you have a vast scope for new progress.

The Gita no doubt has already become the Bible of Hinduism, and it fully deserves to be so; but the personality of Krishna has become so covered with haze that it is impossible today to draw any life-giving inspiration from that life. Moreover, the present age requires new modes of thought and new life.

Hoping this will help you in thinking along these lines.

I am yours with blessings,
Vivekananda.

77 — SARAT CHANDRA

अलमोड़ा।

ॐ नमो भगवते रामकृष्णाय।
यस्य वीर्येण कृतिनो वयं च भुवनानि च।
रामकृष्णं सदा वन्दे शर्वं स्वतन्त्रमीश्वरम्॥

"परभवति भगवान् विधिः" रतियागमनिः अप्रयोगनिपुणाश्च प्रयोगनिपुणाश्च पौरुषं बहुमन्यमानाः। तयोः पौरुषेयापौरुषेयप्रतीकारबलयोः विविकाग्रहनिबन्धनः कलह इति मत्वा यतस्वायुष्मन् शरच्चन्द्र आक्रमितुम् ज्ञानगिरिगुरोर्गरिष्ठं शिखरम्।

यदुक्तं "तत्त्वनिकिषग्रावा विपिदति" उच्येत तदापि शतशः "तत्त्वमसि" तत्त्वाधिकारि। इदमेव तन्नदिनं वैराग्यरुजः। धन्यं कस्यापि जीवनं तल्लक्षणाक्रान्तस्य। अरोचिष्णु अपि नरिदिशर्मा पदं प्रचीनं—"कालः कश्चिति प्रतीक्ष्यताम्" इति समारूढक्षेपणीक्षेपणाश्रमः वश्रिरामयतां तन्निर्भरः पूर्ववाहिती वेगः पारंनेष्यति नावम्। तदेवोक्तं—"तत् स्वयं योगसंसिद्धः कालेनात्मनि विन्दति," "न कर्मणा न प्रजया धनेन त्यागेनैके अमृतत्वमानशुः" इत्यत्र त्यागेन वैराग्यमेव लक्ष्यते। तद्वैराग्यं वस्तुशून्यं वस्तुभूतं वा। प्रथमं यदि, न तत्र यतेत कोऽपि कीटभक्षितिमतिषिकेन

वना; यद्यपरं, तदेतद् आपतति—त्यागः मनसः संकोचनम् अन्यस्मात् वस्तुनः, पर्णीडीकरणं च ईश्वरे वा आत्मनि । सर्वेश्वरस्तु व्यक्तविशिष्यो भवितुं नार्हति, समष्टरित्येव ग्रहणीयम् । आत्मेति वैराग्यवतो जीवात्मा इति नापद्यते, परन्तु सर्वगः सर्वान्तर्यामी सर्वस्यात्मरूपेणावस्थिति सर्वेश्वर एव लक्ष्यीकृतः । स तु समष्टिरूपेण सर्वेषां प्रत्यक्षः । एवं सति जीवेश्वरयोः स्वरूपतः अभेदभावात् तयोः सेवाप्रेमरूपकर्मणोरभेदः । अयमेव विशेषः—जीवे जीवबुद्ध्या या सेवा समर्प्यति सा दया, न प्रेम, यदात्मबुद्ध्या जीवः सेव्यते, तत् प्रेम । आत्मनो हि प्रेमास्पदत्वं श्रुतिस्मृतिप्रत्यक्षप्रसिद्धत्वात् । तत् युक्तमेव यदवादीत् भगवान् चैतन्यः — प्रेम ईश्वरे, दया जीवे इति । द्वैतवादित्वात् तत्र भगवतः सिद्धान्तः जीवेश्वरयोर्भेदविज्ञापकः समीचीनः । अस्माकं तु अद्वैतपराणां जीवबुद्धिरेबन्धनाय इति तदस्माकं प्रेम एव शरणं, न दया । जीवे प्रयुक्तः दयाशब्दोऽपि साहसिकजल्पति इति मन्यामहे । वयं न दयामहे, अपि तु सेवामहे; नानुकम्पानुभूतिरस्माकम्, अपि तु प्रेमानुभवः स्वानुभवः सर्वस्मिन् ।

सेव सर्ववेषम्यसाम्यकरी भवव्याधिनिरूजकरी प्रपञ्चावश्यम्भावव्यतरितापहराकरी सर्ववस्तुस्वरूपप्रकाशकरी मायाध्वान्तवध्वंसकरी आब्रह्मस्तम्भपर्यन्तस्वात्मरूपप्रकटनकरी प्रेमानुभूतिर्वैराग्यरूपा भवतु ते शर्मणे शर्मन् ।

इत्यनुदिवसं प्रार्थयति तवयि धृतचरिप्रेमबन्धः

विवेकानन्दः ।

Translation

Almora,
3rd July, 1897.

Constant salutation be to Shri Ramakrishna, the Free, the Ishvara, the Shiva-form, by whose power we and the whole world are blessed.

Mayest thou live long, O Sharat Chandra[1]!

Those writers of Shâstra who do not tend towards work say that all-powerful destiny prevails; but others who are workers consider the will of man as superior. Knowing that the quarrel between those who believe in the human will as the remover of misery and others who rely on destiny is due to indiscrimination — try to ascend the highest peak of knowledge.

It has been said that adversity is the touchstone of true knowledge, and this may be said a hundred times with regard to the truth: "Thou art That." This truly

---
1. Sharat Chandra Chakravarty, a disciple of Swamiji.

diagnoses the Vairâgya (dispassion) disease. Blessed is the life of one who has developed this symptom. In spite of your dislike I repeat the old saying: "Wait for a short time." You are tired with rowing; rest on your oars. The momentum will take the boat to the other side. This has been said in the Gita (IV. 38), "In good time, having reached perfection in Yoga, one realises That in one's own heart;" and in the Upanishad, "Neither by rituals, nor by progeny, nor by riches, but by renunciation alone a few (rare) people attained immortality" (Kaivalya, 2). Here, by the word renunciation Vairagya is referred to. It may be of two kinds, with or without purpose. If the latter, none but worm-eaten brains will try for it. But if the other is referred to, then renunciation would mean the withdrawal of the mind from other things and concentrating it on God or Atman. The Lord of all cannot be any particular individual. He must be the sum total. One possessing Vairagya does not understand by Atman the individual ego but the All-pervading Lord, residing as the Self and Internal Ruler in all. He is perceivable by all as the sum total. This being so, as Jiva and Ishvara are in essence the same, serving the Jivas and loving God must mean one and the same thing. Here is a peculiarity: when you serve a Jiva with the idea that he is a Jiva, it is Dayâ (compassion) and not Prema (love); but when you serve him with the idea that he is the Self, that is Prema. That the Atman is the one objective of love is known from Shruti, Smriti, and direct perception. Bhagavân Chaitanya was right, therefore, when he said, "Love to God and compassion to the Jivas". This conclusion of the Bhagavan, intimating differentiation between Jiva and Ishvara, was right, as He was a dualist. But for us, Advaitists, this notion of Jiva as distinct from God is the cause of bondage. Our principle, therefore, should be love, and not compassion. The application of the word compassion even to Jiva seems to me to be rash and vain. For us, it is not to pity but to serve. Ours is not the feeling of compassion but of love, and the feeling of Self in all.

For thy good, O Sharman, may thine be Vairagya, the feeling of which is love, which unifies all inequalities, cures the disease of Samsâra, removes the threefold misery, inevitable in this phenomenal world, reveals the true nature of all things, destroys the darkness of Mâyâ, and which brings out the Selfhood of everything from Brahma to the blade of grass!

This is the constant prayer of Vivekananda.

Ever bound to thee in love.

78 — SISTER

Almora,
9th July, 1897.

Dear Sister[1],

I am very sorry to read between the lines the desponding tone of your letter, and I understand the cause; thank you for your warning, I understand your motive perfectly. I had arranged to go with Ajit Singh to England; but the doctors not allowing, it fell thorough. I shall be so happy to learn that Harriet has met him. He will be only too glad to meet any of you.

I had also a lot of cuttings from different American papers fearfully criticising my utterances about American women and furnishing me with the strange news that I had been outcasted! As if I had any caste to lose, being a Sannyâsin!

Not only no caste has been lost, but it has considerably shattered the opposition to sea-voyage — my going to the West. If I should have to be outcasted, it would be with half the ruling princes of India and almost all of educated India. On the other hand, a leading Raja of the caste to which I belonged before my entering the order got up a banquet in my honour, at which were most of the big bugs of that caste. The Sannyasins, on the other hand, may not dine with any one in India, as it would be beneath the dignity of gods to dine with mere mortals. They are regarded as Nârâyanas, while the others are mere men. And dear Mary, these feet have been washed and wiped and worshipped by the descendants of kings, and there has been a progress through the country which none ever commanded in India.

It will suffice to say that the police were necessary to keep order if I ventured out into the street! That is outcasting indeed! Of course, that took the starch out of the missionaries, and who are they here? — Nobodies. We are in blissful ignorance of their existence all the time. I had in a lecture said something about the missionaries and the origin of that species except the English Church gentlemen, and in that connection had to refer to the very churchy women of America and their power of inventing scandals. This the missionaries are parading as an attack on American women en masse to undo my work there, as they well know that anything said against themselves will rather please the U.S. people. My dear Mary, supposing I had said all sorts of fearful things against the "Yanks" — would that be paying off a millionth part of what they say of our mothers and sisters? "Neptune's waters" would be perfectly useless to wash off the hatred the Christian "Yanks" of both sexes bear to us "heathens of India" — and what harm have we done them? Let the "Yanks" learn to be patient under criticism and then criticise others. It is a well-known psychological fact that those who are ever ready to abuse others cannot bear the slightest touch of criticism from others. Then again, what do I owe them? Except your family, Mrs. Bull, the Leggetts, and a few other kind persons, who else has been kind to me? Who came forward to help me work out my ideas? I had to work till I am at death's door and had to spend nearly the whole of that energy in America, so that the Americans may learn to be broader and more spiritual. In England I worked only six months. There was not a breath of scandal save one, and that was the working of an American woman, which greatly relieved my English friends — not only no attacks but many of the best English Church clergymen became my firm friends, and without asking I got much help for my work, and I am sure to get much more. There is a society watching my work and getting help for it, and four respectable persons followed me to India to help my work, and dozens were ready, and the next time I go, hundreds will be.

Dear, dear Mary, do not be afraid for me... The world is big, very big, and there must be some place for me even if the "Yankees" rage. Anyhow, I am quite satisfied with my work. I never planned anything. I

---
1. Miss Mary Hale.

have taken things as they came. Only one idea was burning in my brain — to start the machine for elevating the Indian masses — and that I have succeeded in doing to a certain extent. It would have made your heart glad to see how my boys are working in the midst of famine and disease and misery — nursing by the mat-bed of the cholera stricken Pariah and feeding the starving Chandâla — and the Lord sends help to me and to them all. "What are men?" He is with me, the Beloved, He was when I was in America, in England, when I was roaming about unknown from place to place in India. What do I care about what they talk — the babies, they do not know any better. What! I, who have realised the Spirit and the vanity of all earthly nonsense, to be swerved from my path by babies' prattle! Do I look like that?

I had to talk a lot about myself because I owned that to you. I feel my task is done — at most three or four years more of life are left. I have lost all wish for my salvation. I never wanted earthly enjoyments. I must see my machine in strong working order, and then knowing sure that I have put in a lever for the good of humanity, in India at least, which no power can drive back, I will sleep, without caring what will be next; and may I be born again and again, and suffer thousands of miseries so that I may worship the only God that exists, the only God I believe in, the sum total of all souls — and above all, my God the wicked, my God the miserable, my God the poor of all races, of all species, is the special object of my worship.

"He who is in you and is outside of you, who works through every hand, who walks through every foot, whose body you are, Him worship, and break all other idols.

"He who is the high and the low, the saint and the sinner, the god and the worm, Him worship, the visible, the knowable, the real, the omnipresent, break all other idols.

"In whom there is neither past life nor future birth, nor death nor going or coming, in whom we always have been and always will be one, Him worship, break all other idols.

"Ay, fools, neglecting the living Gods and His infinite reflection with which the world is full, and running after, imaginary shadows! Him worship, the only visible, and break all other idols."

My time is short. I have got to unbreast whatever I have to say, without caring if it smarts some or irritates others. Therefore, my dear Mary, do not be frightened at whatever drops from my lips, for the power behind me is not Vivekananda but He the Lord, and He knows best. If I have to please the world, that will be injuring the world; the voice of the majority is wrong, seeing that they govern and make the sad state of the world. Every new thought must create opposition — in the civilised a polite sneer, in the vulgar savage howls and filthy scandals.

Even these earthworms must stand erect, even children must see light. The Americans are drunk with new wine. A hundred waves of prosperity have come and gone over my country. We have learned the lesson which no child can yet understand. It is vanity. This hideous world is Maya. Renounce and be happy. Give up the idea of sex and possessions. There is no other bond. Marriage and sex and money the only living devils. All earthly love proceeds from the body. No sex, no possessions; as these fall off, the eyes open to spiritual vision. The soul regains its own infinite power. How I wish I were in England to see Harriet. I have one wish left — to see you four sisters before I die, and that must happen.

Yours ever affly.,
Vivekananda.

79 — MOTHER

Almora,
28th July, 1897.

My Dear Mother[2],

Many many thanks for your beautiful and kind letter. I wish I were in London to be able to accept the invitation with the Raja of Khetri. I had a great many dinners to attend in London last season. But it was

---
2. Mrs. Leggett.

fated not to be, and my health did not permit my going over with the Raja.

So Alberta is once more at home in America. I owe her a debt of gratitude for all she did for me in Rome. How is Holli? To both of them my love, and kiss the new baby for me, my youngest sister.

I have been taking some rest in the Himalayas for nine months. Now I am going down to the plains to be harnessed once more for work.

To Frankincense and Joe Joe and Mabel my love, and so to you eternally.

Yours ever in the Lord,
Vivekananda.

80 — JOE

The Math, Belur,
11th August, 1897.

Dear Joe[1],

... Well, the work of the Mother will not suffer; because it has been built and up to date maintained upon truth, sincerity, and purity. Absolute sincerity has been its watchword.

Yours with all love,
Vivekananda.

81 — JAGMOHANLAL

Murree,
11th October, 1897.

My Dear Jagamohanlal,

... Leave words when you start for Bombay to somebody to take care of three Sannyasins I am sending to Jaipur. Give them food and good lodging. They will be there till I come. They are fellows — innocent, not learned. They belong to me, and one is my Gurubhâi

---
1. Miss MacLeod.

(brother-disciple). If they like, take them to Khetri where I will come soon. I am travelling now quietly. I will not even lecture much this year. I have no more faith in all this noise and humbug which brings no practical good. I must make a silent attempt to start my institution in Calcutta; for that I am going to visit different centres quietly to collect funds.

Yours with blessings,
Vivekananda.

82 — M.

Dehra Dun,
24th November, 1897.

My Dear M.[2],

Many many thanks for your second leaflet (leaves from the *Gospel*). It is indeed wonderful. The move is quite original, and never was the life of a great Teacher brought before the public untarnished by the writer's mind, as you are presenting this one. The language also is beyond all praise, so fresh, so pointed, and withal so plain and easy.

I cannot express in adequate terms how I have enjoyed the leaflets. I am really in a transport when I read them. Strange, isn't it? Our Teacher and Lord was so original, and each one of us will have to be original or nothing. I now understand why none of us attempted his life before. It has been reserved for you, this great work. He is with you evidently.

With all love and Namaskâra,
Vivekananda.

PS. The Socratic dialogues are Plato all over; you are entirely hidden. Moreover, the dramatic part is infinitely beautiful. Everybody likes it here and in the West.

---
2. Mahendra Nath Gupta, author of **The Gospel of Sri Ramakrishna**.

83 — YOUR HIGHNESS

Almora,
9th June, 1898.

Your Highness, (Maharaja Of Khetri.)

Very sorry to learn that you are not in perfect health. Sure you will be in a few days.

I am starting for Kashmir on Saturday next. I have your letter of introduction to the Resident, but better still if you kindly drop a line to the Resident telling him that you have already given an introduction to me.

Will you kindly ask Jagamohan to write to the Dewan of Kishangarh reminding him of his promise to supply me with copies of Nimbârka Bhâshya on the *Vyâsa-Sutras* and other Bhashyas (commentaries) through his Pandits.

With all love and blessings,

Yours,
Vivekananda.

PS. Poor Goodwin is dead. Jagamohan knows him well. I want a couple of tiger skins, if I can, to be sent to the Math as present to two European friends. These seem to be most gratifying presents to Westerners.

84 — YOUR HIGHNESS

C/O Risibar Mookerjee,
Chief Judge,
Kashmir,
17th September, 1898.

Your Highness, (Maharaja Of Khetri.)

I have been very ill here for two weeks. Now getting better. I am in want of funds. Though the American; friends are doing everything they can to help me, I feel shame to beg from them all the time, especially as illness makes one incur contingent expenses. I have no shame; to beg of one person in the world and that is yourself. Whether you give or refuse, it is the same to me. If possible send some money kindly. How are you? I am going down by the middle of October.

Very glad to learn from Jagamohan the complete recovery of the Kumâr (Prince) Saheb. Things are going on well with me; hoping it is the same with you.

Ever yours in the Lord,
Vivekananda.

85 — YOUR HIGHNESS

Lahore,
16th October, 1898.

Your Highness, (Maharaja Of Khetri.)

The letter that followed my wire gave the desired information; therefore I did not wire back about my health in reply to yours.

This year I suffered much in Kashmir and am now recovered and going to Calcutta direct today. For the last ten years or so I have not seen the Puja of Shri Durgâ in Bengal which is the great affair there. I hope this year to be present.

The Western friends will come to see Jaipur in a week or two. If Jagamohan be there, kindly instruct him to pay some attention to them and show them over the city and the old arts.

I leave instructions with my brother Saradananda to write to Munshiji before they start for Jaipur.

How are you and the Prince? Ever as usual praying for your welfare,

I remain yours affectionately,
Vivekananda.

PS. My future address is Math, Belur, Howrah Dist. Bengal.

86 — YOUR HIGHNESS

Math, Belur,
Howrah Dist., Bengal,
26th October, 1898.

Your Highness, (Maharaja Of Khetri.)

I am very very anxious about your health. I had a great desire to look in on my way down, but my health failed completely, and I had to run down in all haste. There is some disturbance with my heart, I am afraid.

However I am very anxious to know about your health. If you like I will come over to Khetri to see you. I am praying day and night for your welfare. Do not lose heart if anything befalls, the "Mother" is your protection. Write me all about yourself... How is the Kumar Saheb?

With all love and everlasting blessings,

Ever yours in the Lord,
Vivekananda.

87 — YOUR HIGHNESS

The Math, Belur,
Howrah Dist.,
November (?), 1898.

Your Highness, (Maharaja Of Khetri.)

Very glad to learn that you and the Kumar are enjoying good health As for me, my heart has become very weak. Change, I do not think, will do me any good, as for the last 14 years I do not remember to have stopped at one place for 3 months at a stretch. On the other hand if by some chance I can live for months in one place, I hope it will do me good. I do not mind this. However, I feel that my work in this life is done. Through good and evil, pain and pleasure, my life-boat has been dragged on. The one great lesson I was taught is that life is misery, nothing but misery. Mother knows what is best. Each one of us is in the hands of Karma; it works itself out — and no nay. There is only one element in life which is worth having at any cost, and it is love. Love immense and infinite, broad as the sky and deep as the ocean — this is the one great gain in life. Blessed is he who gets it.

Ever yours in the Lord,
Vivekananda.

88 — YOUR HIGHNESS

Math, Belur,
15th December, 1898.

Your Highness, (Maharaja Of Khetri.)

Your very kind letter received with the order of 500 on Mr. Dulichand. I am a little better now. Don't know whether this improvement will continue or not.

Are you to be in Calcutta this winter, as I hear? Many Rajas are coming to pay their respects to the new Viceroy. The Maharaja of Sikar is here, I learn from the papers already.

Ever praying for you and yours, Yours in the Lord,
Vivekananda.

89 — MOTHER

(Translated from Bengali)

Deoghar, Vaidyanath.
3rd January, 1899.

Dear Mother[1],

Some very important questions have been raised in your letter. It is not possible to answer them fully in a short note, still I reply to them as briefly as possible.

(1) Rishi, Muni, or God — none has power to force an institution on society. When the needs of the times press hard on it, society adopts certain customs for self-preservation. Rishis have only recorded those cus-

---
1. Shrimati Mrinalini Bose.

toms As a man often resorts even to such means as are good for immediate self-protection but which are very injurious in the future, similarly society also not unfrequently saves itself for the time being, but these immediate means which contributed to its preservation turn out to be terrible in the long run.

For example, take the prohibition of widow-marriage in our country. Don't think that Rishis or wicked men introduced the law pertaining to it. Notwithstanding the desire of men to keep women completely under their control, they never could succeed in introducing those laws without betaking themselves to the aid of a social necessity of the time. Of this custom two points should be specially observed: (a) Widow-marriage takes place among the lower classes. (b) Among the higher classes the number of women is greater than that of men.

Now, if it be the rule to marry every girl, it is difficult enough to get one husband apiece; then how to get, in succession, two or three for each? Therefore has society put one party under disadvantage, i.e. it does not let her have a second husband, who has had one; if it did, one maid would have to go without a husband. On the other hand, widow-marriage obtains in communities having a greater number of men than women, as in their case the objection stated above does not exist. It is becoming more and more difficult in the West, too, for unmarried girls to get husbands.

Similar is the case with the caste system and other social customs.

So, if it be necessary to change any social custom the necessity underlying it should be found out first of all, and by altering it, the custom will die of itself. Otherwise no good will be done by condemnation or praise.

(2) Now the question is: Is it for the good of the public at large that social rules are framed or society is formed? Many reply to this in the affirmative; some, again, may hold that it is not so. Some men, being comparatively powerful, slowly bring all others under their control and by stratagem, force, or adroitness gain their own objects. If this be true, what can be the meaning of the statement that there is danger in giving liberty to the ignorant? What, again, is the meaning of liberty?

Liberty does not certainly mean the absence of obstacles in the path of misappropriation of wealth etc. by you and me, but it is our natural right to be allowed to use our own body, intelligence, or wealth according to our will, without doing any harm to others; and all the members of a society ought to have the same opportunity for obtaining wealth, education, or knowledge. The second question is: Those who say that if the ignorant and the poor be given liberty, i.e. full right to their body, wealth, etc., and if their children have the same opportunity to better their condition and acquire knowledge as those of the rich and the highly situated, they would become perverse — do they say this for the good of society or blinded by their selfishness? In England too I have heard, "Who will serve us if the lower classes get education?"

For the luxury of a handful of the rich, let millions of men and women remain submerged in the hell of want and abysmal depth of ignorance, for if they get wealth and education, society will be upset!

Who constitute society? The millions — or you, I, and a few others of the upper classes?

Again, even if the latter be true, what ground is there for our vanity that we lead others? Are we omniscient?

"उध्दरेदात्मनात्मानं — One should raise the self by the self." Let each one work out one's own salvation. Freedom in all matters, i.e. advance towards Mukti is the worthiest gain of man. To advance oneself towards freedom — physical, mental, and spiritual — and help others to do so, is the supreme prize of man. Those social rules which stand in the way of the unfoldment of this freedom are injurious, and steps should be taken to destroy them speedily. Those institutions should be encouraged by which men advance in the path of freedom.

That in this life we feel a deep love at first sight towards a particular person who may not be endowed with extraordinary qualities, is explained by the thinkers of our country as due to the associations of a past incarnation.

Your question regarding the will is very interesting: it is the subject to know. The essence of all religions is the annihilation of desire, along with which comes, of a certainty, the annihilation of the will as well, for desire is only the name of a particular mode of the will. Why, again, is this world? Or why are these manifestations of the will? Some religions hold that the evil will should be destroyed and not the good. The denial of desire here would be compensated by enjoyments hereafter. This reply does not of course satisfy the wise. The Buddhists, on the other hand, say that desire is the cause of misery, its annihilation is quite desirable. But like killing a man in the effort to kill the mosquito on his cheek, they have gone to the length of annihilating their own selves in their efforts to destroy misery according to the Buddhistic doctrine.

The fact is, what we call will is an inferior modification of something higher. Desirelessness means the disappearance of the inferior modification in the form of will and the appearance of that superior state. That state is beyond the range of mind and intellect. But though the look of the gold mohur is quite different from that of the rupee and the pice, yet as we know for certain that the gold mohur is greater than either, so, that highest state — Mukti, or Nirvâna, call it what you like — though out of the reach of the mind and intellect, is greater than the will and all other powers. It is no power, but power is its modification, therefore it is higher. Now you will see that the result of the proper exercise of the will, first with motive for an object and then without motive, is that the will-power will attain a much higher state.

In the preliminary state, the form of the Guru is to be meditated upon by the disciple. Gradually it is to be merged in the Ishta. By Ishta is meant the object of love and devotion... It is very difficult to superimpose divinity on man, but one is sure to succeed by repeated efforts. God is in every man, whether man knows it or not; your loving devotion is bound to call up the divinity in him.

Ever your well-wisher,
Vivekananda.

90 — JOE

The Math, Belur,
Howrah, Bengal,
2nd February, 1899.

My Dear Joe[1],

You must have reached N.Y. by this time and are in the midst of your own after a long absence. Fortune has favoured you at every step of this journey — even the sea was smooth and calm, and the ship nearly empty of undesirable company. Well, with me it is doing otherwise. I am almost desperate I could not accompany you. Neither did the change at Vaidyanath do me any good. I nearly died there, was suffocating for eight days and nights!! I was brought back to Calcutta more dead than alive, and here I am struggling to get back to life again.

Dr. Sarkar is treating me now.

I am not so despondent now as I was. I am reconciled to my fate. This year seems to be very hard for us. Yogananda, who used to live in Mother's house, is suffering for the last month and every day is at death's door. Mother knows best. I am roused to work again, though not personally but am sending the boys all over India to make a stir once more. Above all, as you know, the chief difficulty is of funds. Now that you are in America, Joe, try to raise some funds for our work over here.

I hope to rally again by March, and by April I start for Europe. Again Mother knows best.

I have suffered mentally and physically all my life, but Mother's kindness has been immense. The joy and blessings I had infinitely more than I deserve. And I am struggling not to fail Mother, but that she will always find me fighting, end my last breath will be on the battlefield.

My best love and blessings for you ever and ever.

Ever yours in the Truth,
Vivekananda.

---

1. Miss Josephine MacLeod.

91 — FRIEND

The Math,
Alambazar (?),
14th June, 1899.

My Dear Friend[2],

I want your Highness in that fashion as I am here, you need most of friendship and love just now.

I wrote you a letter a few weeks ago but could not get news of yours. Hope you are in splendid health now. I am starting for England again on the 20th this month.

I hope also to benefit somewhat by this sea-voyage.

May you be protected from all dangers and may all blessings ever attend you!

I am yours in the Lord,
Vivekananda.

PS. To Jagamohan my love and good-bye.

92 — ——

Ridgely,
2nd September, 1899.

Dear ——,

... Life is a series of fights and disillusionments... The secret of life is not enjoyment, but education through experience. But, alas, we are called off the moment we begin really to learn. That seems to be a potent argument for a future existence... Everywhere it is better to have a whirlwind come over the work. That clears the atmosphere and gives us a true insight into the nature of things. It is begun anew, but on adamantine foundations...

Yours with best wishes,
Vivekananda.

93 — SHASHI

(Translated from Bengali)

Math, Belur,
26th December, 1900.

Dear Shashi[3],

I got all the news from your letter. If your health is bad, then certainly you should not come here; and also I am going to Mayavati tomorrow. It is absolutely necessary that I should go there once.

If Alasinga comes here, he will have to await my return. I do not know what those here are deciding about Kanai. I shall return shortly from Almora, and then I may be able to visit Madras. From Vaniyambadi I have received a letter. Write to the people there conveying my love and blessings, and tell them that on my way to Madras I shall surely visit them. Give my love to all. Don't work too hard. All is well here.

Yours affectionately,
Vivekananda.

94 — MOTHER

Prabuddha Bharata Office,
Advaita Ashrama,
Mayavati (Via Almora),
Kumaon, Himalayas,
6th January, 1901.

My Dear Mother[4],

I send you forthwith a translation of the Nâsadiya Hymn sent by Dr. Bose through you. I have tried to make it as literal as possible.

I hope Dr. Bose has recovered his health perfectly by this time.

Mrs. Sevier is a strong woman, and has borne her loss quietly and bravely. She is coming over to Eng-

---

2. Raja Of Khetri.

3. Swami Ramakrishnananda.

4. Mrs. Ole Bull.

land in April, and I am going over with her.

I ought to come to England as early as I can this summer; and as she must go to attend to her husband's affairs, I accompany her.

This place is very, very beautiful, and they have made it simply exquisite. It is a huge place several acres in area, and is very well kept. I hope Mrs. Sevier will be in a position to keep it up in the future. She wishes it ever so much, of course.

My last letter from Joe informed me that she was going up the ... with Mme Calvé.

I am very glad to learn that Margot is leaving her lore for future use. Her book has been very much appreciated here, but the publishers do not seem to make any effort at sale.

The first day's touch of Calcutta brought the asthma back; and every night I used to get a fit during the two weeks I was there. I am, however, very well in the Himalayas.

It is snowing heavily here, and I was caught in a blizzard on the way; but it is not very cold, and all this exposure to the snows for two days on my way here seems to have done me a world of good.

Today I walked over the snow uphill about a mile, seeing Mrs. Sevier's lands; she has made beautiful roads all over. Plenty of gardens, fields, orchards, and large forests, all in her land. The living houses are so simple, so clean, and so pretty, and above all so suited for the purpose.

Are you going to America soon? If not, I hope to see you in London in three months.

Kindly give my best wishes to Miss Olcock and kindly convey my undying love to Miss Müller the next time you see her; so to Sturdy. I have seen my mother, my cousin, and all my people in Calcutta.

Kindly send the remittance you send my cousin to me — in my name so that I shall cash the cheque and give her the money. Saradananda and Brahmananda and the rest were well in the Math when I last left them.

All here send love.

Ever your loving son,
Vivekananda.

PS. Kali has taken two sacrifices; the cause has already two European martyrs. Now, it is going to rise up splendidly.

My love to Alberta and Mrs. Vaughan. The snow is lying all round six inches deep, the sun is bright and glorious, and now in the middle of the day we are sitting outside, reading. And the snow all about us! The winter here is very mild in spite of the snow. The air is dry and balmy, and the water beyond all praise.

95 — STURDY

Mayavati,
Himalayas,
15th January, 1901.

My Dear Sturdy,

I learn from Saradananda that you have sent over Rs. 1,529-5-5 to the Math, being the money that was in hand for work in England. I am sure it will be rightly used.

Capt. Sevier passed away about three months ago. They have made a fine place here in the mountains and Mrs. Sevier means to keep it up. I am on a visit to her, and I may possibly come over to England with her.

I wrote you a letter from Paris. I am afraid you did not get it.

So sorry to learn the passing away of Mrs. Sturdy. She has been a very good wife and good mother, and it is not ordinarily one meets with such in this life.

This life is full of shocks, but the effects pass away anyhow, that is the hope.

It is not because of your free expression of opinion in your last letter to me that I stopped writing. I only let the wave pass, as is my wont. Letters would only have made a wave of a little bubble.

Kindly tender my regards and love to Mrs. Johnson and other friends if you meet them.

And I am ever yours in the Truth,
Vivekananda.

96 — MOTHER

The Math, Belur,
Howrah Dist.,
Bengal,
26th January, 1901.

My Dear Mother[1],

Many thanks for your very encouraging words. I needed them very much just now. The gloom has not lifted with the advent of the new century, it is visibly thickening. I went to see Mrs. Sevier at Mayavati. On my way I learnt of the sudden death of the Raja of Khetri. It appears he was restoring some old architectural monument at Agra, at his own expense, and was up some tower on inspection. Part of the tower came down, and he was instantly killed.

The three cheques have arrived. They will reach my cousin when next I see her.

Joe is here, but I have not seen her yet.

The moment I touch Bengal, especially the Math, the asthmatic fits return! The moment I leave, I recover!

I am going to take my mother on pilgrimage next week. It may take months to make the complete round of pilgrimages. This is the one great wish of a Hindu widow. I have brought only misery to my people all my life. I am trying at least to fulfil this one wish of hers.

I am so glad to learn all that about Margot; everybody here is eager to welcome her back.

I hope Dr. Bose has completely recovered by this time.

I had a beautiful letter also from Mrs. Hammond. She is a great soul.

However, I am very calm and self-possessed this time and find everything better than I ever expected.

With all love,

Ever your son,
Vivekananda.

---

1. Mrs. Ole Bull

97 — SHASHI

Math, Belur

My Dear Shashi, (Swami Ramakrishnananda)

I am going with my mother to Rameswaram, that is all. I don't know whether I shall go to Madras at all. If I go, it will be strictly private. My body and mind are completely worked out; I cannot stand a single person. I do not want anybody. I have neither the strength nor the money, nor the will to take up anybody with me. Bhaktas (devotees) of Guru Maharaj or not, it does not matter. It was very foolish of you even to ask such a question. Let me tell you again, I am more dead than alive, and strictly refuse to see anybody. If you cannot manage this, I don't go to Madras. I have to become a bit selfish to save my body.

Let Yogin-Ma and others go their own way. I shall not take up any company in my present state of health.

Yours in love,
Vivekananda.

98 — MOTHER

The Math, Belur,
Howrah Dist., Bengal,
2nd February, 1901.

My Dear Mother[2],

Several days ago I received your letter and a cheque for Rs. 150 included. I will tear up this one, as the three previous cheques I have handed over to my cousin.

Joe is here, and I have seen her twice; she is busy visiting. Mrs. Sevier is expected here soon en route to England. I expected to go to England with her, but as it now turns out, I must go on a long pilgrimage with my mother.

My health suffers the moment I touch Bengal; anyhow, I don't much mind it now; I am going on well

---

2. Mrs. Ole Bull.

and so do things about me.

Glad to learn about Margot's success, but, says Joe, it is not financially paying; there is the rub. Mere continuance is of little value, and it is a far cry from London to Calcutta. Well, Mother knows. Everybody is praising Margot's Kali the Mother; but alas! they can't get a book to buy; the booksellers are too indifferent to promote the sale of the book.

That this new century may find you and yours in splendid health and equipment for a yet greater future is and always has been the prayer of your son.

Vivekananda.

99 — JOE

Belur Math,
Dist. Howrah,
14th February, 1901.

My Dear Joe, (Miss Josephine MacLeod.)

I am ever so glad to hear that Bois is coming to Calcutta. Send him immediately to the Math. I will be here. If possible I will keep him here for a few days and then let him go again to Nepal.

Yours etc.,
Vivekananda.

100 — JOE

The Math, Belur,
Howrah, Bengal,
17th February, 1901.

Dear Joe, (Miss Josephine MacLeod.)

Just now received your nice long letter. I am so glad that you met and approve Miss Cornelia Sorabji. I knew her father at Poona, also a younger sister who was in America. Perhaps her mother will remember me as the Sannyasin who used to live with the Thakore Sahib of Limbdi at Poona.

I hope you will go to Baroda and see the Maharani.

I am much better and hope to continue so for some time. I have just now a beautiful letter from Mrs. Sevier in which she writes a whole lot of beautiful things about you.

I am so glad you saw Mr. Tata and find him so strong and good.

I will of course accept an invitation if I am strong enough to go to Bombay.

Do wire the name of the steamer you leave by for Colombo. With all love,

Yours affectionately,
Vivekananda.

101 — MOTHER

Dacca,
29th March, 1901.

My Dear Mother[1],

By this time you must have received my other note from Dacca. Saradananda has been suffering badly from fever in Calcutta, which has become simply a hell of demons this year. He has recovered and is now in the Math which, thank God, is one of the healthiest places in our Bengal.

I do not know what conversation took place between you and my mother; I was not present. I suppose it was only an eager desire on her part to see Margot, nothing else.

My advice to Margot would be to mature her plans in England and work them out a good length before she comes back. Good solid work must wait.

Saradananda expects to go to Darjeeling to Mrs. Banerji, who has been in Calcutta for a few days, as soon as he is strong enough.

I have no news yet of Joe from Japan. Mrs. Sevier expects to sail soon. My mother, aunt, and cousin came over five days ago to Dacca, as there was a great

---
1 Mrs. Ole Bull..

sacred bath in the Brahmaputra river. Whenever a particular conjunction of planets takes place, which is very rare, a huge concourse of people gather on the river on a particular spot. This year there has been more than a hundred thousand people; for miles the river was covered with boats.

The river, though nearly a mile broad at the place, was one mass of mud! But it was firm enough, so we had our bath and Pujâ (worship), and all that.

I am rather enjoying Dacca. I am going to take my mother and the other ladies to Chandranath, a holy place at the easternmost corner of Bengal.

I am rather well and hope you and your daughter and Margot are also enjoying splendid health.

With everlasting love,

Ever your son,
Vivekananda.

PS. My cousin and mother send you and Margot their love. PS. I do not know the date.

102 — SWARUP

The Math,
15th May, 1901.

My Dear Swarup (ânanda),

Your letter from Naini Tal is quite exciting. I have just returned from my tour through East Bengal and Assam. As usual I am quite tired and broken down.

If some real good comes out of a visit to H. H. of Baroda I am ready to come over, otherwise I don't want to undergo the expense and exertion of the long journey Think it well over and make inquiries, and write me if you still think it would be best for the Cause for me to come to see H. H...

Yours with love and blessings,
Vivekananda.

103 — MARY

The Math, Belur,
Howrah Dist.,
Bengal, India, 18th May, 1901.

My Dear Mary[2],

Sometimes it is hard work to be tied to the shoe-strings of a great name. And that was just what happened to my letter. You wrote on the 22nd January, 1901. You tied me to the latchet of a great name, Miss MacLeod. Consequently the letter has been following her up and down the world. Now it reached me yesterday from Japan, where Miss MacLeod is at present. Well, this, therefore, is the solution of the sphinx's riddle. "Thou shalt not join a great name with a small one."

So, Mary, you have been enjoying Florence and Italy, and I do not know where you be by this time. So, fat old "laidy", I throw this letter to the mercy of Monroe & Co., 7 rue Scribe.

Now, old "laidy" — so you have been dreaming away in Florence and the Italian lakes. Good; your poet objects to its being empty though.

Well, devoted sister, how about myself? I came to India last fall, suffered all through winter, and went this summer touring through Eastern Bengal and Assam — through a land of giant rivers and hills and malaria — and after hard work of two months had a collapse, and am now back to Calcutta slowly recovering from the effects of it.

The Raja of Khetri died from a fall a few months ago. So you see things are all gloomy with me just now, and my own health is wretched. Yet I am sure to bob up soon and am waiting for the next turn.

I wish I were in Europe, just to have a long chat with you, and then return as quick to India; for, after all, I feel a sort of quiet nowadays, and have done with three-fourths of my restlessness.

My love to Harriet Woolley, to Isabel, to Harriet McKindley; and to mother my eternal love and gratitude. Tell mother, the subtle Hindu's gratitude runs

---

2. Miss Mary Hale.

through generations.

Ever yours in the Lord,
Vivekananda.

PS. Write a line when you feel like it.

104 — SHASHI

(Translated from Bengali)

Math, Belur,
Dist., Howrah,
3rd June, 1901.

My Dear Shashi[1],

Reading your letter I felt like laughing, and also rather sorry. The cause of the laughter is that you had a dream through indigestion and made yourself miserable, taking it to be real. The cause of my sorrow is that it is clear from this that your health is not good, and that your nerves require rest very badly.

Never have I laid a curse on you, and why should I do so now? All your life you have known my love for you, and today are you doubting it? True, my temper was ever bad, and nowadays owing to illness it occasionally becomes terrible — but know this for certain that my love can never cease.

My health nowadays is becoming a little better. Have the rains started in Madras? When the rains begin a little in the South, I may go to Madras via Bombay and Poona. With the onset of the rains the terrible heat of the South will perhaps subside.

My great love to you and all others. Yesterday Sharat returned to the Math from Darjeeling — his health is much better than it was before. I have come here after a tour of East Bengal and Assam. All work has its ups and downs, its periods of intensity and slackness. Again it will rise up. What fear? ...

Whatever that may be, I say that you stop your work for some time and come straight back to the Math. After you have taken a month's rest here, you and I together will make a grand tour via Gujarat, Bombay, Poona, Hyderabad, Mysore to Madras. Would not that be grand? If you cannot do this, stop your lectures in Madras for a month. Take a little good food and sleep well. Within two or three months I shall go there. In any case, reply immediately as to what you decide to do.

Yours with blessings,
Vivekananda.

105 — JOE

The Math, Belur,
Howrah Dist.,
14th June, 1901.

Dear Joe[2],

I am so glad you are enjoying Japan — especially Japanese art. You are perfectly correct in saying that we will have to learn many things from Japan. The help that Japan will give us will be with great sympathy and respect, whereas that from the West unsympathetic and destructive. Certainly it is very desirable to establish a connection between India and Japan.

As for me, I was thrown *hors de combat* in Assam. The climate of the Math is just reviving me a bit. At Shillong — the hill sanatorium of Assam — I had fever, asthma, increase of albumen, and my body swelled to almost twice ills normal size. These symptoms subsided, however, as soon as I reached the Math. It is dreadfully hot this year; but a bit of rain has commenced, and I hope we will soon have the monsoon in full force. I have no plans just now, except that the Bombay Presidency wants me so badly that I think of going there soon. We are thinking of starting touring through Bombay in a week or so.

The 300 dollars you speak of sent by Lady Betty have not reached me yet, nor have I any intimation of its arrival from General Patterson.

He, poor man, was rather miserable, after his wife and children sailed for Europe and asked me to come

---

1. Swami Ramakrishnananda

2. Miss Josephine MacLeod.

and see him, but unfortunately I was so ill, and am so afraid of going into the City that I must wait till the rains have set in.

Now, Joe dear, if I am to go to Japan, this time it is necessary that I take Saradananda with me to carry on the work. Also I must have the promised letter to Li Huang Chang from Mr. Maxim; but Mother knows the rest. I am still undecided.

So you went to Alanquinan to see the foreteller? Did he convince you of his powers? What did he say? Write particular *s'il vous plaît*.

Jules Bois went as far as Lahore, being prevented from entering Nepal. I learn from the papers that he could not bear the heat and fell ill; then he took ship et *bon voyage*. He did not write me a single line since we met in the Math. You also are determined to drag Mrs. Bull down to Japan from Norway all the way — *bien, Mademoiselle, vous êtes use puissante magicienne, sans doute*.[3] Well, Joe, keep health and spirits up; the Alanquinan man's words come out true most of them; and *gloire et honneur* await you — and Mukti. The natural ambition of woman is through marriage to climb up, leaning upon a man; but those days are gone. You shall be great without the help of any man, just as you are, plain, dear Joe — our Joe, everlasting Joe…

We have seen enough of this life to care for any of its bubbles have we not Joe? For months I have been practicing to drive away all sentiments; therefore I stop here, and good-bye just now. It is ordained by Mother we work together; it has been already for the good of many; it shall be for the good of many more; so let it be. It is useless planning, useless high flights; Mother will find Her own way; … rest assured.

Ever yours with love and heart's blessings,
Vivekananda.

PS. Just now came a cheque for Rs. 300 from Mr. Okakura, and the invitation. It is very tempting, but Mother knows all the same.

---

3. Well, Miss, you are undoubtedly a powerful magician.

106 — JOE

The Math, Belur,
18th June, 1901.

Dear Joe, (Miss Josephine MacLeod.)

I enclose with yours an acknowledgement of Mr. Okakura's money — of course I am up to all your tricks.

However, I am really trying to come, but you know — one month to go — one to come — and a few days' stay! Never mind, I am trying my best. Only my terribly poor health, some legal affairs, etc., etc., may make a little delay.

With everlasting love,
Vivekananda.

107 — JOE

The Math, Belur,
Howrah,
Bengal, India,
1901

Dear Joe, (Miss Josephine MacLeod.)

I can't even in imagination pay the immense debt of gratitude I owe you. Wherever you are you never forget my welfare; and, there, you are the only one that bears all my burdens, all my brutal outbursts.

Your Japanese friend has been very kind, but my health is so poor that I am rather afraid I have not much time to spare for Japan. I will drag myself through the Bombay Presidency even if only to say, "How do you do?" to all kind friends.

Then two months will be consumed in coming and going, and only one month to stay; that is not much of a chance for work, is it?

So kindly pay the money your Japanese friend has sent for my passage. I shall give it back to you when you come to India in November.

I have had a terrible collapse in Assam from which I am slowly recovering. The Bombay people have waited and waited till they are sick — must see them this time.

If in spite of all this you wish me to come, I shall start the minute you write.

I had a letter from Mrs. Leggett from London asking whether the £300 have reached me safe. They have, and I had written a week or so before to her the acknowledgment, C/o Monroe & Co., Paris, as per her previous instructions.

Her last letter came to me with the envelope ripped up in a most barefaced manner! The post offices in India don't even try to do the opening of my mail decently.

Ever yours with love,
Vivekananda.

108 — MARY

The Math,
5th July, 1901.

My Dear Mary[1],

I am very thankful for your very long and nice letter, especially as I needed just such a one to cheer me up a bit. My health has been and is very bad. I recover for a few days only; then comes the inevitable collapse. Well, this is the nature of the disease anyway.

I have been touring of late in Eastern Bengal and Assam. Assam is, next to Kashmir, the most beautiful country in India, but very unhealthy. The huge Brahmaputra winding in and out of mountains and hills, studded with islands, is of course worth one's while to see.

My country is, as you know, the land of waters. But never did I realise before what that meant. The rivers of East Bengal are oceans of rolling fresh water, not rivers, and so long that steamers work on them for weeks. Miss MacLeod is in Japan. She is of course charmed with the country and asked me to come

---
1. Miss Mary Hale.

over, but my health not permitting such a long voyage, I desisted. I have seen Japan before.

So you are enjoying Venice. The old man must be delicious; only Venice was the home of old Shylock, was it not?

Sam is with you this year — I am so glad! He must be enjoying the good things of Europe after his dreary experience in the North. I have not made any interesting friends of late, and the old ones that you knew of, have nearly all passed away, even the Raja of Khetri. He died of a fall from a high tower at Secundra, the tomb of Emperor Akbar. He was repairing this old grand piece of architecture at his own expense at Agra, and one day while on inspection, he missed his footing, and it was a sheer fall of several hundred feet. Thus we sometimes come to grief on account of our zeal for antiquity. Take care, Mary, don't be too zealous for your piece of Indian antiquity.

In the Mission Seal, the snake represents mysticism; the sun knowledge; the worked up waters activity; the lotus love; the swan the soul in the midst of all.

With love to Sam and to mother,

Ever with love,
Vivekananda.

PS. My letter had to be short; I am out of sorts all the time; it is the body!

109 — CHRISTINE

The Math, Belur,
6th July, 1901.

Dear Christine,

Things come to me by fits — today I am in a fit of writing. The first thing to do is, therefore, to pen a few lines to you. I am known to be nervous, I worry much; but it seems, dear Christine, you are not far behind in that trick. One of our poets says, "Even the mountains will fly, the fire will be cold, yet the heart of the great will never change." I am small, very, but I know you are great, and my faith is always in your true heart. I worry about everything except you. I have dedicated you to the Mother. She is your shield, your guide. No harm can reach you — nothing hold you down a minute. I know it.

Ever yours in the Lord,
Vivekananda.

110 — MARY

The Math, Belur,
Howrah Dist., Bengal,
27th August, 1901.

My Dear Mary[2],

I would that my health were what you expected — at least to write you a long letter. It is getting worse, in fact, every day, and so many complications and botherations without that. I have ceased to notice it at all.

I wish you all joy in your lovely Swiss chalet — splendid health, good appetite, and a light study of Swiss or other antiquities just to liven things up a bit. I am so glad you are breathing the free air of the mountains, but sorry that Sam is not in the best of health. Well, there is no anxiety about it, he has naturally such a fine physique...

"Women's moods and man's luck — the gods themselves do not know, what to speak of man?" My instincts may be very feminine, but what I am exercised with just this moment is, that you get a little bit of manliness about you. Oh! Mary, your brain, health, beauty, everything is going to waste just for lack of that one essential — assertion of individuality. Your haughtiness, spirit, etc. are all nonsense, only mockery; you are at best a boarding-school girl, no backbone! no backbone!

Alas! this lifelong leading-string business! This is very harsh, very brutal; but I can't help it. I love you, Mary, sincerely, genuinely; I can't cheat you with namby-pamby sugar candies. Nor do they ever come to me.

Then again, I am a dying man; I have no time to fool in. Wake up, girl. I expect now from you letters

---
2. Miss Mary Hale.

of the right slashing order; give it right straight; I need a good deal of rousing.

I did not hear anything of the MacVeaghs when they were here. I have not had any direct message from Mrs. Bull or Nivedità, but I hear regularly from Mrs. Sevier, and they are all in Norway as guests of Mrs. Bull.

I don't know when Nivedita comes to India or if she ever comes back.

I am in a sense a retired man; I don't keep much note of what is going on about the Movement; then the Movement is getting bigger, and it is impossible for one man to know all about it minutely.

I now do nothing, except trying to eat and sleep and nurse my body the rest of the time. Good-bye, dear Mary; hope we shall meet again somewhere in this life, but, meeting or no meeting, I remain,

Ever your loving brother,
Vivekananda.

111 — BLESSED AND BELOVED

The Math, Belur,
Howrah,
29th August, 1901.

Blessed And Beloved[3],

I am getting better, though still very weak... The present disturbance is simply nervous. Anyhow I am getting better every day.

I am so much beholden to mother[4] for her kind proposal, only I am told by everybody in the Math that Nilambar Babu's place and the whole of the village of Belur at that becomes very malarious this month and the next. Then the rent is so extravagant. I would therefore advise mother to take a little house in Calcutta if she decides to come. I may in all probability go and live there, as it is not good for me to catch malaria over and above the present prostration. I have not asked the opinion of Saradananda or Brah-

---
3. Shri M. N. Banerji.
4. Holy Mother — Shri Sarada Devi.

mananda yet. Both are in Calcutta. Calcutta is healthier these two months and very much less expensive.

After all, let her do as she is guided by the Lord. We can only suggest and may be entirely wrong.

If she selects Nilambar's house for residence, do first arrange the rent etc. beforehand. "Mother" knows best. That is all I know too.

With all love and blessings,

Ever yours in the Lord,
Vivekananda.

112 — BLESSED AND BELOVED

The Math, Belur,
Howrah Dist.,
7th September, 1901.

Blessed And Beloved[1],

I had to consult Brahmananda and others, and they were everyone in Calcutta, hence the delay in replying to your last.

The idea of taking a house for a whole year must be worked out with deliberation. As on the one hand there is some risk of catching malaria in Belur this month, in Calcutta on the other hand there is the danger of plague. Then again one is sure to avoid fever if one takes good care not to go into the interior of this village, the immediate bank of the river being entirely free from fever. Plague has not come to the river yet, and all the available places in this village are filled with Marwaris during the plague season.

Then again you ought to mention the maximum rent you can pay, and we seek the house accordingly. The quarter in the city is another suggestion. For myself, I have almost become a foreigner to Calcutta. But others will soon find a house after your mind. The sooner you decide these two points: (1) Whether mother stays at Belur or Calcutta, (2) If Calcutta, what rent and quarter, the better, as it can be done in a trice after receiving your reply.

Yours with love and blessings,
Vivekananda.

PS. We are all right here. Moti has returned after his week's stay in Calcutta. It is raining here day and night last three days. Two of our cows have calved.

113 — JOE

The Math, Belur,
Howrah,
8th November, 1901.

My Dear Joe[2],

By this this time you must have received the letter explaining the word abatement. I did not write the letter nor send the wire. I was too ill at the time to do either. I have been ever since my trip to East Bengal almost bedridden. Now I am worse than ever with the additional disadvantage of impaired eyesight. I would not write these things, but some people require details, it seems.

Well, I am so glad that you are coming over with your Japanese friends — they will have every attention in my power. I will most possibly be in Madras. I have been thinking of leaving Calcutta next week and working my way gradually to the South.

I do not know whether it will be possible to see the Orissan temples in company with your Japanese friends. I do not know whether I shall be allowed inside myself — owing to my eating "Mlechchha" food. Lord Curzon was not allowed inside.

However, your friends are welcome to what I can do always. Miss Müller is in Calcutta. Of course she has not visited us.

Yours with all love,
Vivekananda.

---

1. Shri M. N. Banerji.

2. Miss Josephine MacLeod.

114 — SWARUP

Gopal Lal Villa,
Benares (Varanasi) Cantonment,
9th February, 1902.

My Dear Swarup(ânanda),

... In answer to Châru's letter, tell him to study the *Brahma-Sutras* himself. What does he mean by the *Brahma-Sutras* containing references to Buddhism? He means the Bhâshyas, of course, or rather ought to mean, and Shankara was only the last Bhâshyakâra (commentator). There are references, though in Buddhistic literature, to Vedanta, and the Mahâyâna school of Buddhism is even Advaitistic. Why does Amara Singha, a Buddhist, give as one of the names of Buddha — Advayavâdi? Charu writes, the word Brahman does not occur in the Upanishads! *Quelle bêtise*!

I hold the Mahayana to be the older of the two schools of Buddhism.

The theory of Mâyâ is as old as the Rik-Samhitâ. The Shvetâshvatara Upanishad contains the word "Maya" which is developed out of Prakriti. I hold that Upanishad to be at least older than Buddhism.

I have had much light of late about Buddhism, and I am ready to prove:

(1) That Shiva-worship, in various forms, antedated the Buddhists, that the Buddhists tried to get hold of the sacred places of the Shaivas but, failing in that, made new places in the precincts just as you find now at Bodh-Gayâ and Sârnâth (Varanasi).

(2) The story in the Agni Purâna about Gayâsura does not refer to Buddha at all — as Dr. Rajendralal will have it — but simply to a pre-existing story.

(3) That Buddha went to live on Gayâshirsha mountain proves the pre-existence of the place.

(4) Gaya was a place of ancestor-worship already, and the footprint-worship the Buddhists copied from the Hindus.

(5) About Varanasi, even the oldest records go to prove it as the great place of Shiva-worship; etc., etc.

Many are the new facts I have gathered in Bodh-Gaya and from Buddhist literature. Tell Charu to read for himself, and not be swayed by foolish opinions.

I am rather well here, in Varanasi, and if I go on improving in this way, it will be a great gain.

A total revolution has occurred in my mind about the relation of Buddhism and Neo-Hinduism. I may not live to work out the glimpses, but I shall leave the lines of work indicated, and you and your brethren will have to work it out.

Yours with all blessings and love,
Vivekananda.

115 — MRS. OLE BULL

Gopal Lal Villa,
Benares (Varanasi) Cantonment,
10th February, 1902.

Welcome to India once more, dear mother[3] and daughter. A copy of a Madras journal that I received through the kindness of Joe delighted me exceedingly, as the reception Nivedità had in Madras was for the good of both Nivedita and Madras. Her speech was indeed beautiful.

I hope you are resting well after your long journey, and so is Nivedita. I wish it so much that you should go for a few hours to a few villages west of Calcutta to see the old Bengali structures made of wood, bamboo, cane, mica, and grass.

These are the bungalows, most artistic. Alas! the name is travestied nowadays by every pigsty appropriating the name.

In old days a man who built a palace still built a bungalow for the reception of guests. The art is dying out. I wish I could build the whole of Nivedita's School in that style. Yet it is good to see the few that yet remained, at least one.

Brahmananda will arrange for it, and you have only to take a journey of a few hours.

---

3. Mrs. Ole Bull.

Mr. Okakura has started on his short tour. He intends to visit Agra, Gwalior, Ajanta, Ellora, Chittore, Udaipur, Jaipur, and Delhi.

A very well-educated rich young man of Varanasi, with whose father we had a long-standing friendship, came back to this city yesterday. He is especially interested in art, and spending purposely a lot of money in his attempts to revive dying Indian arts. He came to see me only a few hours after Mr. Okakura left. He is just the man to show him artistic India (i.e. what little is left), and I am sure he will be much benefited by Okakura's suggestions. Okakura just found a common terracotta water-vessel here used by the servants. The shape and the embossed work on it simply charmed him, but as it is common earthenware and would not bear the journey, he left a request with me to have it reproduced in brass. I was at my wit's end as to what to do. My young friend comes a few hours after, and not only undertakes to have it done but offers to show a few hundreds of embossed designs in terracotta infinitely superior to the one Okakura fancied.

He also offers to show us old paintings in that wonderful old style. Only one family is left in Varanasi who can paint after the old style yet. One of them has painted a whole hunting scene on a pea, perfect in detail and action!

I hope Okakura will come to this city on his return and be this gentleman's guest and see a bit of what is left.

Niranjan has gone with Mr. Okakura, and as he is a Japanese, they don't object to his going into any temple. It seems that the Tibetans and the other Northern Buddhists have been coming here to worship Shiva all along.

They allowed him to touch the sign of Shiva and worship. Mrs. Annie Besant tried once, but, poor woman, although she bared her feet, put on a Sari, and humiliated herself to the dust before the priests, she was not admitted even into the compound of the temple. The Buddhists are not considered non-Hindus in any of our great temples. My plans are not settled; I may shift from this place very soon.

Shivananda and the boys send you all their welcome, regards, and love.

I am, as ever, your most affectionate son

Vivekananda.

116 — SISTER NIVEDITA

Benares (Varanasi),
12th February, 1902.

May all powers come unto you[1]! May Mother Herself be your hands and mind! It is immense power — irresistible — that I pray for you, and, if possible, along with it infinite peace...

If there was any truth in Shri Ramakrishna, may He take you into His leading, even as He did me, nay, a thousand times more!

Vivekananda.

117 — RAKHAL

(Translated from Bengali)

Gopal Lal Villa,
Benares (Varanasi) Cantonment,
12th February 1902.

My Dear Rakhal[2],

I was glad to get all the detailed news from your letter. Regarding Nivedita's School, I have written to her what I have to say. My opinion is that she should do what she considers to be best.

Don't ask my opinion on any other matter either. That makes me lose my temper. Just do that work for me — that is all. Send money, for at present only a few rupees are left.

Kanai (Nirbhayananda) lives on Mâdhukari[3], does his Japa at the bathing ghat, and comes and sleeps

---
1. Sister Nivedita.
2. Swami Brahmananda.
3. Cooked food obtained by begging from several houses.

here at night; Nyedâ does a poor man's work and comes and sleeps here at night. "Uncle[4]" and Niranjan have gone to Agra. I may get their letter today.

Continue doing your work as the Lord guides. Why bother about the opinion of this man and that? My love to all.

Yours affectionately.
Vivekananda.

118 — RAKHAL

(Translated from Bengali)

Gopal Lal Villa,
Benares (Varanasi) Cantonment,
18th February, 1902.

My Dear Rakhal, (Swami Brahmananda.)

You must have received by this time my letter of yesterday containing an acknowledgment of the money. The main object of this letter is to write about ——— . You should go and meet him as soon as you get this letter… Get a competent doctor and have the disease diagnosed properly. Now where is Vishnu Mohini, the eldest daughter of Ram Babu[5]? She has recently been widowed…

Anxiety is worse than the disease. Give a little money — whatever is needed. If in this hell of a world one can bring a little joy and peace even for a day into the heart of a single person, that much alone is true; this I have learnt after suffering all my life; all else is mere moonshine…

Reply very soon. "Uncle[6]" and Niranjan have written a letter from Gwalior… Here it is now becoming hot gradually. This place was cooler than Bodh-Gaya… I was very pleased to hear that the Saraswati-Puja was celebrated by Nivedita with great success. If she wants to open the school soon, let her do so. Readings from the sacred books, worship, study — see that all these are being maintained. My love to all.

Yours affectionately,
Vivekananda.

119 — RAKHAL

(Translated from Bengali)

Gopal Lal Villa,
Benares (Varanasi) Cantonment,
21st February, 1902.

My Dear Rakhal,

I received a letter from you just now. If mother and grandmother desire to come, send them over. It is better to get away from Calcutta now when the season of plague is on. There is wide-spread plague in Allahabad; I do not know if it will spread to Varanasi this time … Tell Mrs. Bull from me that a tour to Ellora and other places involves a difficult journey, and it is now very hot. Her body is so tired that it is not proper to go on a tour at present. It is several days since I received a letter from "Uncle[7]" The last news was that he had gone to Ajanta. Mahant also has not replied, perhaps he will do so with the reply to Raja Pyari Mohan's letter…

Write me in detail about the matter of the Nepal Minister. Give my special love and blessings to Mrs. Bull, Miss MacLeod, and all others. My love and greetings to you, Baburam[8] and all others. Has Gopal Dada[9] got the letter? Kindly look after the goat a bit.

Yours affectionately,
Vivekananda.

PS. All the boys here send you their respectful salutations.

---

4. Mr. Okakura was endearingly so called. "Kura" approximating to "Khurhâ" in Bengali which means uncle; Swamiji out of fun calls him uncle.

5. Ram Chandra Datta, a disciple of Shri Ramakrishna.

6. See note (4) previous page.

7. See note (4) previous page.

8. Swami Premananda.

9. Swami Advaitananda.

120 — BRAHMANANDA

(Translated from Bengali)

Gopal Lal Villa,
Benares (Varanasi) Cantonment,
24th February, 1902.

This morning I got a small American parcel sent by you[1]. I have received no letter, neither the registered one you refer to nor any other. Whether the Nepalese gentleman came and what happened — I have not been able to know anything at all about it. To write a simple letter so much trouble and so much delay! ... Now I shall be relieved if I get the accounts. That also I get who knows after how many months! ...

Yours affectionately,
Vivekananda.

121 — JOE

The Math,
21st April, 1902.

Dear Joe, (Miss Josephine MacLeod.)

It seems the plan of going to Japan seems to have come to nought. Mrs. Bull is gone, you are going. I am not sufficiently acquainted with the Japanese.

Sadananda has accompanied the Japanese to Nepal along with Kanai. Christine could not start earlier, as Margot could not go till the end of this month.

I am getting on splendidly, they say, but yet very weak and no water to drink. Anyhow the chemical analysis shows a great improvement. The swelling about the feet and the complaints have all disappeared.

Give my infinite love to Lady Betty and Mr. Leggett, to Alberta and Holly — the baby has my blessings from before birth and will have for ever.

How did you like Mayavati? Write me a line about it.

With everlasting love,
Vivekananda.

122 — JOE

The Math,
Belur, Howrah,
15th May, 1902.

Dear Joe[2],

I send you the letter to Madame Calvé... I am somewhat better, but of course far from what I expected. A great idea of quiet has come upon me. I am going to retire for good — no more work for me. If possible, I will revert to my old days of begging.

All blessings attend you, Joe; you have been a good angel to me.

With everlasting love,
Vivekananda.

123 — DHIRA MATA

The Math,
14th June, 1902.

Dear Dhirâ Mâtâ[3],

... In my opinion, a race must first cultivate a great respect for motherhood, through the sanctification and inviolability of marriage, before it can attain to the ideal of perfect chastity. The Roman Catholics and the Hindus, holding marriage sacred and inviolate, have produced great chaste men and women of immense power. To the Arab, marriage is a contract or a forceful possession, to be dissolved at will, and we do not find there the development of the idea of the virgin or the Brahmachârin. Modern Buddhism —

---

1. Swami Brahmananda.

2. Miss Josephine MacLeod.
3. Mrs. Ole Bull.

having fallen among races who had not yet come up to the evolution of marriage — has made a travesty of monasticism. So until there is developed in Japan a great and sacred ideal about marriage (apart from mutual attraction and love), I do not see how there can be great monks and nuns. As you have come to see that the glory of life is chastity, so my eyes also have been opened to the necessity of this great sanctification for the vast majority, in order that a few lifelong chaste powers may be produced...

I wanted to write many things, but the flesh is weak ... "Whosoever worships me, for whatsoever desire, I meet him with that." . . .

Vivekananda

INTERVIEWS

MIRACLES

(The Memphis Commercial, 15th January, 1894)

Asked by the reporter for his impressions of America, he said:

"I have a good impression of this country especially of the American women. I have especially remarked on the absence of poverty in America."

The conversation afterward turned to the subject of religions. Swami Vive Kananda expressed the opinion that the World's Parliament of Religions had been beneficial in that it had done much toward broadening ideas.

"What", asked the reporter, "is the generally accepted view held by those of your faith as to the fate after death of one holding the Christian religion?"

"We believe that if he is a good man he will be saved. Even an atheist, if he is a good man, we believe must be saved. That is our religion. We believe all religions are good, only those who hold them must not quarrel."

Swami Vive Kananda was questioned concerning the truthfulness of the marvelous stories of the performance of wonderful feats of conjuring, levitation, suspended animation, and the like in India. Vive Kananda said:

"We do not believe in miracles at all but that apparently strange things may be accomplished under the operation of natural laws. There is a vast amount of literature in India on these subjects, and the people there have made a study of these things.

"Thought-reading and the foretelling of events are successfully practiced by the Hathayogis.

"As to levitation, I have never seen anyone overcome gravitation and rise by will into the air, but I have seen many who were trying to do so. They read books published on the subject and spend years trying to accomplish the feat. Some of them in their efforts nearly starve themselves and become so thin that if one presses his finger upon their stomachs he can actually feel the spine.

"Some of these Hathayogis live to a great age."

The subject of suspended animation was broached and the Hindu monk told the Commercial reporter that he himself had known a man who went into a sealed cave, which was then closed up with a trap door, and remained there for many years without food. There was a decided stir of interest among those who heard this assertion. Vive Kananda entertained not the slightest doubt of the genuineness of this case. He says that in the case of suspended animation, growth is for the time arrested. He says the case of the man in India who was buried with a crop of barley raised over his grave and who was finally taken out still alive is perfectly well authenticated. He thinks the studies which enabled persons to accomplish that feat were suggested by the hibernating animals.

Vive Kananda said that he had never seen the feat which some writers have claimed has been accomplished in India, of throwing a rope into the air and the thrower climbing up the rope and disappearing out of sight in the distant heights.

A lady present when the reporter was interviewing the monk said some one had asked her if he, Vive Kananda, could perform wonderful tricks, and if he had been buried alive as a part of his installation in the Brotherhood. The answer to both questions was a positive negative. "What have those things to do with religion?" he asked. "Do they make a man purer? The Satan of your Bible is powerful, but differs from God in not being pure."

Speaking of the sect of Hathayoga, Vive Kananda said there was one thing, whether a coincidence or not, connected with the initiation of their disciples, which was suggestive of the one passage in the life of Christ. They make their disciples live alone for just forty days.

AN INDIAN YOGI IN LONDON

(The Westminster Gazette, 23rd October, 1895)

Indian philosophy has in recent years had a deep and growing fascination for many minds, though up to the present time its exponents in this country have been entirely Western in their thought and training, with the result that very little is really known of the deeper mysteries of the Vedanta wisdom, and that little only by a select few. Not many have the courage or the intuition to seek in heavy translations, made greatly in the interests of philologists, for that sublime knowledge which they really reveal to an able exponent brought up in all the traditions of the East.

It was therefore with interest and not without some curiosity, writes a correspondent, that I proceeded to interview an exponent entirely novel to Western people in the person of the Swami Vivekananda, an actual Indian Yogi, who has boldly undertaken to visit the Western world to expound the traditional teaching which has been handed down by ascetics and Yogis through many ages and who in pursuance of this object, delivered a lecture last night in the Princes' Hall.

The Swami Vivekananda is a striking figure with his turban (or mitre-shaped black cloth cap) and his calm but kindly features.

On my inquiring as to the significance, if any, of his name, the Swami said: "Of the name by which I am now known (Swami Vivekananda), the first word is descriptive of a Sannyâsin, or one who formally renounces the world, and the second is the title I assumed — as is customary with all Sannyasins — on my renunciation of the world, it signifies, literally, 'the bliss of discrimination'."

"And what induced you to forsake the ordinary course of the world, Swami?" I asked.

"I had a deep interest in religion and philosophy from my childhood," he replied, "and our books teach renunciation as the highest ideal to which man can aspire. It only needed the meeting with a great Teacher — Ramakrishna Paramahamsa — to kindle in me the final determination to follow the path he himself had trod, as in him I found my highest ideal realised."

"Then did he found a sect, which you now represent?"

"No", replied the Swami quickly. "No, his whole life was spent in breaking down the barriers of sectarianism and dogma. He formed no sect. Quite the reverse. He advocated and strove to establish absolute freedom of thought. He was a great Yogi."

"Then you are connected with no society or sect in this country? Neither Theosophical nor Christian Scientist, nor any other?"

"None whatever!" said the Swami in clear and impressive tones. (His face lights up like that of a child, it is so simple, straightforward and honest.) "My teaching is my own interpretation of our ancient books, in the light which my Master shed upon them. I claim no supernatural authority. Whatever in my teaching may appeal to the highest intelligence and be accepted by thinking men, the adoption of that will be my reward." "All religions", he continued, "have for their object the teaching either of devotion, knowledge, or Yoga, in a concrete form. Now, the philosophy of Vedanta is the abstract science which embraces all these methods, and this it is that I teach, leaving each one to apply it to his own concrete form. I refer each individual to his own experiences, and where reference is made to books, the latter are procurable, and may be studied by each one for himself. Above all, I teach no authority proceeding from hidden beings speaking through visible agents, any more than I claim learning from hidden books or manuscripts. I am the exponent of no occult societies, nor do I believe that good can come of such bodies. Truth stands on its own authority, and truth can bear the light of day."

"Then you do not propose to form any society. Swami?" I suggested.

"None; no society whatever. I teach only the Self hidden in the heart of every individual and common to all. A handful of strong men knowing that Self and living in Its light would revolutionise the world, even today, as has been the case by single strong men before each in his day."

"Have you just arrived from India?" I inquired — for the Swami is suggestive of Eastern suns.

"No," he replied, "I represented the Hindu religion at the Parliament of Religions held at Chicago in 1893. Since then I have been travelling and lecturing in the United States. The American people have proved most interested audiences and sympathetic friends, and my work there has so taken root that I must shortly return to that country."

"And what is your attitude towards the Western religions, Swami?"

"I propound a philosophy which can serve as a basis to every possible religious system in the world, and my attitude towards all of them is one of extreme sympathy — my teaching is antagonistic to none. I direct my attention to the individual, to make him strong, to teach him that he himself is divine, and I call upon men to make themselves conscious of this divinity within. That is really the ideal — conscious or unconscious — of every religion."

"And what shape will your activities take in this country?"

"My hope is to imbue individuals with the teachings to which I have referred, and to encourage them to express these to others in their own way; let them modify them as they will; I do not teach them as dogmas; truth at length must inevitably prevail.

"The actual machinery through which I work is in the hands of one or two friends. On October 22, they have arranged for me to deliver an address to a British audience at Princes' Hall, Piccadilly, at 8-30 p.m. The event is being advertised. The subject will be on the key of my philosophy — 'Self-Knowledge'. Afterwards I am prepared to follow any course that opens — to attend meetings in people's drawing-rooms or elsewhere, to answer letters, or discuss personally. In a mercenary age I may venture to remark that none of my activities are undertaken for a pecuniary reward."

I then took my leave from one of the most original of men that I have had the honour of meeting.

INDIA'S MISSION

(Sunday Times, London, 1896)

English people are well acquainted with the fact that they send missionaries to India's "coral strands". Indeed, so thoroughly do they obey the behest, "Go ye forth into all the world and preach the Gospel", that none of the chief British sects are behindhand in obedience to the call to spread Christ's teaching. People are not so well aware that India also sends missionaries to England.

By accident, if the term may be allowed, I fell across the Swami Vivekananda in his temporary home at 63 St. George's Road, S. W., and as he did not object to discuss the nature of his work and visit to England, I sought him there and began our talk with an expression of surprise at his assent to my request.

"I got thoroughly used to the interviewer in America. Because it is not the fashion in my country, that is no reason why I should not use means existing in any country I visit, for spreading what I desire to be known! There I was representative of the Hindu religion at the World's Parliament of Religions at Chicago in 1893. The Raja of Mysore and some other friends sent me there. I think I may lay claim to having had some success in America. I had many invitations to other great American cities besides Chicago; my visit was a very long one, for, with the exception of a visit to England last summer, repeated as you see this year, I remained about three years in America. The American civilisation is, in my opinion a very great one. I find the American mind peculiarly susceptible to new ideas; nothing is rejected because it is new. It is examined on its own merits, and stands or falls by these alone."

"Whereas in England — you mean to imply something?"

"Yes, in England, civilisation is older, it has gathered many accretions as the centuries have rolled on. In particular, you have many prejudices that need to be broken through, and whoever deals with you in ideas must lay this to his account."

"So they say. I gather that you did not found anything like a church or a new religion in America."

"That is true. It is contrary to our principles to multiply organizations, since, in all conscience, there are enough of them. And when organizations are created they need individuals to look after them. Now, those who have made Sannyâsa — that is, renunciation of all worldly position, property, and name — whose aim is to seek spiritual knowledge, cannot undertake this work, which is, besides, in other hands."

"Is your teaching a system of comparative religion?"

"It might convey a more definite idea to call it the kernel of all forms of religion, stripping from them the non-essential, and laying stress on that which is the real basis. I am a disciple of Ramakrishna Paramahamsa, a perfect Sannyâsin whose influence and ideas I fell under. This great Sannyasin never assumed the negative or critical attitude towards other religions, but showed their positive side — how they could be carried into life and practiced. To fight, to assume the antagonistic attitude, is the exact contrary of his teaching, which dwells on the truth that the world is moved by love. You know that the Hindu religion never persecutes. It is the land where all sects may live in peace and amity. The Mohammedans brought murder and slaughter in their train, but until their arrival peace prevailed. Thus the Jains, who do not believe in a God and who regard such belief as a delusion, were tolerated, and still are there today. India sets the example of real strength, that is meekness. Dash, pluck, fight, all these things are weakness."

"It sounds very like Tolstoy's doctrine; it may do for individuals, though personally I doubt it. But how will it answer for nations?"

"Admirably for them also. It was India's Karma, her fate, to be conquered, and in her turn, to conquer her conqueror. She has already done so with her Mohammedan victors: Educated Mohammedans are Sufis, scarcely to be distinguished from Hindus. Hindu thought has permeated their civilisation; they assumed the position of learners. The great Akbar, the Mogul Emperor, was practically a Hindu. And England will be conquered in her turn. Today she has the sword, but it is worse than useless in the world of ideas. You know what Schopenhauer said of Indian thought. He foretold that its influence would be as momentous in Europe, when it became well known, as the revival of Greek and Latin; culture after the Dark Ages."

"Excuse me saying that there do not seem many signs; of it just now."

"Perhaps not", said the Swami, gravely. "I dare say a good many people saw no signs of the old Renaissance and did not know it was there, even after it had come. But there is a great movement, which can be discerned by those who know the signs of the times. Oriental research has of recent years made great progress. At present it is in the hands of scholars, and it seems dry and heavy in the work they have achieved. But gradually the light of comprehension will break"

"And India is to be the great conqueror of the future? Yet she does not send out many missionaries to preach her ideas. I presume she will wait until the world comes to her feet?"

"India was once a great missionary power. Hundreds' of years before England was converted to Christianity, Buddha sent out missionaries to convert the world of Asia to his doctrine. The world of thought is being converted. We are only at the beginning as yet. The number of those who decline to adopt any special form of religion is greatly increasing, and this movement is among the educated classes. In a recent American census, a large number of persons declined to class themselves as belonging to any form of religion. All religions are different expressions of the same truth; all march on or die out. They are the radii of the same truth, the expression that variety of minds requires."

"Now we are getting near it. What is that central truth?"

"The Divine within; every being, however degraded, is the expression of the Divine. The Divinity becomes covered, hidden from view. I call to mind an incident of the Indian Mutiny. A Swami, who for years had fulfilled a vow of eternal silence, was stabbed by a Mohammedan. They dragged the murderer before his victim and cried out, 'Speak the word, Swami, and he shall die.' After many years of silence, he broke it to say with his last breath: 'My children, you are all mistaken. That man is God Himself.' The great lesson is, that unity is behind all. Call it God, Love, Spirit. Allah, Jehovah — it is the same unity that animates all life from the lowest animal to the noblest man. Picture to yourself an ocean ice-bound, pierced with many different holes. Each of these is a soul, a man, emancipated according to his degree of intelligence, essaying to break through the ice."

"I think I see one difference between the wisdom of the East and that of the West. You aim at producing very perfect individuals by Sannyasa, concentration, and so forth. Now the ideal of the West seems to be the perfecting of the social state; and so we work at political and social questions, since we think that the permanence of our civilisation depends upon the well-being of the people."

"But the basis of all systems, social or political," said the Swami with great earnestness, "rests upon the goodness of men. No nation is great or good because Parliament enacts this or that, but because its men are great and good. I have visited China which had the most admirable organisation of all nations. Yet today China is like a disorganised mob, because her men are not equal to the system contrived in the olden days. Religion goes to the root of the matter. If it is right, all is right."

"It sounds just a little vague and remote from practical life, that the Divine is within everything but covered. One can't be looking for it all the time."

"People often work for the same ends but fail to recognise the fact. One must admit that law, government, politics are phases not final in any way. There is a goal beyond them where law is not needed. And by the way, the very word Sannyasin means the divine outlaw, one might say, divine nihilist, but that miscomprehension pursues those that use such a word. All great Masters teach the same thing. Christ saw that the basis is not law, that morality and purity are the only strength. As for your statement that the East aims at higher self-development and the West at the perfecting of the social state, you do not of course forget that there is an apparent Self and a real Self."

"The inference, of course, being that we work for the apparent, you for the real?"

"The mind works through various stages to attain its fuller development. First, it lays hold of the concrete, and only gradually deals with abstractions. Look, too, how the idea of universal brotherhood is reached. First it is grasped as brotherhood within a sect — hard, narrow, and exclusive. Step by step we reach broad generalizations and the world of abstract ideas."

"So you think that those sects, of which we English are so fond, will die out. You know what the Frenchman said, 'England, the land of a thousand sects and but one sauce'."

"I am sure that they are bound to disappear. Their existence is founded on non-essentials; the essential part of them will remain and be built up into another edifice. You know the old saying that it is good to be born in a church, but not to die in it."

"Perhaps you will say how your work is progressing in England?"

"Slowly, for the reasons I have already named. When you deal with roots and foundations, all real progress must be slow. Of course, I need not say that these ideas are bound to spread by one means or another, and to many of us the right moment for their dissemination seems now to have come."

Then I listened to an explanation of how the work is carried on. Like many an old doctrine, this new one is offered without money and without price, depending entirely upon the voluntary efforts of those who embrace it.

The Swami is a picturesque figure in his Eastern dress. His simple and cordial manner, savouring of anything but the popular idea of asceticism, an unusual command of English and great conversational powers add not a little to an interesting personality... His vow of Sannyasa implies renunciation of position, property, and name, as well as the persistent search for spiritual knowledge.

INDIA AND ENGLAND

(India, London, 1896)

During the London season, Swami Vivekananda has been teaching and lecturing to considerable numbers of people who have been attracted by his doctrine and philosophy. Most English people fancy that England has the practical monopoly of missionary enterprise, almost unbroken save for a small effort on the part of France. I therefore sought the Swami in his temporary home in South Belgravia to enquire what message India could possibly send to England, apart from the remonstrances she has too often had to make on the subject of home charges, judicial and executive functions combined in one person, the settlement of expenses connected with Sudanese and other expeditions.

"It is no new thing", said the Swami composedly, "that India should send forth missionaries. She used to do so under the Emperor Asoka, in the days when the Buddhist faith was young, when she had something to teach the surrounding nation."

"Well, might one ask why she ever ceased doing so, and why she has now begun again?"

"She ceased because she grew selfish, forgot the principle that nations and individuals alike subsist and prosper by a system of give and take. Her mission to the world has always been the same. It is spiritual, the realm of introspective thought has been hers through all the ages; abstract science, metaphysics, logic, are her special domain. In reality, my mission to England is an outcome of England's to India. It has been hers to conquer, to govern, to use her knowledge of physical science to her advantage and ours. In trying to sum up India's contribution to the world, I am reminded of a Sanskrit and an English idiom. When you say a man dies, your phrase is, 'He gave up the ghost', whereas we say, 'He gave up the body'. Similarly, you more than imply that the body is the chief part of man by saying it possesses a soul. Whereas we say a man is a soul and possesses a body. These are but small ripples on the surface, yet they show the current of your national thought. I should like to remind you how Schopenhauer predicted that the influence of Indian philosophy upon Europe would be as momentous when it became well known as was the revival of Greek and Latin learning at the close of the Dark Ages. Oriental research is making great progress; a new world of ideas is opening to the seeker after truth."

"And is India finally to conquer her conquerors?"

"Yes, in the world of ideas. England has the sword, the material world, as our Mohammedan conquerors had before her. Yet Akbar the Great became practically a Hindu; educated Mohammedans, the Sufis, are hardly to be distinguished from the Hindus; they do not eat beef, and in other ways conform to our usages. Their thought has become permeated by ours."

"So, that is the fate you foresee for the lordly Sahib? Just at this moment he seems to be a long way off it."

"No, it is not so remote as you imply. In the world of religious ideas, the Hindu and the Englishman have much in common, and there is proof of the same thing among other religious communities. Where the English ruler or civil servant has had any knowledge of India's literature, especially her philosophy, there exists the ground of a common sympathy, a territory constantly widening. It is not too much to say that only ignorance is the cause of that exclusive — sometimes even contemptuous — attitude assumed by some."

"Yes, it is the measure of folly. Will you say why you went to America rather than to England on your mission?"

"That was a mere accident — a result of the World's Parliament of Religions being held in Chicago at the time of the World's Fair, instead of in London, as it ought to have been. The Raja of Mysore and some other friends sent me to America as the Hindu representative. I stayed there three years, with the exception of last summer and this summer, when I came to lecture in London. The Americans are a great people, with a future before them. I admire them very much, and found many kind friends among them. They are less prejudiced than the English, more ready to weigh end examine anew idea, to value it in spite of its newness. They are most hospitable too; far less time is lost in showing one's credentials, as it were. You travel in America, as I did, from city to city, always lecturing among friends. I saw Boston, New York, Philadelphia, Baltimore, Washington, Des Moines, Memphis, and numbers of other places."

"And leaving disciples in each of them?"

"Yes, disciples, but not organizations. That is no part of my work. Of these there are enough in all conscience. Organisations need men to manage them; they must seek power, money, influence. Often they struggle for domination, and even fight."

"Could the gist of this mission of yours be summed up in a few words? Is it comparative religion you want to preach?"

"It is really the philosophy of religion, the kernel of all its outward forms. All forms of religion have an essential and a non-essential part. If we strip from them the latter, there remains the real basis of all religion, which all forms of religion possess in common. Unity is behind them all. We may call it God, Allah, Jehovah, the Spirit, Love; it is the same unity that animates all life, from its lowest form to its noblest manifestation in man. It is on this unity that we need to lay stress, whereas in the West, and indeed everywhere, it is on the non-essential that men are apt to lay stress. They will fight and kill each other for these forms, to make their fellows conform. Seeing that the essential is love of God and love of man, this is curious, to say the least."

"I suppose a Hindu could never persecute."

"He never yet has done so; he is the most tolerant of all the races of men. Considering how profoundly religious he is, one might have thought that he would persecute those who believe in no God. The Jains regard such belief as sheer delusion, yet no Jain has ever been persecuted. In India the Mohammedans were the first who ever took the sword."

"What progress does the doctrine of essential unity make in England? Here we have a thousand sects."

"They must gradually disappear as liberty and knowledge increase. They are founded on the nonessential, which by the nature of things cannot survive. The sects have served their purpose, which was that of an exclusive brotherhood on lines comprehended by those within it. Gradually we reach the idea of universal brotherhood by flinging down the walls of partition which separate such aggregations of individuals. In England the work proceeds slowly, possibly because the time is not yet ripe for it; but all the same, it makes progress. Let me call your attention to the similar work that England is engaged upon in India. Modern caste distinction is a barrier to India's progress. It narrows, restricts, separates. It will crumble before the advance of ideas.

"Yet some Englishmen, and they are not the least sympathetic to India nor the most ignorant of her history, regard caste as in the main beneficent. One may easily be too much Europeanised. You yourself condemn many of our ideals as materialistic."

"True. No reasonable person aims at assimilating India to England; the body is made by the thought that lies behind it. The body politic is thus the expression of national thought, and in India, of thousands of years of thought. To Europeanise India is therefore an impossible and foolish task: the elements of progress were always actively present in India. As soon as a peaceful government was there, these have always shown themselves. From the time of the Upanishads down to the present day, nearly all our great Teachers have wanted to break through the barriers of caste, i.e. caste in its degenerate state, not the original system. What little good you see in the present caste clings to it from the original caste, which was the most glorious social institution. Buddha tried to re-establish caste in its original form. At every period of India's awakening, there have always been great efforts made to break down caste. But it must always be we who build up a new India as an effect and continuation of her past, assimilating helpful foreign ideas wherever they may be found. Never can it be they; growth must proceed from within. All that England can do is to help India to work out her own salvation. All progress at the dictation of another, whose hand is at India's throat, is valueless in my opinion. The highest work can only degenerate when slave-labour produces it."

"Have you given any attention to the Indian National Congress movement?"

"I cannot claim to have given much; my work is in

another part of the field. But I regard the movement as significant, and heartily wish it success. A nation is being made out of India's different races. I sometimes think they are no less various than the different peoples of Europe. In the past, Europe has struggled for Indian trade, a trade which has played a tremendous part in the civilisation of the world; its acquisition might almost be called a turning-point in the history of humanity. We see the Dutch, Portuguese, French, and English contending for it in succession. The discovery of America may be traced to the indemnification the Venetians sought in the far distant West for the loss they suffered in the East."

"Where will it end?"

"It will certainly end in the working out of India's homogeneity, in her acquiring what we may call democratic ideas. Intelligence must not remain the monopoly of the cultured few; it will be disseminated from higher to lower classes. Education is coming, and compulsory education will follow. The immense power of our people for work must be utilised. India's potentialities are great and will be called forth"

"Has any nation ever been great without being a great military power?"

"Yes," said the Swami without a moment's hesitation, "China has. Amongst other countries, I have travelled in China and Japan. Today, China is like a disorganised mob; but in the heyday of her greatness she possessed the most admirable organisation any nation has yet known Many of the devices and methods we term modern were practiced by the Chinese for hundreds and even thousands of years. Take competitive examination as an illustration."

"Why did she become disorganized?"

"Because she could not produce men equal to the system. You have the saying that men cannot be made virtuous by an Act of Parliament; the Chinese experienced it before you. And that is why religion is of deeper importance than politics, since it goes to the root, and deals with the essential of conduct."

"Is India conscious of the awakening that you allude to?"

"Perfectly conscious. The world perhaps sees it chiefly in the Congress movement and in the field of social reform; but the awakening is quite as real in religion, though it works more silently."

"The West and East have such different ideals of life. Ours seems to be the perfecting of the social state. Whilst we are busy seeing to these matters, Orientals are meditating on abstractions. Here has Parliament been discussing the payment of the Indian army in the Sudan. All the respectable section of the Conservative press has made a loud outcry against the unjust decision of the Government, whereas you probably think the whole affair not worth attention."

"But you are quite wrong", said the Swami, taking the paper and running his eyes over extracts from the Conservative Journals. "My sympathies in this matter are naturally with my country. Yet it reminds one of the old Sanskrit proverb: 'You have sold the elephant, why quarrel over the goad?' India always pays. The quarrels of politicians are very curious. It will take ages to bring religion into politics."

"One ought to make the effort very soon all the same."

"Yes, it is worth one's while to plant an idea in the heart of this great London, surely the greatest governing machine that has ever been set in motion. I often watch it working, the power and perfection with which the minutest vein is reached, its wonderful system of circulation and distribution. It helps one to realise how great is the Empire and how great its task. And with all the rest, it distributes thought. It would be worth a man's while to place some ideas in the heart of this great machine, so that they might circulate to the remotest part."

The Swami is a man of distinguished appearance. Tall, broad, with fine features enhanced by his picturesque Eastern dress, his personality is very striking. By birth, he is a Bengali, and by education, a graduate of the Calcutta University. His gifts as an orator are high. He can speak for an hour and a half without a note or the slightest pause for a word.

C.S.B

INDIAN MISSIONARY'S MISSION TO ENGLAND

(The Echo, London, 1896)

... I presume that in his own country the Swami would live under a tree, or at most in the precincts of a temple, his head shaved, dressed in the costume of his country. But these things are not done in London, so that I found the Swami located much like other people, and, save that he wears a long coat of a dark orange shade, dressed like other mortals likewise. He laughingly related that his dress, especially when he wears a turban, does not commend itself to the London street arab, whose observations are scarcely worth repeating. I began by asking the Indian Yogi to spell his name very slowly...

"Do you think that nowadays people are laying much stress on the non-essential?"

"I think so among the backward nations, and among the less cultured portion of the civilised people of the West. Your question implies that among the cultured and the wealthy, matters are on a different footing. So they are; the wealthy are either immersed in the enjoyment of health or grubbing for more. They, and a large section of the busy people, say of religion that it is rot, stuff, nonsense, and they honestly think so The only religion that is fashionable is patriotism and Mrs. Grundy. People merely go to church when they are marrying or burying somebody."

"Will your message take them oftener to church?"

"I scarcely think it will. Since I have nothing whatever to do with ritual or dogma; my mission is to show that religion is everything and in everything... And what can we say of the system here in England? Everything goes to show that Socialism or some form of rule by the people, call it what you will, is coming on the boards. The people will certainly want the satisfaction of their material needs, less work, no oppression, no war, more food. What guarantee have we that this or any civilisation will last, unless it is based on religion, on the goodness of man? Depend on it, religion goes to the root of the matter. If it is right, all is right."

"It must be difficult to get the essential, the metaphysical, part of religion into the minds of the people. It is remote from their thoughts and manner of life."

"In all religions we travel from a lesser to a higher truth, never from error to truth. There is a Oneness behind all creation, but minds are very various. 'That which exists is One, sages call It variously.' What I mean is that one progresses from a smaller to a greater truth. The worst religions are only bad readings of the froth. One gets to understand bit by bit. Even devil-worship is but a perverted reading of the ever-true and immutable Brahman. Other phases have more or less of the truth in them. No form of religion possesses it entirely."

"May one ask if you originated this religion you have come to preach to England?"

"Certainly not. I am a pupil of a great Indian sage, Ramakrishna Paramahamsa. He was not what one might call a very learned man, as some of our sages are, but a very holy one, deeply imbued with the spirit of the Vedanta philosophy. When I say philosophy, I hardly know whether I ought not to say religion, for it is really both. You must read Professor Max Müller's account of my Master in a recent number of the Nineteenth Century. Ramakrishna was born in the Hooghly district in 1836 and died in 1886. He produced a deep effect on the life of Keshab Chandra Sen and others. By discipline of the body and subduing of the mind he obtained a wonderful insight into the spiritual world. His face was distinguished by a childlike tenderness, profound humility, and remarkable sweetness of expression. No one could look upon it unmoved."

"Then your teaching is derived from the Vedas?"

"Yes, Vedanta means the end of the Vedas, the third section or Upanishads, containing the ripened ideas which we find more as germs in the earlier portion. The most ancient portion of the Vedas is the Samhitâ, which is in very archaic Sanskrit, only to be understood by the aid of a very old dictionary, the Nirukta of Yâska."

"I fear that we English have rather the idea that India has much to learn from us; the average man is pretty ignorant as to what may be learnt from India."

"That is so, but the world of scholars know well how much is to be learnt and how important the lesson. You would not find Max Müller, Monier Williams, Sir William Hunter, or German Oriental scholars making light of Indian abstract science."

... The Swami gives his lecture at 39 Victoria Street. All are made welcome, and as in ancient apostolic times, the new teaching is without money and without price. The Indian missionary is a mall of exceptionally fine physique; his command of English can only be described as perfect.

C.S.B

WITH THE SWAMI VIVEKANANDA AT MADURA

(The Hindu, Madras, February, 1897)

Q. — The theory that the universe is false seems to be understood in the following senses: (a) the sense in which the duration of perishing forms and names is infinitesimally small with reference to eternity; (b) the sense in which the period between any two Pralayas (involution of the universe) is infinitesimally small with reference to eternity; (c) the sense in which the universe is ultimately false though it has an apparent reality at present, depending upon one sort of consciousness, in the same way as the idea of silver superimposed on a shell or that of a serpent on a rope, is true for the time being, and, in effect, is dependent upon a particular condition of mind; (d) the sense in which the universe is a phantom just like the son of a barren woman or like the horns of a hare.

In which of these senses is the theory understood in the Advaita philosophy?

A. — There are many classes of Advaitists and each has understood the theory in one or the other sense. Shankara taught the theory in the sense (c), and it is his teaching that the universe, as it appears, is real for all purposes for every one in his present consciousness, but it vanishes when the consciousness assumes a higher form. You see the trunk of a tree standing before you, and you mistake it for a ghost. The idea of a ghost is for the time being real, for it works on your mind and produces the same result upon it as if it were a ghost. As soon as you discover it to be a stump, the idea of the ghost disappears. The idea of a stump and that of the ghost cannot co-exist, and when one is present, the other is absent.

Q. — Is not the sense (d) also adopted in some of the writings of Shankara?

A. — No. Some other men who, by mistake, carried Shankara's notion to an extreme have adopted the sense (d) in their writing. The senses (a) and (b) are peculiar to the writings of some other classes of Advaita philosophers but never received Shankara's sanction.

Q. — What is the cause of the apparent reality?

A. — What is the cause of your mistaking a stump for a ghost? The universe is the same, in fact, but it is your mind that creates various conditions for it.

Q. — What is the true meaning of the statement that the Vedas are beginningless and eternal? Does it refer to the Vedic utterances or the statements contained in the Vedas? If it refers to the truth involved in such statements, are not the sciences, such as Logic, Geometry, Chemistry, etc., equally beginningless and eternal, for they contain an everlasting truth?

A. — There was a time when the Vedas themselves were considered eternal in the sense in which the divine truths contained therein were changeless and permanent and were only revealed to man. At a subsequent time, it appears that the utterance of the Vedic hymns with the knowledge of its meaning was important, and it was held that the hymns themselves must have had a divine origin. At a still later period the meaning of the hymns showed that many of them could not be of divine origin, because they inculcated upon mankind performance of various unholy acts, such as torturing animals, and we can also find many ridiculous stories in the Vedas. The correct meaning of the statement "The Vedas are beginningless and eternal" is that the law or truth revealed by them to man is permanent and changeless. Logic, Geometry, Chemistry, etc., reveal also a law or truth which is permanent and changeless, and in that sense they are also beginningless and eternal. But no truth or law is absent from the Vedas, and I ask any one of you to point out to me any truth which is not treated of in them.

Q. — What is the notion of Mukti, according to the Advaita philosophy, or in other words, is it a conscious state? Is there any difference between the Mukti of the Advaitism and the Buddhistic Nirvâna?

A. — There is a consciousness in Mukti, which we call superconsciousness. It differs from your present consciousness. It is illogical to say that there is no consciousness in Mukti. The consciousness is of three sorts — the dull, mediocre, and intense — as is the case of light. When vibration is intense, the brilliancy is so very powerful as to dazzle the sight itself and in effect is as ineffectual as the dullest of lights. The Buddhistic Nirvana must have the same degree of consciousness whatever the Buddhists may say. Our definition of Mukti is affirmative in its nature, while the Buddhistic Nirvana has a negative definition.

Q. — Why should the unconditioned Brahman choose to assume a condition for the purpose of manifestation of the world's creation?

A. — The question itself is most illogical. Brahman is Avângmanasogocharam, meaning that which is incapable of being grasped by word and mind. Whatever lies beyond the region of space, time and causation cannot be conceived by the human mind, and the function of logic and enquiry lies only within the region of space, time, and causation. While that is so, it is a vain attempt to question about what lies beyond the possibilities of human conception.

Q. — Here and there attempts are made to import into the Purânas hidden ideas which are said to have been allegorically represented. Sometimes it is said that the Puranas need not contain any historical truth, but are mere representations of the highest ideals illustrated with fictitious characters. Take for instance, Vishnupurâna, Râmâyana, or Bhârata. Do they contain historical veracity or are they mere allegorical representations of metaphysical truths, or are they representations of the highest ideals for the conduct of humanity, or are they mere epic poems such as those of Homer?

A. — Some historical truth is the nucleus of every Purana. The object of the Puranas is to teach mankind the sublime truth in various forms; and even if they do not contain any historical truth, they form a great authority for us in respect of the highest truth which they inculcate. Take the Râmâyana, for illustration, and for viewing it as an authority on building character, it is not even necessary that one like Rama should have ever lived. The sublimity of the law propounded by Ramayana or Bharata does not depend upon the truth of any personality like Rama or Krishna, and one can even hold that such personages never lived, and at the same time take those writings as high authorities in respect of the grand ideas which they place before mankind. Our philosophy does not depend upon any personality for its truth. Thus Krishna did not teach anything new or original to the world, nor does Ramayana profess anything which is not contained in the Scriptures. It is to be noted that Christianity cannot stand without Christ, Mohammedanism without Mohammed, and Buddhism without Buddha, but Hinduism stands independent of any man, and for the purpose of estimating the philosophical truth contained in any Purana, we need not consider the question whether the personages treated of therein were really material men or were fictitious characters. The object of the Puranas was the education of mankind, and the sages who constructed them contrived to find some historical personages and to superimpose upon them all the best or worst qualities just as they wanted to, and laid down the rules of morals for the conduct of mankind. Is it necessary that a demon with ten heads (Dashamukha) should have actually lived as stated in the Ramayana? It is the representation of some truth which deserves to be studied, apart from the question whether Dashamukha was a real or fictitious character. You can now depict Krishna in a still more attractive manner, and the description depends upon the sublimity of your ideal, but there stands the grand philosophy contained in the Puranas.

Q. — Is it possible for a man, if he were an adept, to remember the events connected with his past incarnations? The physiological brain, which he owned in his previous incarnation, and in which the impressions of his experience were stored, is no longer present. In this birth he is endowed with a new physiological brain, and while that is so, how is it possible for the present brain to get at the impressions received by another apparatus which is not existence at present?

Swami — What do you mean by an adept?

Correspondent — One that has developed the hidden powers of his nature.

Swami — I cannot understand how the hidden powers can be developed. I know what you mean, but I should always desire that the expressions used are precise and accurate. You may say that the powers hidden are uncovered. It is possible for those that have uncovered the hidden powers of their nature to remember the incidents connected with their past incarnations, for their present brain had its Bija (seed) in the Sukshma man after death.

Q. — Does the spirit of Hinduism permit the proselytism of strangers into it? And can a Brâhmin listen to the exposition of philosophy made by a Chandâla?

A. — Proselytism is tolerated by Hinduism. Any man, whether he be a Shudra or Chandala, can expound philosophy even to a Brahmin. The truth can be learnt from the lowest individual, no matter to what caste or creed he belongs.

Here the Swami quoted Sanskrit verses of high authority in support of his position.

The discourse ended, as the time appointed in the programme for his visiting the Temple had already arrived. He accordingly took leave of the gentlemen present and proceeded to visit the Temple.

THE ABROAD AND THE PROBLEMS AT HOME

(The Hindu, Madras, February, 1897)

Our representative met the Swami Vivekananda in the train at the Chingleput Station and travelled with him to Madras. The following is the report of the interview:

"What made you go to America, Swamiji?"

"Rather a serious question to answer in brief. I can only answer it partly now. Because I travelled all over India, I wanted to go over to other countries. I went to America by the Far East."

"What did you see in Japan, and is there any chance of India following in the progressive steps of Japan?"

"None whatever, until all the three hundred millions of India combine together as a whole nation. The world has never seen such a patriotic and artistic race as the Japanese, and one special feature about them is this that while in Europe and elsewhere Art generally goes with dirt, Japanese Art is Art plus absolute cleanliness. I would wish that every one of our young men could visit Japan once at least in his lifetime. It is very easy to go there. The Japanese think that everything Hindu is great and believe that India is a holy land. Japanese Buddhism is entirely different from what you see in Ceylon. It is the same as Vedanta. It is positive and theistic Buddhism, not the negative atheistic Buddhism of Ceylon.

"What is the key to Japan's sudden greatness?"

"The faith of the Japanese in themselves, and their love for their country. When you have men who are ready to sacrifice their everything for their country, sincere to the backbone — when such men arise, India will become great in every respect. It is the men that make the country! What is there in the country? If you catch the social morality and the political morality of the Japanese, you will be as great as they are. The Japanese are ready to sacrifice everything for their country, and they have become a great people. But you are not; you cannot be, you sacrifice everything only for your own families and possessions."

"Is it your wish that India should become like Japan?"

"Decidedly not. India should continue to be what she is. How could India ever become like Japan, or any nation for the matter of that? In each nation, as in music, there is a main note, a central theme, upon which all others turn. Each nation has a theme: everything else is secondary. India's theme is religion. Social reform and everything else are secondary. Therefore India cannot be like Japan. It is said that when 'the heart breaks', then the flow of thought comes. India's heart must break, and the flow of spirituality will come out. India is India. We are not like the Japanese, we are Hindus. India's very atmosphere is soothing. I have been working incessantly here, and amidst this work I am getting rest. It is only from spiritual work that we can get rest in India. If your work is material here, you die of — diabetes!"

"So much for Japan. What was your first experience of America, Swamiji?"

"From first to last it was very good. With the exception of the missionaries and 'Church-women' the Americans are most hospitable, kind-hearted, generous, and good-natured."

"Who are these 'Church-women' that you speak of, Swamiji?"

"When a woman tries her best to find a husband, she goes to all the fashionable seaside resorts and tries all sorts of tricks to catch a man. When she fails in her attempts, she becomes, what they call in America, an 'old maid', and joins the Church. Some of them become very 'Churchy'. These 'Church-women' are awful fanatics. They are under the thumb of the priests there. Between them and the priests they make hell of earth and make a mess of religion. With the exception of these, the Americans are a very good people. They loved me, and I love them a great deal. I felt as if I was one of them."

"What is your idea about the results of the Parliament of Religions?"

"The Parliament of Religions, as it seems to me, was intended for a 'heathen show' before the world: but it turned out that the heathens had the upper hand and made it a Christian show all around. So the Parliament of Religions was a failure from the Christian standpoint, seeing that the Roman Catholics, who were the organisers of that Parliament, are, when there is a talk of another Parliament at Paris, now steadily opposing it. But the Chicago Parliament was a tremendous success for India and Indian thought. It helped on the tide of Vedanta, which is flooding the world. The American people — of course, minus the fanatical priests and Church-women — are very glad of the results of the Parliament."

"What prospects have you, Swamiji, for the spread of your mission in England?"

"There is every prospect. Before many years elapse a vast majority of the English people will be Vedantins. There is a greater prospect of this in England than there is in America. You see, Americans make a fanfaronade of everything, which is not the case with Englishmen. Even Christians cannot understand their New Testament, without understanding the Vedanta. The Vedanta is the rationale of all religions. Without the Vedanta every religion is superstition; with it everything becomes religion."

"What is the special trait you noticed in the English character?"

"The Englishman goes to practical work as soon as he believes in something. He has tremendous energy for practical work. There is in the whole world no human being superior to the English gentleman or lady. That is really the reason of my faith in them. John Bull is rather a thick-headed gentleman to deal with. You must push and push an idea till it reaches his brain, but once there, it does not get out. In England, there was not one missionary or anybody who said anything against me; not one who tried to make a scandal about me. To my astonishment, many of my friends belong to the Church of England. I learn, these missionaries do not come from the higher classes in England. Caste is as rigorous there as it is here, and the English churchmen belong to the class of gentlemen. They may differ in opinion from you, but that is no bar to their being friends with you; therefore, I would give a word of advice to my countrymen, which is, not to take notice of the vituperative missionaries, now that I have known that they are. We have 'sized' them, as the Americans say. Non-recognition is the only attitude to assume towards them."

"Will you kindly enlighten me, Swamiji, on the Social Reform movements in America and England?"

"Yes. All the social upheavalists, at least the leaders of them, are trying to find that all their communistic or equalising theories must have a spiritual basis, and that spiritual basis is in the Vedanta only. I have been told by several leaders, who used to attend my lectures, that they required the Vedanta as the basis of the new order of things."

"What are your views with regard to the Indian masses?"

"Oh, we are awfully poor, and our masses are very ignorant about secular things. Our masses are very good because poverty here is not a crime. Our masses are not violent. Many times I was near being mobbed in America and England, only on account of my dress. But I never heard of such a thing in India as a man being mobbed because of peculiar dress. In every other respect, our masses are much more civilised than the European masses."

"What will you propose for the improvement of our masses?"

"We have to give them secular education. We have to follow the plan laid down by our ancestors, that is, to bring all the ideals slowly down among the masses. Raise them slowly up, raise them to equality. Impart even secular knowledge through religion."

"But do you think, Swamiji, it is a task that can be easily accomplished?"

"It will, of course, have gradually to be worked out. But if there are enough self-sacrificing young fellows, who, I hope, will work with me, it can be done tomorrow. It all depends upon the zeal and the self-sacrifice brought to the task."

"But if the present degraded condition is due to their past Karma, Swamiji, how do you think they could get out of it easily, and how do you propose to help them?"

The Swamiji readily answered "Karma is the eternal assertion of human freedom. If we can bring ourselves down by our Karma, surely it is in our power to raise ourselves by it. The masses, besides, have not brought themselves down altogether by their own Karma. So we should give them better environments to work in. I do not propose any levelling of castes. Caste is a very good thing. Caste is the plan we want to follow. What caste really is, not one in a million understands. There is no country in the world without caste. In India, from caste we reach to the point where there is no caste. Caste is based throughout on that principle. The plan in India is to make everybody a Brahmin, the Brahmin being the ideal of humanity. If you read the history of India you will find that attempts have always been made to raise the lower classes. Many are the classes that have been raised. Many more will follow till the whole will become Brahmin. That is the plan. We have only to raise them without bringing down anybody. And this has mostly to be done by the Brahmins themselves, because it is the duty of every aristocracy to dig its own grave; and the sooner it does so, the better for all. No time should be lost. Indian caste is better than the caste which prevails in Europe or America. I do not say it is absolutely good. Where would you be if there were no caste? Where would be your learning and other things, if there were no caste? There would be nothing left for the Europeans to study if caste had never existed! The Mohammedans would have smashed everything to pieces. Where do you find the Indian society standing still? It is always on the move. Sometimes, as in the times of foreign invasions, the movement has been slow, at other times quicker. This is what I say to my countrymen. I do not condemn them. I look into their past. I find that under the circumstances no nation could do more glorious work. I tell them that they have done well. I only ask them to do better."

"What are your views, Swamiji, in regard to the relation of caste to rituals?"

"Caste is continually changing, rituals are continually changing, so are forms. It is the substance, the principle, that does not change. It is in the Vedas that we have to study our religion. With the exception of the Vedas every book must change. The authority of the Vedas is for all time to come; the authority of every one of our other books is for the time being.

For instance; one Smriti is powerful for one age, another for another age. Great prophets are always coming and pointing the way to work. Some prophets worked for the lower classes, others like Madhva gave to women the right to study the Vedas. Caste should not go; but should only be readjusted occasionally. Within the old structure is to be found life enough for the building of two hundred thousand new ones. It is sheer nonsense to desire the abolition of caste. The new method is — evolution of the old."

"Do not Hindus stand in need of social reform?"

"We do stand in need of social reform. At times great men would evolve new ideas of progress, and kings would give them the sanction of law. Thus social improvements had been in the past made in India, and in modern times to effect such progressive reforms, we will have first to build up such an authoritative power. Kings having gone, the power is the people's. We have, therefore, to wait till the people are educated, till they understand their needs and are ready and able to solve their problems. The tyranny of the minority is the worst tyranny in the world. Therefore, instead of frittering away our energies on ideal reforms, which will never become practical, we had better go to the root of the evil and make a legislative body, that is to say, educate our people, so that they may be able to solve their own problems. Until that is done all these ideal reforms will remain ideals only. The new order of things is the salvation of the people by the people, and it takes time to make it workable, especially in India, which has always in the past been governed by kings."

"Do you think Hindu society can successfully adopt European social laws?"

"No, not wholly. I would say, the combination of the Greek mind represented by the external European energy added to the Hindu spirituality would be an ideal society for India. For instance, it is absolutely necessary for you, instead of frittering away your energy and often talking of idle nonsense, to learn from the Englishman the idea of prompt obedience to leaders, the absence of jealousy, the indomitable perseverance and the undying faith in himself. As soon as he selects a leader for a work, the Englishman sticks to him through thick and thin and obeys him. Here in India, everybody wants to become a leader, and there is nobody to obey. Everyone should learn to obey before he can command. There is no end to our jealousies; and the more important the Hindu, the more jealous he is. Until this absence of jealousy and obedience to leaders are learnt by the Hindu, there will be no power of organization. We shall have to remain the hopelessly confused mob that we are now, hoping and doing nothing. India has to learn from Europe the conquest of external nature, and Europe has to learn from India the conquest of internal nature. Then there will be neither Hindus nor Europeans — there will be the ideal humanity which has conquered both the natures, the external and the internal. We have developed one phase of humanity, and they another. It is the union of the two that is wanted. The word freedom which is the watchword of our religion really means freedom physically, mentally, and spiritually."

"What relation, Swamiji, does ritual bear to religion?"

"Rituals are the kindergarten of religion. They are absolutely necessary for the world as it is now; only we shall have to give people newer and fresher rituals. A party of thinkers must undertake to do this. Old rituals must be rejected and new ones substituted."

"Then you advocate the abolition of rituals, don't you?"

"No, my watchword is construction, not destruction. Out of the existing rituals, new ones will have to be evolved. There is infinite power of development in everything; that is my belief. One atom has the power of the whole universe at its back. All along, in the history of the Hindu race, there never was any attempt at destruction, only construction. One sect wanted to destroy, and they were thrown out of India: They were the Buddhists. We have had a host of reformers — Shankara, Râmânuja, Madhva, and Chaitanya. These were great reformers, who always were constructive and built according to the circumstances of their time. This is our peculiar method of work. All the modern reformers take to European destructive reformation, which will never do good to anyone and never did. Only once was a modern reformer mostly constructive, and that one was Raja Ram Mohan Ray. The progress of the Hindu race has been towards the realisation of the Vedantic ideals. All history of Indian life is the struggle for the realisation of the ideal of the Vedanta through good or bad fortune. Whenever there was any reforming sect or religion which rejected the Vedantic ideal, it was smashed into nothing."

"What is your programme of work here?"

"I want to start two institutions, one in Madras and one in Calcutta, to carry out my plan; and that plan briefly is to bring the Vedantic ideals into the everyday practical life of the saint or the sinner, of the sage or the ignoramus, of the Brahmin or the Pariah."

Our representative here put to him a few questions relative to Indian politics; but before the Swami could attempt anything like an answer, the train steamed up to the Egmore platform, and the only hurried remark that fell from the Swami was that he was dead against all political entanglements of Indian and European problems. The interview then terminated.

THE MISSIONARY WORK OF THE FIRST HINDU SANNYASIN TO THE WEST AND HIS PLAN OF REGENERATION OF INDIA

(Madras Times, February, 1897)

For the past few weeks, the Hindu public of Madras have been most eagerly expecting the arrival of Swami Vivekananda, the great Hindu monk of world-wide fame. At the present moment his name is on everybody's lips. In the school, in the college, in the High Court, on the marina, and in the streets and bazars of Madras, hundreds of inquisitive spirits may be seen asking when the Swami will be coming. Large numbers of students from the mofussil, who have come up for the University examinations are staying here, awaiting the Swami, and increasing their hostelry bills, despite the urgent call of their parents to return home immediately. In a few days the Swami will be in our midst. From the nature of the receptions received elsewhere in this Presidency, from the preparations being made here, from the triumphal arches erected at Castle Kernan, where the "Prophet" is to be lodged at the cost of the Hindu public, and from the interest taken in the movement by the leading Hindu gentlemen of this city, like the Hon'ble Mr. Justice Subramaniya Iyer, there is no doubt that the Swami will have a grand reception. It was Madras that first recognised the superior merits of the Swami and equipped him for Chicago. Madras will now have again the honour of welcoming the undoubtedly great man who has done so much to raise the prestige of his motherland. Four year ago, when the Swami arrived here, he was practically an obscure individual. In an unknown bungalow at St. Thome he spent nearly two months, all along holding conversations on religious topics and teaching and instructing all comers who cared to listen to him. Even then a few educated young men with "a keener eye" predicted that there was something in the man, "a power", that would lift him above all others, that would pre-eminently enable him to be the leader of men. These young men, who were then despised as "misguided enthusiasts", "dreamy revivalists", have now the supreme satisfaction of seeing their Swami, as they love to call him, return to them with a great European and American fame. The mission of the Swami is essentially spiritual. He firmly believes that India, the motherland of spirituality, has a great future before her. He is sanguine that the West will more and more come to appreciate what he regards as the sublime truths of Vedanta. His great motto is "Help, and not Fight" "Assimilation, and not Destruction", "Harmony and Peace, and not Dissension". Whatever difference of opinion followers of other creeds may have with him, few will venture to deny that the Swami has done yeoman's service to his country in opening the eyes of the Western world to "the good in the Hindu". He will always be remembered as the first Hindu Sannyâsin who dared to cross the sea to carry to the West the message of what he believes in as a religious peace.

A representative of our paper interviewed the Swami Vivekananda, with a view to eliciting from him an account of the success of his mission in the West. The Swami very courteously received our representative and motioned him to a chair by his side. The Swami was dressed in yellow robes, was calm, serene, and dignified, and appeared inclined to answer any questions that might be put to him. We have given the Swami's words as taken down in shorthand by our representative.

"May I know a few particulars about your early life?" asked our representative.

The Swami said: "Even while I was a student at Calcutta, I was of a religious temperament. I was critical even at that time of my life, mere words would not satisfy me. Subsequently I met Ramakrishna Paramahamsa, with whom I lived for a long time and under whom I studied. After the death of my father I gave myself up to travelling in India and started a little monastery in Calcutta. During my travels, I came to Madras, where I received help from the Maharaja of Mysore and the Raja of Ramnad."

"What made Your Holiness carry the mission of Hinduism to Western countries?"

"I wanted to get experience. My idea as to the keynote of our national downfall is that we do not mix with other nations — that is the one and the sole cause. We never had opportunity to compare notes. We were Kupa-Mandukas (frogs in a well)."

"You have done a good deal of travelling in the West?"

"I have visited a good deal of Europe, including Germany and France, but England and America were the chief centres of my work. At first I found myself in a critical position, owing to the hostile attitude assumed against the people of this country by those who went there from India. I believe the Indian nation is by far the most moral and religious nation in the whole world, and it would be a blasphemy to compare the Hindus with any other nation. At first, many fell foul of me, manufactured huge lies against me by saying that I was a fraud, that I had a harem of wives and half a regiment of children. But my experience of these missionaries opened my eyes as to what they are capable of doing in the name of religion. Missionaries were nowhere in England. None came to fight me. Mr. Lund went over to America to abuse me behind my back, but people would not listen to him. I was very popular with them. When I came back to England, I thought this missionary would be at me, but the Truth silenced him. In England the social status is stricter than caste is in India. The English Church people are all gentlemen born, which many of the missionaries are not. They greatly sympathised with me. I think that about thirty English Church clergymen agree entirely with me on all points of religious discussion. I was agreeably surprised to find that the English clergymen, though they differed from me, did not abuse me behind my back and stab me in the dark. There is the benefit of caste and hereditary culture."

"What has been the measure of your success in the West?"

"A great number of people sympathised with me in America — much more than in England. Vituperation by the low-caste missionaries made my cause succeed better. I had no money, the people of India having given me my bare passage-money, which was spent in a very short time. I had to live just as here on the charity of individuals. The Americans are a very hospitable people. In America one-third of the people are Christians, but the rest have no religion, that is they do not belong to any of the sects, but amongst them are to be found the most spiritual persons. I think the work in England is sound. If I die tomorrow and cannot send any more Sannyasins, still the English work will go on. The Englishman is a very good man. He is taught from his childhood to suppress all his feelings. He is thickheaded, and is not so quick as the Frenchman or the American. He is immensely practical. The American people are too young to understand renunciation. England has enjoyed wealth and luxury for ages. Many people there are ready for renunciation. When I first lectured in England I had a little class of twenty or thirty, which was kept going when I left, and when I went back from America I could get an audience of one thousand. In America I could get a much bigger one, as I spent three years in America and only one year in England. I have two Sannyasins — one in England and one in America, and I intend sending Sannyasins to other countries.

"English people are tremendous workers. Give them an idea, and you may be sure that that idea is not going to be lost, provided they catch it. People here have given up the Vedas, and all your philosophy is in the kitchen. The religion of India at present is 'Don't-touchism' — that is a religion which the English people will never accept. The thoughts of our forefathers and the wonderful life-giving principles that they discovered, every nation will take. The biggest guns of the English Church told me that I was putting Vedantism into the Bible. The present Hinduism is a degradation. There is no book on philosophy, written today, in which something of our Vedantism is not touched upon — even the works of Herbert Spencer contain it. The philosophy of the age is Advaitism, everybody talks of it; only in Europe, they try to be original. They talk of Hindus with contempt, but at the same time swallow the truths given out by the Hindus. Professor Max Müller is a perfect Vedantist, and has done splendid work in Vedantism. He believes in re-incarnation."

"What do you intend doing for the regeneration of India?"

"I consider that the great national sin is the neglect of the masses, and that is one of the causes of our downfall. No amount of politics would be of any avail until the masses in India are once more well educated, well fed, and well cared for. They pay for our education, they build our temples, but in return they get kicks. They are practically our slaves. If we want to regenerate India, we must work for them. I want to start two central institutions at first — one at Madras and the other at Calcutta — for training young men as preachers. I have funds for starting the Calcutta one. English people will find funds for my purpose.

"My faith is in the younger generation, the modern generation, out of them will come my workers. They will work out the whole problem, like lions. I have formulated the idea and have given my life to it. If I do not achieve success, some better one will come after me to work it out, and I shall be content to struggle. The one problem you have is to give to the masses their rights. You have the greatest religion which the world ever saw, and you feed the masses with stuff and nonsense. You have the perennial fountain flowing, and you give them ditch-water. Your Madras graduate would not touch a low-caste man, but is ready to get out of him the money for his education. I want to start at first these two institutions for educating missionaries to be both spiritual and secular instructors to our masses. They will spread from centre to centre, until we have covered the whole of India. The great thing is to have faith in oneself, even before faith in God; but the difficulty seems to be that we are losing faith in ourselves day by day. That is my objection against the reformers. The orthodox have more faith and more strength in themselves, in spite of their crudeness; but the reformers simply play into the hands of Europeans and pander to their vanity. Our masses are gods as compared with those of other countries. This is the only country where poverty is not a crime. They are mentally and physically handsome; but we hated and hated them till they have lost faith in themselves. They think they are born slaves. Give them their rights, and let them stand on their rights. This is the glory of the American civilization. Compare the Irishman with knees bent, half-starved, with a little stick and bundle of clothes, just arrived from the ship, with what he is, after a few months' stay in America. He walks boldly and bravely. He has come from a country where he was a slave to a country where he is a brother.

"Believe that the soul is immortal, infinite and all-powerful. My idea of education is personal contact with the teacher - Gurugriha-Vâsa. Without the personal life of a teacher there would be no education. Take your Universities. What have they done during the fifty years of their existences. They have not produced one original man. They are merely an examining body. The idea of the sacrifice for the common weal is not yet developed in our nation."

"What do you think of Mrs. Besant and Theosophy?"

"Mrs. Besant is a very good woman. I lectured at her Lodge in London. I do not know personally much about her. Her knowledge of our religion is very limited; she picks up scraps here and there; she never had time to study it thoroughly. That she is one of the most sincere of women, her greatest enemy will concede. She is considered the best speaker in England.

She is a Sannyâsini. But I do not believe in Mahâtmâs and Kuthumis. Let her give up her connection with the Theosophical Society, stand on her own footing, and preach what she thinks right."

Speaking of social reforms, the Swami expressed himself about widow-marriage thus: "I have yet to see a nation whose fate is determined by the number of husbands their widows get."

Knowing as he did that several persons were waiting downstairs to have an interview with the Swami, our representative withdrew, thanking the Swami for the kindness with which he had consented to the journalistic torture.

The Swami, it may be remarked, is accompanied by Mr. and Mrs. J. H. Sevier, Mr. T. G. Harrison, a Buddhist gentleman of Colombo, and Mr. J. J. Goodwin. It appears that Mr. and Mrs. Sevier accompany the Swami with a view to settling in the Himalayas, where they intend building a residence for the Western disciples of the Swami, who may have an inclination to reside in India. For twenty years, Mr. and Mrs. Sevier had followed no particular religion, finding satisfaction in none of those that were preached; but on listening to a course of lectures by the Swami, they professed to have found a religion that satisfied their heart and intellect. Since then they have accompanied the Swami through Switzerland, Germany, and Italy, and now to India. Mr. Goodwin, a journalist in England, became a disciple of the Swami fourteen months ago, when he first met him at New York. He gave up his journalism and devotes himself to attending the Swami and taking down his lectures in shorthand. He is in every sense a true "disciple", saying that he hopes to be with the Swami till his death.

REAWAKENING OF HINDUISM ON A NATIONAL BASIS

(Prabuddha Bharata, September, 1898)

In an interview which a representative of Prabuddha Bharata had recently with the Swami Vivekananda, that great Teacher was asked: "What do you consider the distinguishing feature of your movement, Swamiji?"

"Aggression," said the Swami promptly, "aggression in a religious sense only. Other sects and parties have carried spirituality all over India, but since the days of Buddha we have been the first to break bounds and try to flood the world with missionary zeal."

"And what do you consider to be the function of your movement as regards India?'

"To find the common bases of Hinduism and awaken the national consciousness to them. At present there are three parties in India included under the term 'Hindu' — the orthodox, the reforming sects of the Mohammedan period, and the reforming sects of the present time. Hindus from North to South are only agreed on one point, viz. on not eating beef."

"Not in a common love for the Vedas?"

"Certainly not. That is just what we want to reawaken. India has not yet assimilated the work of Buddha. She is hypnotised by his voice, not made alive by it."

"In what way do you see this importance of Buddhism in India today?"

"It is obvious and overwhelming. You see India never loses anything; only she takes time to turn everything into bone and muscle. Buddha dealt a blow at animal sacrifice from which India has never recovered; and Buddha asked people not to kill cows for sacrifice… not to kill beyond what they needed for consumption.', and cow-killing is an impossibility with us."[1]

"With which of the three parties you name do you

---

1. Source- http://qz.com/366659/history-says-most-hindus-never-had-any-beef-with-beef/

identify yourself, Swamiji?"

"With all of them. We are orthodox Hindus," said the Swami, "but", he added suddenly with great earnestness and emphasis, "we refuse entirely to identify ourselves with 'Don't-touchism'. That is not Hinduism: it is in none of our books; it is an unorthodox superstition which has interfered with national efficiency all along the line."

"Then what you really desire is national efficiency?"

"Certainly. Can you adduce any reason why India should lie in the ebb-tide of the Aryan nations? Is she inferior in intellect? Is she inferior in dexterity? Can you look at her art, at her mathematics, at her philosophy, and answer 'yes'? All that is needed is that she should de-hypnotise herself and wake up from her age-long sleep to take her true rank in the hierarchy of nations."

"But India has always had her deep inner life. Are you not afraid, Swamiji, that in attempting to make her active you may take from her, her one great treasure?"

"Not at all. The history of the past has gone to develop the inner life of India and the activity (i.e. the outer life) of the West. Hitherto these have been divergent. The time has now come for them to unite. Ramakrishna Paramahamsa was alive to the depths of being, yet on the outer plane who was more active? This is the secret. Let your life be as deep as the ocean, but let it also be as wide as the sky.

"It is a curious thing", continued the Swami, "that the inner life is often most profoundly developed where the outer conditions are most cramping and limiting. But this is an accidental — not an essential — association, and if we set ourselves right here in India, the world will be 'tightened'. For are we not all one?"

"Your last remarks, Swamiji, raise another question. In what sense is Shri Ramakrishna a part of this awakened Hinduism?"

"That is not for me to determine", said the Swami. "I have never preached personalities. My own life is guided by the enthusiasm of this great soul; but others will decide for themselves how far they share in this attitude. Inspiration is not filtered out to the world through one channel, however great. Each generation should be inspired afresh. Are we not all God?"

"Thank you. I have only one question more to ask you. You have defined the attitude and function of your movement with regard to your own people. Could you in the same way characterise your methods of action as a whole?"

"Our method", said the Swami, "is very easily described. It simply consists in reasserting the national life. Buddha preached renunciation. India heard, and yet in six centuries she reached heir greatest height. The secret lies there. The national ideals of India are renunciation and service. Intensify her in those channels, and the rest will take carte of itself. The banner of the spiritual cannot be raised too high in this country. In it alone is salvation.

ON INDIAN WOMEN — THEIR PAST, PRESENT AND FUTURE

(Prabuddha Bharata, December, 1898)

It was early one Sunday morning, writes our representative, in a beautiful Himalayan valley, that I was at last able to carry out the order of the Editor, and call on the Swami Vivekananda, to ascertain something of his views on the position and prospects of Indian Women.

"Let us go for a walk", said the Swami, when I had announced my errand, and we set out at once amongst some of the most lovely scenery in the world.

By sunny and shady ways we went, through quiet villages, amongst playing children and across the golden cornfields. Here the tall trees seemed to pierce the blue above, and there a group of peasant girls stooped, sickle in hand, to cut and carry off the plume-tipped stalks of maize-straw for the winter stores. Now the road led into an apple orchard, where great heaps of crimson fruit lay under the trees for sorting, and again we were out in the open, facing the snows that rose in august beauty above the white clouds against the sky.

At last my companion broke the silence. "The Aryan and Semitic ideals of woman", he said, "have always been diametrically opposed. Amongst the Semites the presence of woman is considered dangerous to devotion, and she may not perform any religious function, even such as the killing of a bird for food: according to the Aryan a man cannot perform a religious action without a wife."

"But Swamiji!" said I — startled at an assertion so sweeping and so unexpected — "is Hinduism not an Aryan faith?"

"Modern Hinduism", said the Swami quietly, "is largely Paurânika, that is, post-Buddhistic in origin. Dayânanda Saraswati pointed out that though a wife is absolutely necessary in the Sacrifice of the domestic fire, which is a Vedic rite, she may not touch the Shâlagrâma Shilâ, or the household-idol, because that dates from the later period of the Purânas."

"And so you consider the inequality of woman amongst us as entirely due to the influence of Buddhism?"

"Where it exists, certainly," said the Swami, "but we should not allow the sudden influx of European criticism and our consequent sense of contrast to make us acquiesce too readily in this notion of the inequality of our women. Circumstances have forced upon us, for many centuries, the woman's need of protection. This, and not her inferiority, is the true reading of our customs."

"Are you then entirely satisfied with the position of women amongst us, Swamiji?"

"By no means," said the Swami, "but our right of interference is limited entirely to giving education. Women must be put in a position to solve their own problems in their own way. No one can or ought to do this for them. And our Indian women are as capable of doing it as any in the world."

"How do you account for the evil influence which you attribute to Buddhism?"

"It came only with the decay of the faith", said the Swami. "Every movement triumphs by dint of some unusual characteristic, and when it falls, that point of pride becomes its chief element of weakness. The Lord Buddha — greatest of men — was a marvellous organiser and carried the world by this means. But his religion was the religion of a monastic order. It had, therefore, the evil effect of making the very robe of the monk honoured. He also introduced for the first time the community life of religious houses and thereby necessarily made women inferior to men, since the great abbesses could take no important step without the advice of certain abbots. It ensured its immediate object, the solidarity of the faith, you see, only its far-reaching effects are to be deplored."

"But Sannyâsa is recognised in the Vedas!"

"Of course it is, but without making any distinction between men and women. Do you remember how Yâjnavalkya was questioned at the Court of King Janaka? His principal examiner was Vâchaknavi, the maiden orator — Brahmavâdini, as the word of the day was. 'Like two shining arrows in the hand of the skilled archer', she says, 'are my questions.' Her sex is not even commented upon. Again, could anything be more complete than the equality of boys and girls in our old forest universities? Read our Sanskrit dramas — read the story of Shakuntala, and see if Tennyson's 'Princess' has anything to teach us! "

"You have a wonderful way of revealing the glories of our past, Swamiji!"

"Perhaps, because I have seen both sides of the world," said the Swami gently, "and I know that the race that produced Sitâ — even if it only dreamt of her — has a reverence for woman that is unmatched on the earth. There is many a burden bound with legal tightness on the shoulders of Western women that is utterly unknown to ours. We have our wrongs and our exceptions certainly, but so have they. We must never forget that all over the globe the general effort is to express love and tenderness and uprightness, and that national customs are only the nearest vehicles of this expression. With regard to the domestic virtues I have no hesitation in saying that our Indian methods have in many ways the advantage over all others."

"Then have our women any problems at all, Swamiji?"

"Of course, they have many and grave problems, but none that are not to be solved by that magic word 'education'. The true education, however, is not yet conceived of amongst us."

"And how would you define that?"

"I never define anything", said the Swami, smiling. "Still, it may be described as a development of faculty, not an accumulation of words, or as a training of individuals to will rightly and efficiently. So shall we bring to the need of India great fearless women — women worthy to continue the traditions of Sanghamittâ, Lîlâ, Ahalyâ Bâi, and Mirâ Bâi — women fit to be mothers of heroes, because they are pure and selfless, strong with the strength that comes of touching the feet of God."

"So you consider that there should be a religious element in education, Swamiji?"

"I look upon religion as the innermost core of education", said the Swami solemnly. "Mind, I do not mean my own, or any one else's opinion about religion. I think the teacher should take the pupil's starting-point in this, as in other respects, and enable her to develop along her own line of least resistance."

"But surely the religious exaltation of Brahmacharya, by taking the highest place from the mother and wife and giving it to those who evade those relations, is a direct blow dealt at woman?"

"You should remember", said the Swami, "that if religion exalts Brahmacharya for woman, it does exactly the same for man Moreover, your question shows a certain confusion in your own mind. Hinduism indicates one duty, only one, for the human soul. It is to seek to realise the permanent amidst the evanescent. No one presumes to point out any one way in which this may be done. Marriage or non-marriage, good or evil, learning or ignorance, any of these is justified, if it leads to the goal. In this respect lies the great contrast between it and Buddhism, for the latter's outstanding direction is to realise the impermanence of the external, which, broadly speaking, can only be done in one way. Do you recall the story of the young Yogi in the Mahâbhârata who prided himself on his psychic powers by burning the bodies of a crow and crane by his intense will, produced by anger? Do you remember that the young saint went into the town and found first a wife nursing her sick husband and then the butcher Dharma-Vyâdha, both of whom had obtained enlightenment in the path of common faithfulness and duty?"

"And so what would you say, Swamiji, to the women of this country?

"Why, to the women of this country." said the Swami, "I would say exactly what I say to the men. Believe in India and in our Indian faith. Be strong and hopeful and unashamed, and remember that with something to take, Hindus have immeasurably more to give than any other people in the world."

ON THE BOUNDS OF HINDUISM

(Prabuddha Bharata, April, 1899)

Having been directed by the Editor, writes our representative, to interview Swami Vivekananda on the question of converts to Hinduism, I found an opportunity one evening on the roof of a Ganga houseboat. It was after nightfall, and we had stopped at the embankments of the Ramakrishna Math, and there the Swami came down to speak with me.

Time and place were alike delightful. Overhead the stars, and around — the rolling Ganga; and on one side stood the dimly lighted building, with its background of palms and lofty shade-trees.

"I want to see you, Swami", I began, "on this matter of receiving back into Hinduism those who have been perverted from it. Is it your opinion that they should be received?"

"Certainly," said the Swami, "they can and ought to be taken."

He sat gravely for a moment, thinking, and then resumed. "Besides," he said, "we shall otherwise decrease in numbers. When the Mohammedans first came, we are said — I think on the authority of Ferishta, the oldest Mohammedan historian — to have been six hundred millions of Hindus. Now we are about two hundred millions. And then every man going out of the Hindu pale is not only a man less, but an enemy the more.

"Again, the vast majority of Hindu perverts to Islam and Christianity are perverts by the sword, or the descendants of these. It would be obviously unfair to subject these to disabilities of any kind. As to the case of born aliens, did you say? Why, born aliens have been converted in the past by crowds, and the process is still going on.

"In my own opinion, this statement not only applies to aboriginal tribes, to outlying nations, and to almost all our conquerors before the Mohammedan conquest, but also in the Purânas. I hold that they have been aliens thus adopted.

"Ceremonies of expiation are no doubt suitable in the case of willing converts, returning to their Mother-Church, as it were; but on those who were alienated by conquest — as in Kashmir and Nepal — or on strangers wishing to join us, no penance should be imposed."

"But of what caste would these people be, Swamiji?" I ventured to ask. "They must have some, or they can never be assimilated into the great body of Hindus. Where shall we look for their rightful place?"

"Returning converts", said the Swami quietly, "will gain their own castes, of course. And new people will make theirs. You will remember," he added, "that this has already been done in the case of Vaishnavism. Converts from different castes and aliens were all able to combine under that flag and form a caste by themselves — and a very respectable one too. From Râmânuja down to Chaitanya of Bengal, all great Vaishnava Teachers have done the same."

"And where should these new people expect to marry?" I asked.

"Amongst themselves, as they do now", said the Swami quietly.

"Then as to names," I enquired, "I suppose aliens and perverts who have adopted non-Hindu names should be named newly. Would you give them caste-names, or what?"

"Certainly," said the Swami, thoughtfully, "there is a great deal in a name!" and on this question he would say no more.

But my next enquiry drew blood. "Would you leave these new-comers, Swamiji, to choose their own form of religious belief out of many-visaged Hinduism, or would you chalk out a religion for them?"

"Can you ask that?" he said. "They will choose for themselves. For unless a man chooses for himself, the very spirit of Hinduism is destroyed. The essence of our Faith consists simply in this freedom of the Ishta."

I thought the utterance a weighty one, for the man before me has spent more years than any one else living I fancy, in studying the common bases of Hinduism in a scientific and sympathetic spirit — and the freedom of the Ishta is obviously a principle big enough to accommodate the world.

But the talk passed to other matters, and then with a cordial good night this great teacher of religion lifted his lantern and went back into the monastery, while I by the pathless paths of the Ganga, in and out amongst her crafts of many sizes, made the best of my way back to my Calcutta home.

NOTES FROM LECTURES AND DISCOURSES

ON KARMA-YOGA

Isolation of the soul from all objects, mental and physical, is the goal; when that is attained, the soul will find that it was alone all the time, and it required no one to make it happy. As long as we require someone else to make us happy, we are slaves. When the Purusha finds that It is free, and does not require anything to complete Itself, that this nature is quite unnecessary, then freedom (Kaivalya) is attained.

Men run after a few dollars and do not think anything of cheating a fellow-being to get those dollars; but if they would restrain themselves, in a few years they would develop such characters as would bring them millions of dollars — if they wanted them. Then their will would govern the universe. But we are all such fools!

What is the use of talking of one's mistakes to the world? They cannot thereby be undone. For what one has done one must suffer; one must try and do better. The world sympathises only with the strong and the powerful.

It is only work that is done as a free-will offering to humanity and to nature that does not bring with it any binding attachment.

Duty of any kind is not to be slighted. A man who does the lower work is not, for that reason only, a lower man than he who does the higher work; a man should not be judged by the nature of his duties, but by the manner in which he does them. His manner of doing them and his power to do them are indeed the test of a man. A shoemaker who can turn out a strong, nice pair of shoes in the shortest possible time is a better man, according to his profession and his work, than a professor who talks nonsense every day of his life.

Every duty is holy, and devotion to duty is the highest form of the worship of God; it is certainly a source of great help in enlightening and emancipating the deluded and ignorance-encumbered souls of the Baddhas — the bound ones.

By doing well the duty which is nearest to us, the duty which is in our hands now, we make ourselves stronger and improving our strength in this manner step by step, we may even reach a state in which it shall be our privilege to do the most coveted and honoured duties in life and in society.

Nature's justice is uniformly stern and unrelenting.

The most practical man would call life neither good nor evil.

Every successful man must have behind him somewhere tremendous integrity, tremendous sincerity, and that is the cause of his signal success in life. He may not have been perfectly unselfish; yet he was tending towards it. If he had been perfectly unselfish, his would have been as great a success as that of the Buddha or of the Christ. The degree of unselfishness marks the degree of success everywhere.

The great leaders of mankind belong to higher fields than the field of platform work.

However we may try, there cannot be any action which is perfectly pure or any which is perfectly impure, taking purity or impurity in the sense of injury or non-injury. We cannot breathe or live without injuring others, and every morsel of food we eat is taken from another's mouth; our very lives are crowding out some other lives. It may be those of men, or animals, or small fungi, but someone somewhere we have to crowd out. That being the case, it naturally follows that perfection can never be attained by work. We may work through all eternity, but there will be no way out of this intricate maze: we may work on and on and on, but there will be no end.

The man who works through freedom and love cares nothing for results. But the slave wants his whipping; the servant wants his pay. So with all life; take for instance the public life. The public speaker wants a little applause or a little hissing and hooting. If you keep him in a corner without it, you kill him, for he requires it. This is working through slavery. To expect something in return, under such conditions, becomes second nature. Next comes the work of the servant, who requires some pay; I give this, and you give me that. Nothing is easier to say, "I work for work's sake", but nothing is so difficult to attain. I would go twenty miles on my hands and knees to look on the face of the man who can work for work's sake. There is a motive somewhere. If it is not money, it is power. If it is not power, it is gain. Somehow, somewhere, there is a motive power. You are my friend, and I want to work for you and with you. This is all very well, and every moment I may make protestation of my sincerity. But take care, you must be sure to agree with me! If you do not, I shall no longer take care of you or live for you! This kind of work for a motive brings misery. That work alone brings unattachment and bliss, wherein we work as masters of our own minds.

The great lesson to learn is that I am not the standard by which the whole universe is to be judged; each man is to be judged by his own idea, each race by its own standard and ideal, each custom of each country by its own reasoning and conditions. American customs are the result of the environment in which the Americans live and Indian customs are the result of the environment in which the Indians are; and so of China, Japan, England, and every other country.

We all find ourselves in the position for which we are fit, each ball finds its own hole; and if one has some capacity above another, the world will find that out too, in this universal adjusting that goes on. So it is no use to grumble. There may be a rich man who is wicked, yet there must be in that man certain qualities that made him rich; and if any other man has the same qualities, he will also become rich. What is the use of fighting and complaining? That will not help us to better things. He who grumbles at the little thing that has fallen to his lot to do will grumble at everything. Always grumbling, he will lead a miserable life, and everything will be a failure. But that man who does his duty as he goes, putting, his shoulder to the wheel, will see the light, and higher and higher duties will fall to his share.

ON FANATICISM

There are fanatics of various kinds. Some people are wine fanatics and cigar fanatics. Some think that if men gave up smoking cigars, the world would arrive at the millennium. Women are generally amongst these fanatics. There was a young lady here one day, in this class. She was one of a number of ladies in Chicago who have built a house where they take in the working people and give them music and gymnastics. One day this young lady was talking about the evils of the world and said she knew the remedy. I asked, "How do you know?" and she answered, "Have you seen Hull House?" In her opinion, this Hull House is the one panacea for all the evils that flesh is heir to. This will grow upon her. I am sorry for her. There are some fanatics in India who think that if a woman could marry again when her husband died, it would cure all evil. This is fanaticism.

When I was a boy I thought that fanaticism was a great element in work, but now, as I grow older, I find out that it is not.

There may be a woman who would steal and make no objection to taking someone else's bag and going away with it. But perhaps that woman does not smoke. She becomes a smoke fanatic, and as soon as she finds a man smoking, she strongly disapproves of him, because he smokes a cigar. There may be a man who goes about cheating people; there is no trusting him; no woman is safe with him. But perhaps this scoundrel does not drink wine. If so, he sees nothing good in anyone who drinks wine. All these wicked things that he himself does are of no consideration. This is only natural human selfishness and one-sidedness.

You must also remember that the world has God to govern it, and He has not left it to our charity. The Lord God is its Governor and Maintainer, and in spite of these wine fanatics and cigar fanatics, and all sorts of marriage fanatics, it would go on. If all these persons were to die, it would go on none the worse.

Do you not remember in your own history how the "Mayflower" people came out here, and began to call themselves Puritans? They were very pure and good as far as they went, until they began to persecute other people; and throughout the history of mankind it has been the same. Even those that run away from persecution indulge in persecuting others as soon as a favourable opportunity to do so occurs.

In ninety cases out of a hundred, fanatics must have bad livers, or they are dyspeptics, or are in some way diseased. By degrees even physicians will find out that fanaticism is a kind of disease. I have seen plenty of it. The Lord save me from it!

My experience comes to this, that it is rather wise to avoid all sorts of fanatical reforms. This world is slowly going on; let it go slowly. Why are you in a hurry? Sleep well and keep your nerves in good order; eat right food, and have sympathy with the world. Fanatics only make hatred. Do you mean to say that the temperance fanatic loves these poor people who become drunkards? A fanatic is a fanatic simply because he expects to get something for himself in return. As soon as the battle is over, he goes for the spoil. When you come out of the company of fanatics you may learn how really to love and sympathise. And the more you attain of love and sympathy, the less will be your power to condemn these poor creatures; rather you will sympathise with their faults. It will become possible for you to sympathise with the drunkard and to know that he is also a man like yourself. You will then try to understand the many circumstances that are dragging him down, and feel that if you had been in his place you would perhaps have committed suicide. I remember a woman whose husband was a great drunkard, and she complained to me of his becoming so. I replied, "Madam, if there were twenty millions of wives like yourself, all husbands would become drunkards." I am convinced that a large number of drunkards are manufactured by their wives. My business is to tell the truth and not to flatter anyone. These unruly women from whose minds the words bear and forbear are gone for ever, and whose false ideas of independence lead them to think that men should be at their feet, and who begin to howl as soon as men dare to say anything to them which they do not like — such women are becoming the bane of the world, and it is a wonder that they do not drive half the men in it to commit suicide. In this way things should not go on. Life is not so easy as they believe it to be; it is a more serious business!

A man must not only have faith but intellectual faith too. To make a man take up everything and believe it, would be to make him a lunatic. I once had a book sent me, which said I must believe everything told in it. It said there was no soul, but that there were gods and goddesses in heaven, and a thread of light going from each of our heads to heaven! How did the writer know all these things? She had been inspired, and wanted me to believe it too; and because I refused, she said, "You must be a very bad man; there is no hope for you!" This is fanaticism.

WORK IS WORSHIP

The highest man cannot work, for there is no binding element, no attachment, no ignorance in him. A ship is said to have passed over a mountain of magnet ore, and all the bolts and bars were drawn out, and it went to pieces. It is in ignorance that struggle remains, because we are all really atheists. Real theists cannot work. We are atheists more or less. We do not see God or believe in Him. He is G-O-D to us, and nothing more. There are moments when we think He is near, but then we fall down again. When you see Him, who struggles for whom? Help the Lord! There is a proverb in our language, "Shall we teach the Architect of the universe how to build?" So those are the highest of mankind who do not work. The next time you see these silly phrases about the world and how we must all help God and do this or that for Him, remember this. Do not think such thoughts; they are too selfish. All the work you do is subjective, is done for your own benefit. God has not fallen into a ditch for you and me to help Him out by building a hospital or something of that sort. He allows you to work. He allows you to exercise your muscles in this great gymnasium, not in order to help Him but that you may help yourself. Do you think even an ant will die for want of your help? Most arrant blasphemy! The world does not need you at all. The world goes on you are like a drop in the ocean. A leaf does not move, the wind does not blow without Him. Blessed are we that we are given the privilege of working for Him, not of helping Him. Cut out this word "help" from your mind. You cannot help; it is blaspheming. You are here yourself at His pleasure. Do you mean to say, you help Him? You worship. When you give a morsel of food to the dog, you worship the dog as God. God is in that dog. He is the dog. He is all and in all. We are allowed to worship Him. Stand in that reverent attitude to the whole universe, and then will come perfect non-attachment. This should be your duty. This is the proper attitude of work. This is the secret taught by Karma-Yoga.

WORK WITHOUT MOTIVE

At the forty-second meeting of the Ramakrishna Mission held at the premises No. 57 Râmkânta Bose Street, Baghbazar, Calcutta, on the 20th March, 1898, Swami Vivekananda gave an address on "Work without Motive", and spoke to the following effect:

When the Gita was first preached, there was then going on a great controversy between two sects. One party considered the Vedic Yajnas and animal sacrifices and such like Karmas to constitute the whole of religion. The other preached that the killing of numberless horses and cattle cannot be called religion. The people belonging to the latter party were mostly Sannyâsins and followers of Jnâna. They believed that the giving up of all work and the gaining of the knowledge of the Self was the only path to Moksha By the preaching of His great doctrine of work without motive, the Author of the Gita set at rest the disputes of these two antagonistic sects.

Many are of opinion that the Gita was not written at the time of the Mahâbhârata, but was subsequently added to it. This is not correct. The special teachings of the Gita are to be found in every part of the Mahabharata, and if the Gita is to be expunged, as forming no part of it, every other portion of it which embodies the same teachings should be similarly treated.

Now, what is the meaning of working without motive? Nowadays many understand it in the sense that one is to work in such a way that neither pleasure nor pain touches his mind. If this be its real meaning, then the animals might be said to work without motive. Some animals devour their own offspring, and they do not feel any pangs at all in doing so. Robbers ruin other people by robbing them of their possessions; but if they feel quite callous to pleasure or pain, then they also would be working without motive. If the meaning of it be such, then one who has a stony heart, the worst of criminals, might be considered to be working without motive. The walls have no feelings of pleasure or pain, neither has a stone, and it cannot be said that they are working without motive. In the above sense the doctrine is a potent instrument in the hands of the wicked. They would go on doing wicked deeds, and would pronounce themselves as working without a motive. If such be the significance of working without a motive, then a fearful doctrine has been put forth by the preaching of the Gita. Certainly this is not the meaning. Furthermore, if we look into the lives of those who were connected with the preaching of the Gita, we should find them living quite a different life. Arjuna killed Bhishma and Drona in battle, but withal, he sacrificed all his self-interest and desires and his lower self millions of times.

Gita teaches Karma-Yoga. We should work through Yoga (concentration). In such concentration in action (Karma-Yoga), there is no consciousness of the lower ego present. The consciousness that I am doing this and that is never present when one works through Yoga. The Western people do not understand this. They say that if there be no consciousness of ego, if this ego is gone, how then can a man work? But when one works with concentration, losing all consciousness of oneself the work that is done will be infinitely better, and this every one may have experienced in his own life. We perform many works subconsciously, such as the digestion of food etc., many others consciously, and others again by becoming immersed in Samâdhi as it were, when there is no consciousness of the smaller ego. If the painter, losing the consciousness of his ego, becomes completely immersed in his painting, he will be able to produce masterpieces. The good cook concentrates his whole self on the food-material he handles; he loses all other consciousness for the time being. But they are only able to do perfectly a single work in this way, to which they are habituated. The Gita teaches that all works should be done thus. He who is one with the Lord through Yoga performs all his works by becoming immersed in concentration, and does not seek any personal benefit. Such a performance of work brings only good to the world, no evil can come out of it. Those who work thus never do anything for themselves.

The result of every work is mixed with good and evil. There is no good work that has not a touch of evil in it. Like smoke round the fire, some evil always clings to work. We should engage in such works as bring the largest amount of good and the smallest measure of evil. Arjuna killed Bhishma and Drona; if this had not been done Duryodhana could not have been conquered, the force of evil would have triumphed over the force of good, and thus a great calamity would have fallen on the country. The government of the country would have been usurped by a body of proud unrighteous kings, to the great misfortune of the people. Similarly, Shri Krishna killed Kamsa, Jarâsandha, and others who were tyrants, but not a single one of his deeds was done for himself. Every one of them was for the good of others. We are reading the Gita by candle-light, but numbers of insects are being burnt to death. Thus it is seen that some evil clings to work. Those who work without any consciousness of their lower ego are not affected with evil, for they work for the good of the world. To work without motive, to work unattached, brings the highest bliss and freedom. This secret of Karma-Yoga is taught by the Lord Shri Krishna in the Gita.

SADHANAS OR PREPARATIONS FOR HIGHER LIFE

If atavism gains, you go down; if evolution gains, you go on. Therefore, we must not allow atavism to take place. Here, in my own body, is the first work of the study. We are too busy trying to mend the ways of our neighbours, that is the difficulty. We must begin with our own bodies. The heart, the liver, etc., are all atavistic; bring them back into consciousness, control them, so that they will obey your commands and act up to your wishes. There was a time when we had control of the liver; we could shake the whole skin, as can the cow. I have seen many people bring the control back by sheer hard practice. Once an impress is made, it is there. Bring back all the submerged activities — the vast ocean of action. This is the first part of the great study, and it is absolutely necessary for our social well-being. On the other hand, only the consciousness need not be studied all the time.

Then there is the other part of study, not so necessary in our social life, which tends to liberation. Its direct action is to free the soul, to take the torch into the gloom, to clean out what is behind, to shake it up or even defy it, and to make us march onward piercing the gloom. That is the goal — the superconscious. Then when that state is reached, this very man becomes divine, becomes free. And to the mind thus trained to transcend all, gradually this universe will begin to give up its secrets; the book of nature will be read chapter after chapter, till the goal is attained, and we pass from this valley of life and death to that One, where death and life do not exist, and we know the Real and become the Real.

The first thing necessary is a quiet and peaceable life. If I have to go about the world the whole day to make a living, it is hard for me to attain to anything very high in this life. Perhaps in another life I shall be born under more propitious circumstances. But if I am earnest enough, these very circumstances will change even in this birth. Was there anything you did not get which you really wanted? It could not be. For it is the want that creates the body. It is the light that has bored the holes, as it were, in your head, called the eyes. If the light had not existed, you would have had no eyes. It is sound that had made the ears. The object of perception existed first, before you made the organ. In a few hundred thousand years or earlier, we may have other organs to perceive electricity and other things. There is no desire for a peaceful mind. Desire will not come unless there is something outside to fulfil it. The outside something just bores a hole in the body, as it were, and tries to get into the mind. So, when the desire will arise to have a peaceful, quiet life, that shall come where everything shall be propitious for the development of the mind — you may take that as my experience. It may come after thousands of lives, but it must come. Hold on to that, the desire. You cannot have the strong desire if its object was not outside for you already. Of course you must understand, there is a difference between desire and desire. The master said, "My child, if you desire after God, God shall come to you." The disciple did not understand his master fully. One day both went to bathe in a river, and the master said, "Plunge in", and the boy did so. In a moment the master was upon him, holding him down. He would not let the boy come up. When the boy struggled and was exhausted, he let him go. "Yes, my child, how did you feel there;" "Oh, the desire for a breath of air!" "Do you have that kind of desire for God?" "No, sir." "Have that kind of desire for God and you shall have God."

That, without which we cannot live, must come to us. If it did not come to us, life could not go on.

If you want to be a Yogi, you must be free and place yourself in circumstances where you are alone and free from all anxiety. He who desires for a comfortable and nice life and at the same time wants to realise the Self is like the fool who, wanting to cross the river, caught hold of a crocodile mistaking it for a log of wood. "Seek ye first the Kingdom of God and His righteousness, and all these things shall be added unto you." Unto him everything who does not care for anything. Fortune is like a flirt; she cares not for him who wants her, but she is at the feet of him who does not care for her. Money comes and showers itself upon one who does not care for it; so does fame come in abundance until it is a trouble and a burden. They always come to the Master. The slave never gets anything. The Master is he who can live in spite of them, whose life does not depend upon the little, foolish things of the world. Live for an ideal, and that one ideal alone. Let it be so great, so strong, that there may be nothing else left in the mind; no place for anything else, no time for anything else.

How some people give all their energies, time, brain, body, and everything, to become rich! They have no time for breakfast! Early in the morning they are out and at work! They die in the attempt — ninety per cent of them — and the rest when they make money, cannot enjoy it. That is grand! I do not say it is bad to try to be rich. It is marvellous, wonderful. Why, what does it show? It shows that one can have the same amount of energy and struggle for freedom as one has for money. We know we have to give up money and all other things when we die, and yet, see the amount of energy we can put forth for them. But we, the same human beings, should we not put forth a thousandfold more strength and energy to acquire that which never fades, but which remains to us for ever? For this is the one great friend, our own good deeds, our own spiritual excellence, that follows us beyond the grave. Everything else is left behind here with the body.

That is the one great first step — the real desire for the ideal. Everything comes easy after that. That the Indian mind found out; there, in India, men go to any length to find truth. But here, in the West, the difficulty is that everything is made so easy. It is not truth, but development, that is the great aim. The struggle is the great lesson. Mind you, the great benefit in this life is struggle. It is through that we pass. If there is any road to Heaven, it is through Hell. Through Hell to Heaven is always the way. When the soul has wrestled with circumstance and has met death, a thousand times death on the way, but nothing daunted has struggled forward again and again and yet again — then the soul comes out as a giant and laughs at the ideal he has been struggling for, because he finds how much greater is he than the ideal. I am the end, my own Self, and nothing else, for what is there to compare to me own Self? Can a bag of gold be the ideal of my Soul? Certainly not! My Soul is the highest ideal that I can have. Realising my own real nature is the one goal of my life.

There is nothing that is absolutely evil. The devil has a place here as well as God, else he would not be here. Just as I told you, it is through Hell that we pass to Heaven. Our mistakes have places here. Go on! Do not look back if you think you have done something that is not right. Now, do you believe you could be what you are today, had you not made those mistakes before? Bless your mistakes, then. They have been angels unawares. Blessed be torture! Blessed be happiness! Do not care what be your lot. Hold on to the ideal. March on! Do not look back upon little mistakes and things. In this battlefield of ours, the dust of mistakes must be raised. Those who are so thin-skinned that they cannot bear the dust, let them get out of the ranks.

So, then, this tremendous determination to struggle a hundredfold more determination than that which you put forth to gain anything which belongs to this life, is the first great preparation.

And then along with it, there must be meditation Meditation is the one thing. Meditate! The greatest thing is meditation. It is the nearest approach to spiritual life — the mind meditating. It is the one moment in our daily life that we are not at all material — the Soul thinking of Itself, free from all matter — this marvellous touch of the Soul!

The body is our enemy, and yet is our friend. Which of you can bear the sight of misery? And which of you cannot do so when you see it only as a painting? Because it is unreal, we do not identify ourselves with it, eve know it is only a painting; it cannot bless us, it cannot hurt us. The most terrible misery painted upon a price of canvas, we may even enjoy; we praise the technique of the artist, we wonder at his marvellous genius, even though the scene he paints is most horrible. That is the secret; that non-attachment. Be the Witness.

No breathing, no physical training of Yoga, nothing is of any use until you reach to the idea, "I am the Witness." Say, when the tyrant hand is on your neck, "I am the Witness! I am the Witness!" Say, "I am the Spirit! Nothing external can touch me." When evil thoughts arise, repeat that, give that sledge-hammer blow on their heads, "I am the Spirit! I am the Witness, the Ever-Blessed! I have no reason to do, no reason to suffer, I have finished with everything, I am the Witness. I am in my picture gallery — this universe is my museum, I am looking at these successive paintings. They are all beautiful. Whether good or evil. I see the marvellous skill, but it is all one. Infinite flames of the Great Painter!" Really speaking, there is naught — neither volition, nor desire. He is all. He — She — the Mother, is playing, and we are like dolls, Her helpers in this play. Here, She puts one now in the garb of a beggar, another moment in the garb of a king, the next moment in the garb of a saint, and again in the garb of a devil. We are putting on different garbs to help the Mother Spirit in Her play.

When the baby is at play, she will not come even if called by her mother. But when she finishes her play, she will rush to her mother, and will have no play. So there come moments in our life, when we feel our play is finished, and we want to rush to the Mother. Then all our toil here will be of no value; men, women, and children — wealth, name, and fame, joys and glories of life — punishments and successes — will be no more, and the whole life will seem like a show. We shall see only the infinite rhythm going on, endless and purposeless, going we do not know where. Only this much shall we say; our play is done.

THE COSMOS AND THE SELF

Everything in nature rises from some fine seed-forms, becomes grosser and grosser, exists for a certain time, and again goes back to the original fine form. Our earth, for instance, has come out of a nebulous form which, becoming colder and colder, turned into this crystallised planet upon which we live, and in the future it will again go to pieces and return to its rudimentary nebulous form. This is happening in the universe, and has been through time immemorial. This is the whole history of man, the whole history of nature, the whole history of life.

Every evolution is preceded by an involution. The whole of the tree is present in the seed, its cause. The whole of the human being is present in that one protoplasm. The whole of this universe is present in the cosmic fine universe. Everything is present in its cause, in its fine form. This evolution, or gradual unfolding of grosser and grosser forms, is true, but each case has been preceded by an involution. The whole of this universe must have been involute before it came out, and has unfolded itself in all these various forms to be involved again once more. Take, for instance, the life of a little plant. We find two things that make the plant a unity by itself — its growth and development, its decay and death. These make one unity the plant life. So, taking that plant life as only one link in the chain of life, we may take the whole series as one life, beginning in the protoplasm and ending in the most perfect man. Man is one link, and the various beasts, the lower animals, and plants are other links. Now go back to the source, the finest particles from which they started, and take the whole series as but one life, and you will find that every evolution here is the evolution of something which existed previously.

Where it begins, there it ends. What is the end of this universe? Intelligence, is it not? The last to come in the order of creation, according to the evolutionists, was intelligence. That being so, it must be the cause, the beginning of creation also. At the beginning that intelligence remains involved, and in the end it gets evolved. The sum total of the intelligence displayed in the universe must therefore be the involved universal intelligence unfolding itself, and this universal intelligence is what we call God, from whom we come and to whom we return, as the scriptures say. Call it by any other name, you cannot deny that in the beginning there is that infinite cosmic intelligence.

What makes a compound? A compound is that in which the causes have combined and become the effect. So these compound things can be only within the circle of the law of causation; so far as the rules of cause and effect go, so far can we have compounds and combinations. Beyond that it is impossible to talk of combinations, because no law holds good therein. Law holds good only in that universe which we see, feel, hear, imagine, dream, and beyond that we cannot place any idea of law. That is our universe which we sense or imagine, and we sense what is within our direct perception, and we imagine what is in our mind. What is beyond the body is beyond the senses, and what is beyond the mind is beyond the imagination, and therefore is beyond our universe, and therefore beyond the law of causation. The Self of man being beyond the law of causation is not a compound, is not the effect of any cause, and therefore is ever free and is the ruler of everything that is within law. Not being a compound, it will never die, because death means going back to the component parts, destruction means going back to the cause. Because it cannot die, it cannot live; for both life and death are modes of manifestation of the same thing. So the Soul is beyond life and death. You were never born, and you will never die. Birth and death belong to the body only.

The doctrine of monism holds that this universe is all that exists; gross or fine, it is all here; the effect and the cause are both here; the explanation is here. What is known as the particular is simply repetition in a minute form of the universal. We get our idea of the universe from the study of our own Souls, and what is true there also holds good in the outside universe. The ideas of heaven and all these various places, even if they be true, are in the universe. They altogether make this Unity. The first idea, therefore, is that of a Whole, a Unit, composed of various minute particles, and each one of us is a part, as it were, of this Unit. As manifested beings we appear separate, but as a reality we are one. The more we think ourselves separate from this Whole, the more miserable we become. So, Advaita is the basis of ethics.

WHO IS A REAL GURU?

A real Guru is one who is born from time to time as a repository of spiritual force which he transmits to future generations through successive links of Guru and Shishya (disciple). The current of this spirit-force changes its course from time to time, just as a mighty stream of water opens up a new channel and leaves the old one for good. Thus it is seen that old sects of religion grow lifeless in the course of time, and new sects arise with the fire of life in them. Men who are truly wise commit themselves to the mercy of that particular sect through which the current of life flows. Old forms of religion are like the skeletons of once mighty animals, preserved in museums. They should be regarded with the due honour. They cannot satisfy the true cravings of the soul for the Highest, just as a dead mango-tree cannot satisfy the cravings of a man for luscious mangoes.

The one thing necessary is to be stripped of our vanities — the sense that we possess any spiritual wisdom — and to surrender ourselves completely to the guidance of our Guru. The Guru only knows what will lead us towards perfection. We are quite blind to it. We do not know anything. This sort of humility will open the door of our heart for spiritual truths. Truth will never come into our minds so long as there will remain the faintest shadow of Ahamkâra (egotism). All of you should try to root out this devil from your heart. Complete self-surrender is the only way to spiritual illumination.

ON ART

The secret of Greek Art is its imitation of nature even to the minutest details; whereas the secret of Indian Art is to represent the ideal. The energy of the Greek painter is spent in perhaps painting a piece of flesh, and he is so successful that a dog is deluded into taking it to be a real bit of meat and so goes to bite it. Now, what glory is there in merely imitating nature? Why not place an actual bit of flesh before the dog?

The Indian tendency, on the other hand, to represent the ideal, the supersensual, has become degraded into painting grotesque images. Now, true Art can be compared to a lily which springs from the ground, takes its nourishment from the ground, is in touch with the ground, and yet is quite high above it. So Art must be in touch with nature — and wherever that touch is gone, Art degenerates — yet it must be above nature.

Art is — representing the beautiful. There must be Art in everything.

The difference between architecture and building is that the former expresses an idea, while the latter is merely a structure built on economical principles. The value of matter depends solely on its capacities of expressing ideas.

The artistic faculty was highly developed in our Lord Shri Ramakrishna, and he used to say that without this faculty none can be truly spiritual.

ON LANGUAGE

Simplicity is the secret. My ideal of language is my Master's language, most colloquial and yet most expressive. It must express the thought which is intended to be conveyed.

The attempt to make the Bengali language perfect in so short a time will make it cut and dried. Properly speaking, it has no verbs. Michael Madhusudan Dutt attempted to remedy this in poetry. The greatest poet in Bengal was Kavikankana. The best prose in Sanskrit is Patanjali's Mahâbhâshya. There the language is vigorous. The language of Hitopadesha is not bad, but the language of Kâdambari is an example of degradation.

The Bengali language must be modelled not after the Sanskrit, but rather after the Pâli, which has a strong resemblance to it. In coining or translating technical terms in Bengali, one must, however, use all Sanskrit words for them, and an attempt should be made to coin new words. For this purpose, if a collection is made from a Sanskrit dictionary of all those technical terms, then it ill help greatly the constitution of the Bengali language.

THE SANNYASIN

In explanation of the term Sannyâsin, the Swami in the course of one of his lectures in Boston said:

When a man has fulfilled the duties and obligations of that stage of life in which he is born, and his aspirations lead him to seek a spiritual life and to abandon altogether the worldly pursuits of possession, fame, or power, when, by the growth of insight into the nature of the world, he sees its impermanence, its strife, its misery, and the paltry nature of its prizes, and turns away from all these — then he seeks the True, the Eternal Love, the Refuge. He makes complete renunciation (Sannyâsa) of all worldly position, property, and name, and wanders forth into the world to live a life of self-sacrifice and to persistently seek spiritual knowledge, striving to excel in love and compassion and to acquire lasting insight. Gaining these pearls of wisdom by years of meditation, discipline, and inquiry, he in his turn becomes a teacher and hands on to disciples, lay or professed, who may seek them from him, all that he can of wisdom and beneficence.

A Sannyasin cannot belong to any religion, for his is a life of independent thought, which draws from all religions; his is a life of realisation, not merely of theory or belief, much less of dogma.

THE SANNYASIN AND THE HOUSEHOLDER

The men of the world should have no voice in the affairs of the Sannyâsins. The Sannyasin should have nothing to do with the rich, his duty is with the poor. He should treat the poor with loving care and serve them joyfully with all his might. To pay respects to the rich and hang on them for support has been the bane of all the Sannyasin communities of our country. A true Sannyasin should scrupulously avoid that. Such conduct becomes a public woman rather than one who professes to have renounced the world. How should a man immersed in Kâma-Kânchana (lust and greed) become a devotee of one whose central ideal is the renunciation of Kama-Kanchana? Shri Ramakrishna wept and prayed to the Divine Mother to send him such a one to talk with as would not have in him the slightest tinge of Kama-Kanchana; for he would say, "My lips burn when I talk with the worldly-minded." He also used to say that he could not even bear the touch of the worldly-minded and the impure. That King of Sannyasins (Shri Ramakrishna) can never be preached by men of the world. The latter can never be perfectly sincere; for he cannot but have some selfish motives to serve. If Bhagavân (God) incarnates Himself as a householder, I can never believe Him to be sincere. When a householder takes the position of the leader of a religious sect, he begins to serve his own interests in the name of principle, hiding the former in the garb of the latter, and the result is the sect becomes rotten to the core. All religious movements headed by householders have shared the same fate. Without renunciation religion can never stand.

Here Swamiji was asked — What are we Sannyasins to understand by renunciation of Kanchana (wealth)? He answered as follows: With a view to certain ends we have to adopt certain means. These means vary according to the conditions of time, place, individual, etc.; but the end always remains unaltered. In the case of the Sannyasin, the end is the liberation of the Self and doing good to humanity — "आत्मनो मोक्षार्थं जगद्धिताय च"; and of the ways to attain it, the renunciation of Kama-Kanchana is the most important. Remember, renunciation consists in the total absence of all selfish motives and not in mere abstinence from external contact, such as avoiding to touch one's money kept with another at the same time enjoying all its benefits. Would that be renunciation? For accomplishing the two above-mentioned ends, the begging excursion would be a great help to a Sannyasin at a time when the householders strictly obeyed the injunctions of Manu and other law-givers, by setting apart every day a portion of their meal for ascetic guests. Nowadays things have changed considerably, especially, as in Bengal, where no Mâdhukari[1] system prevails. Here it would be mere waste of energy to try to live on Madhukari, and you would profit nothing by it. The injunction of Bhikshâ (begging) is a means to serve the above two ends, which will not be served by that way now. It does not, therefore, go against the principle of renunciation under such circumstances if a Sannyasin provides for mere necessaries of life and devotes all his energy to the accomplishment of his ends for which he took Sannyasa. Attaching too much importance ignorantly to the means brings confusion. The end should never be lost sight of.

---

1. Literally, 'bee-like'. The system of begging one's food piecemeal from several houses, so as not to tax the householder, as a bee gathers honey from different flowers.

THE EVILS OF ADHIKARIVADA

In one of his question classes the talk drifted on to the Adhikârivâda, or the doctrine of special rights and privileges, and Swamiji in pointing out vehemently the evils that have resulted from it spoke to the following effect:

With all my respects for the Rishis of yore, I cannot but denounce their method in instructing the people. They always enjoined upon them to do certain things but took care never to explain to them the reason for it. This method was pernicious to the very core; and instead of enabling men to attain the end, it laid upon their shoulders a mass of meaningless nonsense. Their excuse for keeping the end hidden from view was that the people could not have understood their real meaning even if they had presented it to them, not being worthy recipients. The Adhikarivada is the outcome of pure selfishness. They knew that by this enlightenment on their special subject they would lose their superior position of instructors to the people. Hence their endeavour to support this theory. If you consider a man too weak to receive these lessons, you should try the more to teach and educate him; you should give him the advantage of more teaching, instead of less, to train up his intellect, so as to enable him to comprehend the more subtle problems. These advocates of Adhikarivada ignored the tremendous fact of the infinite possibilities of the human soul. Every man is capable of receiving knowledge if it is imparted in his own language. A teacher who cannot convince others should weep on account of his own inability to teach the people in their own language, instead of cursing them and dooming them to live in ignorance and superstition, setting up the plea that the higher knowledge is not for them. Speak out the truth boldly, without any fear that it will puzzle the weak. Men are selfish; they do not want others to come up to the same level of their knowledge, for fear of losing their own privilege and prestige over others. Their contention is that the knowledge of the highest spiritual truths will bring about confusion in the understanding of the weak-minded men, and so the Shloka goes:

"न बुद्धभिदं जनयेदज्ञानां कर्मसङ्गिनाम् ।
जोषयेत्सर्वकर्माणि विद्वान्युक्तः समाचरन् ॥३- २६॥"

— "One should not unsettle the understanding of the ignorant, attached to action (by teaching them Jnâna): the wise man, himself steadily acting, should engage the ignorant in all work" (Gita, III. 26).

I cannot believe in the self-contradictory statement that light brings greater darkness. It is like losing life in the ocean of Sachchidânanda, in the ocean of Absolute Existence and Immortality. How absurd! Knowledge means freedom from the errors which ignorance leads to. Knowledge paving the way to error! Enlightenment leading to confusion! Is it possible? Men are not bold enough to speak out broad truths, for fear of losing the respect of the people. They try to make a compromise between the real, eternal truths and the nonsensical prejudices of the people, and thus set up the doctrine that Lokâchâras (customs of the people) and Deshâchâras (customs of the country) must be adhered to. No compromise! No whitewashing! No covering of corpses beneath flowers! Throw away such texts as, "तथापि लोकाचारः —Yet the customs of the people have to be followed." Nonsense! The result of this sort of compromise is that the grand truths are soon buried under heaps of rubbish, and the latter are eagerly held as real truths. Even the grand truths of the Gita, so boldly preached by Shri Krishna, received the gloss of compromise in the hands of future generations of disciples, and the result is that the grandest scripture of the world is now made to yield many things which lead men astray.

This attempt at compromise proceeds from arrant downright cowardice. Be bold! My children should be brave, above all. Not the least compromise on any account. Preach the highest truths broadcast. Do not fear losing your respect or causing unhappy friction. Rest assured that if you serve truth in spite of temptations to forsake it, you will attain a heavenly strength in the face of which men will quail to speak before you things which you do not believe to be true. People will be convinced of what you will say to them if you can strictly serve truth for fourteen years continually, without swerving from it. Thus you will confer the greatest blessing on the masses, unshackle their bandages, and uplift the whole nation.

ON BHAKTI-YOGA

The dualist thinks you cannot be moral unless you have a God with a rod in His hand, ready to punish you. How is that? Suppose a horse had to give us a lecture on morality, one of those very wretched cab-horses who move only with the whip, to which he has become accustomed. He begins to speak about human beings and says that they must be very immoral. Why? "Because I know they are not whipped regularly." The fear of the whip only makes one more immoral.

You all say there is a God and that He is an omnipresent Being. Close your eyes and think what He is. What do you find? Either you are thinking, in bringing the idea of omnipresence in your mind, of the sea, or the blue sky, or an expanse of meadow, or such things as you have seen in your life. If that is so, you do not mean anything by omnipresent God; it has no meaning at all to you. So with every other attribute of God. What idea have we of omnipotence or omniscience? We have none. Religion is realising, and I shall call you a worshipper of God when you have become able to realise the Idea. Before that it is the spelling of words and no more. It is this power of realisation that makes religion; no amount of doctrines or philosophies, or ethical books, that you may have stuffed into your brain, will matter much — only what you are and what you have realised.

The Personal God is the same Absolute looked at through the haze of Mâyâ. When we approach Him with the five senses, we can see Him only as the Personal God. The idea is that the Self cannot be objectified. How can the Knower know Itself? But It can cast a shadow, as it were, if that can be called objectification. So the highest form of that shadow, that attempt at objectifying Itself, is the Personal God. The Self is the eternal subject, and we are struggling all the time to objectify that Self. And out of that struggle has come this phenomenal universe and what we call matter, and so on. But these are very weak attempts, and the highest objectification of the Self possible to us is the Personal God. This objectification is an attempt to reveal our own nature. According to the Sânkhya, nature is showing all these experiences to the soul, and when it has got real experience it will know its own nature. According to the Advaita Vedantist, the soul is struggling to reveal itself. After long struggle, it finds that the subject must always remain the subject; and then begins non-attachment, and it becomes free.

When a man has reached that perfect state, he is of the same nature as the Personal God. "I and my Father are one." He knows that he is one with Brahman, the Absolute, and projects himself as the Personal God does. He plays — as even the mightiest of kings may sometimes play with dolls.

Some imaginations help to break the bondage of the rest. The whole universe is imagination, but one set of imaginations will cure another set. Those that tell us that there is sin and sorrow and death in the world are terrible. But the other set — thou art holy, there is God, there is no pain — these are good, and help to break the bondage of the others. The highest imagination that can break all the links of the chain is that of the Personal God.

To go and say, "Lord, take care of this thing and give me that; Lord, I give you my little prayer and you give me this thing of daily necessity; Lord, cure my headache", and all that — these are not Bhakti. They are the lowest states of religion. They are the lowest form of Karma. If a man uses all his mental energy in seeking to satisfy his body and its wants, show me the difference between him and an animal. Bhakti is a higher thing higher than even desiring heaven. The idea of heaven is of a place of intensified enjoyment. How can that be God?

Only the fools rush after sense-enjoyments. It is easy to live in the senses. It is easier to run in the old groove, eating and drinking; but what these modern philosophers want to tell you is to take these comfortable ideas and put the stamp of religion on them. Such a doctrine is dangerous. Death lies in the senses. Life on the plane of the Spirit is the only life, life on any other plane is mere death; the whole of this life can be only described as a gymnasium. We must go beyond it to enjoy real life.

As long as touch-me-not-ism is your creed and the kitchen-pot your deity, you cannot rise spiritually. All the petty differences between religion and religion are mere word-struggles, nonsense. Everyone thinks, "This is my original idea", and wants to have things his own way. That is how struggles come.

In criticising another, we always foolishly take one especially brilliant point as the whole of our life and compare that with the dark ones in the life of another. Thus we make mistakes in judging individuals.

Through fanaticism and bigotry a religion can be propagated very quickly, no doubt, but the preaching of that religion is firm-based on solid ground, which gives everyone liberty to his opinions and thus uplifts him to a higher path, though this process is slow

First deluge the land (India) with spiritual ideas, then other ideas will follow The gift of spirituality and spiritual knowledge is the highest, for it saves from many and many a birth; the next gift is secular knowledge, as it opens the eyes of human beings towards that spiritual knowledge; the next is the saving of life; and the fourth is the gift of food.

Even if the body goes in practicing Sâdhanâs (austerities for realisation), let it go; what of that? Realisation will come in the fullness of time, by living constantly in the company of Sâdhus (holy men). A time comes when one understands that to serve a man even by preparing a Chhilam (earthen pipe) of tobacco is far greater than millions of meditations. He who can properly prepare a Chhilam of tobacco can also properly meditate.

Gods are nothing but highly developed dead men. We can get help from them.

Anyone and everyone cannot be an Âchârya (teacher of mankind); but many may become Mukta (liberated). The whole world seems like a dream to the liberated, but the Acharya has to take up his stand between the two states. He must have the knowledge that the world is true, or else why should he teach? Again, if he has not realised the world as a dream, then he is no better than an ordinary man, and what could he teach? The Guru has to bear the disciple's burden of sin; and that is the reason why diseases and other ailments appear even in the bodies of powerful Acharyas. But if he be imperfect, they attack his mind also, and he falls. So it is a difficult thing to be an Acharya.

It is easier to become a Jivanmukta (free in this very life) than to be an Acharya. For the former knows the world as a dream and has no concern with it; but an Acharya knows it as a dream and yet has to remain in it and work. It is not possible for everyone to be an Acharya. He is an Acharya through whom the divine power acts. The body in which one becomes an Acharya is very different from that of any other man. There is a science for keeping that body in a perfect state. His is the most delicate organism, very susceptible, capable of feeling intense joy and intense suffering. He is abnormal.

In every sphere of life we find that it is the person within that triumphs, and that personality is the secret of all success.

Nowhere is seen such sublime unfoldment of feeling as in Bhagavân Shri Krishna Chaitanya, the Prophet of Nadia.

Shri Ramakrishna is a force. You should not think that his doctrine is this or that. But he is a power, living even now in his disciples and working in the world. I saw him growing in his ideas. He is still growing. Shri Ramakrishna was both a Jivanmukta and an Acharya.

ISHVARA AND BRAHMAN

In reply to a question as to the exact position of Ishvara in Vedantic Philosophy, the Swami Vivekananda, while in Europe, gave the following definition: "Ishvara is the sum total of individuals, yet He is an Individual, as the human body is a unit, of which each cell is an individual. Samashti or collected equals God; Vyashti or analysed equals the Jiva. The existence of Ishvara, therefore, depends on that of Jiva, as the body on the cell, and vice versa. Thus, Jiva and Ishvara are coexistent beings; when one exists, the other must. Also, because, except on our earth, in all the higher spheres, the amount of good being vastly in excess of the amount of evil, the sum total (Ishvara) may be said to be all-good. Omnipotence and omniscience are obvious qualities and need no argument to prove from the very fact of totality. Brahman is beyond both these and is not a conditioned state; it is the only Unit not composed of many units, the principle which runs through all from a cell to God, without which nothing can exist; and whatever is real is that principle, or Brahman. When I think I am Brahman, I alone exist; so with others. Therefore, each one is the whole of that principle."

ON JNANA-YOGA

All souls are playing, some consciously, some unconsciously. Religion is learning to play consciously.

The same law which holds good in our worldly life also holds good in our religious life and in the life of the cosmos. It is one, it is universal. It is not that religion is guided by one law and the world by another. The flesh and the devil are but degrees of difference from God Himself.

Theologians, philosophers, and scientists in the West are ransacking everything to get a proof that they live afterwards! What a storm in a tea-cup! There are much higher things to think of. What silly superstition is this, that you ever die! It requires no priests or spirits or ghosts to tell us that we shall not die. It is the most self-evident of all truths. No man can imagine his own annihilation. The idea of immortality is inherent in man.

Wherever there is life, with it there is death. Life is the shadow of death, and death, the shadow of life. The line of demarcation is too fine to determine, too difficult to grasp, and most difficult to hold on to.

I do not believe in eternal progress, that we are growing on ever and ever in a straight line. It is too nonsensical to believe. There is no motion in a straight line. A straight line infinitely projected becomes a circle. The force sent out will complete the circle and return to its starting place.

There is no progress in a straight line. Every soul moves in a circle, as it were, and will have to complete it; and no soul can go so low but that there will come a time when it will have to go upwards. It may start straight down, but it has to take the upward curve to complete the circuit. We are all projected from a common centre, which is God, and will come back after completing the circuit to the centre from which we started.

Each soul is a circle. The centre is where the body is, and the activity is manifested there. You are omnipresent, though you have the consciousness of being concentrated in only one point. That point has taken up particles of matter and formed them into a machine to express itself. That through which it expresses itself is called the body. You are everywhere. When one body or machine fails you, the centre moves on and takes up other particles of matter, finer or grosser, and works through them. Here is man. And what is God? God is a circle with circumference nowhere and centre everywhere. Every point in that circle is living, conscious, active, and equally working. With our limited souls only one point is conscious, and that point moves forward and backward.

The soul is a circle whose circumference is nowhere (limitless), but whose centre is in some body. Death is but a change of centre. God is a circle whose circumference is nowhere, and whose centre is everywhere. When we can get out of the limited centre of body, we shall realise God, our true Self.

A tremendous stream is flowing towards the ocean, carrying little bits of paper and straw hither and thither on it. They may struggle to go back, but in the long run they; must flow down to the ocean. So you and I and all nature are like these little straws carried in mad currents towards that ocean of Life, Perfection, and God. We may struggle to go back, or float against the current and play all sorts of pranks, but in the long run we must go and join this great ocean of Life and Bliss.

Jnâna (knowledge) is "creedlessness"; but that does not mean that it despises creeds. It only means that a stage above and beyond creeds has been gained. The Jnâni (true philosopher) strives to destroy nothing but to help all. All rivers roll their waters into the sea and become one. So all creeds should lead to Jnana and become one. Jnana teaches that the world should be renounced but not on that account abandoned. To live in the world and not to be of it is the true test of renunciation.

I cannot see how it can be otherwise than that all knowledge is stored up in us from the beginning. If you and I are little waves in the ocean, then that ocean is the background.

There is really no difference between matter, mind, and Spirit. They are only different phases of experiencing the One. This very world is seen by the five senses as matter, by the very wicked as hell, by the good as heaven, and by the perfect as God.

We cannot bring it to sense demonstration that Brahman is the only real thing; but we can point out that this is the only conclusion that one can come to. For instance, there must be this oneness in everything, even in common things. There is the human generalisation, for example. We say that all the variety is created by name and form; yet when we want to grasp and separate it, it is nowhere. We can never see name or form or causes standing by themselves. So this phenomenon is Mâyâ — something which depends on the noumenon and apart from it has no existence. Take a wave in the ocean. That wave exists so long as that quantity of water remains in a wave form; but as soon as it goes down and becomes the ocean, the wave ceases to exist. But the whole mass of water does not depend so much on its form. The ocean remains, while the wave form becomes absolute zero.

The real is one. It is the mind which makes it appear as many. When we perceive the diversity, the unity has gone; and as soon as we perceive the unity, the diversity has vanished. Just as in everyday life, when you perceive the unity, you do not perceive the diversity. At the beginning you start with unity. It is a curious fact that a Chinaman will not know the difference in appearance between one American and another; and you will not know the difference between different Chinamen.

It can be shown that it is the mind which makes things knowable. It is only things which have certain peculiarities that bring themselves within the range of the known and knowable. That which has no qualities is unknowable. For instance, there is some external world, X, unknown and unknowable. When I look at it, it is X plus mind. When I want to know the world, my mind contributes three quarters of it. The internal world is Y plus mind, and the external world X plus mind. All differentiation in either the external or internal world is created by the mind, and that which exists is unknown and unknowable. It is beyond the range of knowledge, and that which is beyond the range of knowledge can have no differentiation. Therefore this X outside is the same as the Y inside, and therefore the real is one.

God does not reason. Why should you reason if you know? It is a sign of weakness that we have to go on crawling like worms to get a few facts, and then the whole thing tumbles down again. The Spirit is reflected in mind and in everything. It is the light of the Spirit that makes the mind sentient. Everything is an expression of the Spirit; the minds are so many mirrors. What you call love, fear, hatred, virtue, and vice are all reflections of the Spirit. When the reflector is base, the reflection is bad.

The real Existence is without manifestation. We cannot conceive It, because we should have to conceive through the mind, which is itself a manifestation. Its glory is that It is inconceivable. We must remember that in life the lowest and highest vibrations of light we do not see, but they are the opposite poles of existence. There are certain things which we do not know now, but which we can know. It is due to our ignorance that we do not know them. There are certain things which we can never know, because they are much higher than the highest vibrations of knowledge. But we are the Eternal all the time, although we cannot know it. Knowledge will be impossible there. The very fact of the limitations of the conception is the basis for its existence. For instance, there is nothing so certain in me as my Self; and yet I can only conceive of it as a body and mind, as happy or unhappy, as a man or a woman. At the same time, I try to conceive of it as it really is and find that there is no other way of doing it but by dragging it down; yet I am sure of that reality. "No one, O beloved, loves the husband for the husband's sake, but because the Self is there. It is in and through the Self that she loves the husband. No one, O beloved, loves the wife for the wife's sake, but in and through the Self." And that Reality is the only thing we know, because in and through It we know everything else; and yet we cannot conceive of It. How can we know the Knower? If we knew It, It would not be the knower, but the known; It would be objectified.

The man of highest realisation exclaims, "I am the King of kings; there is no king higher than I, I am the God of gods; there is no God higher than II I alone exist, One without a second." This monistic idea of the Vedanta seems to many, of course, very terrible, but that is on account of superstition.

We are the Self, eternally at rest and at peace. We must not weep; there is no weeping for the Soul. We in our imagination think that God is weeping on His throne out of sympathy. Such a God would not be worth attaining. Why should God weep at all? To weep is a sign of weakness, of bondage.

Seek the Highest, always the Highest, for in the Highest is eternal bliss. If I am to hunt, I will hunt the lion. If I am to rob, I will rob the treasury of the king. Seek the Highest.

Oh, One that cannot be confined or described! One that can be perceived in our heart of hearts! One beyond all compare, beyond limit, unchangeable like the blue sky! Oh, learn the All, holy one I Seek for nothing else!

Where changes of nature cannot reach, thought beyond all thought, Unchangeable, Immovable; whom all books declare, all sages worship; Oh, holy one, seek for nothing else!

Beyond compare, Infinite Oneness! No comparison is possible. Water above, water below, water on the right, water on the left; no wave on that water, no ripple, all silence; all eternal bliss. Such will come to thy heart. Seek for nothing else!

Why weepest thou, brother? There is neither death nor disease for thee. Why weepest thou, brother? There is neither misery nor misfortune for thee. Why weepest thou, brother? Neither change nor death was predicated of thee. Thou art Existence Absolute.

I know what God is—I cannot speak Him to you. I know not what God is—how can I speak Him to you? But seest thou not, my brother, that thou art He, thou art; He? Why go seeking God here and there? Seek not, and that is God. Be your own Self.

Thou art Our Father, our Mother, our dear Friend. Thou bearest the burden of the world. Help us to bear the burden of our lives. Thou art our Friend, our Lover, our Husband, Thou art ourselves!

THE CAUSE OF ILLUSION

The question — what is the cause of Mâyâ (illusion)? — has been asked for the last three thousand years; and the only answer is: when the world is able to formulate a logical question, we shall answer it. The question is contradictory. Our position is that the Absolute has become this relative only apparently, that the Unconditioned has become the conditioned only in Maya. By the very admission of the Unconditioned, we admit that the Absolute cannot be acted upon by anything else. It is uncaused, which means that nothing outside Itself can act upon It. First of all, if It is unconditioned, It cannot have been acted upon by anything else. In the Unconditioned there cannot be time, space, or causation. That granted your question will be: "What caused that which cannot be caused by anything to be changed into this?" Your question is only possible in the conditioned. But you take it out of the conditioned, and want to ask it in the Unconditioned. Only when the Unconditioned becomes conditioned, and space, time, and causation come in, can the question be asked. We can only say ignorance makes the illusion. The question is impossible. Nothing can have worked on the Absolute. There was no cause. Not that we do not know, or that we are ignorant; but It is above knowledge, and cannot be brought down to the plane of knowledge. We can use the words, "I do not know" in two senses. In one way, they mean that we are lower than knowledge, and in the other way, that the thing is above knowledge. The X-rays have become known now. The very causes of these are disputed, but we are sure that we shall know them. Here we can say we do not know about the X-rays. But about the Absolute we cannot know. In the case of the X-rays we do not know, although they are within the range of knowledge; only we do not know them yet. But, in the other case, It is so much beyond knowledge that It ceases to be a matter of knowing. "By what means can the Knower be known?" You are always yourself and cannot objectify yourself. This was one of the arguments used by our philosophers to prove immortality. If I try to think I am lying dead, what have I to imagine? That I am standing and looking down at myself, at some dead body. So that I cannot objectify myself.

EVOLUTION

In the matter of the projection of Akâsha and Prâna into manifested form and the return to fine state, there is a good deal of similarity between Indian thought and modern science. The moderns have their evolution, and so have the Yogis. But I think that the Yogis' explanation of evolution is the better one. "The change of one species into another is attained by the infilling of nature." The basic idea is that we are changing from one species to another, and that man is the highest species. Patanjali explains this "infilling of nature" by the simile of peasants irrigating fields. Our education and progression simply mean taking away the obstacles, and by its own nature the divinity will manifest itself. This does away with all the struggle for existence. The miserable experiences of life are simply in the way, and can be eliminated entirely. They are not necessary for evolution. Even if they did not exist, we should progress. It is in the very nature of things to manifest themselves. The momentum is not from outside, but comes from inside. Each soul is the sum total of the universal experiences already coiled up there; and of all these experiences, only those will come out which find suitable circumstances.

So the external things can only give us the environments. These competitions and struggles and evils that we see are not the effect of the involution or the cause, but they are in the way. If they did not exist, still man would go on and evolve as God, because it is the very nature of that God to come out and manifest Himself. To my mind this seems very hopeful, instead of that horrible idea of competition. The more I study history, the more I find that idea to be wrong. Some say that if man did not fight with man, he would not progress. I also used to think so; but I find now that every war has thrown back human progress by fifty years instead of hurrying it forwards. The day will come when men will study history from a different light and find that competition is neither the cause nor the effect, simply a thing on the way, not necessary to evolution at all.

The theory of Patanjali is the only theory I think a rational man can accept. How much evil the modern system causes! Every wicked man has a licence to be wicked under it. I have seen in this country (America) physicists who say that all criminals ought to be exterminated and that that is the only way in which criminality can be eliminated from society. These environments can hinder, but they are not necessary to progress. The most horrible thing about competition is that one may conquer the environments, but that where one may conquer, thousands are crowded out. So it is evil at best. That cannot be good which helps only one and hinders the majority. Patanjali says that these struggles remain only through our ignorance, and are not necessary, and are not part of the evolution of man. It is just our impatience which creates them. We have not the patience to go and work our way out. For instance, there is a fire in a theatre, and only a few escape. The rest in trying to rush out crush one another down. That crush was not necessary for the salvation of the building nor of the two or three who escaped. If all had gone out slowly, not one would have been hurt. That is the case in life. The doors are open for us, and we can all get out without the competition and struggle; and yet we struggle. The struggle we create through our own ignorance, through impatience; we are in too great a hurry. The highest manifestation of strength is to keep ourselves calm and on our own feet.

BUDDHISM AND VEDANTA

The Vedanta philosophy is the foundation of Buddhism and everything else in India; but what we call the Advaita philosophy of the modern school has a great many conclusions of the Buddhists. Of course, the Hindus will not admit that—that is the orthodox Hindus, because to them the Buddhists are heretics. But there is a conscious attempt to stretch out the whole doctrine to include the heretics also.

The Vedanta has no quarrel with Buddhism. The idea of the Vedanta is to harmonise all. With the Northern Buddhists we have no quarrel at all. But the Burmese and Siamese and all the Southern Buddhists say that there is a phenomenal world, and ask what right we have to create a noumenal world behind this. The answer of the Vedanta is that this is a false statement. The Vedanta never contended that there was a noumenal and a phenomenal world. There is one. Seen through the senses it is phenomenal, but it is really the noumenal all the time. The man who sees the rope does not see the snake. It is either the rope or the snake, but never the two. So the Buddhistic statement of our position, that we believe there are two worlds, is entirely false. They have the right to say it is the phenomenal if they like, but no right to contend that other men have not the right to say it is the noumenal.

Buddhism does not want to have anything except phenomena. In phenomena alone is desire. It is desire that is creating all this. Modern Vedantists do not hold this at all. We say there is something which has become the will. Will is a manufactured something, a compound, not a "simple". There cannot be any will without an external object. We see that the very position that will created this universe is impossible. How could it? Have you ever known will without external stimulus? Desire cannot arise without stimulus, or in modern philosophic language, of nerve stimulus. Will is a sort of reaction of the brain, what the Sânkhya philosophers call Buddhi. This reaction must be preceded by action, and action presupposes an external universe. When there is no external universe, naturally there will be no will; and yet, according to your theory, it is will that created the universe. Who creates the will? Will is coexistent with the universe. Will is one phenomenon caused by the same impulse which created the universe. But philosophy must not stop there. Will is entirely personal; therefore we cannot go with Schopenhauer at all. Will is a compound—a mixture of the internal and the external. Suppose a man were born without any senses, he would have no will at all. Will requires something from outside, and the brain will get some energy from inside; therefore will is a compound, as much a compound as the wall or anything else. We do not agree with the will-theory of these German philosophers at all. Will itself is phenomenal and cannot be the Absolute. It is one of the many projections. There is something which is not will, but is manifesting itself as will. That I can understand. But that will is manifesting itself as everything else, I do not understand, seeing that we cannot have any conception of will, as separate from the universe. When that something which is freedom becomes will, it is caused by time, space, and causation. Take Kant's analysis. Will is within time, space, and causation. Then how can it be the Absolute? One cannot will without willing in time.

If we can stop all thought, then we know that we are beyond thought. We come to this by negation. When every phenomenon has been negatived, whatever remains, that is It. That cannot be expressed, cannot be manifested, because the manifestation will be, again, will.

ON THE VEDANTA PHILOSOPHY

The Vedantist says that a man is neither born nor dies nor goes to heaven, and that reincarnation is really a myth with regard to the soul. The example is given of a book being turned over. It is the book that evolves, not the man. Every soul is omnipresent, so where can it come or go? These births and deaths are changes in nature which we are mistaking for changes in us.

Reincarnation is the evolution of nature and the manifestation of the God within.

The Vedanta says that each life is built upon the past, and that when we can look back over the whole past we are free. The desire to be free will take the form of a religious disposition from childhood. A few years will, as it were, make all truth clear to one. After leaving this life, and while waiting for the next, a man is still in the phenomenal.

We would describe the soul in these words: This soul the sword cannot cut, nor the spear pierce; the fire cannot burn nor water melt it; indestructible, omnipresent is this soul. Therefore weep not for it.

If it has been very bad, we believe that it will become good in the time to come. The fundamental principle is that there is eternal freedom for every one. Every one must come to it. We have to struggle, impelled by our desire to be free. Every other desire but that to be free is illusive. Every good action, the Vedantist says, is a manifestation of that freedom.

I do not believe that there will come a time when all the evil in the world will vanish. How could that be? This stream goes on. Masses of water go out at one end, but masses are coming in at the other end.

The Vedanta says that you are pure and perfect, and that there is a state beyond good and evil, and that is your own nature. It is higher even than good. Good is only a lesser differentiation than evil.

We have no theory of evil. We call it ignorance.

So far as it goes, all dealing with other people, all ethics, is in the phenomenal world. As a most complete statement of truth, we would not think of applying such things as ignorance to God. Of Him we say that He is Existence, Knowledge, and Bliss Absolute. Every effort of thought and speech will make the Absolute phenomenal and break Its character.

There is one thing to be remembered: that the assertion—I am God—cannot be made with regard to the sense-world. If you say in the sense-world that you are God, what is to prevent your doing wrong? So the affirmation of your divinity applies only to the noumenal. If I am God, I am beyond the tendencies of the senses and will not do evil. Morality of course is not the goal of man, but the means through which this freedom is attained. The Vedanta says that Yoga is one way that makes men realise this divinity. The Vedanta says this is done by the realisation of the freedom within and that everything will give way to that. Morality and ethics will all range themselves in their proper places.

All the criticism against the Advaita philosophy can be summed up in this, that it does not conduce to sense-enjoyments; and we are glad to admit that.

The Vedanta system begins with tremendous pessimism, and ends with real optimism. We deny the sense-optimism but assert the real optimism of the Supersensuous. That real happiness is not in the senses but above the senses; and it is in every man. The sort of optimism which we see in the world is what will lead to ruin through the senses.

Abnegation has the greatest importance in our philosophy. Negation implies affirmation of the Real Self. The Vedanta is pessimistic so far as it negatives the world of the senses, but it is optimistic in its assertion of the real world.

The Vedanta recognises the reasoning power of man a good deal, although it says there is something higher than intellect; but the road lies through intellect.

We need reason to drive out all the old superstitions; and what remains is Vedantism. There is a beautiful Sanskrit poem in which the sage says to himself: "Why weepest thou, my friend? There is no fear nor death for thee. Why weepest thou? There is no misery for thee, for thou art like the infinite blue sky, unchangeable in thy nature. Clouds of all colours come before it, play for a moment, and pass away; it is the same sky. Thou hast only to drive away the clouds."

We have to open the gates and clear the way. The water will rush in and fill in by its own nature, because it is there already.

Man is a good deal conscious, partly unconscious, and there is a possibility of getting beyond consciousness. It is only when we become men that we can go beyond all reason. The words higher or lower can be used only in the phenomenal world. To say them of the noumenal world is simply contradictory, because there is no differentiation there. Man-manifestation is the highest in the phenomenal world. The Vedantist says he is higher than the Devas. The gods will all have to die and will become men again, and in the man-body alone they will become perfect.

It is true that we create a system, but we have to admit that it is not perfect, because the reality must be beyond all systems. We are ready to compare it with other systems and are ready to show that this is the only rational system that can be; but it is not perfect, because reason is not perfect. It is, however, the only possible rational system that the human mind can conceive.

It is true to a certain extent that a system must disseminate itself to be strong. No system has disseminated itself so much as the Vedanta. It is the personal contact that teaches even now. A mass of reading does not make men; those who were real men were made so by personal contact. It is true that there are very few of these real men, but they will increase. Yet you cannot believe that there will come a day when we shall all be philosophers. We do not believe that there will come a time when there will be all happiness and no unhappiness.

Now and then we know a moment of supreme bliss, when we ask nothing, give nothing, know nothing but bliss. Then it passes, and we again see the panorama of the universe moving before us; and we know that it is but a mosaic work set upon God, who is the background of all things.

The Vedanta teaches that Nirvâna can be attained here and now, that we do not have to wait for death to reach it. Nirvana is the realisation of the Self; and after having once known that, if only for an instant, never again can one be deluded by the mirage of personality. Having eyes, we must see the apparent, but all the time we know what it is; we have found out its true nature. It is the screen that hides the Self, which is unchanging. The screen opens, and we find the Self behind it. All change is in the screen. In the saint the screen is thin, and the reality can almost shine through. In the sinner the screen is thick, and we are liable to lose sight of the truth that the Atman is there, as well as behind the saint's screen. When the screen is wholly removed, we find it really never existed—that we were the Atman and nothing else, even the screen is forgotten.

The two phases of this distinction in life are—first, that the man who knows the real Self, will not be affected by anything; secondly, that that man alone can do good to the world. That man alone will have seen the real motive of doing good to others, because there is only one, it cannot be called egoistic, because that would be differentiation. It is the only selflessness. It is the perception of the universal, not of the individual. Every case of love and sympathy is an assertion of this universal. "Not I, but thou." Help another because you are in him and he is in you, is the philosophical way of putting it. The real Vedantist alone will give up his life for a fellow-man without any compunction, because he knows he will not die. As long as there is one insect left in the world, he is living; as long as one mouth eats, he eats. So he goes on doing good to others; and is never hindered by the modern ideas of caring for the body. When a man reaches this point of abnegation, he goes beyond the moral struggle, beyond everything. He sees in the most learned priest, in the cow, in the dog, in the most miserable places, neither the learned man, nor the cow, nor the dog, nor the miserable place, but the same divinity manifesting itself in them all. He alone is the happy man; and the man who has acquired that sameness has, even in this life, conquered all existence. God is pure; therefore such a man is said to be living in God. Jesus says, "Before Abraham was, I am." That means that Jesus and others like him are free spirits; and Jesus of Nazareth took human form, not by the compulsion of his past actions, but just to do good to mankind. It is not that when a man becomes free, he will stop and become a dead lump; but he will be more active than any other being, because every other being acts only under compulsion, he alone through freedom.

If we are inseparable from God, have we no individuality? Oh, yes: that is God. Our individuality is God. This is not the individuality you have now; you are coming towards that. Individuality means what cannot be divided. How can you call this individuality? One hour you are thinking one way, and the next hour another way, and two hours after, another way. Individuality is that which changes not—is beyond all things, changeless. It would be tremendously dangerous for this state to remain in eternity, because then the thief would always remain a thief and the blackguard a blackguard. If a baby died, he would have to remain a baby. The real individuality is that which never changes and will never change; and that is the God within us.

Vedantism is an expansive ocean on the surface of which a man-of-war could be near a catamaran. So in the Vedantic ocean a real Yogi can be by the side of an idolater or even an atheist. What is more, in the Vedantic ocean, the Hindu, Mohammedan, Christian, and Parsee are all one, all children of the Almighty God.

LAW AND FREEDOM

The struggle never had meaning for the man who is free. But for us it has a meaning, because it is name-and-form that creates the world.

We have a place for struggle in the Vedanta, but not for fear. All fears will vanish when you begin to assert your own nature. If you think that you are bound, bound you will remain. If you think you are free, free you will be.

That sort of freedom which we can feel when we are yet in the phenomenal is a glimpse of the real but not yet the real.

I disagree with the idea that freedom is obedience to the laws of nature. I do not understand what it means. According to the history of human progress, it is disobedience to nature that has constituted that progress. It may be said that the conquest of lower laws was through the higher. But even there, the conquering mind was only trying to be free; and as soon as it found that the struggle was also through law, it wanted to conquer that also. So the ideal was freedom in every case. The trees never disobey law. I never saw a cow steal. An oyster never told a lie. Yet they are not greater than man. This life is a tremendous assertion of freedom; and this obedience to law, carried far enough, would make us simply matter—either in society, or in politics, or in religion. Too many laws are a sure sign of death. Wherever in any society there are too many laws, it is a sure sign that that society will soon die. If you study the characteristics of India, you will find that no nation possesses so many laws as the Hindus, and national death is the result. But the Hindus had one peculiar idea—they never made any doctrines or dogmas in religion; and the latter has had the greatest growth. Eternal law cannot be freedom, because to say that the eternal is inside law is to limit it.

There is no purpose in view with God, because if there were some purpose, He would be nothing better than a man. Why should He need any purpose? If He had any, He would be bound by it. There would be something besides Him which was greater. For instance, the carpet-weaver makes a piece of carpet. The idea was outside of him, something greater. Now where is the idea to which God would adjust Himself? Just as the greatest emperors sometimes play with dolls, so He is playing with this nature; and what we call law is this. We call it law, because we can see only little bits which run smoothly. All our ideas of law are within the little bit. It is nonsense to say that law is infinite, that throughout all time stones will fall. If all reason be based upon experience, who was there to see if stones fell five millions of years ago? So law is not constitutional in man. It is a scientific assertion as to man that where we begin, there we end. As a matter of fact, we get gradually outside of law, until we get out altogether, but with the added experience of a whole life. In God and freedom we began, and freedom and God will be the end. These laws are in the middle state through which we have to pass. Our Vedanta is the assertion of freedom always. The very idea of law will frighten the Vedantist; and eternal law is a very dreadful thing for him, because there would be no escape. If there is to be an eternal law binding him all the time, where is the difference between him and a blade of grass? We do not believe in that abstract idea of law.

We say that it is freedom that we are to seek, and that that freedom is God. It is the same happiness as in everything else; but when man seeks it in something which is finite, he gets only a spark of it. The thief when he steals gets the same happiness as the man who finds it in God; but the thief gets only a little spark with a mass of misery. The real happiness is God. Love is God, freedom is God; and everything that is bondage is not God.

Man has freedom already, but he will have to discover it. He has it, but every moment forgets it. That discovering, consciously or unconsciously, is the whole life of every one. But the difference between the sage and the ignorant man is that one does it consciously and the other unconsciously. Every one is struggling for freedom—from the atom to the star. The ignorant man is satisfied if he can get freedom within a certain limit—if he can get rid of the bondage of hunger or of being thirsty. But that sage feels that there is a stronger bondage which has to be thrown off. He would not consider the freedom of the Red Indian as freedom at all.

According to our philosophers, freedom is the goal. Knowledge cannot be the goal, because knowledge is a compound. It is a compound of power and freedom, and it is freedom alone that is desirable. That is what men struggle after. Simply the possession of power would not be knowledge. For instance, a scientist can send an electric shock to a distance of some miles; but nature can send it to an unlimited distance. Why do we not build statues to nature then? It is not law that we want but ability to break law. We want to be outlaws. If you are bound by laws, you will be a lump of clay. Whether you are beyond law or not is not the question; but the thought that we are beyond law—upon that is based the whole history of humanity. For instance, a man lives in a forest, and never has had any education or knowledge. He sees a stone falling down—a natural phenomenon happening— and he thinks it is freedom. He thinks it has a soul, and the central idea in that is freedom. But as soon as he knows that it must fall, he calls it nature—dead, mechanical action. I may or may not go into the street. In that is my glory as a man. If I am sure that I must go there, I give myself up and become a machine. Nature with its infinite power is only a machine; freedom alone constitutes sentient life.

The Vedanta says that the idea of the man in the forest is the right one; his glimpse is right, but the explanation is wrong. He holds to this nature as freedom and not as governed by law. Only after all this human experience we will come back to think the same, but in a more philosophical sense. For instance, I want to go out into the street. I get the impulse of my will, and then I stop; and in the time that intervenes between the will and going into the street, I am working uniformly. Uniformity of action is what we call law. This uniformity of my actions, I find, is broken into very short periods, and so I do not call my actions under law. I work through freedom. I walk for five minutes; but before those five minutes of walking, which are uniform, there was the action of the will, which gave the impulse to walk. Therefore man says he is free, because all his actions can be cut up into small periods; and although there is sameness in the small periods, beyond the period there is not the same sameness. In this perception of non-uniformity is the idea of freedom. In nature we see only very large periods of uniformity; but the beginning and end must be free impulses. The impulse of freedom was given just at the beginning, and that has rolled on; but this, compared with our periods, is much longer. We find by analysis on philosophic grounds that we are not free. But there will remain this factor, this consciousness that I am free. What we have to explain is, how that comes. We will find that we have these two impulsions in us. Our reason tells us that all our actions are caused, and at the same time, with every impulse we are asserting our freedom. The solution of the Vedanta is that there is freedom inside—that the soul is really free—but that that soul's actions are percolating through body and mind, which are not free.

As soon as we react, we become slaves. A man blames me, and I immediately react in the form of anger. A little vibration which he created made me a slave. So we have to demonstrate our freedom. They alone are the sages who see in the highest, most learned man, or the lowest animal, or the worst and most wicked of mankind, neither a man nor a sage nor an animal, but the same God in all of them. Even in this life they have conquered relativity, and have taken a firm stand upon this equality. God is pure, the same to all. Therefore such a sage would be a living God. This is the goal towards which we are going; and every form of worship, every action of mankind, is a method of attaining to it. The man who wants money is striving for freedom —to get rid of the bondage of poverty. Every action of man is worship, because the idea is to attain to freedom, and all action, directly or indirectly, tends to that. Only, those actions that deter are to be avoided. The whole universe is worshipping, consciously or unconsciously; only it does not know that even while it is cursing, it is in another form worshipping the same God it is cursing, because those who are cursing are also struggling for freedom. They never think that in reacting from a thing they are making themselves slaves to it. It is hard to kick against the pricks.

If we could get rid of the belief in our limitations, it would be possible for us to do everything just now. It is only a question of time. If that is so, add power, and so diminish time. Remember the case of the professor who learnt the secret of the development of marble and who made marble in twelve years, while it took nature centuries.

THE GOAL AND METHODS OF REALISATION

The greatest misfortune to befall the world would be if all mankind were to recognise and accept but one religion, one universal form of worship, one standard of morality. This would be the death-blow to all religious and spiritual progress. Instead of trying to hasten this disastrous event by inducing persons, through good or evil methods, to conform to our own highest ideal of truth, we ought rather to endeavour to remove all obstacles which prevent men from developing in accordance with their own highest ideals, and thus make their attempt vain to establish one universal religion.

The ultimate goal of all mankind, the aim and end of all religions, is but one—re-union with God, or, what amounts to the same, with the divinity which is every man's true nature. But while the aim is one, the method of attaining may vary with the different temperaments of men.

Both the goal and the methods employed for reaching it are called Yoga, a word derived from the same Sanskrit root as the English "yoke", meaning "to join", to join us to our reality, God. There are various such Yogas, or methods of union—but the chief ones are—Karma-Yoga, Bhakti-Yoga, Râja-Yoga, and Jnâna-Yoga.

Every man must develop according to his own nature. As every science has its methods, so has every religion. The methods of attaining the end of religion are called Yoga by us, and the different forms of Yoga that we teach, are adapted to the different natures and temperaments of men. We classify them in the following way, under four heads:

(1) Karma-Yoga—The manner in which a man realises his own divinity through works and duty.

(2) Bhakti-Yoga—The realisation of the divinity through devotion to, and love of, a Personal God.

(3) Raja-Yoga—The realisation of the divinity through the control of mind.

(4) Jnana-Yoga—The realisation of a man's own divinity through knowledge.

These are all different roads leading to the same centre—God. Indeed, the varieties of religious belief are an advantage, since all faiths are good, so far as they encourage man to lead a religious life. The more sects there are, the more opportunities there are for making successful appeals to the divine instinct in all men.

WORLD-WIDE UNITY

Speaking of the world-wide unity, before the Oak Beach Christian Unity, Swami Vivekananda said: All religions are, at the bottom, alike. This is so, although the Christian Church, like the Pharisee in the parable, thanks God that it alone is right and thinks that all other religions are wrong and in need of Christian light. Christianity must become tolerant before the world will be willing to unite with the Christian Church in a common charity. God has not left Himself without a witness in any heart, and men, especially men who follow Jesus Christ, should be willing to admit this. In fact, Jesus Christ was willing to admit every good man to the family of God. It is not the man who believes a certain something, but the man who does the will of the Father in heaven, who is right. On this basis—being right and doing right—the whole world can unite.

THE AIM OF RAJA-YOGA

Yoga has essentially to do with the meditative side of religion, rather than the ethical side, though, of necessity, a little of the latter has to be considered. Men and women are growing to desire more than mere revelation, so called. They want facts in their own consciousness. Only through experience can there be any reality in religion. Spiritual facts are to be gathered mostly from the superconscious state of mind. Let us put ourselves into the same condition as did those who claim to have had special experiences; then if we have similar experiences, they become facts for us. We can see all that another has seen; a thing that happened once can happen again, nay, must, under the same circumstances. Raja-Yoga teaches us how to reach the superconscious state. All the great religions recognise this state in some form; but in India, special attention is paid to this side of religion. In the beginning, some mechanical means may help us to acquire this state; but mechanical means alone can never accomplish much. Certain positions, certain modes of breathing, help to harmonise and concentrate the mind, but with these must go purity and strong desire for God, or realisation. The attempt to sit down and fix the mind on one idea and hold it there will prove to most people that there is some need for help to enable them to do this successfully. The mind has to be gradually and systematically brought under control. The will has to be strengthened by slow, continuous, and persevering drill. This is no child's play, no fad to be tried one day and discarded the next. It is a life's work; and the end to be attained is well worth all that it can cost us to reach it; being nothing less than the realisation of our absolute oneness with the Divine. Surely, with this end in view, and with the knowledge that we can certainly succeed, no price can be too great to pay.

QUESTIONS AND ANSWERS

I — DISCUSSION AT THE GRADUATE PHILOSOPHICAL SOCIETY OF HARVARD UNIVERSITY

Q.—I should like to know something about the present activity of philosophic thought in India. To what extent are these questions discussed?

A.—As I have said, the majority of the Indian people are practically dualists, and the minority are monists. The main subject of discussion is Mâyâ and Jiva. When I came to this country, I found that the labourers were informed of the present condition of politics; but when I asked them, "What is religion, and what are the doctrines of this and that particular sect?" they said, "We do not know; we go to church." In India if I go to a peasant and ask him, "Who governs you?" he says, "I do not know; I pay my taxes." But if I ask him what is his religion, he says, "I am a dualist", and is ready to give you the details about Maya and Jiva. He cannot read or write, but he has learned all this from the monks and is very fond of discussing it. After the day's work, the peasants sit under a tree and discuss these questions.

Q.—What does orthodoxy mean with the Hindus?

A.—In modern times it simply means obeying certain caste laws as to eating, drinking, and marriage. After that the Hindu can believe in any system he likes. There was never an organised church in India; so there was never a body of men to formulate doctrines of orthodoxy. In a general way, we say that those who believe in the Vedas are orthodox; but in reality we find that many of the dualistic sects believe more in the Purânas than in the Vedas alone.

Q.—What influence had your Hindu philosophy on the Stoic philosophy of the Greeks?

A.—It is very probable that it had some influence on it through the Alexandrians. There is some suspicion of Pythagoras' being influenced by the Sânkhya thought. Anyway, we think the Sankhya philosophy is the first attempt to harmonise the philosophy of the Vedas through reason. We find Kapila mentioned even in the Vedas: "Knowledge, the first-born sage Kapila."

Q.—What is the antagonism of this thought with Western science?

A.—No antagonism at all. We are in harmony with it. Our theory of evolution and of Âkâsha and Prâna is exactly what your modern philosophies have. Your belief in evolution is among our Yogis and in the Sankhya philosophy. For instance, Patanjali speaks of one species being changed into another by the in-filling of nature—""जात्यन्तरपरिणामः प्रकृत्यापूरात्"; only he differs from you in the explanation. His explanation of this evolution is spiritual. He says that just as when a farmer wants to water his field from the canals that pass near, he has only to lift up gate — "निमित्तमप्रयोजकं प्रकृतीनां वरणभेदस्तु ततः क्षेत्रिकवत्" — so each man is the Infinite already, only these bars and bolts and different circumstances shut him in; but as soon as they are removed, he rushes out and expresses himself. In the animal, the man was held in abeyance; but as soon as good circumstances came, he was manifested as man. And again, as soon as fitting circumstances came, the God in man manifested itself. So we have very little to quarrel with in the new theories. For instance, the theory of the Sankhya as to perception is very little different from modern physiology.

Q.—But your method is different?

A.—Yes. We claim that concentrating the powers of the mind is the only way to knowledge. In external science, concentration of mind is—putting it on something external; and in internal science, it is—drawing towards one's Self. We call this concentration of mind Yoga.

Q.—In the state of concentration does the truth of these principles become evident?

A.—The Yogis claim a good deal. They claim that by concentration of the mind every truth in the universe becomes evident to the mind, both external and internal truth.

Q.—What does the Advaitist think of cosmology?

A.—The Advaitist would say that all this cosmology

and everything else are only in Maya, in the phenomenal world. In truth they do not exist. But as long as we are bound, we have to see these visions. Within these visions things come in a certain regular order. Beyond them there is no law and order, but freedom.

Q.—Is the Advaita antagonistic to dualism?

A.—The Upanishads not being in a systematised form, it was easy for philosophers to take up texts when they liked to form a system. The Upanishads had always to be taken, else there would be no basis. Yet we find all the different schools of thought in the Upanishads. Our solution is that the Advaita is not antagonistic to the Dvaita (dualism). We say the latter is only one of three steps. Religion always takes three steps. The first is dualism. Then man gets to a higher state, partial non-dualism. And at last he finds he is one with the universe. Therefore the three do not contradict but fulfil.

Q.—Why does Maya or ignorance exist?

A.—"Why" cannot be asked beyond the limit of causation. It can only be asked within Maya. We say we will answer the question when it is logically formulated. Before that we have no right to answer.

Q.—Does the Personal God belong to Maya?

A.—Yes; but the Personal God is the same Absolute seen through Maya. That Absolute under the control of nature is what is called the human soul; and that which is controlling nature is Ishvara, or the Personal God. If a man starts from here to see the sun, he will see at first a little sun; but as he proceeds he will see it bigger and bigger, until he reaches the real one. At each stage of his progress he was seeing apparently a different sun; yet we are sure it was the same sun he was seeing. So all these things are but visions of the Absolute, and as such they are true. Not one is a false vision, but we can only say they were lower stages.

Q.—What is the special process by which one will come to know the Absolute?

A.—We say there are two processes. One is the positive, and the other, the negative. The positive is that through which the whole universe is going— that of love. If this circle of love is increased indefinitely, we reach the one universal love. The other is the "Neti", "Neti"—"not this", "not this"—stopping every wave in the mind which tries to draw it out; and at last the mind dies, as it were, and the Real discloses Itself. We call that Samâdhi, or superconsciousness.

Q.—That would be, then, merging the subject in the object!

A.—Merging the object in the subject, not merging the subject in the object. Really this world dies, and I remain. I am the only one that remains.

Q.—Some of our philosophers in Germany have thought that the whole doctrine of Bhakti (Love for the Divine) in India was very likely the result of occidental influence.

A.—I do not take any stock in that—the assumption was ephemeral. The Bhakti of India is not like the Western Bhakti. The central idea of ours is that there is no thought of fear. It is always, love God. There is no worship through fear, but always through love, from beginning to end. In the second place, the assumption is quite unnecessary. Bhakti is spoken of in the oldest of the Upanishads, which is much older than the Christian Bible. The germs of Bhakti are even in the Samhitâ (the Vedic hymns). The word Bhakti is not a Western word. It was suggested by the word Shraddhâ.

Q.—What is the Indian idea of the Christian faith?

A.—That it is very good. The Vedanta will take in every one. We have a peculiar idea in India. Suppose I had a child. I should not teach him any religion; I should teach him breathings—the practice of concentrating the mind, and just one line of prayer—not prayer in your sense, but simply something like this, "I meditate on Him who is the Creator of this universe: may He enlighten my mind!" That way he would be educated, and then go about hearing different philosophers and teachers. He would select one who, he thought, would suit him best; and this man would become his Guru or teacher, and he would become a Shishya or disciple. He would say to that man, "This form of philosophy which you preach is the best; so teach me." Our fundamental idea is that your doctrine cannot be mine, or mine yours. Each one must have his own way. My daughter may have one method, and my son another, and I again another. So each one has an Ishta or chosen way, and we keep it to ourselves. It is between me and my teacher, because we do not want to create a fight. It will not help any one to tell it to others, because each one will have to find his own way. So only general philosophy and general methods can be taught universally. For instance, giving a ludicrous example, it may help me to stand on one leg. It would be ludicrous to you if I said every one must do that, but it may suit me. It is quite possible for me to be a dualist and for my wife to be a monist, and so on. One of my son may worship Christ or Buddha or Mohammed, so long as he obeys the caste laws. That is his own Ishta.

Q.—Do all Hindus believe in caste?

A.—They are forced to. They may not believe, but they have to obey.

Q.—Are these exercises in breathing and concentration universally practiced?

A.—Yes; only some practice only a little, just to satisfy the requirements of their religion. The temples in India are not like the churches here. They may all vanish tomorrow, and will not be missed. A temple is built by a man who wants to go to heaven, or to get a son, or something of that sort. So he builds a large temple and employs a few priests to hold services there. I need not go there at all, because all my worship is in the home. In every house is a special room set apart, which is called the chapel. The first duty of the child, after his initiation, is to take a bath, and then to worship; and his worship consists of this breathing and meditating and repeating of a certain name. And another thing is to hold the body straight. We believe that the mind has every power over the body to keep it healthy. After one has done this, then another comes and takes his seat, and each one does it in silence. Sometimes there are three or four in the same room, but each one may have a different method. This worship is repeated at least twice a day.

Q.—This state of oneness that you speak of, is it an ideal or something actually attained?

A.—We say it is within actuality; we say we realise that state. If it were only in talk, it would be nothing. The Vedas teach three things: this Self is first to be heard, then to be reasoned, and then to be meditated upon. When a man first hears it, he must reason on it, so that he does not believe it ignorantly, but knowingly; and after reasoning what it is, he must meditate upon it, and then realise it. And that is religion. Belief is no part of religion. We say religion is a superconscious state.

Q.—If you ever reach that state of superconsciousness, can you ever tell about it?

A.—No; but we know it by its fruits. An idiot, when he goes to sleep, comes out of sleep an idiot or even worse. But another man goes into the state of meditation, and when he comes out he is a philosopher, a sage, a great man. That shows the difference between these two states.

Q. —I should like to ask, in continuation of Professor—'s question, whether you know of any people who have made any study of the principles of self-hypnotism, which they undoubtedly practiced to a great extent in ancient India, and what has been recently stated and practiced in that thing. Of course you do not have it so much in modern India.

A.—What you call hypnotism in the West is only a part of the real thing. The Hindus call it self-hypnotisation. They say you are hypnotised already, and that you should get out of it and de-hypnotise yourself. "There the sun cannot illume, nor the moon, nor the stars; the flash of lightning cannot illume that; what to speak of this mortal fire! That shining, everything else shines" (Katha Upanishad, II ii. 15). That is not hypnotisation, but de-hypnotisation. We say that every other religion that preaches these things as real is practicing a form of hypnotism. It is the Advaitist alone that does not care to be hypnotised. His is the only system that more or less understands that hypnotism comes with every form of dualism. But the Advaitist says, throw away even the Vedas, throw away even the Personal God, throw away even the universe, throw away even your own body and mind, and let nothing remain, in order to get rid of hypnotism perfectly. "From where the mind comes back with speech, being unable to reach, knowing the Bliss of Brahman, no more is fear." That is de-hypnotisation. "I have neither vice nor virtue, nor misery nor happiness; I care neither for the Vedas nor sacrifices nor ceremonies; I am neither food nor eating nor eater, for I am Existence Absolute, Knowledge Absolute, Bliss Absolute; I am He, I am He." We know all about hypnotism. We have a psychology which the West is just beginning to know, but not yet adequately, I am sorry to say.

Q.—What do you call the astral body?

A.—The astral body is what we call the Linga Sharira. When this body dies, how can it come to take another body? Force cannot remain without matter. So a little part of the fine matter remains, through which the internal organs make another body—for each one is making his own body; it is the mind that makes the body. If I become a sage, my brain gets changed into a sage's brain; and the Yogis say that even in this life a Yogi can change his body into a god-body.

The Yogis show many wonderful things. One ounce of practice is worth a thousand pounds of theory. So I have no right to say that because I have not seen this or that thing done, it is false. Their books say that with practice you can get all sorts of results that are most wonderful. Small results can be obtained in a short time by regular practice, so that one may know that there is no humbug about it, no charlatanism. And these Yogis explain the very wonderful things mentioned in all scriptures in a scientific way. The question is, how these records of miracles entered into every nation. The man, who says that they are all false and need no explanation, is not rational. You have no right to deny them until you can prove them false. You must prove that they are without any foundation, and only then have you the right to stand up and deny them. But you have not done that. On the other hand, the Yogis say they are not miracles, and they claim that they can do them even today. Many wonderful things are done in India today. But none of them are done by miracles. There are many books on the subject. Again, if nothing else has been done in that line except a scientific approach towards psychology, that credit must be given to the Yogis.

Q.—Can you say in the concrete what the manifestations are which the Yogi can show?

A.—The Yogi wants no faith or belief in his science but that which is given to any other science, just enough gentlemanly faith to come and make the experiment. The ideal of the Yogi is tremendous. I have seen the lower things that can be done by the power of the mind, and therefore, I have no right to disbelieve that the highest things can be done. The ideal of the Yogi is eternal peace and love through omniscience and omnipotence. I know a Yogi who was bitten by a cobra, and who fell down on the ground. In the evening he revived again, and when asked what happened, he said: "A messenger came from my Beloved." All hatred and anger and jealousy have been burnt out of this man. Nothing can make him react; he is infinite love all the time, and he is omnipotent in his power of love. That is the real Yogi. And this manifesting different things is accidental on the way. That is not what he wants to attain. The Yogi says, every man is a slave except the Yogi. He is a slave of food, to air, to his wife, to his children, to a dollar, slave to a nation, slave to name and fame, and to a thousand things in this world. The man who is not controlled by any one of these bandages is alone a real man, a real Yogi. "They have conquered relative existence in this life who are firm-fixed in sameness. God is pure and the same to all. Therefore such are said to be living in God" (Gita, V. 19).

Q.—Do the Yogis attach any importance to caste?

A.—No; caste is only the training school for undeveloped minds.

Q.—Is there no connection between this idea of super. consciousness and the heat of India?

A.—I do not think so; because all this philosophy was thought out fifteen thousand feet above the level of the sea, among the Himalayas, in an almost Arctic temperature.

Q.—Is it practicable to attain success in a cold climate?

A.—It is practicable, and the only thing that is practicable in this world. We say you are a born Vedantist, each one of you. You are declaring your oneness with everything each moment you live. Every time that your heart goes out towards the world, you are a true Vedantist, only you do not know it. You are moral without knowing why; and the Vedanta is the philosophy which analysed and taught man to be moral consciously. It is the essence of all religions.

Q.—Should you say that there is an unsocial principle in our Western people, which makes us so pluralistic, and that Eastern people are more sympathetic than we are?

A.—I think the Western people are more cruel, and the Eastern people have more mercy towards all beings. But that is simply because your civilisation is very much more recent. It takes time to make a thing come under the influence of mercy. You have a great deal of power, and the power of control of the mind has especially been very little practiced. It will take time to make you gentle and good. This feeling tingles in every drop of blood in India. If I go to the villages to teach the people politics, they will not understand; but if I go to teach them Vedanta, they will say, "Now, Swami, you are all right". That Vairâgya, non-attachment, is everywhere in India, even today. We are very much degenerated now; but kings will give up their thrones and go about the country without anything.

In some places the common village-girl with her spinning-wheel says, "Do not talk to me of dualism; my spinning-wheel says 'Soham, Soham'—'I am He, I am He.'" Go and talk to these people, and ask them why it is that they speak so and yet kneel before that stone. They will say that with you religion means dogma, but with them realisation. "I will be a Vedantist", one of them will say, "only when all this has vanished, and I have seen the reality. Until then there is no difference between me and the ignorant. So I am using these stones and am going to temples, and so on, to come to realisation. I have heard, but I want to see and realise." "Different methods of speech, different manners of explaining the meaning of the scriptures—these are only for the enjoyment of the learned, not for freedom" (Shankara). It is realisation which leads us to that freedom.

Q.—Is this spiritual freedom among the people consistent with attention to caste?

A.—Certainly not. They say there should be no caste. Even those who are in caste say it is not a very perfect institution. But they say, when you find us another and a better one, we will give it up. They say, what will you give us instead? Where is there no caste? In your nation you are struggling all the time to make a caste. As soon as a man gets a bag of dollars, he says, "I am one of the Four Hundred." We alone have succeeded in making a permanent caste. Other nations are struggling and do not succeed. We have superstitions and evils enough. Would taking the superstitions and evils from your country mend matters? It is owing to caste that three hundred millions of people can find a piece of bread to eat yet. It is an imperfect institution, no doubt. But if it had not been for caste, you would have had no Sanskrit books to study. This caste made walls, around which all sorts of invasions rolled and surged, but found it impossible to break through. That necessity has not gone yet; so caste remains. The caste we have now is not that of seven hundred years ago. Every blow has riveted it. Do you realise that India is the only country that never went outside of itself to conquer? The great emperor Asoka insisted that none of his descendants should go to conquer. If people want to send us teachers, let them help, but not injure. Why should all these people come to conquer the Hindus? Did they do any injury to any nation? What little good they could do, they did for the world. They taught it science, philosophy, religion, and civilised the savage hordes of the earth. And this is the return—only murder and tyranny, and calling them heathen rascals. Look at the books written on India by Western people and at the stories of many travellers who go there; in retaliation for what injuries are these hurled at them?

Q.—What is the Vedantic idea of civilisation?

A.—You are philosophers, and you do not think that a bag of gold makes the difference between man and man. What is the value of all these machines and sciences? They have only one result: they spread knowledge. You have not solved the problem of want, but only made it keener. Machines do not solve the poverty question; they simply make men struggle the more. Competition gets keener. What value has nature in itself? Why do you go and build a monument to a man who sends electricity through a wire? Does not nature do that millions of times over? Is not everything already existing in nature? What is the value of your getting it? It is already there. The only value is that it makes this development. This universe is simply a gymnasium in which the soul is taking exercise; and after these exercises we become gods. So the value of everything is to be decided by how far it is a manifestation of God. Civilisation is the manifestation of that divinity in man.

Q.—Have the Buddhists any caste laws?

A.—The Buddhists never had much caste, and there are very few Buddhists in India. Buddha was a social reformer. Yet in Buddhistic countries I find that there have been strong attempts to manufacture caste, only they have failed. The Buddhists' caste is practically nothing, but they take pride in it in their own minds.

Buddha was one of the Sannyâsins of the Vedanta. He started a new sect, just as others are started even today. The ideas which now are called Buddhism were not his. They were much more ancient. He was a great man who gave the ideas power. The unique element in Buddhism was its social element. Brahmins and Kshatriyas have always been our teachers, and most of the Upanishads were written by Kshatriyas, while the ritualistic portions of the Vedas came from the Brahmins. Most of our great teachers throughout India have been Kshatriyas, and were always universal in their teachings; whilst the Brahmana prophets with two exceptions were very exclusive. Râma, Krishna, and Buddha—worshipped as Incarnations of God—were Kshatriyas.

Q.—Are sects, ceremonies, and scriptures helps to realisation?

A.—When a man realises, he gives up everything. The various sects and ceremonies and books, so far as they are the means of arriving at that point, are all right. But when they fail in that, we must change them. "The knowing one must not despise the condition of those who are ignorant, nor should the knowing one destroy the faith; of the ignorant in their own particular method, but by proper action lead them and show them the path to comes to where he stands" (Gita, III. 26).

Q.—How does the Vedanta explain individuality and ethics?

A.—The real individual is the Absolute; this personalisation is through Maya. It is only apparent; in reality it is always the Absolute. In reality there is one, but ins Maya it is appearing as many. In Maya there is this variation. Yet even in this Maya there is always the tendency to, get back to the One, as expressed in all ethics and all morality of every nation, because it is the constitutional necessity of the soul. It is finding its oneness; and this struggle to find this oneness is what we call ethics and morality. Therefore we must always practice them.

Q.—Is not the greater part of ethics taken up with the relation between individuals?

A.—That is all it is. The Absolute does not come within Maya.

Q.—You say the individual is the Absolute, and I was going to ask you whether the individual has knowledge.

A.—The state of manifestation is individuality, and the light in that state is what we call knowledge. To use, therefore, this term knowledge for the light of the Absolute is not precise, as the absolute state transcends relative knowledge.

Q.—Does it include it?

A.—Yes, in this sense. Just as a piece of gold can be changed into all sorts of coins, so with this. The state can be broken up into all sorts of knowledge. It is the state of superconsciousness, and includes both consciousness and unconsciousnes. The man who attains that state has all that we call knowledge. When he wants to realise that consciousness of knowledge, he has to go a step lower. Knowledge is a lower state; it is only in Maya that we can have knowledge.

II — AT THE TWENTIETH CENTURY CLUB OF BOSTON

Q.—Did Vedanta exert any influence over Mohammedanism?

A.—This Vedantic spirit of religious liberality has very much affected Mohammedanism. Mohammedanism in India is quite a different thing from that in any other country. It is only when Mohammedans come from other countries and preach to their co-religionists in India about living with men who are not of their faith that a Mohammedan mob is aroused and fights.

Q.—Does Vedanta recognise caste?

A.—The caste system is opposed to the religion of the Vedanta. Caste is a social custom, and all our great preachers have tried to break it down. From Buddhism downwards, every sect has preached against caste, and every time it has only riveted the chains. Caste is simply the outgrowth of the political institutions of India; it is a hereditary trade guild. Trade competition with Europe has broken caste more than any teaching.

Q.—What is the peculiarity of the Vedas?

A.—One peculiarity of the Vedas is that they are the only scriptures that again and again declare that you must go beyond them. The Vedas say that they were written just for the child mind; and when you have grown, you must go beyond them.

Q.—Do you hold the individual soul to be eternally real?

A.—The individual soul consists of a man's thoughts, and they are changing every moment. Therefore, it cannot be eternally real. It is real only in the phenomenal. The individual consists of memory and thought, how can that be real?

Q.—Why did Buddhism as a religion decline in India?

A.—Buddhism did not really decline in India; it was only a gigantic social movement. Before Buddha great numbers of animals were killed for sacrifice and other reasons, and people drank wine and ate meat in large quantities. Since Buddha's teaching drunkenness has almost disappeared, and the killing of animals has almost gone.

III — AT THE BROOKLYN ETHICAL SOCIETY, BROOKLYN

Q.—How can you reconcile your optimistic views with the existence of evil, with the universal prevalence of sorrow and pain?

A. —I can only answer the question if the existence of evil be first proved; but this the Vedantic religion does not admit. Eternal pain unmixed with pleasure would be a positive evil; but temporal pain and sorrow, if they have contributed an element of tenderness and nobility tending towards eternal bliss, are not evils: on the contrary, they may be supreme good. We cannot assert that anything is evil until we have traced its sequence into the realm of eternity.

Devil worship is not a part of the Hindu religion. The human race is in process of development; all have not reached the same altitude. Therefore some are nobler and purer in their earthly lives than others. Every one has an opportunity within the limits of the sphere of his present development of making himself better. We cannot unmake ourselves; we cannot destroy or impair the vital force within us, but we have the freedom to give it different directions.

Q.—Is not the reality of cosmic matter simply the imagining of our own minds?

A.—In my opinion the external world is certainly an entity and has an existence outside of our mental conceptions. All creation is moving onwards and upwards, obedient to the great law of spirit evolution, which is different from the evolution of matter. The latter is symbolical of, but does not explain, the process of the former. We are not individuals now, in our present earthly environment. We shall not have reached individuality until we shall have ascended to the higher state, when the divine spirit within us will have a perfect medium for the expression of its attributes.

Q.—What is your explanation of the problem presented to Christ, as to whether it was the infant itself or its parents that had sinned, that it was born blind?

A.—While the question of sin does not enter into the problem, I am convinced that the blindness was due to some act on the part of the spirit of the child in a previous incarnation. In my opinion such problems are only explicable on the hypothesis of a prior earthly existence.

Q.—Do our spirits pass at death into a state of happiness?

A.—Death is only a change of condition: time and space are in you, you are not in time and space. It is enough to know that as we make our lives purer and nobler, either in the seen or the unseen world, the nearer we approach God, who is the centre of all spiritual beauty and eternal joy.

Q.—What is the Hindu theory of the transmigration of souls?

A.—It is on the same basis as the theory of conservation is to the scientist. This theory was first produced by a philosopher of my country. The ancient sages did not believe in a creation. A creation implies producing something out of nothing. That is impossible. There was no beginning of creation as there was no beginning of time. God and creation are as two lines without end, without beginning, and parallel. Our theory of creation is "It is, it was, and is to be". All punishment is but reaction. People of the West should learn one thing from India and that is toleration. All the religions are good, since the essentials are the same.

Q.—Why are the women of India not much elevated?

A.—It is in a great degree owing to the barbarous invaders through different ages; it is partly due to the people of India themselves.

When it was pointed out to Swamiji in America that Hinduism is not a proselytising religion, he replied:

"I have a message to the West as Buddha had a message to the East."

Q.—Do you intend to introduce the practices and rituals of the Hindu religion into this country (America)?

A.—I am preaching simply philosophy.

Q.—Do you not think if the fear of future hell-fire were taken from man there would be no controlling him?

A.—No! On the contrary, I think he is made far better through love and hope than through fear.

IV — SELECTIONS FROM THE MATH DIARY

Q.—Whom can we call a Guru?

A.—He who can tell your past and future is your Guru.

Q.—How can one have Bhakti?

A.—There is Bhakti within you, only a veil of lust-and-wealth covers it, and as soon as that is removed Bhakti will manifest by itself.

Q.—What is the true meaning of the assertion that we should depend on ourselves?

A.—Here self means the eternal Self. But even dependence on the non-eternal self may lead gradually to the right goal, as the individual self is really the eternal Self under delusion.

Q.—If unity is the only reality, how could duality which is perceived by all every moment have arisen?

A.—Perception is never dual; it is only the representation of perception that involves duality. If perception were dual, the known could have existed independently of the knower, and vice versa.

Q.—How is harmonious development of character to be best effected?

A.—By association with persons whose character has been so developed.

Q.—What should be our attitude to the Vedas?

A.—The Vedas, i.e. only those portions of them which agree with reason, are to be accepted as authority. Other Shâstras, such as the Purânas etc., are only to be accepted so far as they do not go against the Vedas. All the religious thoughts that have come subsequent to the Vedas, in the world, in whatever part of it have been derived from the Vedas.

Q.—Is the division of time into four Yugas astronomical or arbitrary calculation?

A.—There is no mention of such divisions in the Vedas. They are arbitrary assumptions of Paurânika times.

Q.—Is the relation between concepts and words necessary and immutable, or accidental and conventional?

A.—The point is exceedingly debatable. It seems that there is a necessary relation, but not absolutely so, as appears from the diversity of language. There may be some subtle relation which we are not yet able to detect.

Q.—What should be the principle to be followed in working within India?

A.— First of all, men should be taught to be practical and physically strong. A dozen of such lions will conquer the world, and not millions of sheep can do so. Secondly, men should not be taught to imitate a personal ideal, however great.

Then Swamiji went on to speak of the corruptions of some of the Hindu symbols. He distinguished between the path of knowledge and the path of devotion. The former belonged properly to the Aryas, and therefore was so strict in the selection of Adhikâris (qualified aspirants), and the latter coming from the South, or non-Aryan sources, made no such distinction.

Q.—What part will the Ramakrishna Mission take in the regenerating work of India?

A.—From this Math will go out men of character who will deluge the world with spirituality. This will be followed by revivals in other lines. Thus Brahmins, Kshatriyas, and Vaishyas will be produced. The Shudra caste will exist no longer—their work being done by machinery. The present want of India is the Kshatriya force.

Q.—Is retrograde reincarnation from the human stage possible?

A.—Yes. Reincarnation depends on Karma. If a man accumulates Karma akin to the beastly nature, he will be drawn thereto.

In one of the question-classes (1898) Swamiji traced image-worship to Buddhistic sources. First, there was the Chaitya; second, the Stupa ; and then came the temple of Buddha. Along with it arose the temples of the Hindu deities.

Q.—Does the Kundalini really exist in the physical body?

A.—Shri Ramakrishna used to say that the so celled lotuses of the Yogi do not really exist in the human body, but that they are created within oneself by Yoga powers.

Q.—Can a man attain Mukti by image-worship?

A.—Image-worship cannot directly give Mukti; it may be an indirect cause, a help on the way. Image-worship should not be condemned, for, with many, it prepares the mind for the realisation of the Advaita which alone makes man perfect.

Q.—What should be our highest ideal of character?

A.—Renunciation.

Q.—How did Buddhism leave the legacy of corruption in India?

A.—The Bauddhas tried to make everyone in India a monk or a nun. We cannot expect that from every one. This led to gradual relaxation among monks and nuns. It was also caused by their imitating Tibetan and other barbarous customs in the name of religion. They went, to preach in those places and assimilated their corruptions, and then introduced them into India.

Q.—Is Mâyâ without beginning and end?

A.—Maya is eternal both ways, taken universally, ask genus; but it is non-eternal individually.

Q.—Brahman and Maya cannot be cognised simultaneously. How could the absolute reality of either be proved as arising out of the one or the other?

A.—It could be proved only by realisation. When one realises Brahman, for him Maya exists no longer, just as once the identity of the rope is found out, the illusion of the serpent comes no more.

Q.—What is Maya?

A.—There is only one thing, call it by any name—matter, or spirit. It is difficult or rather impossible to think the one independent of the other. This is Maya, or ignorance.

Q.—What is Mukti (liberation)?

A.—Mukti means entire freedom—freedom from the bondages of good and evil. A golden chain is as much a chain as an iron one. Shri Ramakrishna used to say that, to pick out one thorn which has stuck into the foot, another thorn is requisitioned, and when the thorn is taken out, both are thrown away. So the bad tendencies are to be counteracted by the good ones, but after that, the good tendencies have also to be conquered.

Q.—Can salvation (Mukti) be obtained without the grace of God?

A.—Salvation has nothing to do with God. Freedom already is.

Q.—What is the proof of the self in us not being the product of the body etc.?

A.—The "ego" like its correlative "non-ego", is the product of the body, mind etc. The only proof of the existence of the real Self is realisation.

Q.—Who is a true Jnâni, and who is a true Bhakta?

A.—The true Jnani is he who has the deepest love within his heart and at the same time is a practical seer of Advaita in his outward relations. And the true Bhakta (lover) is he who, realising his own soul as identified with the universal Soul, and thus possessed of the true Jnana within, feels for and loves everyone. Of Jnana and Bhakti he who advocates one and denounces the other cannot be either a Jnani or a Bhakta, but he is a thief and a cheat.

Q.—Why should a man serve Ishvara?

A.—If you once admit that there is such a thing as Ishvara (God), you have numberless occasions to serve Him. Service of the Lord means, according to all the scriptural authorities, remembrance (Smarana). If you believe in the existence of God, you will be reminded of Him at every step of your life.

Q.—Is Mâyâvâda different from Advaitâvada?

A.—No. They are identical. There is absolutely no other explanation of Advaitavada except Mayavada.

Q.—How is it possible for God who is infinite to be limited in the form of a man (as an Avatâra)?

A.—It is true that God is infinite, but not in the sense in which you comprehend it. You have confounded your idea of infinity with the materialistic idea of vastness. When you say that God cannot take the form of a man, you understand that a very, very large substance or form (as if material in nature), cannot be compressed into a very, very small compass. God's infinitude refers to the unlimitedness of a purely spiritual entity, and as such, does not suffer in the least by expressing itself in a human form.

Q.—Some say, "First of all become a Siddha (one who has realised the Truth), and then you have the right to Karma, or work for others", while others say that one should work for others even from the beginning. How can both these views be reconciled?

A.—You are confusing one thing with the other. Karma means either service to humanity or preaching. To real preaching, no doubt, none has the right except the Siddha Purusha, i.e. one who has realised the Truth. But to service every one has the right, and not only so, but every one is under obligation to serve others, so long as he is accepting service from others.

V — YOGA, VAIRAGYA, TAPASYA, LOVE

Q. — Does Yoga serve to keep the body in its full health and vitality?

A. — It does. It staves off disease. As objectification of one's own body is difficult, it is very effective in regard to others. Fruit and milk are the best food for Yogis.

Q. — Is the attainment of bliss synchronous with that of Vairagya?

A. — The first step in Vairagya is very painful. When perfected, it yields supreme bliss.

Q. — What is Tapasyâ?

A. — Tapasya is threefold — of the body, of speech and of mind. The first is service of others; the second truthfulness; and third, control and concentration.

Q. — Why do we not see that the same consciousness pervades the ant as well as the perfected sage?

A. — Realising the unity of this manifestation is a question of time only.

Q. — Is preaching possible without gaining perfection?

A. — No. May the Lord grant that all the Sannyasin disciples of my Master and of myself be perfected, so that they may be fit for missionary work!

Q. — Is the divine majesty expressed in the Universal Form of Shri Krishna in the Gita superior to the expression of love unattended with other attributes, embodied in the form of Shri Krishna, for instance, in His relation with the Gopis?

A. — The feeling of love, unattended with the idea of divinity, in respect to the person loved, is assuredly inferior to the expression of divine majesty. If it were not so, all lovers of the flesh would have obtained freedom.

VI — IN ANSWER TO NIVEDITA

Q.—I cannot remember what parts Prithvi Rai and Chând disguised themselves to play, when they determined to attend the Svayamvara at Kanauj.

A.—Both went as minstrels.

Q.—Also did Prithvi Rai determine to marry Samyuktâ partly because she was the daughter of his rival and partly for the fame of her great beauty? Did he then send a woman-servant to obtain the post of her maid? And did this old nurse set herself to make the princess fall in love with Prithvi Rai?

A.—They had fallen in love with each other, hearing deeds and beauty and seeing portraits. Falling in love through portraits is an old Indian game.

Q.—How did Krishna come to be brought up amongst the shepherds?

A.—His father had to flee with the baby to save it from the tyrant Kamsa, who ordered all the babes (male) from that year to be killed, as (through prophecy) he was afraid one of them would be Krishna and dethrone him. He kept Krishna's father and mother in prison (who were his cousins) for fear of that prophecy.

Q.—How did this part of his life terminate?

A.—He came with his brother Baladeva and Nanda, his foster-father, invited by the tyrant to a festival. (The tyrant had plotted his destruction.) He killed the tyrant and instead of taking the throne placed the nearest heir on it. Himself he never took any fruit of action.

Q.—Can you give me any dramatic incident of this period?

A.—This period is full of miracles. He as a baby was once naughty and the cowherd-mother tried to tie him with her churning string and found she could not bind him with all the strings she had. Then her eyes opened and she saw that she was going to bind him who had the whole universe in his body. She began to pray and tremble. Immediately the Lord touched her with his Maya and she saw only the child.

Brahmâ, the chief of gods, disbelieving that the Lord had become a cowherd, stole one day all the cows and cowherd boys and put them to sleep in a cave. When he came back, he found the same boys and cows round Krishna. Again he stole the new lot and hid them away. He came back and saw there the same again. Then his eyes opened and began to see numerous worlds and heavens and Brahmans by the thousands, one greater than the preceding, in the body of the Lord.

He danced on the serpent Kâliya who had been poisoning the water of the Yamunâ, and he held up the mount Govardhana in defiance of Indra whose worship he had forbidden and who in revenge wanted to kill all the people of Vraja by deluge of rain. They were all sheltered by Krishna under the hill Govardhana which he upheld with a finger on their head.

He from his childhood was against snake-worship and Indra-worship. Indra-worship is a Vedic ritual. Throughout the Gita he is not favourable to Vedic ritual.

This is the period of his love to Gopis. He was eleven years of age.

VII — GURU, AVATARA, YOGA, JAPA, SEVA

Q.—How can Vedanta be realised?

A.—By "hearing, reflection, and meditation". Hearing must take place from a Sad-guru. Even if one is not a regular disciple, but is a fit aspirant and hears the Sad-guru's words, he is liberated.

Q.—Who is a Sad-guru?

A.—A Sad-guru is one on whom the spiritual power has descended by Guru-paramparâ, or an unbroken chain of discipleship.

To play the role of a spiritual teacher is a very difficult thing. One has to take on oneself the sins of others. There is every chance of a fall in less advanced men. If merely physical pain ensues, then he should consider himself fortunate.

Q.—Cannot the spiritual teacher make the aspirant fit?

A.—An Avatâra can. Not an ordinary Guru.

Q.—Is there no easy way to liberation?

A.—"There is no royal road to Geometry"—except for those who have been fortunate enough to come in contact with an Avatara. Paramahamsa Deva used to say, "One who is having his last birth shall somehow or other see me."

Q.—Is not Yoga an easy path to that?

A.—(Jokingly) You have said well, I see!—Yoga an easy path! If your mind be not pure and you try to follow Yoga, you will perhaps attain some supernatural power, but that will be a hindrance. Therefore purity of mind is the first thing necessary.

Q.—How can this be attained?

A.—By good work. Good work is of two kinds, positive and negative. "Do not steal"—that is a negative mandate, and "Do good to others"—is a positive one.

Q.—Should not doing good to others be performed in a higher stage, for if performed in a lower stage, it may bind one to the world?

A.—It should be performed in the first stage. One who has any desire at first gets deluded and becomes bound, but not others. Gradually it will become very natural.

Q.—Sir, last night you said, "In you is everything." Now, if I want to be like Vishnu, shall I have to meditate on the form also, or only on the idea?

A.—According to capacity one may follow either way.

Q.—What is the means of realisation?

A.—The Guru is the means of realisation. "There is no knowledge without a teacher."

Q.—Some say that there is no necessity of practicing meditation in a worship-room. How far is it true?

A.—Those who have already realised the Lord's

presence may not require it, but for others it is necessary. One, however, should go beyond the form and meditate on the impersonal aspect of God, for no form can grant liberation. You may get worldly prosperity from the sight of the form. One who ministers to his mother succeeds in this world; one who worships his father goes to heaven; but the worshipper of a Sâdhu (holy man) gets knowledge and devotion.

Q.—What is the meaning of "कृषणामहि सज्जनसंगतिरिका"—"Even a moment's association with the holy ones serves to take one beyond this relative existence"?

A.—A fit person coming in contact with a true Sadhu attains to liberation. True Sadhus are very rare, but their influence is such that a great writer has said, "Hypocrisy is the tribute which vice pays to virtue." But Avataras are Kapâlamochanas, that is, they can alter the doom of people. They can stir the whole world. The least dangerous and best form of worship is worshipping man. One who has got the idea of Brahman in a man has realised it in the whole universe. Monasticism and the householder's life are both good, according to different circumstances. Knowledge is the only thing necessary.

Q.—Where should one meditate—inside the body or outside it? Should the mind be withdrawn inside or held outside?

A.—We should try to meditate inside. As for the mind being here or there, it will take a long time before we reach the mental plane. Now our struggle is with the body. When one acquires a perfect steadiness in posture, then and then alone one begins to struggle with the mind. Âsana (posture) being conquered, one's limbs remain motionless, and one can sit as long as one pleases.

Q.—Sometimes one gets tired of Japa (repetition of the Mantra). Should one continue it or read some good book instead?

A. —One gets tired of Japa for two reasons. Sometimes one's brain is fatigued, sometimes it is the result of idleness. If the former, then one should give up Japa for the time being, for persistence in it at the time results in seeing hallucinations, or in lunacy etc. But if the latter, the mind should be forced to continue Japa.

Q.—Sometimes sitting at Japa one gets joy at first, but then one seems to be disinclined to continue the Japa owing to that joy. Should it be continued then?

A.—Yes, that joy is a hindrance to spiritual practice, its name being Rasâsvâdana (tasting of the sweetness). One must rise above that.

Q.—Is it good to practice Japa for a long time, though the mind may be wandering?

A.—Yes. As some people break a wild horse by always keeping his seat on his back.

Q.—You have written in your Bhakti-Yoga that if a weak-bodied man tries to practice Yoga, a tremendous reaction comes. Then what to do?

A.—What fear if you die in the attempt to realise the Self! Man is not afraid of dying for the sake of learning and many other things, and why should you fear to die for religion?

Q.—Can Jiva-sevâ (service to beings) alone give Mukti?

A.—Jiva-seva can give Mukti not directly but indirectly, through the purification of the mind. But if you wish to do a thing properly, you must, for the time being, think that that is all-sufficient. The danger in any sect is want of zeal. There must be constancy (Nishthâ), or there will be no growth. At present it has become necessary to lay stress on Karma.

Q.—What should be our motive in work—compassion, or any other motive?

A.—Doing good to others out of compassion is good, but the Seva (service) of all beings in the spirit of the Lord is better.

Q.—What is the efficacy of prayer?

A.—By prayer one's subtle powers are easily roused, and if consciously done, all desires may be fulfilled by it; but done unconsciously, one perhaps in ten is fulfilled. Such prayer, however, is selfish and should therefore be discarded.

Q.—How to recognise God when He has assumed

a human form?

A.—One who can alter the doom of people is the Lord. No Sadhu, however advanced, can claim this unique position. I do not see anyone who realises Ramakrishna as God. We sometimes feel it hazily, that is all. To realise Him as God and yet be attached to the world is inconsistent.

CONVERSATIONS AND DIALOGUES

The Conversations and Dialogues are translated from the contributions of disciples to the Udbodhan, the Bengali organ of the Ramakrishna Math and Mission.

I — SHRI SURENDRA NATH DAS GUPTA

I — Think of Death Always and New Life Will Come within—Work for Others—God the Last Refuge

Shri Suredra Nath Das Gupta

One day, with some of my young friends belonging to different colleges, I went to the Belur Math to see Swamiji. We sat round him; talks on various subjects were going on. No sooner was any question put to him than he gave the most conclusive answer to it. Suddenly he exclaimed, pointing to us, "You are all studying different schools of European philosophy and metaphysics and learning new facts about nationalities and countries; can you tell me what is the grandest of all the truths in life?"

We began to think, but could not make out what he wanted us to say. As none put forth any reply, he exclaimed in his inspiring language:

"Look here—we shall all die! Bear this in mind always, and then the spirit within will wake up. Then only, meanness will vanish from you, practicality in work will come, you will get new vigour in mind and body, and those who come in contact with you will also feel that they have really got something uplifting from you."

Then the following conversation took place between him and myself:

Myself: But, Swamiji, will not the spirit break down at the thought of death and the heart be overpowered by despondency?

Swamiji: Quite so. At first, the heart will break down, and despondency and gloomy thoughts will occupy your mind. But persist; let days pass like that —and then? Then you will see that new strength has come into the heart, that the constant thought of death is giving you a new life and is making you more and more thoughtful by bringing every moment before your mind's eye the truth of the saying, "Vanity of vanities, all is vanity!" Wait! Let days, months, and years pass, and you will feel that the spirit within is waking up with the strength of a lion, that the little power within has transformed itself into a mighty power! Think of death always, and you will realise the truth of every word I say. What more shall I say in words!

One of my friends praised Swamiji in a low voice.

Swamiji: Do not praise me. Praise and censure have no value in this world of ours. They only rock a man as if in a swing. Praise I have had enough of; showers of censure I have also had to bear; but what avails thinking of them! Let everyone go on doing his own duty unconcerned. When the last moment arrives, praise and blame will be the same to you, to me, and to others. We are here to work, and will have to leave all when the call comes

Myself: How little we are, Swamiji!

Swamiji: True! You have well said! Think of this infinite universe with its millions and millions of solar systems, and think with what an infinite, incomprehensible power they are impelled, running as if to touch the Feet of the One Unknown—and how little we are! Where then is room here to allow ourselves to indulge in vileness and mean-mindedness? What should we gain here by fostering mutual enmity and party-spirit? Take my advice: Set yourselves wholly to the service of others, when you come from your colleges. Believe me, far greater happiness would then be yours than if you had had a whole treasury full of money and other valuables at your command. As you go on your way, serving others, you will advance accordingly in the path of knowledge.

Myself: But we are so very poor, Swamiji!

Swamiji: Leave aside your thoughts of poverty! In what respect are you poor? Do you feel regret because you have not a coach and pair or a retinue of servants at your beck and call? What of that? You little know how nothing would be impossible for you in life if you labour day and night for others with your heart's blood! And lo and behold! the other side of the hallowed river of life stands revealed before your eyes—the screen of Death has vanished, and you are the inheritors of the wondrous realm of immortality!

Myself: Oh, how we enjoy sitting before you, Swamiji, and hearing your life-giving words!

Swamiji: You see, in my travels throughout India all these years, I have come across many a great soul, many a heart overflowing with loving kindness, sitting at whose feet I used to feel a mighty current of strength coursing into my heart, and the few words I speak to you are only through the force of that current gained by coming in contact with them! Do not think I am myself something great!

Myself: But we look upon you, Swamiji, as one who has realised God!

No sooner did I say these words than those fascinating eyes of his were filled with tears (Oh, how vividly I, see that scene before my eyes even now), and he with a heart overflowing with love, softly and gently spoke: "At those Blessed Feet is the perfection of Knowledge, sought by the Jnanis! At those Blessed Feet also is the fulfilment of Love sought by the Lovers! Oh, say, where else will men and women go for refuge but to those Blessed Feet!"

After a while he again said, "Alas! what folly for men in this world to spend their days fighting and quarrelling with one another as they do! But how long can they go in that way? In the evening of life[1] they must all come home, to the arms of the Mother."

II — V SHRI SURENDRA NATH SEN

II — The Loss of Shraddha in India and Need of Its Revival—Men We Want—Real Social Reform

Shri Surendra Nath Sen —from private dairy

Saturday, the 22nd January, 1898.

Early in the morning I came to Swamiji who was then staying in the house of Balaram Babu at 57 Ramkanta Bose Street, Calcutta. The room was packed full

---
1. At the end of one's whole course of transmigratory existence.

with listeners. Swamiji was saying, "We want Shraddhâ, we want faith in our own selves. Strength is life, weakness is death. 'We are the Âtman, deathless and free; pure, pure by nature. Can we ever commit any sin? Impossible!'—such a faith is needed. Such a faith makes men of us, makes gods of us. It is by losing this idea of Shraddha that the country has gone to ruin."

Question: How did we come to lose this Shraddha?

Swamiji: We have had a negative education all along from our boyhood. We have only learnt that we are nobodies. Seldom are we given to understand that great men were ever born in our country. Nothing positive has been taught to us. We do not even know how to use our hands and feet! We master all the facts and figures concerning the ancestors of the English, but we are sadly unmindful about our own. We have learnt only weakness. Being a conquered race, we have brought ourselves to believe that we are weak and have no independence in anything. So, how can it be but that the Shraddha is lost? The idea of true Shraddha must be brought back once more to us, the faith in our own selves must be reawakened, and, then only, all the problems which face our country will gradually be solved by ourselves.

Q. How can that ever be? How will Shraddha alone remedy the innumerable evils with which our society is beset? Besides, there are so many crying evils in the country, to remove which the Indian National Congress and other patriotic associations are carrying on a strenuous agitation and petitioning the British government. How better can their wants be made known? What has Shraddha to do with the matter?

Swamiji: Tell me, whose wants are those—yours or the ruler's? If yours, will the ruler supply them for you, or will you have to do that for yourselves?

Q. But it is the ruler's duty to see to the wants of the subject people. Whom should we look up to for everything, if not to the king?

Swamiji: Never are the wants of a beggar fulfilled. Suppose the government give you all you need, where are the men who are able to keep up the things demanded? So make men first. Men we want, and how can men be made unless Shraddha is there?

Q. But such is not the view Of the majority, sir.

Swamiji: What you call majority is mainly composed of fools and men of common intellect. Men who have brains to think for themselves are few, everywhere. These few men with brains are the real leaders in everything and in every department of work; the majority are guided by them as with a string, and that is good, for everything goes all right when they follow in the footsteps of these leaders. Those are only fools who think themselves too high to bend their heads to anyone, and they bring on their own ruin by acting on their own judgment. You talk of social reform? But what do you do? All that you mean by your social reform is either widow remarriage, or female emancipation, or something of that sort. Do you not? And these again are directed within the confines of a few of the castes only. Such a scheme of reform may do good to a few no doubt, but of what avail is that to the whole nation? Is that reform or only a form of selfishness—somehow to cleanse your own room and keep it tidy and let others go from bad to worse!

Q. Then, you mean to say that there is no need of social reform at all?

Swamiji: Who says so? Of course there is need of it. Most of what you talk of as social reform does not touch the poor masses; they have already those things—the widow remarriage, female emancipation, etc.—which you cry for. For this reason they will not think of those things as reforms at all. What I mean to say is that want of Shraddha has brought in all the evils among us, and is bringing in more and more. My method of treatment is to take out by the roots the very causes of the disease and not to keep them merely suppressed. Reforms we should have in many ways; who will be so foolish as to deny it? There is, for example, a good reason for intermarriage in India, in the absence of which the race is becoming physically weaker day by day.

Since it was a day of a solar eclipse, the gentleman who was asking these questions saluted Swamiji and left saying "I must go now for a bath in the Ganga. I shall, however, come another day."

III — Reconciliation of Jnana-Yoga and Bhakti-Yoga—God in Good and in Evil Too—Use Makes a Thing Good or Evil—Karma—Creation—God—Maya

Shri Surendra Nath Sen —from private dairy

Sunday, The 23rd January, 1898.

It was evening and the occasion of the weekly meeting of the Ramakrishna Mission, at the house of Balaram Babu of Baghbazar. Swami Turiyananda, Swami Yogananda, Swami Premananda, and others had come from the Math. Swamiji was seated in the verandah to the east, which was now full of people, as were the northern and the southern sections of the verandah. But such used to be the case every day when Swamiji stayed in Calcutta.

Many of the people who came to the meeting had heard that Swamiji could sing well, and so were desirous of hearing him. Knowing this, Master Mahâshaya (M.) whispered to a few gentlemen near him to request Swamiji to sing; but he saw through their intention and playfully asked, "Master Mahashaya, what are you talking about among yourselves in whispers? Do speak out." At the request of Master Mahashaya, Swamiji now began in his charming voice the song— "Keep with loving care the darling Mother Shyâmâ in thy heart... " It seemed as if a Vinâ was playing. At its close, he said to Master Mahashaya, "Well, are you now satisfied? But no more singing! Otherwise, being in the swing of it, I shall be carried away by its intoxication. Moreover, my voice is now spoilt be frequent lecturing in the West. My voice trembles a great deal... "

Swamiji then asked one of his Brahmacharin disciples to speak on the real nature of Mukti. So, the Brahmacharin stood up and spoke at some length. A few others followed him. Swamiji then invited discussion on the subject of the discourse, and called upon one of his householder disciples to lead it; but as the latter tried to advocate the Advaita and Jnâna and assign a lower place to dualism and Bhakti, he met with a protest from one of the audience. As each of the two opponents tried to establish his own viewpoint, a lively word-fight ensued. Swamiji watched them for a while but, seeing that they were getting excited, silenced them with the following words:

Why do you get excited in argument and spoil everything? Listen! Shri Ramakrishna used to say that pure knowledge and pure Bhakti are one and the same. According to the doctrine of Bhakti, God is held to be "All-Love". One cannot even say, "I love Him", for the reason that He is All-Love. There is no love outside of Himself; the love that is in the heart with which you love Him is even He Himself. In a similar way, whatever attractions or inclinations one feels drawn by, are all He Himself. The thief steals, the harlot sells her body to prostitution, the mother loves her child—in each of these too is He! One world system attracts another—there also is He. Everywhere is He. According to the doctrine of Jnana also, He is realised by one everywhere. Here lies the reconciliation of Jnana and Bhakti. When one is immersed in the highest ecstasy of divine vision (Bhâva), or is in the state of Samâdhi, then alone the idea of duality ceases, and the distinction between the devotee and his God vanishes. In the scriptures on Bhakti, five different paths of relationship are mentioned, by any of which one can attain to God; but another one can very well be added to them, viz. the path of meditation on the non-separateness, or oneness with God. Thus the Bhakta can call the Advaitins Bhaktas as well, but of the non-differentiating type. As long as one is within the region of Mâya, so long the idea of duality will no doubt remain. Space-time-causation, or name-and-form, is what is called Maya. When one goes beyond this Maya, then only the Oneness is realised, and then man is neither a dualist nor an Advaitist—to him all is One. All this difference that you notice between a Bhakta and a Jnani is in the preparatory stage—one sees God outside, and the other sees Him within. But there is another point: Shri Ramakrishna used to say that there is another stage of Bhakti which is called the Supreme Devotion (Parâbhakti) i.e. to love Him after becoming established in the consciousness of Advaita and after having attained Mukti. It may seem paradoxical, and the question may be raised here why such a one who has already attained Mukti should be desirous of retaining the spirit of Bhakti? The answer is: The Mukta or the Free is beyond all law; no law applies in his case, and hence no question can be asked regarding him. Even becoming Mukta, some, out of their own free will, retain Bhakti to taste of its sweetness.

Q. God may be in the love of the mother for her child; but, sir, this idea is really perplexing that God is even in thieves and the harlots in the form of their natural inclinations to sin! It follows then that God is as responsible for the sin as for all the virtue in this world.

Swamiji: That consciousness comes in a stage of highest realization, when one sees that whatever is of the nature of love or attraction is God. But one has to reach that state to see and realise that idea for oneself in actual life.

Q. But still one has to admit that God is also in the sin!

Swamiji: You see, there are, in reality, no such different things as good and evil. They are mere conventional terms. The same thing we call bad, and again another time we call good, according to the way we make use of it. Take for example this lamplight; because of its burning, we are able to see and do various works of utility; this is one mode of using the light. Again, if you put your fingers in it, they will be burnt; that is another mode of using the same light. So we should know that a thing becomes good or bad according to the way we use it. Similarly with virtue and vice. Broadly speaking, the proper use of any of the faculties of our mind and body is termed virtue, and its improper application or waste is called vice.

Thus questions after questions were put and answered. Someone remarked, "The theory that God is even there, where one heavenly body attracts another, may or may not be true as a fact, but there is no denying the exquisite poetry the idea conveys."

Swamiji: No, my dear sir, that is not poetry. One can see for oneself its truth when one attains knowledge.

From what Swamiji further said on this point, I understood him to mean that matter and spirit, though to all appearances they seem to be two distinct things, are really two different forms of one substance; and similarly, all the different forces that are known to us, whether in the material or in the internal world, are but varying forms of the manifestation of one Force. We call a thing matter, where that spirit force is manifested less; and living, where it shows itself more; but there is nothing which is absolutely matter at all times and in all conditions. The same Force which presents itself in the material world as attraction or gravitation is felt in its finer and subtler state as love and the like in the higher spiritual stages of realisation.

Q. Why should there be even this difference relating to individual use? Why should there be at all this tendency in man to make bad or improper use of any of his faculties?

Swamiji: That tendency comes as a result of one's own past actions (Karma); everything one has is of his own doing. Hence it follows that it is solely in the hands of every individual to control his tendencies and to guide them properly.

Q. Even if everything is the result of our Karma, still it must have had a beginning, and why should our tendencies have been good or bad at the beginning?

Swamiji: How do you know that there is a beginning? The Srishti (creation) is without beginning—this is the doctrine of the Vedas. So long as there is God, there is creation as well.

Q. Well, sir, why is this Maya here, and whence has it come?

Swamiji: It is a mistake to ask "why" with respect to God; we can only do so regarding one who has wants or imperfections. How can there be an, "why" concerning Him who has no wants and who is the One Whole? No such question as "Whence has Maya come?" can be asked. Time-space-causation is what is called Maya. You, I, and everyone else are within this Maya; and you are asking about what is beyond Maya! How can you do so while living within Maya?

Again, many questions followed. The conversation turned on the philosophies of Mill, Hamilton, Herbert Spencer, etc., and Swamiji dwelt on them to the satisfaction of all. Everyone wondered at the vastness of his Western philosophical scholarship and the promptness of his replies.

The meeting dispersed after a short conversation on miscellaneous subjects.

IV — Intermarriage Among Subdivisions of a Varna—Against Early Marriage—The Education that Indians Need—Brahmacharya

*Shri Surendra Nath Sen
—from private dairy*

Monday, The 24th January, 1898.

The same gentleman who was asking questions of Swamiji on Saturday last came again. He raised again the topic of intermarriage and enquired, "How should intermarriage be introduced between different nationalities?"

Swamiji: I do not advise our intermarriage with nations professing an alien religion. At least for the present, that will, of a certainty, slacken the ties of society and be a cause of manifold mischief. It is the intermarriage between people of the same religion that I advocate.

Q. Even then, it will involve much perplexity. Suppose I have a daughter who is born and brought up in Bengal, and I marry her to a Marathi or a Madrasi. Neither will the girl understand her husband's language nor the husband the girl's. Again, the difference in their individual habits and customs is so great. Such are a few of the troubles in the case of the married couple. Then as regards society, it will make confusion worse confounded.

Swamiji: The time is yet very long in coming when marriages of that kind will be widely possible. Besides, it is not judicious now to go in for that all of a sudden. One of the secrets of work is to go along the line of least resistance. So, first of all, let there be marriages within the sphere of one's own caste-people. Take for instance, the Kayasthas of Bengal. They have several subdivisions amongst them, such as, the Uttar-rârhi, Dakshin-rârhi, Bangaja, etc., and they do not intermarry with each other. Now, let there be intermarriages between the Uttar-rarhis and the Dakshin-rarhis, and if that is not possible at present, let it be between the Bangajas and the Dakshin-rarhis. Thus we are to build up that which is already existing, and which is in our hands to reduce into practice—reform does not mean wholesale breaking down.

Q. Very well, let it be as you say: but what corresponding good can come of it?

Swamiji: Don't you see how in our society, marriage, being restricted for several hundreds of years within the same subdivisions of each caste, has come to such a pass nowadays as virtually to mean marital alliance between cousins and near relations; and how for this very reason the race is getting deteriorated physically, and consequently all sorts of disease and other evils are finding a ready entrance into it? The blood having had to circulate within the narrow circle of a limited number of individuals has become vitiated; so the new-born children inherit from their very birth the constitutional diseases of their fathers. Thus, born with poor blood, their bodies have very little power to resist the microbes of any disease, which are ever ready to prey upon them. It is only by widening the circle of marriage that we can infuse a new and a different kind of blood into our progeny, so that they may be saved from the clutches of many of our present-day diseases and other consequent evils.

Q. May I ask you, sir, what is your opinion about early marriage?

Swamiji: Amongst the educated classes in Bengal, the custom of marrying their boys too early is dying out gradually. The girls are also given in marriage a year or two older than before, but that has been under compulsion —from pecuniary want. Whatever might be the reason for it, the age of marrying girls should be raised still higher. But what will the poor father do? As soon as the girl grows up a little, every one of the female sex, beginning with the mother down to the relatives and neighbours even, will begin to cry out that he must find a bridegroom for her, and will not leave him in peace until he does so! And, about your religious hypocrites, the less said the better. In these days no one hears them, but still they will take up the role of leaders themselves. The rulers passed the Age of Consent Bill prohibiting a man under the threat of penalty to live with a girl of twelve years, and at once all these so-called leaders of your religion raised a tremendous hue and cry against it, sounding the alarm, "Alas, our religion is lost! As if religion consisted in making a girl a mother at the age of twelve or thirteen! So the rulers also naturally think, "Goodness gracious! What a religion is theirs! And these people lead political agitations and demand political rights!"

Q. Then, in your opinion, both men and women should be married at an advanced age?

Swamiji: Certainly. But education should be imparted along with it, otherwise irregularity and corruption will ensue. By education I do not mean the present system, but something in the line of positive teaching. Mere book-learning won't do. We want that education by which character is formed, strength of mind is increased, the intellect is expanded, and by which one can stand on one's own feet.

Q. We have to reform our women in many ways.

Swamiji: With such an education women will solve their own problems. They have all the time been trained in helplessness, servile dependence on others, and so they are good only to weep their eyes out at the slightest approach of a mishap or danger. Along with other things they should acquire the spirit of valour and heroism. In the present day it has become necessary for them also to learn self-defence. See how grand was the Queen of Jhansi!

Q. What you advise is quite a new departure, and it will, I am afraid, take a very long time yet to train our women in that way.

Swamiji: Anyhow, we have to try our best. We have not only to teach them but to teach ourselves also. Mere begetting children does not make a father; a great many responsibilities have to be taken upon one's shoulders as well. To make a beginning in women's education: our Hindu women easily understand what chastity means, because it is their heritage. Now, first of all, intensify that ideal within them above everything else, so that they may develop a strong character by the force of which, in every stage of their life, whether married, or single if they prefer to remain so, they will not be in the least afraid even to give up their lives rather than flinch an inch from their chastity. Is it little heroism to be able to sacrifice one's life for the sake of one's ideal whatever that ideal may be? Studying the present needs of the age, it seems imperative to train some women up in the ideal of renunciation, so that they will take up the vow of lifelong virginity, fired with the strength of that virtue of chastity which is innate in their life-blood from hoary antiquity. Along with that they should be taught sciences and other things which would be of benefit, not only to them but to others as well, and knowing this they would easily learn these things and feel pleasure in doing so. Our motherland requires for her well-being some of her children to become such pure-souled Brahmachârins and Brahmachârinis.

Q. In what way will that conduce to her well-being?

Swamiji: By their example and through their endeavours to hold the national ideal before the eyes of the people, a revolution in thoughts and aspirations will take place. How do matters stand now? Somehow, the parents must dispose of a girl in marriage, if she he nine or ten years of age! And what a rejoicing of the whole family if a child is born to her at the age of thirteen! If the trend of such ideas is reversed, then only there is some hope for the ancient Shraddhâ to return. And what to talk of those who will practice Brahmacharya as defined above—think how much faith in themselves will be theirs! And what a power for good they will be!

The questioner now saluted Swamiji and was ready to take leave. Swamiji asked him to come now and then "Certainly, sir," replied the gentleman, "I feel so much benefited. I have heard from you many new things, which I have not been told anywhere before." I also went home as it was about time for dinner.

V — Madhura-Bhava—Prema—Namakirtana—Its Danger—Bhakti Tempered With Jnana—A Curious Dream

Shri Surendra Nath Sen —from private dairy

Monday, The 24th January, 1898.

In the afternoon I came again to Swamiji and saw quite a good gathering round him. The topic was the Madhura-Bhâva or the way of worshipping God as husband, as in vogue with some followers of Shri Chaitanya. His occasional bons mots were raising laughter, when someone remarked, "What is there to make so much fun of about the Lord's doings? Do you think that he was not a great saint, and that he did not do everything for the good of humanity?"

Swamiji: Who is that! Should I poke fun at you then, my dear sir! You only see the fun of it, do you? And you, sir, do not see the lifelong struggle through which I have passed to mould this life after his burning ideal of renunciation of wealth and lust, and my endeavours to infuse that ideal into the people at large! Shri Chaitanya was a man of tremendous renunciation and had nothing to do with woman and carnal appetites. But, in later times, his disciples admitted women into their order, mixed indiscriminately with them in his name, and made an awful mess of the whole thing. And the ideal of love which the Lord exemplified in his life was perfectly selfless and bereft of any vestige of lust; that sexless love can never be the property of the masses. But the subsequent Vaishnava Gurus, instead of laying particular stress first on the aspect of renunciation in the Master's life, bestowed all their zeal on preaching and infusing his ideal of love among the masses, and the consequence was that the common people could not grasp and assimilate that high ideal of divine love, and naturally made of it the worst form of love between man and woman.

Q. But, sir, he preached the name of the Lord Hari to all, even to the Chandâlas; so why should not the common masses have a right to it?

Swamiji: I am talking not of his preaching, but

of his great ideal of love —the Râdhâ-prema[1], with which he used to remain intoxicated day and night, losing his individuality in Radha.

Q. Why may not that be made the common property of all?

Swamiji: Look at this nation and see what has been the outcome of such an attempt. Through the preaching of that love broadcast, the whole nation has become effeminate—a race of women! The whole of Orissa has been turned into a land of cowards; and Bengal, running after the Radha-prema, these past four hundred years, has almost lost all sense of manliness! The people are very good only at crying and weeping; that has become their national trait. Look at their literature, the sure index of a nation's thoughts and ideas. Why, the refrain of the Bengali literature for these four hundred years is strung to that same tune of moaning and crying. It has failed to give birth to any poetry which breathes a true heroic spirit!

Q. Who are then truly entitled to possess that Prema (love)?

Swamiji: There can be no love so long as there is lust—even as speck of it, as it were, in the heart. None but men of great renunciation, none but mighty giants among men, have a right to that Love Divine. If that highest ideal of love is held out to the masses, it will indirectly tend to stimulate its worldly prototype which dominates the heart of man—for, meditating on love to God by thinking of oneself as His wife or beloved, one would very likely be thinking most of the time of one's own wife—the result is too obvious to point out.

Q. Then is it impossible for householders to realise God through that path of love, worshipping God as one's husband or lover and considering oneself as His spouse?

Swamiji : With a few exceptions; for ordinary householders it is impossible no doubt. And why lay so much stress on this delicate path, above all others? Are there no other relationships by which to worship God, except this Madhura idea of love? Why not follow the four other paths, and take the name of the Lord with all your heart? Let the heart be opened first, and all else will follow of itself. But know this for certain, that Prema cannot come while there is lust. Why not try first to get rid of carnal desires? You will say, "How is that possible? I am a householder." Nonsense! Because one is a householder, does it mean that one should be a personification of incontinence, or that one has to live in marital relations all one's life? And, after all, how unbecoming of a man to make of himself a woman, so that he may practice this Madhura love!

Q. True, sir. Singing God's name in a party (Nâmakirtana) is an excellent help and gives one a joyous feeling. So say our scriptures, and so did Shri Chaitanya Deva also preach to the masses. When the Khole (drum) is played upon, it makes the heart leap with such a transport that one feels inclined to dance.

Swamiji: That is all right, but don't think that Kirtana means dancing only. It means singing the glories of God, in whatever way that suits you. That vehement stirring up of feeling and that dancing of the Vaishnavas are good and very catching no doubt; but there is also a danger in practising them, from which you must save yourself. The danger lies here—in the reaction. On the one hand, the feelings are at once roused to the highest pitch, tears flow from the eyes, the head reels as it were under intoxication—on the other hand, as soon as the Sankirtan stops, that mass of feeling sinks down as precipitately as it rose. The higher the wave rises on the ocean, the lower it falls, with equal force. It is very difficult at that stage to contain oneself against the shock of reaction; unless one has proper discrimination, one is likely to succumb to the lower propensities of lust etc. I have noticed the same thing in America also. Many would go to church, pray with much devotion, sing with great feeling, and even burst into tears when hearing the sermons; but after coming out of church, they would have a great reaction and succumb to carnal tendencies.

Q. Then, sir, do instruct us which of the ideas preached by Shri Chaitanya we should take up as well suited to us, so that we may not fall into errors.

Swamiji: Worship God with Bhakti tempered with

---

1. The divine love which Radha had towards Shri Krishna.

Jnâna. Keep the spirit of discrimination along with Bhakti. Besides this, gather from Shri Chaitanya, his heart, his loving kindness to all beings, his burning passion for God, and make his renunciation the ideal of your life.

The questioner now addressed the Swamiji with folded hands, "I beg your pardon, sir. Now I come to see you are right. Seeing you criticise in a playful mood the Madhura love of the Vaishnavas, I could not at first understand the drift of your remarks; hence I took exception to them."

Swamiji: Well, look here, if we are to criticise at all, it is better to criticise God or God-men. If you abuse me I shall very likely get angry with you, and if I abuse you, you will try to retaliate. Isn't it so? But God or God-men will never return evil for evil. The gentleman now left, after bowing down at the feet of Swamiji. I have already said that such a gathering was an everyday occurrence when Swamiji used to stay in Calcutta. From early in the morning till eight or nine at night, men would flock to him at every hour of the day. This naturally occasioned much irregularity in the time of his taking his meals; so, many desiring to put a stop to this state of things, strongly advised Swamiji not to receive visitors except at appointed hours. But the loving heart of Swamiji, ever ready to go to any length to help others, was so melted with compassion at the sight of such a thirst for religion in the people, that in spite of ill health, he did not comply with any request of the kind. His only reply was, "They take so much trouble to come walking all the way from their homes, and can I, for the consideration of risking my health a little, sit here and not speak a few words to them?"

At about 4 p.m. the general conversation came to a close, and the gathering dispersed, except for a few gentlemen with whom Swamiji continued his talk on different subjects, such as England and America, and so on. In the course of conversation he said:

"I had a curious dream on my return voyage from England. While our ship was passing through the Mediterranean Sea, in my sleep, a very old and venerable looking person, Rishi-like in appearance, stood before me and said, 'Do ye come and effect our restoration. I am one of that ancient order of Therâputtas (Theraputae) which had its origin in the teachings of the Indian Rishis. The truths and ideals preached by us have been given out by Christians as taught by Jesus; but for the matter of that, there was no such personality by the name of Jesus ever born. Various evidences testifying to this fact will be brought to light by excavating here.' 'By excavating which place can those proofs and relics you speak of be found?' I asked. The hoary-headed one, pointing to a locality in the vicinity of Turkey, said, 'See here.' Immediately after, I woke up, and at once rushed to the upper deck and asked the Captain, 'What neighbourhood is the ship in just now?' 'Look yonder', the Captain replied, 'there is Turkey and the Island of Crete.'"

Was it but a dream, or is there anything in the above vision? Who knows!

VI — X SHRI PRIYA NATH SINHA

VI — Reminiscences—The Problem of Famines in India and Self-Sacrificing Workers—East and West—Is it Sattva or Tamas—A Nation of Mendicants—The "Give and Take" Policy—Tell a Man his Defects Directly but Praise his Virtues Before Others—Vivekananda Everyone may Become—Unbroken Brahmacharya is the Secret of Power—Samadhi and Work

Shri Priya Nath Sinha

Our house was very close to Swamiji's, and since we were boys of the same section of the town, I often used to play with him. From my boyhood I had a special attraction for him, and I had a sincere belief that he would become a great man. When he became a Sannyasin we thought that the promise of a brilliant career for such a man was all in vain.

Afterwards, when he went to America, I read in

newspapers reports of his lectures at the Chicago Parliament of Religions and others delivered in various place, of America, and I thought that fire can never remain hidden under a cloth; the fire that was within Swamiji had now burst into a flame; the bud after so many years had blossomed.

After a time I came to know that he had returned to India, and had been delivering fiery lectures at Madras. I read them and wondered that such sublime truths existed in the Hindu religion and that they could be explained so lucidly. What an extraordinary power he had! Was he a man or a god?

A great enthusiasm prevailed when Swamiji came to Calcutta, and we followed him to the Sil's garden-house, on the Ganga, at Cossipore. A few days later, at the residence of Raja Radhakanta Dev, the "Calcutta boy" delivered an inspiring lecture to a huge concourse of people in reply to an address of welcome, and Calcutta heard him for the first time and was lost in admiration. But these are facts known to all.

After his coming to Calcutta, I was very anxious to see him once alone and be able to talk freely with him as in our boyhood. But there was always a gathering of eager inquirers about him, and conversations were going on without a break; so I did not get an opportunity for some time, until one day when we went out for a walk in the garden on the Ganga side. He at once began to talk, as of old, to me, the playmate of his boyhood. No sooner had a few words passed between us than repeated calls came, informing him that many gentlemen had come to see him. He became a little impatient at last and told the messenger, "Give me a little respite, my son; let me speak a few words with this companion of my boyhood; let me stay in the open air for a while. Go and give a welcome to those who have come, ask them to sit down, offer them tobacco, and request them to wait a little."

When we were alone again, I asked him, "Well, Swamiji, you are a Sâdhu (holy man). Money was raised by subscription for your reception here, and I thought, in view of the famine in this country, that you would wire, before arriving in Calcutta, saying, 'Don't spend a single pice on my reception, rather contribute the whole sum to the famine relief fund'; but I found that you did nothing of the kind. How was that?"

Swamiji: Why, I wished rather that a great enthusiasm should be stirred up. Don't you see, without some such thing how would the people be drawn towards Shri Ramakrishna and be fired in his name? Was this ovation done for me personally, or was not his name glorified by this? See how much thirst has been created in the minds of men to know about him! Now they will come to know of him gradually, and will not that be conducive to the good of the country? If the people do not know him who came for the welfare of the country, how can good befall them? When they know what he really was, then men—real men—will be made; and when will be such men, how long will it take to drive away famines etc. from the land? So I say that I rather desired that there should be some bustle and stir in Calcutta, so that the public might be inclined to believe in the mission of Shri Ramakrishna; otherwise what was the use of making so much fuss for my sake? What do I care for it? Have I become any greater now than when I used to play with you at your house? I am the same now as I was before. Tell me, do you find any change in me?

Though I said, "No, I do not find much change to speak of", yet in my mind I thought, "You have now, indeed, become a god."

Swamiji continued: "Famine has come to be a constant quantity in our country, and now it is, as it were, a sort of blight upon us. Do you find in any other country such frequent ravages of famine? No, because there are men in other countries, while in ours, men have become akin to dead matter, quite inert. Let the people first learn to renounce their selfish nature by studying Shri Ramakrishna, by knowing him as he really was, and then will proceed from them real efforts trying to stop the frequently recurring famines. By and by I shall make efforts in that direction too; you will see."

Myself: That will be good. Then you are going to deliver many lectures here, I presume; otherwise, how will his name be preached?

Swamiji: What nonsense! Nothing of the kind!

Has anything left undone by which his name can be known? Enough has been done in that line. Lectures won't do any good in this country. Our educated countrymen would hear them and, at best, would cheer and clap their hands, saying, "Well done"; that is all. Then they would go home and digest, as we say, everything they had heard, with their meal! What good will hammering do on a piece of rusty old iron? It will only crumble into pieces. First, it should be made red-hot, and then it can be moulded into any shape by hammering. Nothing will avail in our country without setting a glowing and living example before the people. What we want are some young men who will renounce everything and sacrifice their lives for their country's sake. We should first form their lives and then some real work can be expected.

Myself: Well, Swamiji, it has always puzzled me that, while men of our country, unable to understand their own religion, were embracing alien religions, such as Christianity, Mohammedanism, etc., you, instead of doing anything for them, went over to England and America to preach Hinduism.

Swamiji: Don't you see that circumstances have changed now? Have the men of our country the power left in them to take up and practice true religion? What they have is only pride in themselves that they are very Sâttvika. Time was when they were Sattvika, no doubt, but now they have fallen very low. The fall from Sattva brings one down headlong into Tamas! That is what has happened to them. Do you think that a man who does not exert himself at all, who only takes the name of Hari, shutting himself up in a room, who remains quiet and indifferent even when seeing a huge amount of wrong and violence done to others before his very eyes, possesses the quality of Sattva? Nothing of the kind, he is only enshrouded in dark Tamas. How can the people of a country practice religion who do not get even sufficient food to appease their hunger? How can renunciation come to the people of a country in whose minds the desires for Bhoga (enjoyment) have not been in the least satisfied? For this reason, find out, first of all, the ways and means by which men may get enough to eat and have enough luxuries to enable them to enjoy life a little; and then gradually, true Vairâgya (dispassion) will come, and they will be fit and ready to realise religion in life. The people of England and America, how full of Rajas they are! They have become satiated with all sorts of worldly enjoyment. Moreover, Christianity, being a religion of faith and superstition, occupies the same rank as our religion of the Purânas. With the spread of education and culture, the people of the West can no more find peace in that. Their present condition is such that, giving them one lift will make them reach the Sattva. Then again, in these days, would you accept the words of a Sannyasin clad in rags, in the same degree as you would the words of a white-face (Westerner) who might come and speak to you on your own religion?

Myself: Just so, Swamiji! Mr. N. N. Ghosh[1] also speaks exactly to the same effect.

Swamiji: Yes, when my Western disciples after acquiring proper training and illumination will come in numbers here and ask you, "What are you all doing? Why are you of so little faith? How are your rites and religion, manners, customs, and morals in any way inferior? We even regard your religion to be the highest!"—then you will see that lots of our big and influential folk will hear them. Thus they will be able to do immense good to this country. Do not think for a moment that they will come to take up the position of teachers of religion to you. They will, no doubt, be your Guru regarding practical sciences etc., for the improvement of material conditions, and the people of our country will be their Guru in everything pertaining to religion. This relation of Guru and disciple in the domain of religion will for ever exist between India and the rest of the world. Myself: How can that be, Swamiji? Considering the feeling of hatred with which they look upon us, it does not seem probable that they will ever do good to us, purely from an unselfish motive.

Swamiji: They find many reasons to hate us, and so they may justify themselves in doing so. In the first place, we are a conquered race, and moreover there is nowhere in the world such a nation of mendicants as we are! The masses who comprise the lowest castes, through ages of constant tyranny of the higher castes and by being treated by them with blows and kicks at

---

1. A celebrated barrister, journalist, and educationalist of Calcutta.

every step they took, have totally lost their manliness and become like professional beggars; and those who are removed one stage higher than these, having read a few pages of English, hang about the thresholds of public offices with petitions in their hands. In the case of a post of twenty or thirty rupees falling vacant, five hundred B.A.s and M.A.s will apply for it! And, dear me! how curiously worded these petitions are! "I have nothing to eat at home, sir, my wife and children are starving; I most humbly implore you, sir, to give me some means to provide for myself and my family, or we shall die of starvation!" Even when they enter into service, they cast all self-respect to the winds, and servitude in its worst form is what they practice. Such is the condition, then, of the masses. The highly-educated, prominent men among you form themselves into societies and clamour at the top of their voices: "Alas, India is going to ruin, day by day! O English rulers, admit our country men to the higher offices of the State, relieve us from famines" and so on, thus rending the air, day and night, with the eternal cry of "Give" and "Give"! The burden of all their speech is, "Give to us, give more to us, O Englishmen!" Dear me! what more will they give to you? They have given railways, telegraphs, well-ordered administration to the country—have almost entirely suppressed robbers, have given education in science—what more will they give? What does anyone give to others with perfect unselfishness? Well, they have given you so much; let me ask, what have you given to them in return?

Myself: What have we to give, Swamiji? We pay taxes.

Swamiji: Do you, really? Do you give taxes to them of your own will, or do they exact them by compulsion because they keep peace in the country? Tell me plainly, what do you give them in return for all that they have done for you? You also have something to give them that they have not. You go to England, but that is also in the garb of a beggar—praying for education. Some go, and what they do there at the most is, perchance, to applaud the Westerner's religion in some speeches and then come back. What an achievement, indeed! Why, have you nothing to give them? An inestimable treasure you have, which you can give—give them your religion, give them your philosophy! Study the history of the whole world, and you will see that every high ideal you meet with anywhere had its origin in India. From time immemorial India has been the mine of precious ideas to human society; giving birth to high ideas herself, she has freely distributed them broadcast over the whole world. The English are in India today, to gather those higher ideals, to acquire a knowledge of the Vedanta, to penetrate into the deep mysteries of that eternal religion which is yours. Give those invaluable gems in exchange for what you receive from them. The Lord took me to their country to remove this opprobrium of the beggar that is attributed by them to us. It is not right to go to England for the purpose of begging only. Why should they always give us alms? Does anyone do so for ever? It is not the law of nature to be always taking gifts with outstretched hands like beggars. To give and take is the law of nature. Any individual or class or nation that does not obey this law never prospers in life. We also must follow that law That is why I went to America. So great is now the thirst for religion in the people there that there is room enough even if thousands of men like me go. They have been for a long time giving you of what wealth they possess, and now is the time for you to share your priceless treasure with them. And you will see how their feelings of hatred will be quickly replaced by those of faith, devotion, and reverence towards you, and how they will do good to your country even unasked. They are a nation of heroes —never do they forget any good done to them.

Myself: Well, Swamiji, in your lectures in the West you have frequently and eloquently dwelt on our characteristic talents and virtues, and many convincing proofs you have put forward to show our whole-souled love of religion; but now you say that we have become full of Tamas; and at the same time you are accrediting us as the teachers of the eternal religion of the Rishis to the world! How is that?

Swamiji: Do you mean to say that I should go about from country to country, expatiating on your failings before the public? Should I not rather hold up before them the characteristic virtues that mark you as a nation? It is always good to tell a man his defects in a direct way and in a friendly spirit to make him convinced of them, so that he may correct himself—but you should trumpet forth his virtues before others. Shri Ramakrishna used to say that if you repeatedly tell a bad man that he is good, he turns in time to be good; similarly, a good man becomes bad if he is incessantly called so. There, in the West, I have said enough to the people of their shortcomings. Mind, up to my time, all who went over to the West from our country have sung paeans to them in praise of their virtues and have trumpeted out only our blemishes to their ears. Consequently, it is no wonder that they have learnt to hate us. For this reason I have laid before them your virtues, and pointed out to them their vices, just as I am now telling you of your weaknesses and their good points. However full of Tamas you may have become, something of the nature of the ancient Rishis, however little it may be, is undoubtedly in you still—at least the framework of it. But that does not show that one should be in a hurry to take up at once the role of a teacher of religion and go over to the West to preach it. First of all, one must completely mould one's religious life in solitude, must be perfect in renunciation and must preserve Brahmacharya without a break. The Tamas has entered into you—what of that? Cannot the Tamas be destroyed? It can be done in less than no time! It was for the destruction of this Tamas that Bhagavân Shri Ramakrishna came to us.

Myself: But who can aspire to be like you, Swamiji?

Swamiji: Do you think that there will be no more Vivekanandas after I die! That batch of young men who came and played music before me a little while ago, whom you all despise for being addicted to intoxicating drugs and look upon as worthless fellows, if the Lord wishes, each and everyone of them may become a Vivekananda! There will be no lack of Vivekanandas, if the world needs them—thousands and millions of Vivekanandas will appear—from where, who knows! Know for certain that the work done by me is not the work of Vivekananda, it is His work—the Lord's own work! If one governor-general retires, another is sure to be sent in his place by the Emperor. Enveloped in Tamas however much you may be, know all that will clear away if you take refuge in Him by being sincere to the core of your heart. The time is opportune now, as the physician of the world-disease has come. Taking His name, if you set yourself to work, He will accomplish everything Himself through you. Tamas itself will be transformed into the highest Sattva!

Myself: Whatever you may say, I cannot bring myself to believe in these words. Who can come by that oratorical power of expounding philosophy which you have?

Swamiji: You don't know! That power may come to all. That power comes to him who observes unbroken Brahmacharya for a period of twelve years, with the sole object of realising God I have practiced that kind of Brahmacharya myself, and so a screen has been removed, as it were, from my brain. For that reason, I need not any more think over or prepare myself for any lectures on such a subtle subject as philosophy. Suppose I have to lecture tomorrow; all that I shall speak about will pass tonight before my eyes like so many pictures; and the next day I put into words during my lecture all those things that I saw. So you will understand now that it is not any power which is exclusively my own. Whoever will practice unbroken Brahmacharya for twelve years will surely have it. If you do so, you too will get it. Our Shâstras do not say that only such and such a person will get it and not others!

Myself: Do you remember, Swamiji, one day, before you took Sannyâsa, we were sitting in the house of—, and you were trying to explain the mystery of Samâdhi to us. And when I called in question the truth of your words, saying that Samadhi was not possible in this Kali Yuga, you emphatically demanded: "Do you want to see Samadhi or to have it yourself? I get Samadhi myself, and I can make you have it!" No sooner had you finished saying so than a stranger came up and we did not pursue that subject any further.

Swamiji: Yes, I remember the occasion.

Later, on my pressing him to make me get Samadhi, he said, "You see, having continually lectured and worked hard for several years, the quality of Rajas has become too predominant in me. Hence that power is lying covered, as it were, in me now. If I leave all work and go to the Himalayas and meditate in solitude for some time, then that power will again come out in me."

VII — Reminiscences—Pranayama—Thought-Reading—Knowledge of Previous Births

A day or two later, as I was coming out of my house intending to pay a visit to Swamiji, I met two of my friends who expressed a wish to accompany me, for they wanted to ask Swamiji something about Prânâyâma. I had heard that one should not visit a temple or a Sannyâsin without taking something as an offering; so we took some fruits and sweets with us and placed them before him. Swamiji took them in his hands, raised them to his head, and bowed to us before even we made our obeisance to him. One of the two friends with me had been a fellow-student of his. Swamiji recognised him at once and asked about his health and welfare Then he made us sit down by him. There were many others there who had come to see and hear him. After replying to a few questions put by some of the gentlemen, Swamiji, in the course of his conversation, began to speak about Pranayama. First of all, he explained through modern science the origin of matter from the mind, and then went on to show what Pranayama is. All three of us had carefully read beforehand his book called Râja-Yoga. But from what we heard from him that day about Pranayama, it seemed to me that very little of the knowledge that was in him had been recorded in that book. I understand also that what he said was not mere book-learning, for who could explain so lucidly and elaborately all the intricate problems of religion, even with the help of science, without himself realising the Truth?

His conversation on Pranayama went on from half past three o'clock till half past seven in the evening. When the meeting dissolved and we came away, my companions asked me how Swamiji could have known the questions that were in their hearts, and whether I had communicated to him their desire for asking those questions.

A few days after this occasion, I saw Swamiji in the house of the late Priya Nath Mukherjee at Baghbazar. There were present Swami Brahmananda, Swami Yogananda, Mr. G. C. Ghosh, Atul Babu, and one or two other friends. I said, "Well, Swamiji, the two gentlemen who went to see you the other day wanted to ask you some questions about Pranayama, which had been raised in their minds by reading your book on Raja-Yoga some time before you returned to this country, and they had then told me of them. But that day, before they asked you anything, you yourself raised those doubts that had occurred to them and solved them! They were very much surprised and inquired of me if I had let you know their doubts beforehand." Swamiji replied: "Similar occurrences having come to pass many times in the West, people often used to ask me, 'How could you know the questions that were agitating our minds?' This knowledge does not happen to me so often, but with Shri Ramakrishna it was almost always there."

In this connection Atul Babu asked him: "You have said in Raja-Yoga that one can come to know all about one's previous births. Do you know them yourself?"

Swamiji: Yes, I do.

Atul Babu: What do you know? Have you any objection to tell?

Swamiji: I can know them—I do know them—but I prefer not to say anything in detail.

VIII — The Art and Science of Music, Eastern and Western

It was an evening in July 1898, at the Math, in Nilambar Mukerjee's garden-house, Belur. Swamiji with all his disciples had been meditating, and at the close of the meditation came out and sat in one of the rooms. As it was raining hard and a cold wind was blowing, he shut the door and began to sing to the accompaniment of Tânpurâ. The singing being over, a long conversation on music followed. Swami Shivananda asked him, "What is Western music like?"

Swamiji: Oh, it is very good; there is in it a perfection of harmony, which we have not attained. Only, to our untrained ears, it does not sound well, hence we do not like it, and think that the singers howl like jackals. I also had the same sort of impression, but when I began to listen to the music with attention and study it minutely, I came more and more to understand it, and I was lost in admiration. Such is the case with every art. In glancing at a highly finished painting we cannot understand where its beauty lies. Moreover, unless the eye is, to a certain extent, trained, one cannot appreciate the subtle touches and blendings, the inner genius of a work of art. What real music we have lies in Kirtana and Dhrupada; the rest has been spoiled by being modulated according to the Islamic methods. Do you think that singing the short and light airs of Tappâ songs in a nasal voice and flitting like lightning from one note to another by fits and starts are the best things in the world of music? Not so. Unless each note is given full play in every scale, all the science of music is marred. In painting, by keeping in touch with nature, you can make it as artistic as you like; there is no harm in doing that, and the result will be nothing but good. Similarly, in music, you can display any amount of skill by keeping to science, and it will be pleasing to the ear. The Mohammedans took up the different Râgas and Râginis after coming into India. But they put such a stamp of their own colouring on the art of Tappa songs that all the science in music was destroyed.

Q. Why, Mahârâj (sir)? Who has not a liking for music in Tappa?

Swamiji: The chirping of crickets sounds very good to some. The Santâls think their music also to be the best of all. You do not seem to understand that when one note comes upon another in such quick succession, it not only robs music of all grace, but, on the other hand, creates discordance rather. Do not the permutation and combination of the seven keynotes form one or other of the different melodies of music, known as Ragas and Raginis? Now, in Tappa, if one slurs over a whole melody (Raga) and creates a new tune, and over and above that, if the voice is raised to the highest pitch by tremulous modulation, say, how can the Raga be kept intact? Again, the poetry of music is completely destroyed if there be in it such profuse use of light and short strains just for effect. To sing by keeping to the idea, meant to be conveyed by a song, totally disappeared from our country when Tappas came into vogue. Nowadays, it seems, the true art is reviving a little with the improvement in theatres; but, on the other hand, all regard for Ragas and Raginis is being more and more flung to the winds.

Accordingly, to those who are past masters in the art of singing Dhrupada, it is painful to hear Tappas. But in our music the cadence, or a duly regulated rise and fall of voice or sound, is very good. The French detected and appreciated this trait first, and tried to adapt and introduce it in their music. After their doing this, the whole of Europe has now thoroughly mastered it.

Q. Maharaj, their music seems to be pre-eminently martial, whereas that element appears to be altogether absent in ours.

Swamiji: Oh, no, we have it also. In martial music, harmony is greatly needed. We sadly lack harmony, hence it does not show itself so much. Our music had been improving steadily. But when the Mohammedans came, they took possession of it in such a way that the tree of music could grow no further. The music of the Westerners is much advanced. They have the sentiment of pathos as well as of heroism in their music, which is as it should be. But our antique musical instrument made from the gourd has been improved no further.

Q. Which of the Ragas and Raginis are martial in tune?

Swamiji: Every Raga may be made martial if it is set in harmony and the instruments are tuned accordingly. Some of the Raginis can also become martial.

The conversation was then closed, as it was time for supper. After supper, Swamiji enquired as to the sleeping arrangements for the guests who had come from Calcutta to the Math to pass the night, and he then retired to his bedroom.

IX — The Old Institution of Living with the Guru—The Present University System—Lack of Shraddha—We have a National History—Western Science Coupled with Vedanta—The So-called Higher Education—The Need of Technical Education and Education on National Lines—The Story of Satyakama—Mere Book-Learning and Education under Tyagis—Shri Ramakrishna and the Pandits—Establishment of Maths with Sadhus in Charge of Colleges—Text-Books for Boys to be Compiled—Stop Early Marriage!—Plan of Sending Unmarried Graduates to Japan—The Secret of Japan's Greatness—Art, Asian and European—Art and Utility—Styles of Dress—The Food Question and Poverty

It was about two years after the new Math had been constructed and while all the Swamis were living there that I came one morning to pay a visit to my Guru. Seeing me, Swamiji smiled and after inquiring of my welfare etc., said, "You are going to stay today, are you not?"

"Certainly", I said, and after various inquiries I asked, "Well, Mahârâj, what is your idea of educating our boys?"

Swamiji: Guru-griha-vâsa—living with the Guru.

Q. How?

Swamiji: In the same way as of old. But with this education has to be combined modern Western science. Both these are necessary.

Q. Why, what is the defect in the present university system?

Swamiji: It is almost wholly one of defects. Why, it is nothing but a perfect machine for turning out clerks. I would even thank my stars if that were all. But no! See how men are becoming destitute of Shraddhâ and faith. They assert that the Gita is only an interpolation, and that the Vedas are but rustic songs! They like to master every detail concerning things and nations outside of India, but if you ask them, they do not know even the names of their own forefathers up to the seventh generation, not to speak of the fourteenth!

Q. But what does that matter? What if they do not know the names of their forefathers?

Swamiji: Don't think so. A nation that has no history of its own has nothing in this world. Do you believe that one who has such faith and pride as to feel, "I come of noble descent", can ever turn out to be bad? How could that be? That faith in himself would curb his actions and feelings, so much so that he would rather die than commit wrong. So a national history keeps a nation well-restrained and does not allow it to sink so low. Oh, I know you will say, "But we have not such a history!" No, there is not any, according to those who think like you. Neither is there any, according to your big university scholars; and so also think those who, having travelled through the West in one great rush, come back dressed in European style and assert, "We have nothing, we are barbarians." Of course, we have no history exactly like that of other countries. Suppose we take rice, and the Englishmen do not. Would you for that reason imagine that they all die of starvation, and are going to be exterminated? They live quite well on what they can easily procure or produce in their own country and what is suited to them. Similarly, we have our own history exactly as it ought to have been for us. Will that history be made extinct by shutting your eyes and crying, "Alas! we have no history!" Those who have eyes to see, find a luminous history there, and on the strength of that they know the nation is still alive. But that history has to be rewritten. It should be restated and suited to the understanding and ways of thinking which our men have acquired in the present age through Western education.

Q. How has that to be done?

Swamiji: That is too big a subject for a talk now. However, to bring that about, the old institution of "living with the Guru" and similar systems of imparting education are needed. What we want are Western science coupled with Vedanta, Brahmacharya as the guiding motto, and also Shraddhâ and faith in one's own self. Another thing that we want is the abolition of that system which aims at educating our boys in the same manner as that of the man who battered his ass, being advised that it could thereby be turned into a horse.

Q. What do you mean by that?

Swamiji: You see, no one can teach anybody. The teacher spoils everything by thinking that he is teaching. Thus Vedanta says that within man is all knowledge—even in a boy it is so—and it requires only an awakening, and that much is the work of a teacher. We have to do only so much for the boys that they may learn to apply their own intellect to the proper use of their hands, legs, ears, eyes, etc., and finally everything will become easy. But the root is religion. Religion is as the rice, and everything else, like the curries. Taking only curries causes indigestion, and so is the case with taking rice alone. Our pedagogues are making parrots of our boys and ruining their brains by cramming a lot of subjects into them. Looking from one standpoint, you should rather be grateful to the Viceroy[1] for his proposal of reforming the university system, which means practically abolishing higher education; the country will, at least, feel some relief by having breathing time. Goodness gracious! What a fuss and fury about graduating, and after a few days all cools down! And after all that, what is it they learn but that what religion and customs we have are all bad, and what the Westerners have are all good! At last, they cannot keep the wolf from the door! What does it matter if this higher education remains or goes? It would be better if the people got a little technical education, so that they might find work and earn their bread, instead of dawdling about and crying for service.

Q. Yes, the Marwaris are wiser, since they do not accept service and most of them engage themselves in some trade.

Swamiji: Nonsense! They are on the way to bringing ruin on the country. They have little understanding of their own interests. You are much better, because you have more of an eye towards manufactures. If the money that they lay out in their business and with which they make only a small percentage of profit were utilised in conducting a few factories and workshops, instead of filling the pockets of Europeans by letting them reap the benefit of most of the transactions, then it would not only conduce to the well-being of the country but bring by far the greater amount of profit to them, as well. It is only the Kabulis who do not care for service—the spirit of independence is in their very bone and marrow. Propose to anyone of them to take service, and you will see what follows!

Q. Well, Maharaj, in case higher education is abolished, will not the men become as stupid as cows, as they were before?

Swamiji: What nonsense! Can ever a lion become a jackal? What do you mean? Is it ever possible for the sons of the land that has nourished the whole world with knowledge from time immemorial to turn as stupid as cows, because of the abolition of higher education by Lord Curzon?

Q. But think what our people were before the advent of the English, and what they are now.

Swamiji: Does higher education mean mere study of material sciences and turning out things of everyday use by machinery? The use of higher education is to find out how to solve the problems of life, and this is what is engaging the profound thought of the modern civilised world, but it was solved in our country thousands of years ago.

Q. But your Vedanta also was about to disappear?

Swamiji: It might be so. In the efflux of time the light of Vedanta now and then seems as if about to be extinguished, and when that happens, the Lord has to incarnate Himself in the human body; He then infuses such life and strength into religion that it goes on again for some time with irresistible vigour. That life and strength has come into it again.

Q. What proof is there, Maharaj, that India has freely contributed her knowledge to the rest of the world?

Swamiji: History itself bears testimony to the fact. All the soul-elevating ideas and the different branches of knowledge that exist in the world are found on proper investigation to have their roots in India.

---

1. Lord Curzon, who took steps to raise the standard of university education so high as to make it very expensive and hence almost inaccessible to boys of the middle classes.

Aglow with enthusiasm, Swamiji dwelt at length on this topic. His health was very bad at the time, and moreover owing to the intense heat of summer, he was feeling thirsty and drinking water too often. At last he said "Dear Singhi, get a glass of iced water for me please, I shall explain everything to you clearly." After drinking the iced water he began afresh.

Swamiji: What we need, you know, is to study, independent of foreign control, different branches of the knowledge that is our own, and with it the English language and Western science; we need technical education and all else that may develop industries So that men, instead of seeking for service, may earn enough to provide for themselves, and save something against a rainy day.

Q. What were you going to say the other day about the tol (Sanskrit boarding school) system?

Swamiji: Haven't you read the stories from the Upanishads? I will tell you one. Satyakâma went to live the life of a Brahmachârin with his Guru. The Guru gave into his charge some cows and sent him away to the forest with them. Many months passed by, and when Satyakama saw that the number of cows was doubled he thought of returning to his Guru. On his way back, one of the bulls, the fire, and some other animals gave him instructions about the Highest Brahman. When the disciple came back, the Guru at once saw by a mere glance at his face that the disciple had learnt the knowledge of the Supreme Brahman[1]. Now, the moral this story is meant to teach is that true education is gained by constant living in communion with nature.

Knowledge should be acquired in that way, otherwise by educating yourself in the tol of a Pandit you will be only a human ape all your life. One should live from his very boyhood with one whose character is like a blazing fire and should have before him a living example of the highest teaching. Mere reading that it is a sin to tell a lie will be of no use. Every boy should be trained to practice absolute Brahmacharya, and then, and then only, faith —Shraddha—will come. Otherwise, why will not one who has no Shraddha speak an untruth? In our country, the imparting of knowledge has always been through men of renunciation. Later, the Pandits, by monopolising all knowledge and restricting it to the tols, have only brought the country to the brink of ruin. India had all good prospects so long as Tyâgis (men of renunciation) used to impart knowledge.

Q. What do you mean, Maharaj? There are no Sannyâsins in other countries, but see how by dint of their knowledge India is laid prostrate at their feet!

Swamiji: Don't talk nonsense, my dear, hear what I say. India will have to carry others' shoes for ever on her head if the charge of imparting knowledge to her sons does not again fall upon the shoulders Of Tyagis. Don't you know how an illiterate boy, possessed of renunciation, turned the heads of your great old Pandits? Once at the Dakshineswar Temple the Brâhmana who was in charge of the worship of Vishnu broke a leg of the image. Pandits were brought together at a meeting to give their opinions, and they, after consulting old books and manuscripts, declared that the worship of this broken image could not be sanctioned according to the Shâstras and a new image would have to be consecrated. There was, consequently, a great stir. Shri Ramakrishna was called at last. He heard and asked, "Does a wife forsake her husband in case he becomes lame?" What followed? The Pandits were struck dumb, all their Shâstric commentaries and erudition could not withstand the force of this simple statement. If what you say was true, why should Shri Ramakrishna come down to this earth, and why should he discourage mere book-learning so much? That new life-force which he brought with him has to be instilled into learning and education, and then the real work will be done.

Q. But that is easier said than done.

Swamiji: Had it been easy, it would not have been necessary for him to come. What you have to do now is to establish a Math in every town and in every village. Can you do that? Do something at least. Start a big Math in the heart of Calcutta. A well-educated Sâdhu should be at the head of that centre and under him there should be departments for teaching practical science and arts, with a specialist Sannyasin in charge of each of these departments.

Q. Where will you get such Sadhus?

1. Chhândogya, IV. ix. 2.

Swamiji: We shall have to manufacture them. Therefore, I always say that some young men with burning patriotism and renunciation are needed. None can master a thing perfectly in so short a time as the Tyagis will.

After a short silence Swamiji said, "Singhi, there are so many things left to be done for our country that thousands like you and me are needed. What will mere talk do? See to what a miserable condition the country is reduced; now do something! We haven't even got a single book well suited for the little boys."

Q. Why, there are so many books of Ishwar Chandra Vidyâsâgar for the boys!

No sooner had I said this than he laughed out and said: Yes, there you read "Ishvar Nirakar Chaitanya Svarup"—(God is without form and of the essence of pure knowledge); "Subal ati subodh bâlak"—(Subal is a very good boy), and so on. That won't do. We must compose some books in Bengali as also in English with short stories from the Râmâyana, the Mahâbhârata, the Upanishads, etc., in very easy and simple language, and these are to be given to our little boys to read.

It was about eleven o'clock by this time. The sky became suddenly overcast, and a cool breeze began to blow. Swamiji was greatly delighted at the prospect of rain. He got up and said, "Let us, Singhi, have a stroll by the side of the Ganga." We did so, and he recited many stanzas from the Meghaduta of Kâlidâsa, but the one undercurrent of thought that was all the time running through his mind was the good of India. He exclaimed, "Look here, Singhi, can you do one thing? Can you put a stop to the marriage of our boys for some time?"

I said, "Well, Maharaj, how can we think of that when the Babus are trying, on the other hand, all sorts of means to make marriage cheaper?"

Swamiji : Don't trouble your head on that score; who can stem the tide of time! All such agitations will end in empty sound, that is all. The dearer the marriages become, the better for the country. What a hurry-scurry of passing examinations and marrying right off! It seems as if no one was to be left a bachelor, but it is just the same thing again, next year!

After a short silence, Swamiji again said, "if I can get some unmarried graduates, I may try to send them over to Japan and make arrangements for their technical education there, so that when they come back, they may turn their knowledge to the best account for India. What a good thing that would be!"

Q. Why, Maharaj, is it better for us to go to Japan than to England?

Swamiji: Certainly! In my opinion, if all our rich and educated men once go and see Japan, their eyes will be opened.

Q. How?

Swamiji: There, in Japan, you find a fine assimilation of knowledge, and not its indigestion, as we have here. They have taken everything from the Europeans, but they remain Japanese all the same, and have not turned European; while in our country, the terrible mania of becoming Westernised has seized upon us like a plague.

I said: "Maharaj, I have seen some Japanese paintings; one cannot but marvel at their art. Its inspiration seems to be something which is their own and beyond imitation."

Swamiji: Quite so. They are great as a nation because of their art. Don't you see they are Asians, as we are? And though we have lost almost everything, yet what we still have is wonderful. The very soul of the Asian is interwoven with art. The Asian never uses a thing unless there be art in it. Don't you knew that art is, with us, a part of religion? How greatly is a lady admired, among us, who can nicely paint the floors and walls, on auspicious occasions, with the paste of rice powder? How great an artist was Shri Ramakrishna himself!

Q. The English art is also good, is it not?

Swamiji: What a stupid fool you are! But what is the use of blaming you when that seems to be the prevailing way of thinking! Alas, to such a state is our country reduced! The people will look upon their own gold as brass, while the brass of the foreigner it gold to them! This is, indeed, the magic wrought by modern education! Know that since the time the Europeans have come into contact with Asia, they are trying to infuse art into their own life.

Myself: If others hear you talk like this, Maharaj they will think that you take a pessimistic view of things.

Swamiji: Naturally! What else can they think who move in a rut! How I wish I could show you everything through my eyes! Look at their buildings—how commonplace, how meaningless, they are! Look at those big government buildings; can you, just by seeing their outside, make out any meaning for which each of them stands? No, because they are all so unsymbolical. Take again the dress of Westerners: their stiff coats and straight pants fitting almost tightly to the body, are, in our estimation hardly decent. Is it not so? And, oh, what beauty indeed, in that! Now, go all over our motherland and see if you cannot read aright, from their very appearance, the meaning for which our buildings stand, and how much art there is in them! The glass is their drinking vessel, and ours is the metal Ghati (pitcher-shaped); which of the two is artistic? Have you seen the farmers' homes in our villages?

Myself: Yes, I have, of course.

Swamiji: What have you seen of them?

I did not know what to say. However, I replied, "Maharaj, they are faultlessly neat and clean, the yards and floors being daily well plastered over".

Swamiji: Have you seen their granaries for keeping paddy? What an art is there in them! What a variety of paintings even on their mud walls! And then, if you go and see how the lower classes live in the West, you would at once mark the difference. Their ideal is utility, ours art. The Westerner looks for utility in everything, whereas with us art is everywhere. With the Western education, those beautiful Ghatis of ours have been discarded, and enamel glasses have usurped their place in our homes! Thus the ideal of utility has been imbibed by us to such an extent as to make it look little short of the ridiculous. Now what we need is the combination of art and utility. Japan has done that very quickly, and so she has advanced by giant strides. Now, in their turn, the Japanese are going to teach the Westerners.

Q. Maharaj, which nation in the world dresses best?

Swamiji: The Aryans do; even the Europeans admit that. How picturesquely their dresses hang in folds! The royal costumes of most nations are, to some extent, a sort of imitation of the Aryans,'—the same attempt is made there to keep them in folds, and those costumes bear a marked difference to their national style.

By the by, Singhi, leave off that wretched habit of wearing those European shirts.

Q. Why, Maharaj?

Swamiji: For the reason that they are used by the Westerners only as underwear. They never like to see them worn outside. How mistaken of the Bengalis to do so! As if one should wear anything and everything, as if there was no unwritten law about dress, as if there was no ancestral style to follow! Our people are out-casted by taking the food touched by the lower classes it would have been very well if the same law applied to their wearing any irregular style of dress. Why can't you adapt your dress in some way to our own style? What sense is there in your adopting European shirts and coats?

It began to rain now, and the dinner-bell also rang. So we went in to partake of the Prasâda (consecrated food) with others. During the meal, Swamiji said, addressing me: "Concentrated food should be taken. To fill the stomach with a large quantity of rice is the root of laziness." A little while after he said again, "Look at the Japanese, they take rice with the soup of split peas, twice or thrice a day. But even the strongly built take a little at a time, though the number of meals may be more. Those who are well-to-do among them take meat daily. While we stuff ourselves twice a day up to the throat, as it were, and the whole of our energy is exhausted in digesting such a quantity of rice!"

Q. Is it feasible for us Bengalis, poor as we are, to take meat?

Swamiji: Why not? You can afford to have it in small quantities. Half a pound a day is quite enough. The real evil is idleness, which is the principal cause of our poverty. Suppose the head of a firm gets displeased with someone and decreases his pay; or out of three or four bread-winning sons in a family one suddenly dies; what do they do? Why, they at once curtail the quantity of milk for the children, or live on one meal a day, having a little popped rice or so at night!

Q. But what else can they do under the circumstances?

Swamiji: Why can't they exert themselves and earn more to keep up their standard of food? But no! They must go to their local Âddâs (rendezvous) and idle hours away! Oh, if they only knew how they wasted their time!

X — The Discrimination of the Four Castes According to Jati and Guna—Brahmanas and Kshatriyas in the West—The Kula-Guru System in Bengal

Once I went to see Swamiji while he was staying in Calcutta at the house of the late Balaram Basu. After a long conversation about Japan and America, I asked him, "Well, Swamiji, how many disciples have you in the West?"

Swamiji: A good many.

Q. Two or three thousands?

Swamiji: Maybe more than that.

Q. Are they all initiated by you with Mantras?

Swamiji: Yes.

Q. Did you give them permission to utter Pranava (Om)?

Swamiji: Yes.

Q. How did you, Mahârâj? They say that the Shudras have no right to Pranava, and none has except the Brâhmins. Moreover, the Westerners are Mlechchhas, not even Shudras.

Swamiji: How do you know that those whom I have initiated are not Brahmins?

Myself: Where could you get Brahmins outside India, in the lands of the Yavanas and Mlechchhas?

Swamiji: My disciples are all Brahmins! I quite admit the truth of the words that none except the Brahmins has the right to Pranava. But the son of a Brahmin is not necessarily always a Brahmin; though there is every possibility of his being one, he may not become so. Did you not hear that the nephew of Aghore Chakravarti of Baghbazar became a sweeper and actually used to do all the menial services of his adopted caste? Was he not the son of a Brahmin?

The Brahmin caste and the Brâhmanya qualities are two distinct things. In India, one is held to be a Brahmin by one's caste, but in the West, one should be known as such by one's Brahmanya qualities. As there are three Gunas—Sattva, Rajas, and Tamas—so there are Gunas which show a man to be a Brahmin, Kshatriya, Vaishya or Shudra. The qualities of being a Brahmin or a Kshatriya are dying out from the country; but in the West they have now attained to Kshatriyahood, from which the next step is Brahminhood; and many there are who have qualified themselves for that.

Q. Then you call those Brahmins who are Sâttvika by nature.

Swamiji: Quite so. As there are Sattva, Rajas, and Tamas—one or other of these Gunas more or less—in every man, so the qualities which make a Brahmin, Kshatriya, Vaishya, or Shudra are inherent in every man, more or less. But at times one or other of these qualities predominates in him in varying degrees, and it is manifested accordingly. Take a man in his different pursuits, for example: when he is engaged in serving another for pay, he is in Shudrahood; when he is busy transacting some piece of business for profit, on his own account, he is a Vaishya; when he fights to right wrongs, then the qualities of a Kshatriya come out in him; and when he meditates on God or passes his time in conversation about Him, then he is a Brahmin. Naturally, it is quite possible for one to be changed from one caste into another. Otherwise, how did Vishvâmitra become a Brahmin and Parashurâma a Kshatriya?

Q. What you say seems to be quite right, but why then do not our Pandits and family-Gurus teach us the same thing?

Swamiji: That is one of the great evils of our country. But let the matter rest now.

Swamiji here spoke highly of the Westerners' spirit of practicality, and how, when they take up religion also, that spirit shows itself.

Myself: True, Maharaj, I have heard that their spiritual and psychic powers are very quickly developed when they practice religion. The other day Swami Saradananda showed me a letter written by one of his Western disciples, describing the spiritual powers highly developed in the writer through the Sâdhanâs practiced for only four months.

Swamiji: So you see! Now you understand whether there are Brahmins in the West or not. You have Brahmins here also, but they are bringing the country down to the verge of ruin by their awful tyranny, and consequently what they have naturally is vanishing away by degrees. The Guru initiates his disciple with a Mantra, but that has come to be a trade with him. And then, how wonderful is the relation nowadays between a Guru and his disciple! Perchance, the Guru has nothing to eat at home, and his wife brings the matter to his notice and says, "Pray, go once again to your disciples, dear. Will your playing at dice all day long save us from hunger?" The Brahmin in reply says, "Very well, remind me of it tomorrow morning. I have come to hear that my disciple so-and-so is having a run of luck, and, moreover, I have not been to him for a long time." This is what your Kula-Guru system has come to in Bengal! Priestcraft in the West is not so degenerated, as yet; it is on the whole better than your kind!

XI — XV FROM THE DIARY OF A DISCIPLE, SHRI SARAT CHANDRA CHAKRAVARTY

(Translated from Bengali)

India Wants not Lecturing but Work—The Crying Problem in India is Poverty—Young Sannyasins to be Trained Both as Secular And Spiritual Teachers and Workers for the Masses—Exhortations to Young Men to WORK for Others

(From the Diary of a disciple)

(The disciple in this and the following conversations is Sharat Chandra Chakravarty.)

Disciple: How is it, Swamiji, that you do not lecture in this country? You have stirred Europe and America with your lectures, but coming back here you have kept silence.

Swamiji: In this country, the ground should be prepared first; then if the seed is sown, the plant will come out best. The ground in the West, in Europe and America is very fertile and fit for sowing seeds. There they have reached the climax of Bhoga (enjoyment). Being satiated with Bhoga to the full, their minds are not getting peace now even in those enjoyments, and they feel as if they wanted something else. In this country you have neither Bhoga nor Yoga (renunciation). When one is satiated with Bhoga, then it is that one will listen to and understand the teachings on Yoga. What good will lectures do in a country like India which has become the birthplace of disease, sorrow, and affliction, and where men are emaciated through starvation, and weak in mind?

Disciple: How is that? Do you not say that ours is the land of religion and that here the people understand religion as they do nowhere else? Why then will not this country be animated by your inspiring eloquence and reap to the full the fruits thereof?

Swamiji: Now understand what religion means. The first thing required is the worship of the Kurma (tortoise) Incarnation, and the belly-god is this Kurma, as it were. Until you pacify this, no one will welcome your words about religion. India is restless with the thought of how to face this spectre of hunger. The draining of the best resources of the country by the foreigners, the unrestricted exports of merchandise, and, above all, the abominable jealousy natural to slaves are eating into the vitals of India. First of all, you must remove this evil of hunger and starvation, this constant anxiety for bare existence, from those to whom you want to preach religion; otherwise, lectures and such things will be of no benefit.

Disciple: What should we do then to remove that evil?

Swamiji: First, some young men full of the spirit of renunciation are needed —those who will be ready to sacrifice their lives for others, instead of devoting themselves to their own happiness. With this object in view I shall establish a Math to train young Sannyâsins, who will go from door to door and make the people realise their pitiable condition by means of facts and reasoning, and instruct them in the ways and means for their welfare, and at the same time will explain to them as clearly as possible, in very simple and easy language, the higher truths of religion. The masses in our country are like the sleeping Leviathan. The education imparted by the present university system reaches one or two per cent of the masses only. And even those who get that do not succeed in their endeavours of doing any good to their country. But it is not their fault, poor fellows! As soon as they come out of their college, they find themselves fathers of several children! Somehow or other they manage to secure the position of a clerk, or at the most, a deputy magistrate. This is the finale of education! With the burden of a family on their backs, they find no time to do anything great or think anything high. They do not find means enough to fulfil their personal wants and interests; so what can be expected of them in the way of doing anything for others?

Disciple: Is there then no way out for us?

Swamiji: Certainly there is. This is the land of Religion Eternal. The country has fallen, no doubt, but will as surely rise again, and that upheaval will astound the world. The lower the hollows the billows make, the higher and with greater force will they rise again.

Disciple: How will India rise again?

Swamiji: Do you not see? The dawn has already appeared in the eastern sky, and there is little delay in the sun's rising. You all set your shoulders to the wheel! What is there in making the world all in all, and thinking of "My Samsâra (family and property), my Samsâra"? Your duty at present is to go from one part of the country to another, from village to village, and make the people understand that mere sitting idly won't do any more. Make them understand their real condition and say, "O ye brothers, arise! Awake! How much longer would you remain asleep!" Go and advise them how to improve their own condition, and make them comprehend the sublime truths of the Shâstras (scriptures), by presenting them in a lucid and popular way. So long the Brahmins have monopolised religion; but since they cannot hold their ground against the strong tide of time, go and take steps so that one and all in the land may get that religion. Impress upon their minds that they have the same right to religion as the Brahmins. Initiate all, even down to the Chandâlas (people of the lowest castes), in these fiery Mantras. Also instruct them, in simple words, about the necessities of life, and in trade, commerce, agriculture, etc. If you cannot do this then lie upon your education and culture, and lie upon your studying the Vedas and Vedanta!

Disciple: But where is that strength in us? I should have felt myself blessed if I had a hundredth part of your powers, Swamiji.

Swamiji: How foolish! Power and things like that will come by themselves. Put yourself to work, and you will final such tremendous power coming to you that you will feel it hard to bear. Even the least work done for others awakens the power within; even thinking the least good of others gradually instils into the heart the strength of a lion. I lore you all ever so much, but I wish you all to die working for others—I should rather be glad to see you do that!

Disciple: What will become of those, then, who depend on me?

Swamiji: If you are ready to sacrifice your life for others, God will certainly provide some means for them. Have you not read in the Gita (VI. 40) the words of Shri Krishna, "न हि कल्याणकृत्कश्चित् दुर्गतिं तात गच्छति—Never does a doer of good, O my beloved, come to grief"?

Disciple: I see, sir.

Swamiji: The essential thing is renunciation. Without renunciation none can pour out his whole heart in working for others. The man of renunciation sees all with an equal eye and devotes himself to the service of all. Does not our Vedanta also teach us to see all with an equal eye? Why then do you cherish the idea that the wife and children are your own, more than others? At your very threshold, Nârâyana Himself in the form of a poor beggar is dying of starvation! Instead of giving him anything, would you only satisfy the appetites of your wife and children with delicacies? Why, that is beastly!

Disciple: To work for others requires a good deal of money at times, and where shall I get that?

Swamiji: Why not do as much as lies within your power? Even if you cannot give to others for want of money, surely you can at least breathe into their ears some good words or impart some good instruction, can't you? Or does that also require money?

Disciple: Yes, sir, that I can do.

Swamiji: But saying, "I can", won't do. Show me through action what you can do, and then only I shall know that your coming to me is turned to some good account. Get up, and put your shoulders to the wheel—how long is this life for? As you have come into this world, leave some mark behind. Otherwise, where is the difference between you and the trees and stones? They, too, come into existence, decay and die. If you like to be born and to die like them, you are at liberty to do so. Show me by your actions that your reading the Vedanta has been fruitful of the highest good. Go and tell all, "In every one of you lies that Eternal Power", and try to wake It up. What will you do with individual salvation? That is sheer selfishness. Throw aside your meditation, throw away your salvation and such things! Put your whole heart and soul in the work to which I have consecrated myself.

With bated breath the disciple heard these inspiring words, and Swamiji went on with his usual fire and eloquence.

Swamiji: First of all, make the soil ready, and thousands of Vivekanandas will in time be born into this world to deliver lectures on religion. You needn't worry yourself about that! Don't you see why I am starting orphanages, famine-relief works, etc.? Don't you see how Sister Nivedita, a British lady, has learnt to serve Indians so well, by doing even menial work for them? And can't you, being Indians, similarly serve your own fellow-countrymen? Go, all of you, wherever there is an outbreak of plague or famine, or wherever the people are in distress, and mitigate their sufferings. At the most you may die in the attempt—what of that? How many like you are being born and dying like worms every day? What difference does that make to the world at large? Die you must, but have a great ideal to die for, and it is better to die with a great ideal in life. Preach this ideal from door to door, and you will yourselves be benefited by it at the same time that you are doing good to your country. On you lie the future hopes of our country. I feel extreme pain to see you leading a life of inaction. Set yourselves to work—to work! Do not tarry—the time of death is approaching day by day! Do not sit idle, thinking that everything will be done in time, later on! Mind—nothing will be done that way!

XII — Reconciliation of Jnana and Bhakti—Sat-Chit-Ananda—How Sectarianism Originates—Bring in Shraddha and the Worship of Shakti and avataras—The Ideal of the Hero We Want Now, not the Madhura-Bhava—Shri Ramakrishna—Avataras

Disciple: Pray, Swamiji, how can Jnâna and Bhakti be reconciled? We see the followers of the path of devotion (Bhaktas) close their ears at the name of Shankara, and again, the followers of the path of knowledge (Jnanis) call the Bhaktas fanatics, seeing them weep in torrents, or sing and dance in ecstasy, in the name of the Lord.

Swamiji: The thing is, all this conflict is in the preliminary (preparatory) stages of Jnana and Bhakti. Have you not heard Shri Ramakrishna's story about Shiva's demons and Râma's monkeys[1]?

Disciple: Yes, sir, I have.

Swamiji: But there is no difference between the supreme Bhakti and the supreme Jnana. The supreme Bhakti is to realise God as the form of Prema (love) itself. If you see the loving form of God manifest everywhere and in everything, how can you hate or injure others? That realisation of love can never come so long as there is the least desire in the heart, or what Shri Ramakrishna used to say, attachment for Kâma-Kânchana (sense-pleasure and wealth). In the perfect realisation of love, even the consciousness of

---

1. There was once a fight between Shiva and Rama. Shiva was the Guru of Rama, and Rama was the Guru of Shiva. They fought but became friendly again. But there was no end to the quarrels and wranglings between the demons of Shiva and the monkeys of Rama!

one's own body does not exist. Also, the supreme Jnana is to realise the oneness everywhere, to see one's own self as the Self in everything. That too cannot come so long as there is the least consciousness of the ego (Aham).

Disciple: Then what you call love is the same as supreme knowledge?

Swamiji: Exactly so. Realisation of love comes to none unless one becomes a perfect Jnani. Does not the Vedanta say that Brahman is Sat-Chit-Ânanda—the absolute Existence-Knowledge-Bliss?

Disciple: Yes, sir.

Swamiji: The phrase Sat-Chit-Ananda means—Sat, i.e. existence, Chit, i.e. consciousness or knowledge, and Ananda, i.e. bliss which is the same as love. There is no controversy between the Bhakta and the Jnani regarding the Sat aspect of Brahman. Only, the Jnanis lay greater stress on His aspect of Chit or knowledge, while the Bhaktas keep the aspect of Ananda or love more in view. But no sooner is the essence of Chit realised than the essence of Ananda is also realised. Because what is Chit is verily the same as Ananda.

Disciple: Why then is so much sectarianism prevalent in India? And why is there so much controversy between the scriptures on Bhakti and Jnana?

Swamiji: The thing is, all this waging of war and controversy is concerning the preliminary ideals, i.e. those ideals which men take up to attain the real Jnana or real Bhakti. But which do you think is the higher—the end or the means? Surely, the means can never be higher than the end, because the means to realise the same end must be numerous, as they vary according to the temperament or mental capacities of individual followers. The counting of beads, meditation, worship, offering oblations in the sacred fire—all these and such other things are the limbs of religion; they are but means; and to attain to supreme devotion (Parâ-Bhakti) or to the highest realisation of Brahman is the pre-eminent end. If you look a little deeper, you will understand what they are fighting about. One says, "If you pray to God facing the East, then you will reach Him." "No," says another, "you will have to sit facing the West, and then only you will see Him." Perhaps someone realised God in meditation, ages ago, by sitting with his face to the East, and his disciples at once began to preach this attitude, asserting that none can ever see God unless he assumes this position. Another party comes forward and inquires, "How is that? Such and such a person realised God while facing the West, and we have seen this ourselves." In this way all these sects have originated. Someone might have attained supreme devotion by repeating the name of the Lord as Hari, and at once it entered into the composition of the Shâstra as:

हरेर्नाम हरेर्नाम हरेर्नामैव केवलम् । कलौ नास्त्येव नास्त्येव नास्त्येव गतिरन्यथा ॥

—"The name of the Lord Hari, the name of the Lord Hari, the name of the Lord Hari alone. Verily, there is no other, no other, no other path than this in the age of Kali."

Someone, again, let us suppose, might have attained perfection with the name of Allah, and immediately another creed originated by him began to spread, and so on. But we have to see what is the end to which all these forms of worship and other religious practices are intended to lead. The end is Shraddhâ. We have not any synonym in our Bengali language to express the Sanskrit word Shraddha. The (Katha) Upanishad says that Shraddha entered into the heart of Nachiketâ. Even with the word Ekâgratâ (one-pointedness) we cannot express the whole significance of the word Shraddha. The word Ekâgranishthâ (one-pointed devotion) conveys, to a certain extent, the meaning of the word Shraddha. If you meditate on any truth with steadfast devotion and concentration, you will see that the mind is more and more tending onwards to Oneness, i.e. taking you towards the realisation of the absolute Existence-Knowledge-Bliss. The scriptures on Bhakti or Jnana give special advice to men to take up in life the one or the other of such Nishthas (scrupulous persistence) and make it their own. With the lapse of ages, these great truths become distorted and gradually transform themselves into Deshâchâras or the prevailing customs of a country. It has happened, not only in India, but in every nation and every society in the world. And the common people, lacking in discrimination, make these the bone of contention and fight among themselves. They have lost sight of the end, and hence sectarianism, quarrels, and fights continue.

Disciple: What then is the saving means, Swamiji?

Swamiji: That true Shraddha, as of old, has to be brought back again. The weeds have to be talker up by the roots. In every faith and in every path, there are, no doubt, truths which transcend time and space, but a good deal of rubbish has accumulated over them. This has to be cleared away, and the true eternal principles have to be held before the people; and then only, our religion and our country will be really benefited.

Disciple: How will that be effected?

Swamiji: Why, first of all, we have to introduce the worship of the great saints. Those great-souled ones who have realised the eternal truths are to be presented before the people as the ideas to be followed; as in the case of India—Shri Râmachandra, Shri Krishna, Mahâvira and Shri Ramakrishna, among others. Can you bring in the worship of Shri Ramachandra and Mahavira in this country? Keep aside for the present the Vrindâvan aspect of Shri Krishna, and spread far and wide the worship of Shri Krishna roaring the Gita out, with the voice of a Lion. And bring into daily use the worship of Shakti—the divine Mother, the source of all power.

Disciple: Is the divine play of Shri Krishna with the Gopis of Vrindavan not good, then?

Swamiji: Under the present circumstances, that worship is of no good to you. Playing on the flute and so on will not regenerate the country. We now mostly need the ideal of a hero with the tremendous spirit of Rajas thrilling through his veins from head to foot—the hero who will dare and die to know the Truth—the hero whose armour is renunciation, whose sword is wisdom. We want now the spirit of the brave warrior in the battlefield of life, and not of the wooing lover who looks upon life as a pleasure-garden!

Disciple: Is then the path of love, as depicted in the ideal of the Gopis, false?

Swamiji: Who says so? Not I! That is a very superior form of worship (Sâdhanâ). In this age of tremendous attachment to sense-pleasure and wealth, very few are able even to comprehend those higher ideals.

Disciple: Then are not those who are worshipping God as husband or lover (Madhura) following the proper path?

Swamiji: I dare say not. There may be a few honourable exceptions among them, but know, that the greater part of them are possessed of dark Tâmasika nature. Most of them are full of morbidity and affected with exceptional weakness. The country must be raised. The worship of Mahavira must be introduced; the Shakti-pujâ must form a part of our daily practice; Shri Ramachandra must be worshipped in every home. Therein lies your welfare, therein lies the good of the country—there is no other way.

Disciple: But I have heard that Bhagavan Shri Ramakrishna used to sing the name of God very much?

Swamiji: Quite so, but his was a different case. What comparison can there be between him and ordinary men? He practiced in his life all the different ideals of religion to show that each of them leads but to the One Truth. Shall you or I ever be able to do all that he has done? None of us has understood him fully. So, I do not venture to speak about him anywhere and everywhere. He only knows what he himself really was; his frame was a human one only, but everything else about him was entirely different from others.

Disciple: Do you, may I ask, believe him to be an Avatara (Incarnation of God)?

Swamiji: Tell me first—what do you mean by an Avatara?

Disciple: Why, I mean one like Shri Ramachandra, Shri Krishna, Shri Gauranga, Buddha, Jesus, and others.

Swamiji: I know Bhagavan Shri Ramakrishna to be even greater than those you have just named. What to speak of believing, which is a petty thing—I know! Let us, however, drop the subject now; more of it another time.

After a pause Swamiji continued: To re-establish the

Dharma, there come Mahâpurushas (great teachers of humanity), suited to the needs of the times and society. Call them what you will—either Mahapurushas or Avataras—it matters little. They reveal, each in his life, the ideal. Then, by degrees, shapes are moulded in their matrices—MEN are made! Gradually, sects arise and spread As time goes on, these sects degenerate, and similar reformers come again. This has been the law flowing in uninterrupted succession, like a current, down the ages.

Disciple: Why do you not preach Shri Ramakrishna as an Avatara? You have, indeed, power, eloquence, and everything else needed to do it.

Swamiji: Truly, I tell you, I have understood him very little. He appears to me to have been so great that, whenever I have to speak anything of him, I am afraid lest I ignore or explain away the truth, lest my little power does not suffice, lest in trying to extol him I present his picture by painting him according to my lights and belittle him thereby!

Disciple: But many are now preaching him as an Avatara.

Swamiji: Let them do so if they like. They are doing it in the light in which they have understood him. You too can go and do the same, if you have understood him.

Disciple: I cannot even grasp you, what to say of Shri Ramakrishna! I should consider myself blessed in this life if I get a little of Your grace.

XIII — Brahman and Differentiation—Personal Realisation of Oneness—Supreme Bliss is the Goal of All—Think Always, I am Brahman—Discrimination and Renunciation are the Means—Be Fearless

Disciple: Pray, Swamiji, if the one Brahman is the only Reality, why then exists all this differentiation in the world?

Swamiji: Are you not considering this question from the point of view of phenomenal existence? Looking from the phenomenal side of existence, one can, through reasoning and discrimination, gradually arrive at the very root of Unity. But if you were firmly established in that Unity, how from that standpoint, tell me, could you see this differentiation?

Disciple: True, if I had existed in the Unity, how should I be able to raise this question of "why"? As I put this question, it is already taken for granted that I do so by seeing this diversity.

Swamiji: Very well. To enquire about the root of Oneness through the diversity of phenomenal existence is named by the Shâstras as Vyatireki reasoning, or the process of arguing by the indirect method, that is, Adhyâropa and Apavâda, first taking for granted something that is nonexistent or unreal as existing or real, and then showing through the course of reasoning that that is not a substance existing or real. You are talking of the process of arriving at the truth through assuming that which is not-true as true—are you not?

Disciple: To my mind, the state of the existing or the seen seems to be self-evident, and hence true, and that which is opposite to it seems, on the other hand, to be unreal.

Swamiji: But the Vedas say, "One only without a second". And if in reality there is the One only that exists—the Brahman—then, your differentiation is false. You believe in the Vedas, I suppose?

Disciple: Oh, yes, for me self I hold the Vedas as the highest authority; but if, in argument, one does not accept them to be so, one must, in that case, have to be refuted by other means.

Swamiji: That also can be done. Look here, a time comes when what you call differentiation vanishes, and we cannot perceive it at all. I have experienced that state in my own life.

Disciple: When have you done so?

Swamiji: One day in the temple-garden at Dakshineswar Shri Ramakrishna touched me over the heart, and first of all I began to see that the houses —rooms, doors, windows, verandahs—the trees, the sun, the moon—all were flying off, shattering to pieces as it were—reduced to atoms and molecules —and ultimately became merged in the Âkâsha. Gradually again, the Akasha also vanished, and after that, my consciousness of the ego with it; what happened next I do not recollect. I was at first frightened. Coming back from that state, again I began to see the houses, doors, windows, verandahs, and other things. On another occasion, I had exactly the same realisation by the side of a lake in America.

Disciple: Might not this state as well be brought about by a derangement of the brain? And I do not understand what happiness there can be in realising such a state.

Swamiji: A derangement of the brain! How can you call it so, when it comes neither as the result of delirium from any disease, nor of intoxication from drinking, nor as an illusion produced by various sorts of queer breathing exercises—but when it comes to a normal man in full possession of his health and wits? Then again, this experience is in perfect harmony with the Vedas. It also coincides with the words of realisation of the inspired Rishis and Âchâryas of old. Do you take me, at last, to be a crack-brained man? (smiling).

Disciple: Oh, no, I did not mean that of course. When there are to be found hundreds of illustrations about such realisation of Oneness in the Shastras, and when you say that it can be as directly realised as a fruit in the palm of one's hand, and when it has been your own personal experience in life, perfectly coinciding with the words of the Vedas and other Shastras—how dare I say that it is false? Shri Shankaracharya also realising that state has said, "Where is the universe vanished?" and so on.

Swamiji: Know—this knowledge of Oneness is what the Shastras speak of as realisation of the Brahman, by knowing which, one gets rid of fear, and the shackles of birth and death break for ever. Having once realised that Supreme Bliss, one is no more overwhelmed by pleasure and pain of this world. Men being fettered by base lust-and-wealth cannot enjoy that Bliss of Brahman.

Disciple: If it is so, and if we are really of the essence of the Supreme Brahman, then why do we not exert ourselves to gain that Bliss? Why do we again and again run into the jaws of death, being decoyed by this worthless snare of lust-and-wealth?

Swamiji: You speak as if man does not desire to have that Bliss! Ponder over it, and you will see that whatever anyone is doing, he is doing in the hope of gaining that Supreme Bliss. Only, not everyone is conscious of it and so cannot understand it. That Supreme Bliss fully exists in all, from Brahmâ down to the blade of grass. You are also that undivided Brahman. This very moment you can realise if you think yourself truly and absolutely to be so. It is all mere want of direct perception. That you have taken service and work so hard for the sake of your wife also shows that the aim is ultimately to attain to that Supreme Bliss of Brahman. Being again and again entangled in the intricate maze of delusion and hard hit by sorrows and afflictions, the eye will turn of itself to one's own real nature, the Inner Self. It is owing to the presence of this desire for bliss in the heart, that man, getting hard shocks one after another, turns his eye inwards—to his own Self. A time is sure to come to everyone, without exception, when he will do so to one it may be in this life, to another, after thousands of incarnations.

Disciple: It all depends upon the blessings of the Guru and the grace of the Lord!

Swamiji: The wind of grace of the Lord is blowing on, for ever and ever. You just need to spread your sail. Whenever you do anything, do it with your whole heart concentrated on it. Think day and night, "I am of the essence of that Supreme Existence-Knowledge-Bliss—what fear and anxiety have I? This body, mind, and intellect are all transient, and That which is beyond these is myself."

Disciple: Thoughts like these come only for a while now and then, but quickly vanish, and I think all sorts of trash and nonsense.

Swamiji: It happens like that in the initial stage, but gradually it is overcome. But from the beginning, intensity of desire in the mind is needed. Think always, "I am ever-pure, ever-knowing, and ever-free; how can I do anything evil? Can I ever be befooled like ordinary men with the insignificant charms of lust and wealth?" Strengthen the mind with such thoughts.

This will surely bring real good.

Disciple: Once in a while strength of mind comes. But then again I think that if I would appear at the Deputy Magistrateship Examination, wealth and name and fame would come and I should live well and happy

Swamiji: Whenever such thoughts come in the mind, discriminate within yourself between the real and the unreal. Have you not read the Vedanta? Even when you sleep, keep the sword of discrimination at the head of your bed, so that covetousness cannot approach you even in dream. Practising such strength, renunciation will gradually come, and then you will see—the portals of heaven are wide open to you.

Disciple: If it is so, Swamiji, how is it then that the texts on Bhakti say that too much of renunciation kills the feelings that make for tenderness?

Swamiji: Throw away, I say, texts which teach things like that! Without renunciation, without burning dispassion for sense-objects, without turning away from wealth and lust as from filthy abomination— "न सिध्यति ब्रह्मशतान्तरेऽपि—never can one attain salvation even in hundreds of Brahma's cycles". Repeating the names of the Lord, meditation, worship, offering libations in sacred fire, penance—all these are for bringing forth renunciation. One who has not gained renunciation, know his efforts to be like unto those of the man who is pulling at the oars all the while that the boat is at anchor. "न प्रजया धनेन त्यागेनेके अमृतत्वमानशुः—neither by progeny nor by wealth, but by renunciation alone some (rare ones) attained immortality" (Kaivalya Upanishad, 3).

Disciple: Will mere renouncing of wealth and lust accomplish everything?

Swamiji: There are other hindrances on the path even after renouncing those two; then, for example, comes name and fame. Very few men, unless of exceptional strength, can keep their balance under that. People shower honours upon them, and various enjoyments creep in by degrees. It is owing to this that three-fourths of the Tyâgis are debarred from further progress! For establishing this Math and other things, who knows but that I may have to come back again!

Disciple: If you say things like that, then we are undone!

Swamiji: What fear? "अभीरभीरभीः—Be fearless, be fearless, be fearless!" You have seen Nâg Mahâshaya how even while living the life of a householder, he is more than a Sannyâsin! This is very uncommon; I have rarely seen one like him. If anyone wants to be a householder, let him be like Nag Mahashaya. He shines like a brilliant luminary in the spiritual firmament of East Bengal. Ask the people of that part of the country to visit him often; that will do much good to them.

Disciple: Nag Mahashaya, it seems, is the living personification of humility in the play of Shri Ramakrishna's divine drama on earth.

Swamiji: Decidedly so, without a shadow of doubt! I have a wish to go and see him once. Will you go with, me? I love to see fields flooded over with water in the rains. Will you write to him?

Disciple: Certainly I will. He is always mad with joy when he hears about you, and says that East Bengal will be sanctified into a place of pilgrimage by the dust of your feet.

Swamiji: Do you know, Shri Ramakrishna used to speak of Nag Mahashaya as a "flaming fire"?

Disciple: Yes, so I have heard.

At the request of Swamiji, the disciple partook of some Prasâda (consecrated food), and left for Calcutta late in the evening; he was deeply thinking over the message of fearlessness that he had heard from the lips of the inspired teacher—"I am free!" "I am free!"

XIV — Renunciation of Kamakanchana—God's Mercy Falls on Those Who Struggle for Realisation—Unconditional Mercy and Brahman Are One

Disciple: Shri Ramakrishna used to say, Swamiji, that a man cannot progress far towards religious realisation unless he first relinquishes Kâma-Kânchana (lust and greed). If so, what will become of householders? For their whole minds are set on these two things.

Swamiji: It is true that the mind can never turn to God until the desire for lust and wealth has gone from it, be the man a householder or a Sannyâsin. Know this for a fact, that as long as the mind is caught in these, so long true devotion, firmness, and Shraddhâ (faith) can never come.

Disciple: Where will the householders be, then? What way are they to follow?

Swamiji: To satisfy our smaller desires and have done with them for ever, and to relinquish the greater ones by discrimination—that is the way. Without renunciation God can never be realised—यदि ब्रह्मा स्वयं वदेत्—even if Brahmâ himself enjoined otherwise!

Disciple: But does renunciation of everything come as soon as one becomes a monk?

Swamiji: Sannyasins are at least struggling to make themselves ready for renunciation, whereas householders are in this matter like boatmen who work at their oars while the boat lies at anchor. Is the desire for enjoyment ever appeased? "भूय एवाभिवर्धते—It increases ever and ever" (Bhâgavata, IX. xix. 14).

Disciple: Why? May not world-weariness come, after enjoying the objects of the senses over and over for a long time?

Swamiji: To how many does that come? The mind becomes tarnished by constant contact with the objects of the senses and receives a permanent moulding and impress from them. Renunciation, and renunciation alone, is the real secret, the Mulamantra, of all Realisation.

Disciple: But there are such injunctions of the seers in the scriptures as these: "गृहेषु पञ्चेन्द्रयनिग्रहस्तपः—To restrain the five senses while living with one's wife and children is Tapas." "निवृत्तरागस्य गृहं तपोवनम्—For him whose desires are under control, living in the midst of his family is the same as retiring into a forest for Tapasya."

Swamiji: Blessed indeed are those who can renounce Kama-Kanchana, living in their homes with their family! But how many can do that?

Disciple: But then, what about the Sannyasins? Are they all able to relinquish lust and love for riches fully?

Swamiji: As I said just now, Sannyasins are on the path of renunciation, they have taken the field, at least, to fight for the goal; but householders, on the other hand, having no knowledge as yet of the danger that comes through lust and greed, do not even attempt to realise the Self; that they must struggle to get rid of these is an idea that has not yet entered their minds.

Disciple: But many of them are struggling for it.

Swamiji: Oh, yes, and those who are doing so will surely renounce by degrees; their inordinate attachment for Kama-Kanchana will diminish gradually. But for those who procrastinate, saying, "Oh, not so soon! I shall do it when the time comes", Self-realisation is very far off. "Let me realise the Truth this moment! In this very life!"—these are the words of a hero. Such heroes are ever ready to renounce the very next moment, and to such the scripture (Jâbâla Upanishad, 3.) says, "यदहरेव विरजेत् तदहरेव प्रव्रजेत्—The moment you feel disgust for the vanities of the world, leave it all and take to the life of a monk."

Disciple: But was not Shri Ramakrishna wont to say, "All these attachments vanish through the grace of God when one prays to Him?"

Swamiji: Yes, it is so, no doubt, through His mercy, but one needs to be pure first before one can receive this mercy—pure in thought, word, and deed; then it is that His grace descends on one.

Disciple: But of what necessity is grace to him who can control himself in thought, word, and deed? For then he would be able to develop himself in the path of spirituality by means of his own exertions!

Swamiji: The Lord is very merciful to him whom He sees struggling heart and soul for Realisation. But remain idle, without any struggle, and you will see that His grace will never come.

Disciple: Everyone longs to be good, yet the mind for some inscrutable reasons, turns to evil! Does not everyone wish to be good—to be perfect—to realise God?

Swamiji: Know them to be already struggling who desire this. God bestows His mercy when this struggle is maintained.

Disciple: In the history of the Incarnations, we find many persons who, we should say, had led very dissipated lives and yet were able to realise God without much trouble and without performing any Sâdhanâ or devotion. How is this accounted for?

Swamiji: Yes, but a great restlessness must already have come upon them; long enjoyment of the objects of the senses must already have created in them deep disgust. Want of peace must have been consuming their very hearts. So deeply they had already felt this void in their hearts that life even for a moment had seemed unbearable to them unless they could gain that peace which follows in the train of the Lord's mercy. So God was kind to them. This development took place in them direct from Tamas to Sattva.

Disciple: Then, whatever was the path, they may be said to have realised God truly in that way?

Swamiji: Yes, why not? But is it not better to enter into a mansion by the main entrance than by its doorway of dishonour?

Disciple: No doubt that is true. Yet, the point is established that through mercy alone one can realise God.

Swamiji: Oh, yes, that one can, but few indeed are there who do so!

Disciple: It appears to me that those who seek to realise God by restraining their senses and renouncing lust and wealth hold to the (free-will) theory of self-exertion and self-help; and that those who take the name of the Lord and depend on Him are made free by the Lord Himself of all worldly attachments, and led by Him to the supreme stage of realisation.

Swamiji: True, those are the two different standpoints, the former held by the Jnânis, and the latter by the Bhaktas. But the ideal of renunciation is the keynote of both.

Disciple: No doubt about that! But Shri Girish Chandra Ghosh[1] once said to me that there could be no condition in God's mercy; there could be no law for it! If there were, then it could no longer be termed mercy. The realm of grace or mercy must transcend all law.

Swamiji: But there must be some higher law at work in the sphere alluded to by G. C. of which we are ignorant. Those are words, indeed, for the last stage of development, which alone is beyond time, space, and causation. But, when we get there, who will be merciful, and to whom, where there is no law of causation? There the worshipper and the worshipped, the meditator and the object of meditation, the knower and the known, all become one—call that Grace or Brahman, if you will. It is all one uniform homogeneous entity!

Disciple: Hearing these words from you, Swamiji, I have come to understand the essence of all philosophy and religion (Vedas and Vedanta); it seems as if I had hitherto been living in the midst of high-sounding words without any meaning.

XV — Doctrine of Ahimsa and Meat-Eating—Sattva, Rajas, Tamas in Man—Food And Spirituality—'Âhâra'—Three Defects in Food—Don't-Touchism and Caste-Prejudices—Restoring the Old Chaturvarnya and the Laws of the Rishis

Disciple: Pray, Swamiji, do tell me if there is any relation between the discrimination of food taken and the development of spirituality in man.

Swamiji: Yes, there is, more or less.

Disciple: Is it proper or necessary to take fish and meat?

Swamiji: Ay, take them, my boy! And if there be any harm in doing so, I will take care of that. Look at the masses of our country! What a look of sadness on their faces and want of courage and enthusiasm in their hearts, with large stomachs and no strength in their hands and feet—a set of cowards frightened at every trifle!

---

1. The great Bengali actor-dramatist, a staunch devotee of Shri Ramakrishna.

Disciple: Does the taking of fish and meat give strength? Why do Buddhism and Vaishnavism preach "अहिंसा परमो धर्मः—Non-killing is the highest virtue"?

Swamiji: Buddhism and Vaishnavism are not two different things. During the decline of Buddhism in India, Hinduism took from her a few cardinal tenets of conduct and made them her own, and these have now come to be known as Vaishnavism. The Buddhist tenet, "Non-killing is supreme virtue", is very good, but in trying to enforce it upon all by legislation without paying any heed to the capacities of the people at large, Buddhism has brought ruin upon India. I have come across many a "religious heron"[1] in India, who fed ants with sugar, and at the same time would not hesitate to bring ruin on his own brother for the sake of "filthy lucre"!

Disciple: But in the Vedas as well as in the laws of Manu, there are injunctions to take fish and meat.

Swamiji: Ay, and injunctions to abstain from killing as well. For the Vedas enjoin, "मा हिंस्यात् सर्वभूतानि—Cause no injury to any being"; Manu also says, "निवृत्तिस्तु महाफला—Cessation of desire brings great results." Killing and non-killing have both been enjoined, according to the individual capacity, or fitness and adaptability on those who will observe the one practice or the other.

Disciple: It is the fashion here nowadays to give up fish and meat as soon as one takes to religion, and to many it is more sinful not to do so than to commit such great sins as adultery. How, do you think, such notions came into existence?

Swamiji: What's the use of your knowing how they came, when you see clearly, do you not, that such notions are working ruin to our country and our society? Just see—the people of East Bengal eat much fish, meat, and turtle, and they are much healthier than those of this part of Bengal. Even the rich men of East Bengal have not yet taken to Loochis or Châpâtis at night, and they do not suffer from acidity and dyspepsia like us. I have heard that in the villages of East Bengal the people have not the slightest idea of what dyspepsia means!

Disciple: Quite so, Swamiji. We never complain of dyspepsia in our part of the country. I first heard of it after coming to these parts. We take fish with rice, mornings and evenings.

Swamiji: Yes, take as much of that as you can, without fearing criticism. The country has been flooded with dyspeptic Bâbâjis living on vegetables only. That is no sign of Sattva, but of deep Tamas—the shadow of death. Brightness in the face, undaunted enthusiasm in the heart, and tremendous activity—these result from Sattva; whereas idleness, lethargy, inordinate attachment, and sleep are the signs of Tamas.

Disciple: But do not fish and meat increase Rajas in man?

Swamiji: That is what I want you to have. Rajas is badly needed just now! More than ninety per cent of those whom you now take to be men with the Sattva, quality are only steeped in the deepest Tamas. Enough, if you find one-sixteenth of them to be really Sâttvika! What we want now is an immense awakening of Râjasika energy, for the whole country is wrapped in the shroud of Tamas. The people of this land must be fed and clothed—must be awakened — must be made more fully active. Otherwise they will become inert, as inert as trees and stones. So, I say, eat large quantities of fish and meat, my boy!

Disciple: Does a liking for fish and meat remain when one has fully developed the Sattva quality?

Swamiji: No, it does not. All liking for fish and meat disappears when pure Sattva is highly developed, and these are the signs of its manifestation in a soul: sacrifice of everything for others, perfect non-attachment to lust and wealth, want of pride and egotism. The desire for animal food goes when these things are seen in a man. And where such indications are absent, and yet you find men sidings with the non-killing party, know it for a certainty that herein, there is either hypocrisy or a show of religion. When you yourself come to that stage of pure Sattva, give up fish and meat, by all means.

---

1. Meaning, religious hypocrite. The heron, so the story goes, gave it out to the fishes that he had forsaken his old habit of catching fish and turned highly religious. So he took his stand on the brink of the water and feigned to be meditating, while in reality he was always hatching his opportunity to catch the unwary fish.

Disciple: In the Chhândogya Upanishad (VII. xxvi. 2) there is this passage, "आहारशुद्धौ सत्त्वशुद्धिः—Through pure food the Sattva quality in a man becomes pure."

Swamiji: Yes, I know. Shankarâchârya has said that the word Âhâra there means "objects of the senses", whereas Shri Râmânuja has taken the meaning of Ahara to be "food". In my opinion we should take that meaning of the word which reconciles both these points of view. Are we to pass our lives discussing all the time about the purity and impurity of food only, or are we to practice the restraining of our senses? Surely, the restraining of the senses is the main object; and the discrimination of good and bad, pure and impure foods, only helps one, to a certain extent, in gaining that end. There are, according to our scriptures, three things which make food impure: (1) Jâti-dosha or natural defects of a certain class of food, like onions, garlic, etc.; (2) Nimitta-dosha or defects arising from the presence of external impurities in it, such as dead insects, dust, etc. that attach to sweetmeats bought from shops; (3) Âshraya-dosha or defects that arise by the food coming from evil sources, as when it has been touched and handled by wicked persons. Special care should be taken to avoid the first and second classes of defects. But in this country men pay no regard just to these two, and go on fighting for the third alone, the very one that none but a Yogi could really discriminate! The country from end to end is being bored to extinction by the cry, "Don't touch", "Don't touch", of the non-touchism party. In that exclusive circle of theirs, too, there is no discrimination of good and bad men, for their food may be taken from the hands of anyone who wears a thread round his neck and calls himself a Brâhmin! Shri Ramakrishna was quite unable to take food in this indiscriminate way from the hands of any and all. It happened many a time that he would not accept food touched by a certain person or persons, and on rigorous investigation it would turn out that these had some particular stain to hide. Your religion seems nowadays to be confined to the cooking-pot alone. You put on one side the sublime truths of religion and fight, as they say, for the skin of the fruit and not for the fruit itself!

Disciple: Do you mean, then, that we should eat the food handled by anyone and everyone?

Swamiji: Why so? Look here. You being Brahmin of a certain class, say, of the Bhattâcharya class, why should you not eat rice cooked by Brahmins of all classes? Why should you, who belong to the Rârhi section, object to taking rice cooked by a Brahmin of the Barendra section, or why should a Barendra object to taking your rice? Again, why should not the other subcastes in the west and south of India, e.g. the Marathi, Telangi, Kanouji, do the same? Do you not see that hundreds of Brahmins and Kâyasthas in Bengal now go secretly to eat dainties in public restaurants, and when they come out of those places pose as leaders of society and frame rules to support don't-touchism. Must our society really be guided by laws dictated by such hypocrites? No, I say. On the contrary we must turn them out. The laws laid down by the great Rishis of old must be brought back and be made to rule supreme once more. Then alone can national well-being be ours.

Disciple: Then, do not the laws laid down by the Rishis rule and guide our present society?

Swamiji: Vain delusion! Where indeed is that the case nowadays? Nowhere have I found the laws of the Rishis current in India, even when during my travels I searched carefully and thoroughly. The blind and not unoften meaningless customs sanctioned by the peoples local prejudices and ideas, and the usages and ceremonials prevalent amongst women, are what really govern society everywhere! How many care to read the Shâstras or to lead society according to their ordinances after careful study?

Disciple: What are we to do, then?

Swamiji: We must revive the old laws of the Rishis. We must initiate the whole people into the codes of our old Manu and Yâjnavalkya, with a few modifications here and there to adjust them to the changed circumstances of the time. Do you not see that nowhere in India now are the original four castes (Châturvarnya) to be found? We have to redivide the whole Hindu population, grouping it under the four main castes, of Brahmins, Kshatriyas, Vaishyas, and Shudras, as of old. The numberless modern subdivisions of the Brahmins that split them up into so many castes, as it were, have to be abolished and a single Brahmin caste to be made by uniting them all. Each of the three remaining castes also will have to be brought similarly into single groups, as was the case in Vedic times. Without this will the Motherland be really benefited by your simply crying as you do nowadays, "We won't touch you!; We won't take him back into our caste!"? Never, my boy!

SAYINGS AND UTTERANCES

1. Man is born to conquer nature and not to follow it.
2. When you think you are a body, you are apart from the universe; when you think; you are a soul, you are a spark from the great Eternal Fire; when you think you are the Âtman (Self), you are All.
3. The will is not free—it is a phenomenon bound by cause and effect—but there is something behind the will which is free.
4. Strength is in goodness, in purity.
5. The universe is—objectified God.
6. You cannot believe in God until you believe in yourself.
7. The root of evil is in the illusion that we are bodies. This, if any, is the original sin.
8. One party says thought is caused by matter, and the other says matter is caused by thought. Both statements are wrong; matter and thought are coexistent. There is a third something of which both matter and thought are products.
9. As particles of matter combine in space, so mind-waves combine in time.
10. To define God is—grinding the already ground; for He is the only being we know.
11. Religion is the idea which is raising the brute unto man, and man unto God.
12. External nature is only internal nature writ large.
13. The motive is the measure of your work. What motive can be higher than that you are God, and that the lowest man is also God?
14. The observer in the psychic world needs to be very strong and scientifically trained.
15. To believe that mind is all, that thought is all is only a higher materialism.
16. This world is the great gymnasium where we come to make ourselves strong.
17. You cannot teach a child any more than you can grow a plant. All you can do is on the negative side—you can only help. It is a manifestation from within; it develops its own nature—you can only take away obstructions.
18. As soon as you make a sect, you protest against universal brotherhood. Those who really feel universal brotherhood do not talk much, but their very actions speak aloud.
19. Truth can be stated in a thousand different ways, yet each one can be true.
20. You have to grow from inside out. None can teach you, none can make you spiritual. There is no other teacher but your own soul.
21. If in an infinite chain a few links can be explained, by the same method all can be explained.
22. That man has reached immortality who is disturbed by nothing material.
23. Everything can be sacrificed for truth, but truth cannot be sacrificed for anything.
24. The search for truth is the expression of strength—not the groping of a weak, blind man.
25. God has become man; man will become God again.
26. It is child's talk that a man dies and goes to heaven. We never come nor go. We are where we are. All the souls that have been, are, and will be, are on one geometrical point.
27. He whose book of the heart has been opened needs no other books. Their only value is to create desire in us. They are merely the experiences of others.
28. Have charity towards all beings. Pity those who are in distress. Love all creatures. Do not be jealous of anyone. Look not to the faults of others.
29. Man never dies, nor is he ever born; bodies die, but he never dies.
30. No one is born into a religion, but each one is born for a religion.
31. There is really but one Self in the universe, all else is but Its manifestations.
32. All the worshippers are divided into the common masses and the brave few.

33. If it is impossible to attain perfection here and now, there is no proof that we can attain perfection in any other life.

34. If I know one lump of clay perfectly, I know all the clay there is. This is the knowledge of principles, but their adaptations are various. When you know yourself you know all.

35. Personally I take as much of the Vedas as agrees with reason. Parts of the Vedas are apparently contradictory. They are not considered as inspired in the Western sense of the word, but as the sum total of the knowledge of God, omniscience. This knowledge comes out at the beginning of a cycle and manifests itself; and when the cycle ends, it goes down into minute form. When the cycle is projected again, that knowledge is projected again with it. So far the theory is all right. But that only these books which are called the Vedas are His knowledge is mere sophistry. Manu says in one pace that that part of the Vedas which agrees with reason is the Vedas and nothing else. Many of our philosophers have taken this view.

36. Of all the scriptures of the world it is the Vedas alone that declare that even the study of the Vedas is secondary. The real study is "that by which we realise the Unchangeable". And that is neither reading, for believing, nor reasoning, but superconscious perception, or Samâdhi.

37. We have been low animals once. We think they are something different from us. I hear, Western people say, "The world was created for us." If tigers could write books, they would say, man was created for them and that man is a most sinful animal, because he does not allow him (the tiger) to catch him easily. The worm that crawls under your feet today is a God to be.

38. "I should very much like our women to have your intellectuality, but not if it must be at the cost of purity", said Swami Vivekananda in New York. "I admire you for all that you know, but I dislike the way that you cover what is bad with roses and call it good. Intellectuality is not the highest good. Morality and spirituality are the things for which we strive. Our women are not so learned, but they are more pure.

"To all women every man save her husband should be as her son. To all men every woman save his own wife should be as his mother. When I look about me and see what you call gallantry, my soul is filled with disgust. Not until you learn to ignore the question of sex and to meet on a ground of common humanity will your women really develop. Until then they are playthings, nothing more. All this is the cause of divorce. Your men bow low and offer a chair, but in another breath they offer compliments. They say, 'Oh, madam, how beautiful are your eyes!' What right have they to do this? How dare a man venture so far, and how can you women permit it? Such things develop the less noble side of humanity. They do not tend to nobler ideals.

"We should not think that we are men and women, but only that we are human beings, born to cherish and to help one another. No sooner are a young man and a young woman left alone than he pays compliments to her, and perhaps before he takes a wife, he has courted two hundred women. Bah! If I belonged to the marrying set, I could find a woman to love without all that!

"When I was in India and saw these things from the outside, I was told it was all right, it was mere pleasantry and I believed it. But I have travelled since then, and I know it is not right. It is wrong, only you of the West shut your eyes and call it good. The trouble with the nations of the West is that they are young, foolish, fickle, and wealthy. What mischief can come of one of these qualities; but when all three, all four, are combined beware!"

But severe as the Swami was upon all, Boston received the hardest blow:

"Of all, Boston is the worst. There the women are all faddists, all fickle, merely bent on following something new and strange."

39. "Where is the spirituality one would expect in a country", he said in America, "that is so boastful of its civilisation?"

40. "Here" and "hereafter" are words to frighten children. It is all "here". To live and move in God even here, even in this body, all self should go out, all superstition should be banished. Such persons live in India. Where are such in this country (America)? Your preachers speak against dreamers. The people of this country would be better off if there were more dreamers. There is a good deal of difference between dreaming and the brag of the nineteenth century. The whole world is full of God and not of sin. Let us help one another, let us love one another.

41. Let me die a true Sannyâsin as my Master did, heedless of money, of women, and of fame! And of these the most insidious is the love of fame!

42. I have never spoken of revenge, I have always spoken of strength. Do we dream of revenging ourselves on this drop of sea-spray? But it is a great thing to a mosquito!

43. "This is a great land," said Swamiji on one occasion in America, "but I would not like to live here. Americans think too much of money. They give it preference over anything else. Your people have much to learn. When your nation is as old as ours, you will be wiser."

44. It may be that I shall find it good to get outside of my body—to cast it off like a disused garment. But I shall not cease to work! I shall inspire men everywhere, until the world shall know that it is one with God.

45. All that I am, all that the world itself will some day be, is owing to my Master, Shri Ramakrishna, who incarnated and experienced and taught this wonderful unity which underlies everything, having discovered it alike in Hinduism, in Islam, and in Christianity.

46. Give the organ of taste a free rein, and the other organs will also run on unbridled.

47. Jnâna, Bhakti, Yoga and Karma—these are the four paths which lead to salvation. One must follow the path for which one is best suited; but in this age special stress should be laid on Karma-Yoga.

48. Religion is not a thing of imagination but of direct perception. He who has seen even a single spirit is greater than many a book-learned Pandit.

49. Once Swamiji was praising someone very much; at this, one sitting near by said to him, "But he does not believe in you." Hearing this, Swamiji at once replied: "Is there any legal affidavit that he should have to do so? He is doing good work, and so he is worthy of praise."

50. In the domain of true religion, book-learning has no right to enter.

51. The downfall of a religious sect begins from the day that the worship of the rich enters into it.

52. If you want to do anything evil, do it before the eyes of your superiors.

53. By the grace of the Guru, a disciple becomes a Pandit (scholar) even without reading books.

54. There is no sin nor virtue: there is only ignorance. By realisation of non-duality this ignorance is dispelled.

55. Religious movements come in groups. Each one of them tries to rear itself above the rest. But as a rule only one of them really grows in strength, and this, in the long run, swallows up all the contemporary movements.

56. When Swamiji was at Ramnad, he said in the course of a conversation that Shri Râma was the Paramâtman and that Sitâ was the Jivâtman, and each man's or woman's body was the Lanka (Ceylon). The Jivatman which was enclosed in the body, or captured in the island of Lankâ, always desired to be in affinity with the Paramatman, or Shri Rama. But the Râkshasas would not allow it, and Rakshasas represented certain traits of character. For instance, Vibhishana represented Sattva Guna; Râvana, Rajas; and Kumbhakarna, Tamas. Sattva Guna means goodness; Rajas means lust and passions, and

Tamas darkness, stupor, avarice, malice, and its concomitants. These Gunas keep back Sita, or Jivatman, which is in the body, or Lanka, from joining Paramatman, or Rama. Sita, thus imprisoned and trying to unite with her Lord, receives a visit from Hanumân, the Guru or divine teacher, who shows her the Lord's ring, which is Brahma-Jnâna, the supreme wisdom that destroys all illusions; and thus Sita finds the way to be at one with Shri Rama, or, in other words, the Jivatman finds itself one with the Paramatman.

57. A true Christian is a true Hindu, and a true Hindu is a true Christian.

58. All healthy social changes are the manifestations of the spiritual forces working within, and if these are strong and well adjusted, society will arrange itself accordingly. Each individual has to work out his own salvation; there is no other way, and so also with nations. Again, the great institutions of every nation are the conditions of its very existence and cannot be transformed by the mould of any other race. Until higher institutions have been evolved, any attempt to break the old ones will be disastrous. Growth is always gradual.

59. It is very easy to point out the defects of institutions, all being more or less imperfect, but he is the real benefactor of humanity who helps the individual to overcome his imperfections under whatever institutions he may live. The individuals being raised, the nation and its institutions are bound to rise. Bad customs and laws are ignored by the virtuous, and unwritten but mightier laws of love, sympathy, and integrity take their place. Happy is the nation which can rise to the necessity of but few law books, and needs no longer to bother its head about this or that institution. Good men rise beyond all laws, and will help their fellows to rise under whatever conditions they live.

60. The salvation of India, therefore, depends on the strength of the individual, and the realisation by each man of the divinity within.

61. Spirituality can never be attained until materiality is gone.

62. The first discourse in the Gita can be taken allegorically.

63. "Swami, you have no idea of time", remarked an impatient American devotee, afraid of missing a steamer. "No," retorted Swamiji calmly, "you live in time; we live in eternity!"

64. We are always letting sentiment usurp the place of duty and flatter ourselves that we are acting in response to true love.

65. We must get beyond emotionalism if we want the power to renounce. Emotion belongs to the animals. They are creatures of emotion entirely.

66. It is not sacrifice of a high order to die for one's young. The animals do that, and just as readily as any human mother ever did. It is no sign of real love to do that; it is merely blind emotion.

67. We are for ever trying to make our weakness look like strength, our sentiment like love, our cowardice like courage, and so on.

68. Say to your soul in regard to vanities, weakness, etc., "This does not befit thee. This does not befit thee."

69. Never loved a husband the wife for the wife's sake or the wife the husband for the husband's sake. It is God in the wife the husband loves, and God in the husband the wife loves. It is God in every one that draws us to the one we love, God in everything and in everybody that makes us love. God is the only love.

70. Oh, if only you knew yourselves! You are souls; you are Gods. If ever I feel like blaspheming, it is when I call you man.

71. In everyone is God, the Atman; all else is but dream, an illusion.

72. If I do not find bliss in the life of the Spirit, shall, I seek satisfaction in the life of the senses? If I cannot' get nectar; shall I fall back upon ditch water? The bird called Châtaka drinks from the clouds only, ever calling as it soars, "Pure water! Pure water!" And no storms or tempests make it falter on wing or descend to

drink from the earth.

73. Any sect that may help you to realise God is welcome. Religion is the realising of God.

74. An atheist can be charitable but not religious. But the religious man must be charitable.

75. Everyone makes shipwreck on the rock of would-be Guruism, except those souls that were born to be Gurus.

76. Man is a compound of animality, humanity, and divinity.

77. The term "social progress" has as much meaning as "hot ice" or "dark light". There is no such thing, ultimately, as "social progress"!

78. Things are not bettered, but we are bettered, by making changes in them.

79. Let me help my fellow men; that is all I seek.

80. "No", said the Swami, very softly, in answer to a question in New York, "I do not believe in the occult. If a thing be unreal, it is not. What is unreal does not exist. Strange things are natural phenomena. I know them to be matters of science. Then they are not occult to me. I do not believe in occult societies. They do no good, and can never do good."

81. There are four general types of men—the rational, the emotional, the mystical, and the worker. For each of these we must provide suitable forms of worship. There comes the rational man, who says, "I care not for this form of worship. Give me the philosophical, the rational—that I can appreciate." So for the rational man is the rational philosophic worship.

   There comes the worker. He says, "I care not for the worship of the philosopher. Give me work to do for my fellow men." So for him is provided work as the path of worship. As for the mystical and the emotional, we have their respective modes of devotion. All these men have, in religion, the elements of their faith.

   I stand for truth. Truth will never ally itself with falsehood. Even if all the world should be against me, Truth must prevail in the end.

   Wherever you see the most humanitarian ideas fall into the hands of the multitude, the first result you notice is degradation. It is learning and intellect that help to keep things safe. It is the cultured among a community that are the real custodians of religion and philosophy in their purest form. It is that form which serves as the index for the intellectual and social condition of a community.

82. "I do not come", said Swamiji on one occasion in America, "to convert you to a new belief. I want you to keep your own belief; I want to make the Methodist a better Methodist; the Presbyterian a better Presbyterian; the Unitarian a better Unitarian. I want to teach you to live the truth, to reveal the light within your own soul."

83. Happiness presents itself before man, wearing the crown of sorrow on its head. He who welcomes it must also welcome sorrow.

84. He is free, he is great, who turns his back upon the world, who has renounced everything, who has controlled his passion, and who thirsts for peace. One may gain political and social independence, but if one is a slave to his passions and desires, one cannot feel the pure joy of real freedom.

85. Doing good to others is virtue (Dharma); injuring others is sin. Strength and manliness are virtue; weakness and cowardice are sin. Independence is virtue; dependence is sin. Loving others is virtue; hating others is sin. Faith in God and in one's own Self is virtue; doubt is sin. Knowledge of oneness is virtue; seeing diversity is sin. The different scriptures only show the means of attaining virtue.

86. When, by reasoning, Truth is comprehended by the intellect, then it is realised in the heart, the fountainhead of feeling. Thus the head and the heart become illumined at the same moment; and then only, as says the Upanishad, "The knot of the heart is rent asunder, and all doubts cease" (Mundaka Upanishad, II.ii.8).

   When in ancient times this knowledge (Jnâna) and this feeling (Bhâva) thus blossomed forth simultaneously in the heart of the Rishi, then the Highest Truth became poetic, and then the Vedas and other scriptures were composed. It is for this reason that one finds, in studying them, that the two parallel lines of Bhava and Jnana have at last met, as it were, in the plane of the Vedas and become combined and inseparable.

87. The scriptures of different religions point out different means to attain the ideals of universal love, freedom, manliness, and selfless benevolence. Every religious sect is generally at variance as to its idea of what is virtue and what is vice, and fights with others over the means of attaining virtue and eschewing vice, instead of aiming at realising the end. Every means is helpful more or less, and the Gita (XVIII. says, "Every undertaking is attended with defects as fire with smoke"; so the means will no doubt appear more or less defective. But as we are to attain the highest virtue through the means laid dozen in our respective scriptures, we should try our best to follow them. Moreover, they should be tempered with reason and discrimination. Thus, as we progress, the riddle of virtue and vice will be solved by itself.

88. How many in our country truly understand the Shastras nowadays? They have only learnt such words as Brahman, Maya, Prakriti, and so on, and confuse their heads with them. Setting aside the real meaning and purpose of the Shastras, they fight over the words only. If the Shastras cannot help all men in all conditions at all times, of what use, then, are such Shastras? If the Shastras show the way to the Sannyasins only and not to the householders, then what need has a householder for such one-sided Shastras? If the Shastras can only help men when they give up all work and retire into the forests, and cannot show the way of lighting the lamp of hope in the hearts of men of the workaday world—in the midst of their daily toil, disease, misery, and poverty, in the despondency of the penitent, in the self-reproach of the downtrodden, in the terror of the battlefield, in lust, anger and pleasure, in the joy of victory, in the darkness of defeat, and finally, in the dreaded night of death—then weak humanity has no need of such Shastras, and such Shastras will be no Shastras at all!

89. Through Bhoga (enjoyment) Yoga will come in time. But alas, such is the lot of my countrymen that, not to speak of possessing yoga, they cannot even have a little Bhoga! Suffering all sorts of indignities they can with the utmost difficulty only meet the barest needs of the body—and even that everyone cannot do! It is strange that such a state of affairs does not disturb our sleep and rouse us to our immediate duties.

90. Agitate ever so much for your rights and privileges, but remember that so long as we do not truly elevate ourselves by rousing intensely the feeling of self-respect in the nation, so long our hope of gaining rights and privileges is like the day-dream of Alnascar.

91. When a genius of a man with some special great power is born, all the best and the most creative faculties of his whole heredity are drawn towards the making up of his personality and squeezed dry, as it were. It is for this reason that we find that all those who are subsequently born in such a family are either idiots or men of very ordinary calibre, and that in time such a family in many cases becomes extinct.

92. If you cannot attain salvation in this life, what proof is there that you can attain it in the life or lives to come?

93. While visiting the Taj at Agra he remarked: "If you squeeze a bit of this marble, it will drip drops of royal love and its sorrow." Further he observed, "It takes really six months to study a square inch of its interior works of beauty."

94. When the real history of India will be unearthed, it will be proved that, as in matters of religion, so in fine arts, India is the primal Guru of the whole world.

95. Speaking of architecture he said: "People say Calcutta is a city of palaces, but the houses look much like so many boxes placed one upon

the other! They convey no idea whatever. In Rajputana you can still find much pure Hindu architecture. If you look at a Dharmashala, you will feel as if it calls you with open arms to take shelter within and partake of its unqualified hospitableness. If you look at a temple, you are sure to find a Divine Presence in and about it. If you look about a rural cottage, you will at once be able to comprehend the special meanings of its different portions, and that the whole structure bears evidence to the predominant nature and ideal of the owner thereof. This sort of expressive architecture I have seen nowhere else except in Italy."

WRITINGS: PROSE AND POEMS

REASON, FAITH AND LOVE

Swamiji had made the home of the Hale family his headquarters during almost all of 1894 before the pivot of his activities moved eastward to the Atlantic Coast. It was on George W. Hale's letter paper and thus, presumably, during one of his stays in the latter's home, that Swamiji jotted down in pencil a series of notes on the subjects of reason, faith, and love, which have recently come to light. Unfortunately the date of the manuscript cannot be accurately determined.

Reason—has its limits—its base—
its degeneration. The walls round it—
Agnosticism. Atheism. But must not stop
The beyond is acting upon influencing us every
moment—the sky the stars acting upon us—even
those not seen. Therefore must go beyond—reason
alone can't go—finite cannot get at the infinite

Faith its degeneration when alone—bigotry
fanaticism—sectarianism. Narrowing
finite therefore cannot get to the infinite
Sometimes gain in intensity but loses in
extensity—and in bigots & fanatics become
worship of his own pride & vanity

Is there no other way—there is Love
it never degenerates—peaceful softening
ever widening—the universe is too small
for its expansiveness.

We cannot define it we can only trace
it through its development and describe its surroundings

It is at first—what the gravitation
is to the external world—a tendency to unification
forms and conventionalities are its death.
Worship through forms—methods—services
forms—up to then no love.

When love comes method dies.
Human language and human forms God
as father, God as mother, God as
the lover—Surata-vardhanam etc. Solomon's Song of
Songs—Dependence and independence
Love Love—

Love the chaste wife—Anasuya Sita—
not as hard dry duty but as ever pleasing
love—Sita worship—

The madness of Love—God intoxicated man
The allegory of Radha—misunderstood
The restriction more increase—
Lust is the death of love
Self is the death of love
individual to general
Concrete to abstract—to absolute
The praying Mohammedan and the girl
The Sympathy—Kabir—
The Christian nun from whose hands blood came
The Mohammedan Saint
Every particle seeking its own complement
When it finds that it is at rest
Every man seeking—happiness—& stability
The search is real but the objects are themselves
but happiness is coming to them momentary at least
through the search of these objects.

The only object unchangeable and the only
complement of character and
aspirations of the human Soul is God.

Love is struggle of a human Soul to find its
complement its stable equilibrium its infinite rest.

SIX SANSKRIT MOTTOES

Reproduced from Swami Vivekananda in America: New Discoveries. These together with the English translations, were transcribed by Swamiji in six of his photographs.

1. *Ajarâmaravat prâjnah vidyâm
artham cha chintayet
Grihita iva kesheshu mrityunâ
dharmam âcharet*

When in search of knowledge or prosperity think that thou would never have death or disease, and when worshipping God think that death's hand is in your hair.

2. *Eka eve suhrid dharma
nidhanepyanuyâti yah*

Virtue is the only friend which follows us even beyond the grave. Everything else ends with death.
—Vivekananda.

3. One infinite pure and holy—beyond
thought beyond qualities
I bow down to thee
—Swami Vivekananda.

4. *Samatâ sarva-bhuteshu
etanmuktasya lakshanam.*

Equality in all beings this is the sign of the free
—Vivekananda.

5. Thou art the only treasure in this world
—Vivekananda.

6. Thou art the father the lord the
mother the husband and love
—Swami Vivekananda.

THE MESSAGE OF DIVINE WISDOM

The following three chapters were discovered among Swami Vivekananda's papers. He evidently intended to write a book and jotted down some points for the work.

Bondage

1. Desire is infinite, its fulfilment limited. Desire is unlimited in everyone; the power of fulfilment varies. Thus some are more successful than others in life.

2. This limitation is the bondage we are struggling against all our lives.

3. We desire only the pleasurable, not the painful.

4. The objects of desire are all complex—pleasure-giving and pain-bringing mixed up.

5. We do not or cannot see the painful parts in objects, we are charmed with only the pleasurable portion; and, thus grasping the pleasurable, we unwittingly draw in the painful.

6. At times we vainly hope that in our case only the pleasurable will come, leaving the painful aside, which never happens.

7. Our desires also are constantly changing—what we would prize today we would reject tomorrow. The pleasure of the present will be the pain of the future, the loved hated, and so on.

8. We vainly hope that in the future life we shall be able to gather in only the pleasurable, to the exclusion of the painful.

9. The future is only the extension of the present. Such a thing cannot be!

10. Whosoever seeks pleasure in objects will get it, but he must take the pain with it.

11. All objective pleasure in the long run must bring pain, because of the fact of change or death.

12. Death is the goal of all objects, change is the nature of all objective things.

13. As desire increases, so increases the power of pleasure, so the power of pain.

14. The finer the organism, the higher the culture—the greater is the power to enjoy pleasure and the sharper are the pangs of pain.

15. Mental pleasures are greatly superior to physical joys. Mental pains are more poignant than physical tortures.

16. The power of thought, of looking far away into the future, and the power of memory, of recalling the past to the present, make us live in heaven; they make us live in hell also.

17. The man who can collect the largest amount of pleasurable objects around him is as a rule too unimaginative to enjoy them. The man of great imagination is thwarted by the intensity of his feeling of loss, or fear of loss, or perception of defects.

18. We are struggling hard to conquer pain, succeeding in the attempt, and yet creating new pains at the same time.

19. We achieve success, and we are overthrown by failure; we pursue pleasure and we are pursued by pain.

20. We say we do, we are made to do. We say we work, we are made to labour. We say we live, we are made to die every moment. We are in the crowd, we cannot stop, must go on—it deserves no cheering. Had it not been so, no amount of cheering would make us undertake all this pain and misery for a grain of pleasure—which, alas, in most cases is only a hope!

21. Our pessimism is a dread reality, our optimism is a faint cheering, making the best of a bad job.

The Law

1. The law is never separate from the phenomena, the principle from the person.

2. The law is the method of action or poise of every single phenomenon within its scope.

3. We get our knowledge of law from the massing and welding of changes that occur. We never see law beyond these changes. The idea of law as something separate from phenomena is a mental abstraction, a convenient use of words and nothing more. Law is a part of every change within its range, a manner which resides in the things governed by the law. The power resides in the things, is a part of our idea of that

thing—its action upon something else is in a certain manner—this is our law.

4. Law is in the actual state of things—it is in how they act towards each other, and not in how they should. It might have been better if fire did not burn or water wet; but that they do—this is the law; and if it is a true law, a fire that does not burn or water that does not wet is neither fire nor water.

5. Spiritual laws, ethical laws, social laws, national laws—are laws if they are parts of existing spiritual and human units and the unfailing experience of the action of every unit said to be bound by such laws.

6. We, by turn, are made by law and make it. A generalization of what man does invariably in certain circumstances is a law with regard to man in that particular aspect. It is the invariable, universal human action that is law for man—and which no individual can escape—and yet the summation of the action of each individual is the universal Law. The sum total, or the universal, or the infinite is fashioning the individual, while the individual is keeping by its action the Law alive. Law in this sense is another name for the universal. The universal is dependent upon the individual, the individual dependent upon the universal. It is an infinite made up of finite parts, an infinite of number, though involving the difficulty of assuming an infinity summed up of finites—yet for all practical purposes, it is a fact before us. And as the law, or whole, or the infinite cannot be destroyed—and the destruction of a part of an infinite is an impossibility, as we cannot either add anything to or subtract anything from the infinite—each part persists for ever.

7. Laws regarding the materials of which the body of man is composed have been found out, and also the persistence of these materials through time has been shown. The elements which composed the body of a man a hundred thousand years ago have been proved to be still existing in some place or other. The thoughts which have been projected also are living in other minds.

8. But the difficulty is to find a law about the man beyond the body.

9. The spiritual and ethical laws are not the method of action of every human being. The systems of ethics of morality, even of national laws, are honoured more in the breach than in the observance. If they were laws how could they be broken?

10. No man is able to go against the laws of nature. How is it that we always complain of his breaking the moral laws, national laws?

11. The national laws at best are the embodied will of a majority of the nation—always a state of things wished for, not actually existing.

12. The ideal law may be that no man should covet the belongings of others, but the actual law is that a very large number do.

13. Thus the word law used in regard to laws of nature has a very different interpretation when applied to ethics and human actions generally.

14. Analysing the ethical laws of the world and comparing them with the actual state of things, two laws stand out supreme. The one, that of repelling everything from us—separating ourselves from everyone—which leads to self-aggrandisement even at the cost of everyone else's happiness. The other, that of self-sacrifice—of taking no thought of ourselves—only of others. Both spring from the search for happiness—one, of finding happiness in injuring others and the ability of feeling that happiness only in our own senses. The other, of finding happiness in doing good to others —the ability of feeling happy, as it were, through the senses of others. The great and good of the world are those who have the latter power predominating. Yet both these are working side by side conjointly; in almost everyone they are found in mixture, one or the other predominating. The thief steals, perhaps, for someone he loves.

The Absolute and the attainment of freedom

1. Om Tat Sat—that Being—Knowing—Bliss.

(a) The only real Existence, which alone is—everything else exists inasmuch as it reflects that real Existence.

(b) It is the only Knower—the only Self-luminous—the Light of consciousness. Everything else shines by light borrowed from It. Everything else knows inasmuch as it reflects Its knowing.

(c) It is the only Blessedness—as in It there is no want. It comprehends all—is the essence of all. It is Sat-Chit-Ânanda.

(d) It has no parts, no attributes, neither pleasure nor pain, nor is it matter nor mind. It is the Supreme, Infinite, Impersonal Self in everything, the Infinite Ego of the Universe.

(e) It is the Reality in me, in thee, and in everything—therefore, "That thou art"—Tattvamasi.

2. The same Impersonal is conceived by the mind as the Creator, the Ruler, and the Dissolver of this universe, its material as well as its efficient cause, the Supreme Ruler—the Living, the Loving, the Beautiful, in the highest sense.

(a) The Absolute Being is manifested in Its highest in Isvara, or the Supreme Ruler, as the highest and omnipotent Life or Energy.

(b) The Absolute Knowledge is manifesting Itself in Its highest as Infinite Love, in the Supreme Lord.

(c) The Absolute Bliss is manifested as the Infinite Beautiful, in the Supreme Lord. He is the greatest attraction of the soul.

Satyam-Shivam-Sundaram.

The Absolute or Brahman, the Sat-Chit-Ananda, is Impersonal and the real Infinite

Every existence from the highest to the lowest, all manifest according to their degree as—energy (in the higher life), attraction (in the higher love), and struggle for equilibrium (in the higher happiness). This highest Energy-Love-Beauty is a person, an individual, the Infinite Mother of this universe—the God of gods—the Lord of lords, omnipresent yet separate from the universe—the Soul of souls, yet separate from every soul—the Mother of this universe, because She has produced it—its Ruler, because She guides it with the greatest love and in the long run brings everything back to Herself. Through Her command the sun and moon shine, the clouds rain, and death stalks upon the earth.

She is the power of all causation. She energises every cause unmistakably to produce the effect. Her will is the only law, and as She cannot make a mistake, nature's laws—Her will—can never be changed. She is the life of the Law of Karma or causation. She is the fructifier of every action. Under Her guidance we are manufacturing our lives through our deeds or Karma. Freedom is the motive of the universe, freedom its goal. The laws of nature are the methods through which we are struggling to reach that freedom, under the guidance of Mother. This universal struggle for freedom attains its highest expression in man in the conscious desire to be free.

This freedom is attained by the threefold means of—work, worship, and knowledge.

(a) Work—constant, unceasing effort to help others and love others.

(b) Worship—consists in prayer, praise, and meditation.

(c) Knowledge—that follows meditation.

THE BELUR MATH: AN APPEAL

The success which attended the labours of the disciples of Shri Ramakrishna Paramahamsa in diffusing the principles of Hindu religion and obtaining some respect for our much abused faith in the West, gave rise to the hope of training a number of young Sannyâsins to carry on the propaganda, both in and out of India. And an attempt is being made to educate a number of young men according to the Vedic principle of students living in touch with the Guru.

A Math has already been started on the Ganga near Calcutta, through the kindness of some European and American friends.

The work, to produce any visible results in a short time, requires funds and hence this appeal to those who are in sympathy with our efforts.

It is intended to extend the operations of the Math, by educating in the Math as many young men as the funds can afford, in both Western science and Indian spirituality, so that in addition to the advantages of a University education, they will acquire a manly discipline by living in contact with their teachers.

The central Math near Calcutta will gradually start branches in other parts of the country as men become ready and the means are forthcoming.

It is a work which will take time to bring forth any permanent result and requires a great deal of sacrifice on the part of our young men and on those who have the means of helping this work.

We believe the men are ready, and our appeal therefore is to those who really love their religion and their country and have the means to show their sympathy practically by helping the cause.

Vivekananda.

THE ADVAITA ASHRAMA, HIMALAYAS

These lines there sent in a letter, March, 1899, by Swamiji, for embodying in the prospectus of the Advaita Ashrama, Mayavati, Almora, Himalayas.

In Whom is the Universe, Who is in the Universe, Who is the Universe; in Whom is the Soul, Who is in the Soul, Who is the Soul of Man; knowing Him —and therefore the Universe—as our Self, alone extinguishes all fear, brings an end to misery and leads to Infinite Freedom. Wherever there has been expansion in love or progress in well-being, of individuals or numbers, it has been through the perception, realisation, and the practicalisation of the Eternal Truth— the oneness of all beings. "Dependence is misery. Independence is happiness." The Advaita is the only system which gives unto man complete possession of himself, takes off all dependence and its associated superstitions, thus making us brave to suffer, brave to do, and in the long run attain to Absolute Freedom.

Hitherto it has not been possible to preach this Noble Truth entirely free from the settings of dualistic weakness; this alone, we are convinced, explains why it has not been more operative and useful to mankind at large.

To give this one truth a freer and fuller scope in elevating the lives of individuals and leavening the mass of mankind, we start this Advaita Ashrama on the Himalayan heights, the land of its first expiration.

Here it is hoped to keep Advaita free from all superstitions and weakening contaminations. Here will be taught and practiced nothing but the Doctrine of Unity, pure and simple; and though in entire sympathy with all other systems, this Ashrama is dedicated to Advaita and Advaita alone.

THE RAMAKRISHNA HOME OF SERVICE VARANASI: AN APPEAL

Letter written by Swamiji, to accompany the First Report of the Ramakrishna Home of Service, Varanasi, February, 1902.

Dear—

We beg your acceptance of the past year's Report of the Ramakrishna Home of Service, Varanasi, embodying a short statement of our humble efforts towards the amelioration, however little, of the miserable state into which a good many of our fellow-beings, generally old men and women, are cast in this city.

In these days of intellectual awakening and steadily asserting public opinion, the holy places of the Hindus, their condition, and method of work have not escaped tile keen eye of criticism; and this city, being the holy of holies to all Hindus, has not failed to attract its full share of censure.

In other sacred places people go to purify themselves from sin, and their connection with these places is casual, and of a few day's duration. In this, the nicest ancient and living centre of Aryan religious activity, there come men and women, and as a rule, old and decrepit, waiting to pass unto Eternal Freedom, through the greatest of all sanctifications, death under the shadow of the temple of the Lord of the universe.

And then there are those who have renounced everything for the good of the world and have for ever lost the helping hands of their own flesh and blood and childhood's associations.

They too are overtaken by the common lot of humanity, physical evil in the form of disease.

It may be true that some blame attaches to the management of the place. It may be true that the priests deserve a good part of the sweeping criticism generally heaped upon them; yet we must not forget the great truth—like people, like priests. If the people stand be with folded hands and watch the swift current of misery rushing past their doors, dragging men, women and children, the Sannyâsin and the householder into one common whirlpool of helpless suffering, and make not the least effort to save any from the current, only waxing eloquent at the misdoings of the priests of the holy places not one particle of suffering can ever be lessened, not one ever be helped.

Do we want to keep up the faith of our forefathers in the efficacy of the Eternal City of Shiva towards salvation?

If we do, we ought to be glad to see the number of those increase from year to year who come here to die.

And blessed be the name of the Lord that the poor have this eager desire for salvation, the same as ever.

The poor who come here to die have voluntarily cut themselves off from any help they could have received in the places of their birth, and when disease overtakes them, their condition we leave to your imagination and to your conscience as a Hindu to feel and to rectify.

Brother, does it not make you pause and think of the marvellous attraction of this wonderful place of preparation for final rest? Does it not strike you with a mysterious sense of awe—this age-old and never-ending stream of pilgrims marching to salvation through death?

If it does—come and lend us a helping hand.

Never mind if your contribution is only a mite, your help only a little; blades of grass united into a rope will hold in confinement the maddest of elephants—says the old proverb.

Ever yours in the Lord of the universe,
Vivekananda.

WHO KNOWS HOW MOTHER PLAYS!

Perchance a prophet thou —
Who knows? Who dares touch
The depths where Mother hides
Her silent failless bolts!

Perchance the child had glimpse
Of shades, behind the scenes,
With eager eyes and strained,
Quivering forms—ready
To jump in front and be
Events! resistless, strong.
Who knows but Mother, how,
And where, and when, they come?

Perchance the shining sage
Saw more than he could tell;
Who knows, what soul, and when,
The Mother makes Her throne?

What law would freedom bind?
What merit guide Her will,
Whose freak is greatest order,
Whose will resistless law?

To child may glories ope
Which father never dreamt;
May thousandfold in daughter
Her powers Mother store.

TO THE FOURTH OF JULY

It is well known that Swami Vivekananda's death (or resurrection, as some of us would prefer to call it!) took place on the 4th of July, 1902. On the 4th of July, 1898, he was travelling with some American disciples in Kashmir, and as part of a domestic agreement for the celebration of the day—the anniversary of the American Declaration of Independence — he prepared the following poem, to be read aloud at the early breakfast. The poem itself fell to the keeping of Dhirâ Mâtâ.

Behold, the dark clouds melt away,
That gathered thick at night, and hung
So like a gloomy pall above the earth!
Before thy magic touch, the world
Awakes. The birds in chorus sing.
The flowers raise their star-like crowns—
Dew-set, and wave thee welcome fair.
The lakes are opening wide in love
Their hundred thousand lotus-eyes
To welcome thee, with all their depth.
All hail to thee, thou Lord of Light!
A welcome new to thee, today,
O Sun! Today thou sheddest Liberty!
Bethink thee how the world did wait,
And search for thee, through time and clime.
Some gave up home and love of friends,
And went in quest of thee, self-banished,
Through dreary oceans, through primeval forests,
Each step a struggle for their life or death;
Then came the day when work bore fruit,
And worship, love, and sacrifice,
Fulfilled, accepted, and complete.
Then thou, propitious, rose to shed
The light of Freedom on mankind.
Move on, O Lord, in thy resistless path!
Till thy high noon o'erspreads the world.
Till every land reflects thy light,
Till men and women, with uplifted head,
Behold their shackles broken, and
Know, in springing joy, their life renewed!

THE EAST AND THE WEST

I — INTRODUCTION

Vast and deep rivers—swelling and impetuous—charming pleasure-gardens by the river banks, putting to shame the celestial Nandana-Kânana; amidst these pleasure-gardens rise, towering to the sky, beautiful marble palaces, decorated with the most exquisite workmanship of fine art; on the sides, in front, and behind, clusters of huts, with crumbling mud-walls and dilapidated roofs, the bamboos of which, forming their skeletons, as it were, are exposed to view; moving about here and there emaciated figures of young and old in tattered rags, whose faces bear deep-cut lines of the despair and poverty of hundreds of years; cows, bullocks, buffaloes everywhere—ay, the same melancholy look in their eyes, the same feeble physique; on the wayside refuse and dirt: This is our present-day India!

Worn-out huts by the very side of palaces, piles of refuse in the near proximity of temples, the Sanny-âsin clad with only a little loin-cloth, walking by the gorgeously dressed, the pitiful gaze of lustreless eyes of the hunger-stricken at the well-fed and the amply-provided: This is our native land!

Devastation by violent plague and cholera; malaria eating into the very vitals of the nation; starvation and semi-starvation as second nature; death-like famine often dancing its tragic dance; the Kurukshetra (battlefield) of malady and misery, the huge cremation ground, strewn with the dead bones of lost hope, activity, joy, and courage; and in the midst of that, sitting in august silence, the Yogi, absorbed in deep communion with the Spirit, with no other goal in life than Moksha: This is what meets the eye of the European traveller in India.

A conglomeration of three hundred million souls, resembling men only in appearance, crushed out of life by being downtrodden by their own people and foreign nations, by people professing their own religion and by others of foreign faiths; patient in labour and suffering and devoid of initiative like the slave; without any hope, without any past, without any future; desirous only of maintaining the present life anyhow, however precarious; of malicious nature befitting a slave, to whom the prosperity of their fellow-men is unbearable; bereft of Shraddhâ, like one with whom all hope is dead, faithless; whose weapon of defence is base trickery, treachery, and slyness like that of a fox; the embodiment of selfishness; licking the dust of the feet of the strong, withal dealing a death-blow to those who are comparatively weak; full of ugly, diabolical superstitions which come naturally to those who are weak and hopeless of the future; without any standard of morality as their backbone; three hundred millions of souls such as these are swarming on the body of India like so many worms on a rotten, stinking carcass: This is the picture concerning us, which naturally presents itself to the English official!

Maddened with the wine of newly acquired powers; devoid of discrimination between right and wrong; fierce like wild beasts, henpecked, lustful; drenched in liquor, having no idea of chastity or purity, nor of cleanly ways and habits; believing in matter only, with a civilisation resting on matter and its various applications; addicted to the aggrandisement of self by exploiting others' countries, others' wealth, by force, trick, and treachery; having no faith in the life hereafter, whose Âtman (Self) is the body, whose whole life is only in the senses and creature comforts: Thus, to the Indian, the Westerner is the veriest demon (Asura).

These are the views of observers on both sides—views born of mutual indiscrimination and superficial knowledge or ignorance. The foreigners, the Europeans, come to India, live in palatial buildings in the perfectly clean and healthy quarters of our towns and compare our "native" quarters with their neat and beautifully laid-out cities at home; the Indians with whom they come in contact are only of one class—those who hold some sort of employment under them. And, indeed, distress and poverty are nowhere else to be met with as in India; besides that, there is no gainsaying that dirt and filth are everywhere. To the European mind, it is inconceivable that anything good can possibly be amidst such dirt, such slavery, and such degradation.

We, on the other hand, see that the Europeans eat without discrimination whatever they get, have no idea of cleanliness as we have, do not observe caste distinctions, freely mix with women, drink wine, and shamelessly dance at a ball, men and women held in each other's arms: and we ask ourselves in amazement, what good can there be in such a nation?

Both these views are derived from without, and do not look within and below the surface. We do not allow foreigners to mix in our society, and we call them Mlechchhas; they also in their turn hate us as slaves and call us "niggers". In both of these views there must be some truth, though neither of the parties has seen the real thing behind the other.

With every man, there is an idea; the external man is only the outward manifestation, the mere language of this idea within. Likewise, every nation has a corresponding national idea. This idea is working for the world and is necessary for its preservation. The day when the necessity of an idea as an element for the preservation of the world is over, that very day the receptacle of that idea, whether it be an individual or a nation, will meet destruction. The reason that we Indians are still living, in spite of so much misery, distress, poverty, and oppression from within and without is that we have a national idea, which is yet necessary for the preservation of the world. The Europeans too have a national idea of their own, without which the world will not go on; therefore they are so strong. Does a man live a moment, if he loses all his strength? A nation is the sum total of so many individual men; will a nation live if it has utterly lost all its strength and activity? Why did not this Hindu race die out, in the face of so many troubles and tumults of a thousand years? If our customs and manners are so very bad, how is it that we have not been effaced from the face of the earth by this time? Have the various foreign conquerors spared any pains to crush us out? Why, then, were not the Hindus blotted out of existence, as happened with men in other countries which are uncivilised? Why was not India depopulated and turned into a wilderness? Why, then foreigners would have lost no time to come and settle in India, and till her fertile lands in the same way as they did and are still doing in America, Australia, and Africa! Well, then, my foreigner, you are not so strong as you think yourself to be; it is a vain imagination. First understand that India has strength as well, has a substantial reality of her own yet. Furthermore, understand that India is still living, because she has her own quota yet to give to the general store of the world's civilisation. And you too understand this full well, I mean those of our countrymen who have become thoroughly Europeanised both in external habits and in ways of thought and ideas, and who are continually crying their eyes out and praying to the European to save them—"We are degraded, we have come down to the level of brutes; O ye European people, you are our saviours, have pity on us and raise us from this fallen state!" And you too understand this, who are singing Te Deums and raising a hue and cry that Jesus is come to India, and are seeing the fulfilment of the divine decree in the fullness of time. Oh, dear! No! neither Jesus is come nor Jehovah; nor will they come; they are now busy in saving their own hearths and homes and have no time to come to our country. Here is the selfsame Old Shiva seated as before, the bloody Mother Kâli worshipped with the selfsame paraphernalia, the pastoral Shepherd of Love, Shri Krishna, playing on His flute. Once this Old Shiva, riding on His bull and laboring on His Damaru travelled from India, on the one side, to Sumatra, Borneo, Celebes, Australia, as far as the shores of America, and on the other side, this Old Shiva battened His bull in Tibet, China, Japan, and as far up as Siberia, and is still doing the same. The Mother Kali is still exacting Her worship even in China and Japan: it is She whom the Christians metamorphosed into the Virgin Mary, and worship as the mother of Jesus the Christ. Behold the Himalayas! There to the north is Kailâs, the main abode of the Old Shiva. That throne the ten-headed, twenty-armed, mighty Ravana could not shake—now for the missionaries to attempt the task?—Bless my soul! Here in India will ever be the Old Shiva laboring on his Damaru, the Mother Kali worshipped with animal sacrifice, and the lovable Shri Krishna playing on His flute. Firm as the Himalayas they are; and no attempts of anyone, Christian or other missionaries, will ever be able to remove them. If you cannot bear them—avaunt! For a handful of you, shall a whole nation be wearied out of all patience and bored to death? Why don't you make your way somewhere else where you may find fields to graze upon freely—the wide world is open to you! But no, that they won't do. Where is that strength to do it? They would eat the salt of that Old Shiva and play Him false, slander Him, and sing the glory of a foreign Saviour—dear me! To such of our countrymen who go whimpering before foreigners—"We are very low, we are mean, we are degraded, everything we have is diabolical"—to them we say: "Yes, that may be the truth, forsooth, because you profess to be truthful and we have no reason to disbelieve you; but why do you include the whole nation in that We? Pray, sirs, what sort of good manner is that?"

First, we have to understand that there are not any good qualities which are the privileged monopoly of one nation only. Of course, as with individuals, so with nations, there may be a prevalence of certain good qualities, more or less in one nation than in another.

With us, the prominent idea is Mukti; with the Westerners, it is Dharma. What we desire is Mukti; what they want is Dharma. Here the word "Dharma" is used in the sense of the Mimâmsakas. What is Dharma? Dharma is that which makes man seek for happiness in this world or the next. Dharma is established on work, Dharma is impelling man day and night to run after and work for happiness.

What is Mukti? That which teaches that even the happiness of this life is slavery, and the same is the happiness of the life to come, because neither this world nor the next is beyond the laws of nature; only, the slavery of this world is to that of the next as an iron chain is to a golden one. Again, happiness, wherever it may be, being within the laws of nature, is subject to death and will not last ad infinitum. Therefore man must aspire to become Mukta, he must go beyond the bondage of the body; slavery will not do. This Mokshapath is only in India and nowhere else. Hence is true the oft-repeated saying that Mukta souls are only in India and in no other country. But it is equally true that in future they will be in other countries as well; that is well and good, and a thing of great pleasure to us. There was a time in India when Dharma was compatible with Mukti. There were worshippers of Dharma, such as Yudhishthira, Arjuna, Duryodhana, Bhishma, and Karna, side by side with the aspirants of Mukti, such as Vyâsa, Shuka, and Janaka. On the advent of Buddhism, Dharma was entirely neglected, and the path of Moksha alone became predominant. Hence, we read in the Agni Purâna, in the language of similes, that the demon Gayâsura—that is, Buddha[1]—tried to destroy the world by showing the path of Moksha to all; and therefore the Devas held a council and by stratagem set him at rest for ever. However, the central fact is that the fall of our country, of which we hear so much spoken, is due to the utter want of this Dharma. If the whole nation practices and follows the path of Moksha, that is well and good; but is that possible? Without enjoyment, renunciation can never come; first enjoy and then you can renounce. Otherwise, if the whole nation, all of a sudden, takes up Sannyâsa, it does not gain what it desires, but it loses what it had into the bargain—the bird in the hand is fled, nor is that in the bush caught. When, in the heyday of Buddhistic supremacy, thousands of Sannyâsins lived in every monastery, then it was that the country was just on the verge of its ruin! The Bauddhas, the Christians, the Mussulmans, and the Jains prescribe, in their folly, the same law and the same rule for all. That is a great mistake; education, habits, customs, laws, and rules should be different for different men and nations, in conformity with their difference of temperament. What will it avail, if one tries to make them all uniform by compulsion? The Bauddhas declared, "Nothing is more desirable in life than Moksha; whoever you are, come one and all to take it." I ask, "Is that ever possible?" "You are a householder, you must not concern yourself much with things of that sort: you do your Svadharma (natural duty)"—thus say the Hindu scriptures. Exactly so! He who cannot leap one foot, is going to jump across the ocean to Lankâ in one bound! Is it reason? You cannot feed your own family or dole out food to two of your fellow-men, you cannot do even an ordinary piece of work for the common good, in harmony with others—and you are running after Mukti! The Hindu scriptures say, "No doubt, Moksha is far superior to Dharma; but Dharma should be finished

---

1. Swamiji afterwards changed this view with reference to Buddha, as is evident from the letter dated Varanasi, the 9th February, 1902, in this volume.

first of all". The Bauddhas were confounded just there and brought about all sorts of mischief. Non-injury is right; "Resist not evil" is a great thing—these are indeed grand principles; but the scriptures say, "Thou art a householder; if anyone smites thee on thy cheek, and thou dost not return him an eye for an eye, a tooth for a tooth, thou wilt verily be a sinner." Manu says, "When one has come to kill you, there is no sin in killing him, even though he be a Brâhmin" (Manu, VIII. 350). This is very true, and this is a thing which should not be forgotten. Heroes only enjoy the world. Show your heroism; apply, according to circumstances, the fourfold political maxims of conciliation, bribery, sowing dissensions, and open war, to win over your adversary and enjoy the world—then you will be Dhârmika (righteous). Otherwise, you live a disgraceful life if you pocket your insults when you are kicked and trodden down by anyone who takes it into his head to do so; your life is a veritable hell here, and so is the life hereafter. This is what the Shastras say. Do your Svadharma—this is truth, the truth of truths. This is my advice to you, my beloved co-religionists. Of course, do not do any wrong, do not injure or tyrannise over anyone, but try to do good to others as much as you can. But passively to submit to wrong done by others is a sin—with the householder. He must try to pay them back in their own coin then and there. The householder must earn money with great effort and enthusiasm, and by that must support and bring comforts to his own family and to others, and perform good works as far as possible. If you cannot do that, how do you profess to be a man? You are not a householder even—what to talk of Moksha for you!!

We have said before that Dharma is based on work. The nature of the Dharmika is constant performance of action with efficiency. Why, even the opinion of some Mimamsakas is that those parts of the Vedas which do not enjoin work are not, properly speaking, Vedas at all. One of the aphorisms of Jaimini runs thus: "आम्नायस्य क्रियार्थत्वादानर्थक्यमतदर्थानाम्— The purpose of the Vedas being work, those parts of the Vedas that do not deal with work miss the mark."

"By constant repetition of the syllable Om and by meditating on its meaning, everything can be obtained"; "All sins are washed away by uttering the name of the Lord"; "He gets all, who resigns himself to the Will of God"—yes, these words of the Shastras and the sages are, no doubt, true. But, do you see, thousands of us are, for our whole life, meditating on Om, are getting ecstatic in devotion in the name of the Lord, and are crying, "Thy Will be done, I am fully resigned to Thee!"—and what are they actually getting in return? Absolutely nothing! How do you account for this? The reason lies here, and it must be fully understood. Whose meditation is real and effective? Who can really resign himself to the Will of God? Who can utter with power irresistible, like that of a thunderbolt, the name of the Lord? It is he who has earned Chitta-shuddhi, that is, whose mind has been purified by work, or in other words, he who is the Dharmika.

Every individual is a centre for the manifestation of a certain force. This force has been stored up as the resultant of our previous works, and each one of us is born with this force at his back. So long as this force has not worked itself out, who can possibly remain quiet and give up work? Until then, he will have to enjoy or suffer according to the fruition of his good or bad work and will be irresistibly impelled to do work. Since enjoyment and work cannot be given up till then, is it not better to do good rather than bad works—to enjoy happiness rather than suffer misery? Shri Râmprasâd[1] used to say, "They speak of two works, 'good' and 'bad'; of them, it is better to do the good."

Now what is that good which is to be pursued? The good for him who desires Moksha is one, and the good for him who wants Dharma is another. This is the great truth which the Lord Shri Krishna, the revealer of the Gita, has tried therein to explain, and upon this great truth is established the Varnâshrama[2] system and the doctrine of Svadharma etc. of the Hindu religion.

अद्वेष्टा सर्वभूतानां मैत्रः करुण एव च ।
निर्ममो निरहंकारः समदुःखसुखः क्षमी ॥ (Gita, XII.13.)

---

1. A Bengali saint, devotee of Kâli, and an inspired poet who composed songs in praise of the Deity, expressing the highest truths of religion in the simplest words.

2. Four castes and four stages of life.

—"He who has no enemy, and is friendly and compassionate towards all, who is free from the feelings of 'me and mine', even-minded in pain and pleasure, and forbearing"—these and other epithets of like nature are for him whose one goal in life is Moksha.

क्लैब्यं मा स्म गमः पार्थ नैतत्त्वय्युपपद्यते ।

क्षुद्रं हृदयदौर्बल्यं त्यक्त्वोत्तिष्ठ परन्तप ॥ (Gita, II. 3.)

—"Yield not to unmanliness, O son of Prithâ! Ill cloth it befit thee. Cast off this mean faint-heartedness and arise. O scorcher of thine enemies."

तस्मात्त्वमुत्तिष्ठ यशो लभस्व जित्वा शत्रून् भुङ्क्ष्व राज्यं समृद्धम् ।

मयैवैते निहताः पूर्वमेव निमित्तमात्रं भव सव्यसाचिन् ॥ (Gita, XI. 33.)

—"Therefore do thou arise and acquire fame. After conquering thy enemies, enjoy unrivalled dominion; verily, by Myself have they been already slain; be thou merely the instrument, O Savyasâchin (Arjuna)." In these and similar passages in the Gita the Lord is showing the way to Dharma. Of course, work is always mixed with good and evil, and to work, one has to incur sin, more or less. But what of that? Let it be so. Is not something better than nothing? Is not insufficient food better than going without any? Is not doing work, though mixed with good and evil, better than doing nothing and passing an idle and inactive life, and being like stones? The cow never tells a lie, and the stone never steals, but, nevertheless, the cow remains a cow and the stone a stone. Man steals and man tells lies, and again it is man that becomes a god. With the prevalence of the Sâttvika essence, man becomes inactive and rests always in a state of deep Dhyâna or contemplation; with the prevalence of the Rajas, he does bad as well as good works; and with the prevalence of the Tamas again, he becomes inactive and inert. Now, tell me, looking from outside, how are we to understand, whether you are in a state wherein the Sattva or the Tamas prevails? Whether we are in the state of Sattvika calmness, beyond all pleasure and pain, and past all work and activity, or whether we are in the lowest Tâmasika state, lifeless, passive, dull as dead matter, and doing no work, because there is no power in us to do it, and are, thus, silently and by degrees, getting rotten and corrupted within—I seriously ask you this question and demand an answer. Ask your own mind, and you shall know what the reality is. But, what need to wait for the answer? The tree is known by its fruit. The Sattva prevailing, the man is inactive, he is calm, to be sure; but that inactivity is the outcome of the centralization of great powers, that calmness is the mother of tremendous energy. That highly Sattivka man, that great soul, has no longer to work as we do with hands and feet—by his mere willing only, all his works are immediately accomplished to perfection. That man of predominating Sattva is the Brahmin, the worshipped of all. Has he to go about from door to door, begging others to worship him? The Almighty Mother of the universe writes with Her own hand, in golden letters on his forehead, "Worship ye all, this great one, this son of Mine", and the world reads and listens to it and humbly bows down its head before him in obedience. That man is really—

अद्वेष्टा सर्वभूतानां मैत्रः करुण एव च ।

निर्ममो निरहंकारः समदुःखसुखः क्षमी ॥ (Gita, XII.13.)

—"He who has no enemy, and is friendly and compassionate towards all, who is free from the feelings of 'me and mine', even-minded in pain and pleasure, and forbearing." And mark you, those things which you see in pusillanimous, effeminate folk who speak in a nasal tone chewing every syllable, whose voice is as thin as of one who has been starving for a week, who are like a tattered wet rag, who never protest or are moved even if kicked by anybody—those are the signs of the lowest Tamas, those are the signs of death, not of Sattva—all corruption and stench. It is because Arjuna was going to fall into the ranks of these men that the Lord is explaining matters to him so elaborately in the Gita. Is that not the fact? Listen to the very first words that came out of the mouth of the Lord, "क्लैब्यं मा स्म गमः पार्थ नैतत्त्वय्युपपद्यते—Yield not to unmanliness, O Pârtha! Ill, doth it befit thee!" and then later, "तस्मात्त्वमुत्तिष्ठ यशो लभस्व—Therefore do thou arise and acquire fame." Coming under the influence of the Jains, Buddhas, and others, we have joined the lines of those Tamasika people. During these last thousand years, the whole country is filling the air with the name of the Lord and is sending its prayers to Him; and the Lord is never lending His ears to them. And why should He? When even man never hears the cries of the fool, do you think God will? Now the only way out is to listen to the words of the Lord in the Gita, "क्लैब्यं मा स्म गमः पार्थ—Yield not to unmanliness, O Partha!" "तस्मात्त्वमुत्तिष्ठ यशो लभस्व—Therefore do thou arise and acquire fame."

Now let us go on with our subject-matter—the East and the West. First see the irony of it. Jesus Christ, the God of the Europeans, has taught: Have no enemy, bless them that curse you; whosoever shall smite thee on thy right cheek, turn to him the other also; stop all your work and be ready for the next world; the end of the world is near at hand. And our Lord in the Gita is saying: Always work with great enthusiasm, destroy your enemies and enjoy the world. But, after all, it turned out to be exactly the reverse of what Christ or Krishna implied. The Europeans never took the words of Jesus Christ seriously. Always of active habits, being possessed of a tremendous Râjasika nature, they are gathering with great enterprise and youthful ardour the comforts and luxuries of the different countries of the world and enjoying them to their hearts' content. And we are sitting in a corner, with our bag and baggage, pondering on death day and night, and singing, "नलिनीदलगतजलमतितरलं तद्वज्जीवितमतिशयचपलम्—Very tremulous and unsteady is the water on the lotus-leaf; so is the life of man frail and transient"—with the result that it is making our blood run cold and our flesh creep with the fear of Yama, the god of death; and Yama, too, alas, has taken us at our word, as it were—plague and all sorts of maladies have entered into our country! Who are following the teachings of the Gita?—the Europeans. And who are acting according to the will of Jesus Christ?—The descendants of Shri Krishna! This must be well understood. The Vedas were the first to find and proclaim the way to Moksha, and from that one source, the Vedas, was taken whatever any great Teacher, say, Buddha or Christ, afterwards taught. Now, they were Sannyasins, and therefore they "had no enemy and were friendly and compassionate towards all". That was well and good for them. But why this attempt to compel the whole world to follow the same path to Moksha? "Can beauty be manufactured by rubbing and scrubbing? Can anybody's love be won by threats or force?" What does Buddha or Christ prescribe for the man who neither wants Moksha nor is fit to receive it?—Nothing! Either you must have Moksha or you are doomed to destruction—these are the only two ways held forth by them, and there is no middle course. You are tied hand and foot in the matter of trying for anything other than Moksha. There is no way shown how you may enjoy the world a little for a time; not only all openings to that are hermetically sealed to you, but, in addition, there are obstructions put at every step. It is only the Vedic religion which considers ways and means and lays down rules for the fourfold attainment of man, comprising Dharma, Artha, Kama, and Moksha. Buddha ruined us, and so did Christ ruin Greece and Rome! Then, in due course of time, fortunately, the Europeans became Protestants, shook off the teachings of Christ as represented by Papal authority, and heaved a sigh of relief. In India, Kumârila again brought into currency the Karma-Mârga, the way of Karma only, and Shankara and Râmânuja firmly re-established the Eternal Vedic religion, harmonising and balancing in due proportions Dharma, Artha, Kama, and Moksha. Thus the nation was brought to the way of regaining its lost life; but India has three hundred million souls to wake, and hence the delay. To revive three hundred millions—can it be done in a day?

The aims of the Buddhistic and the Vedic religions are the same, but the means adopted by the Buddhistic are not right. If the Buddhistic means were correct, then why have we been thus hopelessly lost and ruined? It will not do to say that the efflux of time has naturally wrought this. Can time work, transgressing the laws of cause and effect?

Therefore, though the aims are the same, the Bauddhas for want of right means have degraded India. Perhaps my Bauddha brothers will be offended at this remark, and fret and fume; but there's no help for it; the truth ought to be told, and I do not care for the result. The right and correct means is that of the Vedas—the Jâti Dharma, that is, the Dharma enjoined according to the different castes—the Svadharma, that is, one's own Dharma, or set of duties prescribed for man according to his capacity and position—which is the very basis of Vedic religion and Vedic society. Again, perhaps, I am offending many of my friends, who are saying, I suppose, that I am flattering my own countrymen. Here let me ask them once for all: What do I gain by such flattery? Do they support me with any money or means? On the contrary, they try their best to get possession of money which I secure by begging from outside of India for feeding the famine-stricken and the helpless; and if they do not get it, they abuse and slander! Such then, O my educated countrymen, are the people of my country. I know them too well to expect anything from them by flattery. I know they have to be treated like the insane; and anyone who administers medicine to a madman must be ready to be rewarded with kicks and bites; but he is the true friend who forces the medicine down the throats of such and bears with them in patience.

Now, this Jati Dharma, this Svadharma, is the path of welfare of all societies in every land, the ladder to ultimate freedom. With the decay of this Jati Dharma, this Svadharma, has come the downfall of our land. But the Jati Dharma or Svadharma as commonly understood at present by the higher castes is rather a new evil, which has to be guarded against. They think they know everything of Jati Dharma, but really they know nothing of it. Regarding their own village customs as the eternal customs laid down by the Vedas, and appropriating to themselves all privileges, they are going to their doom! I am not talking of caste as determined by qualitative distinction, but of the hereditary caste system. I admit that the qualitative caste system is the primary one; but the pity is qualities yield to birth in two or three generations. Thus the vital point of our national life has been touched; otherwise, why should we sink to this degraded state? Read in the Gita, "संकरस्य च कर्ता स्यामुपहन्यामिमाः प्रजाः—I should then be the cause of the admixture of races, and I should thus ruin these beings." How came this terrible Varna-Sâmkarya—this confounding mixture of all castes—and disappearance of all qualitative distinctions? Why has the white complexion of our forefathers now become black? Why did the Sattva-guna give place to the prevailing Tamas with a sprinkling, as it were, of Rajas in it? That is a long story to tell, and I reserve my answer for some future occasion. For the present, try to understand this, that if the Jati Dharma be rightly and truly preserved, the nation shall never fall. If this is true, then what was it that brought our downfall? That we have fallen is the sure sign that the basis of the Jati Dharma has been tampered with. Therefore, what you call the Jati Dharma is quite contrary to what we have in fact. First, read your own Shastras through and through, and you will easily see that what the Shastras define as caste-Dharma, has disappeared almost everywhere from the land. Now try to bring back the true Jati Dharma, and then it will be a real and sure boon to the country. What I have learnt and understood, I am telling you plainly. I have not been imported from some foreign land to come and save you, that I should countenance all your foolish customs and give scientific explanations for them; it does not cost our foreign friends anything, they can well afford to do so. You cheer them up and heap applause upon them, and that is the acme of their ambition. But if dirt and dust be flung at your faces, it falls on mine too! Don't you see that?

I have said elsewhere that every nation has a national purpose of its own. Either in obedience to the Law of nature, or by virtue of the superior genius of the great ones, the social manners and customs of every nation are being moulded into shape, so as to bring that purpose to fruition. In the life of every nation, besides that purpose and those manners and customs that are essentially necessary to effect that purpose, all others are superfluous. It does not matter much whether those superfluous customs and manners grow or disappear; but a nation is sure to die when the main purpose of its life is hurt.

When we were children, we heard the story of a certain ogress who had her soul living in a small bird, and unless the bird was killed, the ogress would never die. The life of a nation is also like that. Again another thing you will observe, that a nation will never greatly grudge if it be deprived of these rights which have not much to do with its national purpose, nay, even if all of such are wrested from it; but when the slightest blow is given to that purpose on which rests its national life, that moment it reacts with tremendous power.

Take for instance the case of the three living nations, of whose history you know more or less, viz. the French, the English, and the Hindu. Political independence is the backbone of the French character. French subjects bear calmly all oppressions. Burden them with heavy taxes, they will not raise the least voice against them; compel the whole nation to join the army, they never complain; but the instant anyone meddles with that political independence, the whole nation will rise as one man and madly react. No one man shall be allowed to usurp authority over us; whether learned or ignorant, rich or poor, of noble birth or of the lower classes, we have equal share in the Government of our country, and in the independent control of our society—this is the root-principle of the French character. He must suffer Who will try to interfere with this freedom.

In the English character, the "give and take" policy, the business principle of the trader, is principally inherent. To the English, just and equitable distribution of wealth is of essential interest. The Englishman humbly submits to the king and to the privileges of the nobility; only if he has to pay a farthing from his pocket, he must demand an account of it. There is the king; that is all right; he is ready to obey and honour him; but if the king wants money, the Englishman says: All right, but first let me understand why it is needed, what good it will bring; next, I must have my say in the matter of how it is to be spent, and then I shall part with it. The king, once trying to exact money from the English people by force, brought about a great revolution. They killed the king.

The Hindu says that political and social independence are well and good, but the real thing is spiritual independence—Mukti. This is our national purpose; whether you take the Vaidika, the Jaina, or the Bauddha, the Advaita, the Vishishtâdvaita, or the Dvaita—there, they are all of one mind. Leave that point untouched and do whatever you like, the Hindu is quite unconcerned and keeps silence; but if you run foul of him there, beware, you court your ruin. Rob him of everything he has, kick him, call him a "nigger" or any such name, he does not care much; only

keep that one gate of religion free and unmolested. Look here, how in the modern period the Pathan dynasties were coming and going, but could nor get a firm hold of their Indian Empire, because they were all along attacking the Hindu's religion. And see, how firmly based, how tremendously strong was the Mogul Empire. Why? Because the Moguls left that point untouched. In fact, Hindus were the real prop of the Mogul Empire; do you not know that Jahangir, Shahjahan, and Dara Shikoh were all born of Hindu mothers? Now then observe—as soon as the ill-fated Aurangzeb again touched that point, the vast Mogul Empire vanished in an instant like a dream. Why is it that the English throne is so firmly established in India? Because it never touches the religion of the land in any way. The sapient Christian missionaries tried to tamper a little with this point, and the result was the Mutiny of 1857. So long as the English understand this thoroughly and act accordingly, their throne in India will remain unsullied and unshaken. The wise and far-seeing among the English also comprehend this and admit it—read Lord Roberts's Forty-one Years in India[1].

Now you understand clearly where the soul of this ogress is—it is in religion. Because no one was able to destroy that, therefore the Hindu nation is still living, having survived so many troubles and tribulations. Well, One Indian scholar asks, "what is the use of keeping the soul of the nation in religion? Why not keep it in social or political independence, as is the case with other nations?" It is very easy to talk like that. If it be granted, for the sake of argument, that religion and spiritual independence, and soul, God, and Mukti are all false, even then see how the matter stands. As the same fire is manifesting itself in different forms, so the same one great Force is manifesting itself as political independence with the French, as mercantile genius and expansion of the sphere of equity with the English, and as the desire for Mukti or spiritual independence with the Hindu. Be it noted that by the impelling of this great Force, has been moulded the French and the English character, through several centuries of vicissitudes of fortune; and also by the inspiration of that great Force, with

---

1. Vide 30th and 31st Chapters.

the rolling of thousands of centuries, has been the present evolution of the Hindu national character. I ask in all seriousness—which is easier, to give up our national character evolved out of thousands of centuries, or your grafted foreign character of a few hundred years? Why do not the English forget their warlike habits and give up fighting and bloodshed, and sit calm and quiet concentrating their whole energy on making religion the sole aim of their life?

The fact is, that the river has come down a thousand miles from its source in the mountains; does it, or can it go back to its source? If it ever tries to trace back its course, it will simply dry up by being dissipated in all directions. Anyhow the river is sure to fall into the ocean, sooner or later, either by passing through open and beautiful plaints or struggling through grimy soil. If our national life of these ten thousand years has been a mistake, then there is no help for it; and if we try now to form a new character, the inevitable result will be that we shall die.

But, excuse me if I say that it is sheer ignorance and want of proper understanding to think like that, namely, that our national ideal has been a mistake. First go to other countries and study carefully their manners and conditions with your own eyes—not with others'—and reflect on them with a thoughtful brain, if you have it: then read your own scriptures, your ancient literature travel throughout India, and mark the people of her different parts and their ways and habits with the wide-awake eye of an intelligent and keen observer—not with a fool's eye—and you will see as clear as noonday that the nation is still living intact and its life is surely pulsating. You will find there also that, hidden under the ashes of apparent death, the fire of our national life is yet smouldering and that the life of this nation is religion, its language religion, and its idea religion; and your politics, society, municipality, plague-prevention work, and famine-relief work—all these things will be done as they have been done all along here, viz. only through religion; otherwise all your frantic yelling and bewailing will end in nothing, my friend!

Besides, in every country, the means is the same after all, that is, whatever only a handful of powerful men dictate becomes the *fait accompli*; the rest of the men only follow like a flock of sheep, that's all. I have seen your Parliament, your Senate, your vote, majority, ballot; it is the same thing everywhere, my friend. The powerful men in every country are moving society whatever way they like, and the rest are only like a flock of sheep. Now the question is this, who are these men of power in India?—they who are giants in religion. It is they who lead our society; and it is they again who change our social laws and usages when necessity demands: and we listen to them silently anti do what they command. The only difference with ours is, that we have not that superfluous fuss and bustle of the majority, the vote, ballot, and similar concomitant tugs-of-war as in other countries. That is all.

Of course we do not get that education which the common people in the West do, by the system of vote and ballot etc., but, on the other hand, we have not also amongst us that class of people who, in the name of politics, rob others and fatten themselves by sucking the very life-blood of the masses in all European countries. If you ever saw, my friend that shocking sight behind the scene of acting of these politicians—that revelry of bribery, that robbery in broad daylight, that dance of the Devil in man, which are practiced on such occasions—you would be hopeless about man! "Milk goes abegging from door to door, while the grog-shop is crowded; the chaste woman seldom gets the wherewithal to hide her modesty, while the woman of the town flutters about in all her jewelry!" They that have money have kept the government of the land under their thumb, are robbing the people and sending them as soldiers to fight and be slain on foreign shores, so that, in case of victory; their coffers may be full of gold bought by the blood of the subject-people on the field of battle. And the subject-people? Well, theirs is only to shed their blood. This is politics! Don't be startled, my friend; don't be lost in its mazes.

First of all, try to understand this: Does man make laws, or do laws make man? Does man make money, or does money make man? Does man make name and fame, or name and fame make man?

Be a man first, my friend, and you will see how all those things and the rest will follow of themselves after you. Give up that hateful malice, that dog-like bickering and barking at one another, and take your stand on goal purpose, right means, righteous courage, and be brave When you are born a man, leave some indelible mark behind you. "When you first came to this world, O Tulsi[1], the world rejoiced and you cried; now live your life in doing such acts that when you will leave this world, the world will cry for you and you will leave it laughing." If you can do that, then you are a man; otherwise, what good are you?

Next, you must understand this, my friend, that we have many things to learn from other nations. The man who says he has nothing more to learn is already at his last grasp. The nation that says it knows everything is on the very brink of destruction! "As long as I live, so long do I learn." But one point to note here is that when we take anything from others, we must mould it after our own way. We shall add to our stock what others have to teach, but we must always be careful to keep intact what is essentially our own. For instance, Suppose I want to have my dinner cooked in the European fashion. When taking food, the Europeans sit on chairs, and we are accustomed to squat on the floor. To imitate the Europeans, if I order my dinner to be served, on a table and have to sit on a chair more than an hour, my feet will be in a fair way of going to Yama's door, as they say, and I shall writhe in torture; what do you say to that? So I must squat on the floor in my own style, while having their dishes. Similarly, whenever we learn anything from others, we must mould it after our own fashion, always preserving in full our characteristic nationality. Let me ask, "Does man wear clothes or do clothes make the man?" The man of genius in any, dress commands respect; but nobody cares for fools like me, though carrying, like the washerman's ass, a load of clothes on my back.

---
1. A poet and a devotee—the author of the Ramcharitmanasa. Here the poet is addressing himself.

II. CUSTOMS: EASTERN AND WESTERN

The foregoing, by way of an introduction, has come to be rather long; but after all this talk it will be easier for us to compare the two nations. They are good, and we are also good. "You can neither praise the one nor blame the other; both the scales are equal." Of course, there are gradations and varieties of good, this is all.

According to us, there are three things in the make-up of man. There is the body, there is the mind, and there is the soul. First let us consider the body, which is the most external thing about man.

First, see how various are the differences with respect to the body. How many varieties of nose, face, hair, height, complexion, breadth, etc., there are!

The modern ethnologists hold that variety of complexion is due to intermixture of blood. Though the hot or cold climate of the place to a certain extent affects the complexion, no doubt, yet the main cause of its change is heredity. Even in the coldest parts of the world, people with dark complexions are seen, and again in the hottest countries white men are seen to live. The complexion of the aboriginal tribes of Canada, in America, and of the Eskimos of the Northern Polar regions, is not white. While islands, such as Borneo, Celebes, etc., situated in the equatorial regions are peopled by white aborigines.

According to the Hindu Shastras, the three Hindu castes, Brahmana, Kshatriya, and Vaishya, and the several nations outside India, to wit, Cheen, Hun, Darad, Pahlava, Yavana, and Khâsh are all Aryas. This Cheen of our Shastras is not the modern Chinaman. Besides, in those days, the Chinamen did not call themselves Cheen at all. There was a distinct, powerful nation, called Cheen, living in the north-eastern parts of Kashmir, and the Darads lived where are now seen the hill-tribes between India and Afghanistan. Some remnants of the ancient Cheen are yet to be found in very small numbers, and Daradisthan is yet in existence. In the Râjatarangini, the history of Kashmir, references are often made to the supremacy of the powerful Darad-Raj. An ancient tribe of Huns reigned for a long period in the north-western parts of India. The Tibetans now call themselves Hun, but this Hun is perhaps "Hune". The fact is, that the Huns referred to in Manu are not the modern Tibetans, but it is quite probable that the modern Tibetans are the product of a mixture of the ancient Aryan Huns and some other Mogul tribes that came to Tibet from Central Asia. According to Prjevalski and the Duc d' Orleans, the Russian and French travellers, there are still found in some parts of Tibet tribes with faces and eyes of the Aryan type. "Yavana" was the name given to the Greeks. There has been much dispute about the origin of this name. Some say that the name Yavana was first used to designate a tribe of Greeks inhabiting the place called "Ionia", and hence, in the Pâli writs of the Emperor Asoka, the Greeks are named "Yonas", and afterwards from this "Yona" the Sanskrit word Yavana, was derived. Again, according to some of our Indian antiquarians, the word Yavana does not stand for the Greeks. But all these views are wrong. The original word is Yavana itself; for not only the Hindus but the ancient Egyptians and the Babylonians as well called the Greeks by that name. By the word Pahlava is meant the ancient Parsees, speaking the Pahlavi tongue. Even now, Khash denotes the semi-civilised Aryan tribes living in mountainous regions and in the Himalayas, and the word is still used in this sense. In that sense, the present Europeans are the descendants of the Khash; in other words, those Aryan tribes that were uncivilised in ancient days are all Khash.

In the opinion of modern savants, the Aryans had reddish-white complexion, black or red hair, straight noses, well-drawn eyes, etc.; and the formation of the skull varied a little according to the colour of the hair. Where the complexion is dark, there the change has come to pass owing to the mixture of the pure Aryan blood with black races. They hold that there are still some tribes to the west of the Himalayan borders who are of pure Aryan blood, and that the rest are all of mixed blood; otherwise, how could they be dark? But the European Pundits ought to know by this time that, in the southern parts of India, many children are born with red hair, which after two or three years changes into black, and that in the Himalayas many have red hair and blue or grey eyes.

Let the Pundits fight among themselves; it is the Hindus who have all along called themselves Aryas. Whether of pure or mixed blood, the Hindus are Aryas; there it rests. If the Europeans do not like us, Aryas, because we are dark, let them take another name for themselves—what is that to us?

Whether black or white, it does not matter; but of all the nations of the world, the Hindus are the handsomest and finest in feature. I am not bragging nor saying anything in exaggeration because they belong to my own nationality, but this fact is known all over the world. Where else can one find a higher percentage of fine-featured men and women than in India? Besides, it has to be taken into consideration how much more is required in our country to make us look handsome than in other countries, because our bodies are so much more exposed. In other countries, the attempt is always to make ugly persons appear beautiful under cover of elaborate dresses and clothes.

Of course, in point of health, the Westerners are far superior to us. In the West, men of forty years and women of fifty years are still young. This is, no doubt, because they take good food, dress well and live in a good climate, and above all, the secret is that they do not marry at an early age. Ask those few strong tribes among ourselves and see what their marriageable age is. Ask the hill tribes, such as, the Goorkhas, the Punjabis, the Jats, and the Afridis, what their marriageable age is. Then read your own Shastras—thirty is the age fixed for the Brahmana, twenty-five for the Kshatriya, and twenty for the Vaishya. In point of longevity and physical and mental strength, there is a great difference between the Westerners and ourselves. As soon as we attain to forty, our hope and physical and mental strength are on the decline. While, at that age, full of youthful vigour and hope, they have only made a start.

We are vegetarians—most of our diseases are of the stomach; our old men and women generally die of stomach complaints. They of the West take meat—most of their diseases are of the heart; their old men and women generally die of heart or lung diseases. A learned doctor of the West observes that the people who have chronic stomach complaints generally tend to a melancholy and renouncing nature, and the people suffering from complaints of the heart and the upper parts of the body have always hope and faith to the last; the cholera patient is from the very beginning afraid of death, while the consumptive patient hopes to the last moment that he will recover. "Is it owing to this," my doctor friend may with good reasoning ask, "that the Indians always talk and think of death and renunciation?" As yet I have not been able to find a satisfactory answer to this; but the question seems to have an air of truth about it, and demands serious consideration.

In our country, people suffer little from diseases of the teeth and hair; in the West, few people have natural, healthy teeth, and baldness is met with everywhere. Our women bore their noses and ears for wearing ornaments; in the West, among the higher classes, the women do not do those things much, nowadays; but by squeezing the waist, making the spine crooked, and thus displacing the liver and spleen and disfiguring the form, they suffer the torment of death to make themselves shapely in appearance and added to that is the burden of dress, over which they have to show their features to the best advantage. Their Western dress is, however, more suited for work. With the exception of the dress worn in society by the ladies of the wealthy classes, the dress of the women in general is ugly. The Sâri of our women, and the Chogâ, Châpkan, and turban of our men defy comparison as regards beauty in dress. The tight dresses cannot approach in beauty the loose ones that fall in natural folds. But all our dresses being flowing, and in folds, are not suited for doing work; in doing work, they are spoiled and done for. There is such a thing as fashion in the West. Their fashion is in dress, ours in ornaments, though nowadays it is entering a little into clothes also. Paris is the centre of fashion for ladies' dress and London for men's. The actresses of Paris often set the fashions. What new fashion of dress a distinguished actress of the time would wear, the fashionable world would greedily imitate. The big firms of dressmakers set the fashions nowadays. We can form no idea of the millions of pounds that are spent every year in the making of dress in the West. The dress-making business has become a regular science. What colour of dress will suit with the complexion of the girl and the colour of her hair, what special feature of her body should be disguised, and what displayed to the best advantage—these and many other like important points, the dressmakers have seriously to consider. Again, the dress that ladies of very high position wear, others have to wear also, otherwise they lose their caste! This is FASHION.

Then again, this fashion is changing every day, so to say; it is sure to change four times with the four seasons of the year, and, besides, many other times as well. The rich people have their dresses made after the latest fashion by expert firms; those who belong to the middle classes have them often done at home by women-tailors, or do them themselves. If the new fashion approaches very near to their last one, then they just change or adjust their clothes accordingly; otherwise, they buy new ones. The wealthy classes give away their dresses which have gone out of fashion to their dependents and servants. The ladies' maids and valets sell them, and those are exported to the various colonies established by the Europeans in Africa, Asia, and Australia, and there they are used again. The dresses of those who are immensely rich are all ordered from Paris; the less wealthy have them copied in their own country by their own dressmakers. But the ladies' hats must be of French make. As a matter of fact, the dress of the English and the German women is not good; they do not generally follow the Paris fashions—except, of course, a few of the rich and the higher classes. So, the women of other countries indulge in jokes at their expense. But men in England mostly dress very well. The American men and women, without distinction, wear very fashionable dress. Though the American Government imposes heavy duties on all dresses imported from London or Paris, to keep out foreign goods from the country—yet, all the same, the women order their dress from Paris, and men, from London. Thousands of men and women are employed in daily introducing into the market woollen and silk fabrics of various kinds and colours, and thousands, again, are manufacturing all sorts of dresses out of them. Unless the dress is exactly up to date, ladies and gentlemen cannot walk in the street without being remarked upon by the fashionable. Though we have not all this botheration of the fashion in dress in our country, we have, instead, a fashion in ornaments, to a certain extent. The merchants dealing in silk, woollen, and other materials in the West have their watchful eyes always fixed on the way the fashion changes, and what sort of things people have begun to like; or they hit upon a new fashion, out of their own brain, and try to draw the attention of the people thereto. When once a merchant succeeds in gaining the eyes of the people to the fashion brought into the market by him, he is a made man for life. At the time of the Emperor Napoleon III of France, his wife, the Empress Eugenie, was the universally recognised avatar of fashion of the West. The shawl, of Kashmir were her special favourites, and therefore shawls worth millions of rupees used to be exported every year, in her time, from Kashmir to Europe. With the fall of Napoleon III, the fashion has changed, and Kashmir shawls no longer sell. And as for the merchants of our country, they always walk in the old rut. They could not opportunely hit upon any new style to catch the fancy of the West under the altered circumstances, and so the market was lost to them. Kashmir received a severe shock and her big and rich merchants all of a sudden failed.

This world, if you have the eyes to see, is yours—if not, it is mine; do you think that anyone waits for another? The Westerners are devising new means and methods to attract the luxuries and the comforts of different parts of the world. They watch the situation with ten eyes and work with two hundred hands, as it were; while we will never do what the authors of Shastras have not written in books, and thus we are moving in the same old groove, and there is no attempt to seek anything original and new; and the capacity to do that is lost to us now. The whole nation is rending the skies with the cry for food and dying of starvation. Whose fault is it? Ours! What means are we taking in hand to find a way out of the pitiable situation? Zero! Only making great noise by our big and empty talk! That is all that we are doing. Why not come put of your narrow comer and see, with your eyes open, how the world is moving onwards? Then the mind will open and the power of thinking and of timely action will come of itself. You certainly know the story of the Devas and the Asuras. The Devas have faith in their soul, in God, and in the after-life, while the Asuras give importance to this life, and devote themselves to enjoying this world and trying to have bodily comforts in every possible way. We do not mean to discuss here whether the Devas are better than the Asuras, or the Asuras than the Devas, but, reading their descriptions in the Purânas, the Asuras seem to be, truth to tell, more like MEN, and far more manly than the Devas; the Devas are inferior, without doubt, to the Asuras, in many respects. Now, to understand the East and the West, we cannot do better than interpret the Hindus as the sons of the Devas and the Westerners as the sons of the Asuras.

First, let us see about their respective ideas of cleanliness of the body. Purity means cleanliness of mind and body; the latter is effected by the use of water etc. No nation in the world is as cleanly in the body as the Hindu, who uses water very freely. Taking a plunge bath is wellnigh scarce in other nations, with a few exceptions. The English have introduced it into their country after coming in contact with India. Even now, ask those of our students who have resided in England for education, and they will tell you how insufficient the arrangements for bathing are there. When the Westerners bathe—and that is once a week—they change their inner clothing. Of course, nowadays, among those who have means, many bathe daily and among Americans the number is larger; the Germans once in a week, the French and others very rarely! Spain and Italy are warm countries, but there it is still less! Imagine their eating of garlic in abundance, profuse perspiration day and night, and yet no bath! Ghosts must surely run away from them, what to say of men! What is meant by bath in the West? Why, the washing of face, head, and hands, i.e. only those parts which are exposed. A millionaire friend of mine once invited me to come over to Paris: Paris, which is the capital of modern civilisation—Paris, the heaven of luxury, fashion, and merriment on earth—the centre of arts and sciences. My friend accommodated me in a huge palatial hotel, where arrangements for meals were in a right royal style, but, for bath—well, no name of it. Two days I suffered silently—till at last I could bear it no longer, and had to address my friend thus: "Dear brother, let this royal luxury be with you and yours! I am panting to get out of this situation. Such hot weather, and no facility of bathing; if it continues like this, I shall be in imminent danger of turning mad like a rabid dog." Hearing this, my friend became very sorry for me and annoyed with the hotel authorities, and said: "I won't let you stay here any more, let us go and find out a better place". Twelve of the chief hotels were seen, but no place for bathing was there in any of them. There are independent bathing-houses, where one can go and have a bath for four or five rupees. Good heavens! That very afternoon I read in a paper that an old lady entered into the bath-tub and died then and there! Whatever the doctors may say, I am inclined to think that perhaps that was the first occasion in her life to come into contact with so much water, and the frame collapsed by the sudden shock! This is no exaggeration. Then, the Russians and some others are awfully unclean in that line. Starting from Tibet, it is about the same all over those regions. In every boarding house in America, of course, there is a bath-room, and an arrangement of pipe-water.

See, however, the difference here. Why do we Hindus bathe? Because of the fear of incurring sin. The Westerners wash their hands and face for cleanliness' sake. Bathing with us means pouring water over the body, though the oil and the dirt may stick on and show themselves. Again, our Southern Indian brothers decorate themselves with such long and wide caste-marks that it requires, perchance the use of a pumice-stone to rub them off. Our bath, on the other hand, is an easy matter—to have a plunge in, anywhere; but not so, in the West. There they have to put off a load of clothes, and how many buttons and hooks and eyes are there! We do not feel any delicacy to show our body; to them it is awful, but among men, say, between father and son, there is no impropriety; only before women you have to cover yourself cap-a-pie.

This custom of external cleanliness, like all other customs, sometimes turns out to be, in the long run, rather a tyranny or the very reverse of Âchâra (cleanliness). The European says that all bodily matters have to be attended to in private. Well and good. "It is vulgar to spit before other people. To rinse your mouth before others is disgraceful." So, for fear of censure, they do not wash their mouth after meals, and the result is that the teeth gradually decay. Here is non-observance of cleanliness for fear of society or civilisation. With us, it is the other extreme—to rinse and wash the mouth before all men, or sitting in the street, making a noise as if you were sick—this is rather tyranny. Those things should, no doubt, be done privately and silently, but not to do them for fear of society is also equally wrong.

Again, society patiently bears and accommodates itself to those customs which are unavoidable in particular climates. In a warm country like ours, we drink glass after glass of water; now, how can we help eructating; but in the West, that habit is very ungentlemanly. But there, if you blow the nose and use your pocket handkerchief at the time of eating—that is not objectionable, but with us, it is disgusting. In a cold country like theirs, one cannot avoid doing it now and then.

We Hindus hold dirt in abomination very much, but, all the same, we are, in point of fact, frequently dirty ourselves. Dirt is so repugnant to us that if we touch it we bathe; and so to keep ourselves away from it, we leave a heap of it to rot near the house—the only thing to be careful about is not to touch it; but, on the other hand, do we ever think that we are living virtually in hell? To avoid one uncleanliness, we court another and a greater uncleanliness; to escape from one evil, we follow on the heels of another and a greater evil. He who keeps dirt heaped in his house is a sinner, no doubt about that. And for his retribution he has not to wait for the next life; it recoils on his head betimes—in this very life.

The grace of both Lakshmi (goddess of fortune) and Sarasvati (goddess of learning) now shines on the peoples of the Western countries. They do not stop at the mere acquisition of the objects of enjoyment, but in all their actions they seek for a sort of beauty and grace. In eating and drinking, in their homes and surroundings, in everything, they want to see an all-round elegance. We also had that trait once—when there was wealth and prosperity in the land. We have now too much poverty, but, to make matters worse, we are courting our ruin in two ways—namely, we are throwing away what we have as our own, and labouring in vain to make others' ideals and habits ours. Those national virtues that we had are gradually disappearing, and we are not acquiring any of the Western ones either? In sitting, walking, talking, etc., there was in the olden days a traditional, specific trait of our own; that is now gone, and withal we have not the ability to take in the Western modes of etiquette. Those ancient religious rites, practices, studies, etc., that were left to us, you are consigning to the tide-waters to be swept away—and yet something new and suitable to the exigencies of the time, to make up for them, is not striking its roots and becoming stable with us. In oscillating between these two lines, all our present distress lies. The Bengal that is to be has not as yet got a stable footing. It is our arts that have fared the worst of all. In the days gone by, our old women used to paint the floors, doors, and walls of their houses with a paste of rice-powder, drawing various beautiful figures; they used to cut plantain leaves in an artistic manner, to serve the food on; they used to lavish their art in nicely arranging the different comestibles on the plates. Those arts, in these days, have gradually disappeared or are doing so.

Of course new things have to be learnt, have to be introduced and worked out; but is that to be done by sweeping away all that is old, just because it is old? What new things have you learnt? Not any—save and except a jumble of words! What really useful science or art have you acquired? Go, and see, even now in the distant villages, the old woodwork and brickwork. The carpenters of your towns cannot even turn out a decent pair of doors. Whether they are made for a hut or a mansion is hard to make out! They are only good at buying foreign tools, as if that is all of carpentry! Alas! That state of things has come upon all matters in our country. What we possessed as our own is all passing away, and yet, all that we have learnt from foreigners is the art of speechifying. Merely reading and talking! The Bengalis, and the Irish in Europe, are races cast in the same mould—only talking and talking, and bandying words. These two nations are adepts in making grandiloquent speeches. They are nowhere, when a jot of real practical work is required—over and above that, they are barking at each other and fighting among themselves all the days of their life!

In the West, they have a habit of keeping everything about themselves neat and clean, and even the poorest have an eye towards it. And this regard for cleanliness has to be observed; for, unless the people have clean suits of clothes, none will employ them in their service. Their servants, maids, cooks, etc., are all dressed in spotlessly clean clothes. Their houses are kept trim and tidy by being daily brushed, washed and dusted. A part of good breeding consists in not throwing things about, but keeping them in their proper places. Their kitchens look clean and bright—vegetable peelings and such other refuse are placed, for the time being in a separate receptacle, and taken, later on, by a scavenger to a distance and thrown away in a proper place set apart for the purpose. They do not throw such things about in their yards or on the roads.

The houses and other buildings of those who are wealthy are really a sight worth seeing—these are, night and day, a marvel of orderliness and cleanliness! Over and above that, they are in the habit of collecting art treasures from various countries, and adorning their rooms with them. As regards ourselves, we need not, of course, at any rate for the present, go in for collecting works of art as they do; but should we, or should we not, at least preserve those which we possess from going to ruin? It will take up a long time yet to become as good and efficient as they are in the arts of painting and sculpture. We were never very skilful in those two departments of art. By imitating the Europeans we at the utmost can only produce one or two Ravi Varmas among us! But far better than such artists are our Patuas (painter) who do the Châlchitras[1] of our goddesses, in Bengal. They display in their work at least a boldness in the brilliancy of their colours. The paintings of Ravi Varma and others make one hide one's face from shame! Far better are those gilded pictures of Jaipur and the Chalchitra of the goddess Durgâ that we have had from old times. I shall reserve my reflections on the European arts of sculpture and painting for some future occasion. That is too vast a subject to enter upon here.

---

1. Arch shaper frames over the images of deities, with Paurânika pictures.

III. FOOD AND COOKING

Now hear something about the Western art of cooking. There is greater purity observed in our cooking than in any other country; on the other hand, we have not that perfect regularity, method and cleanliness of the English table. Every day our cook first bathes and changes his clothes before entering the kitchen; he neatly cleanses all the utensils and the hearth with water and earth, and if he chances to touch his face, nose, or any part of his body, he washes his hands before he touches again any food. The Western cook scarcely bathes; moreover, he tastes with a spoon the cooking he is engaged in, and does not think much of redipping the spoon into the pot. Taking out his handkerchief he blows his nose vigorously, and again with the same hand he, perchance, kneads the dough. He never thinks of washing his hands when he comes from outside, and begins his cooking at once. But all the same, he has snow-white clothes and cap. Maybe, he is dancing on the dough—why, because he may knead it thoroughly well with the whole pressure of his body, no matter if the sweat of his brow gets mixed with it! (Fortunately nowadays, machines are widely used for the task.) After all this sacrilege, when the bread is finished, it is placed on a porcelain dish covered with a snow-white napkin and is carried by the servant dressed in a spotless suit of clothes with white gloves on; then it is laid upon the table spread over with a clean table-cloth. Mark here, the gloves—lest the man touches anything with his bare fingers!

Observe ours on the other hand. Our Brahmin cook has first purified himself with a bath, and then cooked the dinner in thoroughly cleansed utensils, but he serves it to you on a plate on the bare floor which has been pasted over with earth and cow-dung; and his cloth, albeit daily washed, is so dirty that it looks as if it were never washed. And if the plantain-leaf, which sometimes serves the purpose of a plate, is torn, there is a good chance of the soup getting mixed up with the moist floor and cow-dung paste and giving rise to a wonderful taste!

After taking a nice bath we put on a dirty-looking cloth, almost sticky with oil; and in the West, they put on a perfectly clean suit on a dirty body, without having had a proper bath. Now, this is to be understood thoroughly—for here is the point of essential difference between the Orient and the Occident. That inward vision of the Hindu and the outward vision of the West, are manifest in all their respective manners and customs. The Hindu always looks inside, and the Westerner outside. The Hindu keeps diamonds wrapped in a rag, as it were; the Westerner preserves a lump of earth in a golden casket! The Hindu bathes to keep his body clean, he does not care how dirty his cloth may be; the Westerner takes care to wear clean clothes—what matters it if dirt remains on his body! The Hindu keeps neat and clean the rooms, doors, floors, and everything inside his house; what matters it if a heap of dirt and refuse lies outside his entrance door! The Westerner looks to covering his floors with bright and beautiful carpets, the dirt and dust under them is all right if concealed from view! The Hindu lets his drains run open over the road, the bad smell does not count much! The drains in the West are underground—the hotbed of typhoid fever! The Hindu cleanses the inside, the Westerner cleanses the outside.

What is wanted is a clean body with clean clothes. Rinsing the mouth, cleansing the teeth and all that must be done—but in private. The dwelling-houses must be kept clean, as well as the streets and thoroughfares and all outlying places. The cook must keep his clothes clean as well as his body. Moreover, the meals must be partaken of in spotless cups and plates, sitting in a neat and tidy place. Achara or observance of the established rules of conduct in life is the first step to religion, and of that again, cleanliness of body and mind, cleanliness in everything, is the most important factor. Will one devoid of Achara ever attain to religion? Don't you see before your very eyes the miseries of those who are devoid of Achara? Should we not, thus paying dearly for it, learn the lesson? Cholera, malaria, and plague have made their permanent home in India, and are carrying away their victims by millions. Whose fault is it? Ours, to be sure. We are sadly devoid of Achara!

All our different sects of Hinduism admit the truth

of the celebrated saying of the Shruti[1], "आहारशुद्धौ सत्त्वशुद्धिः सत्त्वशुद्धौ ध्रुवा स्मृतिः—When the food is pure, then the inner-sense gets purified; on the purification of the innersense, memory (of the soul's perfection) becomes steady." Only, according to Shankarâchârya, the word Ahâra means the sense-perceptions, and Râmânuja takes the word to mean food. But what is the solution? All sects agree that both are necessary, and both ought to be taken into account. Without pure food, how can the Indriyas (organs) perform their respective functions properly? Everyone knows by experience that impure food weakens the power of receptivity of the Indriyas or makes them act in opposition to the will. It is a well-known fact that indigestion distorts the vision of things and makes one thing appeal as another, and that want of food makes the eyesight and other powers of the senses dim and weak. Similarly, it is often seen that some particular kind of food brings on some particular state of the body and the mind. This principle is at the root of those many rules which are so strictly enjoined in Hindu society—that we should take this sort and avoid that sort of food—though in many cases, forgetting their essential substance, the kernel, we are now busy only with quarelling about the shell and keeping watch and ward over it.

Râmânujâchârya asks us to avoid three sorts at defects which, according to him, make food impure. The first defect is that of the Jâti, i.e. the very nature or the species to which the food belongs, as onion, garlic, and so on. These have an exciting tendency and, when taken, produce restlessness of the mind, or in other words perturb the intellect. The next is that of Âshraya, i.e. the nature of the person from whom the food comes. The food coming from a wicked person will make one impure and think wicked thoughts, while the food coming from a good man will elevate one's thoughts. Then the other is Nimitta-dosha, i.e. impurity in food due to such agents in it as dirt and dust, worms or hair; taking such food also makes the mind impure. Of these three defects, anyone can eschew the Jati and the Nimitta, but it is not easy for all to avoid the Ashraya. It is only to avoid this Ashraya-dosha, that we have so much of "Don't-touchism" amongst us nowadays. "Don't touch me! Don't touch me!"

But in most cases, the cart is put before the horse; and the real meaning of the principle being misunderstood, it becomes in time a queer and hideous superstition. In these cases, the Acharas of the great Âchâryas, the teachers of mankind, should be followed instead of the Lokâchâras. i.e. the customs followed by the people in general. One ought to read the lives of such great Masters as Shri Chaitanya Deva and other similarly great religious teachers and see how they behaved themselves with their fellow-men in this respect. As regards the Jati-dosha in food, no other country in the world furnishes a better field for its observation than India. The Indians, of all nations, take the purest of foods and, all over the world, there is no other country where the purity as regards the Jati is so well observed as in India. We had better attend to the Nimitta-dosha a little more now in India, as it is becoming a source of serious evil with us. It has become too common with us to buy food from the sweets-vendor's shop in the bazaar, and you can judge for yourselves how impure these confections are from the point of view of the Nimitta-dosha; for, being kept exposed, the dirt and dust of the roads as well as dead insects adhere to them, and how stale and polluted they must sometimes be. All this dyspepsia that you notice in every home and the prevalence of diabetes from which the townspeople suffer so much nowadays are due to the taking of impure food from the bazaars; and that the village-people are not as a rule so subject to these complaints is principally due to the fact that they have not these bazaars near them, where they can buy at their will such poisonous food as Loochi, Kachoori, etc. I shall dwell on this in detail later on.

This is, in short, the old general rule about food. But there were, and still are, many differences of opinion about it. Again, as in the old, so in the present day, there is a great controversy whether it is good or bad to take animal food or live only on a vegetable diet, whether we are benefited or otherwise by taking meat. Besides, the question whether it is right or wrong to kill animals has always been a matter of great dispute. One party says that to take away life is a sin, and on

---

[1]. Chhândogya Upanishad, VII. xxvi. 2.

no account should it be done. The other party replies: "A fig for your opinion! It is simply impossible to live without killing." The Shastras also differ, and rather confuse one, on this point. In one place the Shastra dictates, "Kill animals in Yajnas", and again, in another place it says, "Never take away life". The Hindus hold that it is a sin to kill animals except in sacrifices, but one can with impunity enjoy the pleasure of eating meat after the animal is sacrificed in a Yajna. Indeed, there are certain rules prescribed for the householder in which he is required to kill animals on occasions, such as Shraddha and so on; and if he omits to kill animals at those times, he is condemned as a sinner. Manu says that if those that are invited to Shraddha and certain other ceremonies do not partake of the animal food offered there, they take birth in an animal body in their next.

On the other hand, the Jains, the Buddhists, and the Vaishnavas protest, saying, "We do not believe in the dictates of such Hindu Shastras; on no account should the taking away of life be tolerated." Asoka, the Buddhist emperor, we read, punished those who would perform Yajnas or offer meat to the invited at any ceremony. The position in which the modern Vaishnavas find themselves is rather one of difficulty. Instances are found in the Râmâyana[1] and the Mahâbhârata[2] of the drinking of wine and the taking of meat by Rama and Krishna, whom they worship as God. Sita Devi vows meat, rice, and a thousand jars of wine to the river-goddess, Gangâ[3]!

---

1. सीतामादाय बाहुभ्यां मधुमैरेयकं शुचि।
पाययामास काकुत्स्थः शचीमिन्द्रो यथामृतम् ॥
मांसानि च सुमृष्टानि विविधानि फलानि च ।
रामस्याभ्यवहारार्थं किंकरास्तूर्णमाहरन्॥

"Embracing Sitâ with both his arms, Kâkutstha (Râma) made her drink pure Maireya wine, even as Indra makes Shachi partake of nectar. Servants quickly served flesh-meat variously dressed, and fruits of various kinds for the use of Rama."

2. उभौ मध्वासवक्षप्तिावुभौ चन्दनरूषितौ।
सरग्विणौ वरवस्त्रौ तौ दिव्याभरणभूषितौ ॥

"(I saw) both of them (Krishna and Arjuna) drunk with Madhvâsava (sweet spirituous liquor made from honey), both adorned with sandal paste, garlanded, and wearing costly garments and beautiful ornaments." (Udyoga, LVIII. 5).

3. सुराघटसहस्रेण मांसभूतौदनेन च ।
यक्ष्ये त्वां प्रीयतां देवि पुरीं पुनरुपागता॥

"Be merciful to us, O goddess, and I shall, on my return home, worship thee with a thousand jars of arrack (spirituous liquor) and rice well-dressed with flesh-meat" (Ramayana).

In the West, the contention is whether animal food is injurious to health or not, whether it is more strengthening than vegetable diet or not, and so on. One party says that those that take animal food suffer from all sorts of bodily complaints. The other contradicts this and says, "That is all fiction. If that were true, then the Hindus would have been the healthiest race, and the powerful nations, such as the English, the Americans, and others, whose principal food is meat, would have succumbed to all sorts of maladies and ceased to exist by this time." One says that the flesh of the goat makes the intellect like that of the goat, the flesh of the swine like that of the swine, and fish like that of the fish. The other declares that it can as well be argued then that the potato makes a potato-like brain, that vegetables make a vegetable-like brain—resembling dull and dead matter. Is it not better to have the intelligence of a living animal than to have the brain dull and inert like dead matter? One party says that those things which are in the chemical composition of animal food are also equally present in the vegetables. The other ridicules it and exclaims. "Why, they are in the air too. Go then and live on air only". One argues that the vegetarians are very painstaking and can go through hard and long-sustained labour. The other says, "If that were true, then the vegetarian nations would occupy the foremost rank, which is not the case, the strongest and foremost nations being always those that take animal food." Those who advocate animal food contend: "Look at the Hindus and the Chinamen, how poor they are. They do not take meat, but live somehow on the scanty diet of rice and all sorts of vegetables. Look at their miserable condition. And the Japanese were also in the same plight, but since they commenced taking meat, they turned over a new leaf. In the Indian regiments there are about a lac and a half of native sepoys; see how many of them are vegetarians. The best parts of them, such as the Sikhs and the Goorkhas, are never vegetarians". One party says, "Indigestion is due to animal food". The other says, "That is all stuff and nonsense. It is mostly the vegetarians who suffer from stomach complaints." Again, "It may be the vegetable food acts as an effective purgative to the system. But is that any reason that you should induce the whole world to take it?"

Whatever one or the other may say, the real fact, however, is that the nations who take the animal food are always, as a rule, notably brave, heroic and thoughtful. The nations who take animal food also assert that in those days when the smoke from Yajnas used to rise in the Indian sky and the Hindus used to take the meat of animals sacrificed, then only great religious geniuses and intellectual giants were born among them; but since the drifting of the Hindus into the Bâbâji's vegetarianism, not one great, original man arose midst them. Taking this view into account, the meat-eaters in our country are afraid to give up their habitual diet. The Ârya Samâjists are divided amongst themselves on this point, and a controversy is raging within their fold—one party holding that animal food is absolutely necessary, and the opposite party denouncing it as extremely wrong and unjust.

In this way, discussions of a conflicting character, giving rise to mutual abuses, quarrels, and fights, are going on. After carefully scrutinising all sides of the question and setting aside all fanaticism that is rampant on this delicate question of food, I must say that my conviction tends to confirm this view—that the Hindus are, after all right; I mean that injunction of the Hindu Shastras which lays down the rule that food, like many other things, must be different according to the difference of birth and profession; this is the sound conclusion. But the Hindus of the present day will neither follow their Shastras nor listen to what their great Acharyas taught.

To eat meat is surely barbarous and vegetable food is certainly purer—who can deny that? For him surely is a strict vegetarian diet whose one end is to lead solely a spiritual life. But he who has to steer the boat of his life with strenuous labour through the constant life-and-death struggles and the competition of this world must of necessity take meat. So long as there will be in human society such a thing as the triumph of the strong over the weak, animal food is required; otherwise, the weak will naturally be crushed under the feet of the strong. It will not do to quote solitary instances of the good effect of vegetable food on some particular person or persons: compare one nation with another and then draw conclusions.

The vegetarians, again, are also divided amongst themselves. Some say that rice, potatoes, wheat, barley, maize, and other starchy foods are of no use; these have been produced by man, and are the source of all maladies. Starchy food which generates sugar in the system is most injurious to health. Even horses and cows become sickly and diseased if kept within doors and fed on wheat and rice; but they get well again if allowed to graze freely on the tender and growing herbage in the meadows. There is very little starchy substance in grass and nuts and other green edible herbs. The orang-outang eats grass and nuts and does not usually eat potato and wheat, but if he ever does so, he eats them before they are ripe, i.e. when there is not much starch in them. Others say that taking roast meat and plenty of fruit and milk is best suited to the attainment longevity. More especially, they who take much fruit regularly, do not so soon lose their youth, as the acid of fruit dissolves the foul crust formed on the bones which is mainly the cause of bringing on old age.

All these contentions have no end; they are going on unceasingly. Now the judicious view admitted by all in regard to this vexed question is, to take such food as is substantial and nutritious and at the same time, easily digested. The food should be such as contains the greatest nutriment in the smallest compass, and be at the same time quickly assimilable; otherwise, it has necessarily to be taken in large quantity, and consequently the whole day is required only to digest it. If all the energy is spent only in digesting food, what will there be left to do other works?

All fried things are really poisonous. The sweets-vendor's shop is Death's door. In hot countries, the less oil and clarified butter (ghee) taken the better. Butter is more easily digested than ghee. There is very little substance in snow-white flour; whole-wheat flour is good as food. For Bengal, the style and preparation of food that are still in vogue in our distant villages are commendable. What ancient Bengali poet do you find singing the praise of Loochi and Kachoori? These Loochis and Kachooris have been introduced into Bengal from the North-Western Provinces; but even there, people take them only occasionally. I have never seen even there anyone who lives mainly on things fried in ghee, day after day. The Chaube wrestlers of Mathura are, no doubt, fond of Loochis and sweetmeats; but in a few years Chaubeji's power of digestion is ruined, and he has to drug himself with appetising preparations called Churans.

The poor die of starvation because they can get nothing to eat, and the rich die of starvation because what they take is not food. Any and every stuff eaten is not food; that is real food which, when eaten, is well assimilated. It is better to fast rather than stuff oneself with anything and everything. In the delicacies of the sweetmeat shops there is hardly anything nourishing; on the other hand, there is—poison! Of old, people used to take those injurious things only occasionally; but now, the townspeople, especially those who come from villages to live in towns, are the greatest sinners in this respect, as they take them every day. What wonder is there that they die prematurely of dyspepsia! If you are hungry, throw away all sweets and things fried in ghee into the ditch, and buy a pice worth of Moorhi (popped rice)—that will be cheaper and more nutritious food. It is sufficient food to have rice, Dâl (lentils), whole-wheat Châpâtis (unfermented bread), fish, vegetables, and milk. But Dal has to be taken as the Southern Indians take it, that is, the soup of it only; the rest of the preparation give to the cattle. He may take meat who can afford it, but not making it too rich with heating spices, as the North-Western people do. The spices are no food at all; to take them in abundance is only due to a bad habit. Dal is a very substantial food but hard to digest. Pea-soup prepared of tender peas is easily digested and pleasant to the taste. In Paris this pea-soup is a favourite dish. First, boil the peas well, then make a paste of them and mix them with water. Now strain the soup through a wire-strainer, like that in which milk is strained and all the outer skin will be separated. Then add some spices, such as turmeric, black pepper, etc., according to taste, and broil it with a little ghee in the pan—and you get a pleasant and wholesome Dal. The meat-eaters can make it delicious by cooking it with the head of a goat or fish.

That we have so many cases of diabetes in India is chiefly due to indigestion; of course there are solitary instances in which excessive brain work is the cause, but with the majority it is indigestion. Pot-belly is the foremost sign of indigestion. Does eating mean stuffing oneself? That much which on can assimilate is proper food for one. Growing thin or fat is equally due to indigestion. Do not give yourself up as lost because some symptoms of diabetes are noticeable in you; those are nothing in our country anti should not be taken seriously into account. Only, pay more attention to your diet so that you may avoid indigestion. Be in the open air as much as possible, and take good long walks and work hard. The muscles of the leg should be as hard as iron. If you are in service, take leave when possible and make a pilgrimage to the Badarikâshrama in the Himalayas. If the journey is accomplished on foot through the ascent and descent of two hundred miles in the hills, you will see that this ghost of diabetes will depart from you. Do not let the doctors come near you; most of them will harm you more than do any good; and so far as possible, never take medicines, which in most cases kill the patient sooner than the illness itself. If you can, walk all the way from town to your native village every year during the Puja vacation. To be rich in our country has come to be synonymous with being the embodiment of laziness and dependence. One who has to walk being supported by another, or one who has to be fed by another, is doomed to be miserable—is a veritable in valid. He who eats cautiously only the finer coating of the Loochi, for fear that the whole will not agree with him, is already dead in life. Is he a man or a worm who cannot walk twenty miles at a stretch. Who can save one who invites illness and premature death of his own will?

And as for fermented bread, it is also poison; do not touch it at all! Flour mixed with yeast becomes injurious. Never take any fermented thing; in this respect the prohibition in our Shastras of partaking of any such article of food is a fact of great importance. Any sweet thing which has turned sour is called in the Shastras "Shukta", and that is prohibited to be taken, excepting curd, which is good and beneficial. If you have to take bread, toast it well over the fire.

Impure water and impure food are the cause of all maladies. In America, nowadays, it has become a craze to purify the drinking water. The filter has had its day and is now discredited, because it only strains the water through, while all the finer germs of diseases such as cholera, plague, remain intact in it; moreover, the filter itself gradually becomes the hotbed of these germs. When the filter was first introduced in Calcutta, for five years, it is said there was no outbreak of cholera; since then it has become as bad as ever, for the reason that the huge filter itself has now come to be the vehicle of cholera germs. Of all kinds, the simple method that we have of placing three earthen jars one over another on a three-footed bamboo frame, is the best; but every second or third day the sand and charcoal should be changed, or used again after heating them. The method of straining water through a cloth containing a lump of alum in it, that we find in vogue in the villages along the banks of the Ganga in the vicinity of Calcutta, is the best of all. The particles of alum taking with them all earth and impurities and the disease germs, gradually settle at the bottom of the deep jar as sediment; this simple system brings into disrepute pipewater and excels all your foreign filters. Moreover, if the water is boiled it becomes perfectly safe. Boil the water when the impurities are settled down by the alum, and then drink it, and throw away filters and such other things into the ditch. Now in America, the drinking water is first turned into vapour by means of huge machines; then the vapour is cooled down into water again, and through another machine pure air is pressed into it to substitute that air which goes out during the process of vaporization. This water is very pure and is used in every home.

In our country, he who has some means, feeds his children with all sorts of sweets and ghee-fried things, because, perchance, it is a shame—just think what the people will say!—to let them have only rice and Chapatis! What can you expect children fed like that to be but disproportionate in figure, lazy, worthless idiots, with no backbone of their own? The English people, who are so strong a race, who work so hard day and night, and whose native place is a cold country—even they hold in dread the very name of sweetmeats and food fried in butter! And we, who live in the zone of fire, as it were, who do not like to move from one place to another—what do we eat?—Loochis, Kachooris, sweets, and other things, all fried in ghee or oil! Formerly, our village zemindars in Bengal would think nothing of walking twenty or thirty miles, and would eat twice-twenty Koi-fish, bones and all—and they lived to a hundred years. Now their sons and grandsons come to Calcutta and put on airs, wear spectacles, eat the sweets from the bazaars, hire a carriage to go from one street to another, and then complain of diabetes—and their life is cut short; this is the result of their being "civilised, Calcutta-ised" people. And doctors and Vaidyas hasten their ruin too. They are all-knowing, they think they can cure anything with medicine. If there is a little flatulence, immediately some medicine is prescribed. Alas, it never enters into the heads of these Vaidyas to advise them to keep away from medicine, and go and have a good walk of four or five miles, or so.

I am seeing many countries, and many ways and preparations of food; but none of them approaches the admirable cooking of our various dishes of Bengal, and it is not too much to say that one should like to take rebirth for the sake of again enjoying their excellence. It is a great pity that one does not appreciate the value of teeth when one has them! Why should we imitate the West as regards food—and how many can afford to do so? The food which is suitable in our part of the country is pure Bengali food, cheap, wholesome, and nourishing, like that of the people of Eastern Bengal. Imitate their food as much as you can; the more you lean westwards to copy the modes of food, the worse you are, and the more uncivilized you become. You are Calcutta-ites, civilised, forsooth! Carried away by the charm of that destructive net which is of your own creation, the bazaar sweets, Bankura has consigned its popped-rice to the river Damodar, its Kalâi Dâl has been cast into the ditch, and Dacca and Vikrampur have thrown to the dogs their old dishes—or in other words, they have become "civilised"! You have gone to rack and ruin, and are leading others in the same path, toll townspeople, and you pride yourselves on your being "civilized"! And these provincial people are so foolish that they will eat all the refuse of Calcutta and suffer from dyspepsia and dysentery, but will not admit that it is not suiting them, and will defend themselves by saying that the air of Calcutta is damp and "saline"! They must by all means be townspeople in every respect!

So far, in brief, about the merits of food and other customs. Now I shall say something in the matter of what the Westerners generally eat, and how by degrees it has changed.

The food of the poor in all countries is some species of corn; herbs, vegetables, and fish and meat fall within the category of luxuries and are used in the shape of chutney. The crop which grows in abundance and is the chief produce of a country is the staple food of its poorer classes; as in Bengal, Orissa, Madras, and the Malabar coasts, the prime food is rice, pulse, and vegetables, and sometimes, fish and meat are used for chutney only. The food of the well-to-do class in other parts of India is Chapatis (unfermented bread) of wheat, and rice, of the people in general, mainly Chapatis of Bazrâ, Marhuâ, Janâr, Jhingorâ, and other corns.

All over India, herbs, vegetables, pulse, fish, and meat are used only to make tasteful the Roti (unfermented bread), or the rice, as the case may be, and hence they are called in Sanskrit, "Vyanjana", i.e. that which seasons food. In the Punjab, Rajputana, and the Deccan, though the rich people and the princes take many kinds of meat every day, yet with them even, the principal food is Roti or rice. He who takes daily one pound of meat, surely takes two pounds of Chapatis along with it.

Similarly in the West, the chief foods of the people in poor countries, and especially of the poor class in the rich parts, are bread and potatoes; meat is rarely taken, and, if taken, is considered as a chutney. In Spain, Portugal, Italy, and in other comparatively warm countries, grapes grow profusely, and the wine made of grapes is very cheap. These wines are not intoxicating (i.e.. unless one drinks a great quantity, one will not get intoxicated) and are very nutritious. The poor of those countries, therefore, use grape juice as a nourishment instead of fish and meat. But in the northern parts of Europe, such as Russia, Sweden, and Norway, bread made of rye, potatoes, and a little dried fish form the food of the poor classes.

The food of the wealthy classes of Europe, and of all the classes of America is quite different, that is to say, their chief food is fish and meat, and bread, rice, and other things are taken as chutney. In America, bread is taken very little. When fish is served, it is served by itself, or when meat is served, it is served by itself and is often taken without bread or rice. Therefore the plate has to be changed frequently; if there are ten sorts of food, the plate has to be changed as many times. If we were to take our food in this way, we should have to serve like this—suppose the Shukta (bitter curry) is first brought, and, changing that plate, Dal is served on another; in the same way the soup arrives; and again a little rice by itself, or a few Loochis, and so on. One benefit of this way of serving is that a little only of many varieties is taken, and it saves one from eating too much of anything. The French take coffee, and one or two slices of bread and butter in the morning, fish and meat, etc., in a moderate way about midday, and the principal meal comes at night. With the Italians and Spaniards, the custom is the same as that of the French. The Germans eat a good deal, five or six times a day, with more or less meat every time; the English, three times, the breakfast being rather small, but tea or coffee between; and the Americans also three times, but the meal is rather large every time, with plenty of meat. In all these countries, the principal meal is, however, dinner; the rich have French cooks and have food cooked after the French fashion. To begin with, a little salted fish or roe, or some sort of chutney or vegetable—this is by way of stimulating the appetite; soup follows; then, according to the present day fashion, fruit; next comes fish; then a meat-curry; after which a joint of roast meat, and with it some vegetables; afterwards game birds, or venison, etc., then sweets, and finally, delicious ice-cream. At the table of the rich, the wine is changed every time the dish changes—and hock, claret, and iced champagne are served with the different courses. The spoon and knife and fork are also changed each time with the plate. After dinner—coffee without milk and liqueurs in very tiny glasses are brought in, and smoking comes last. The greater the variety of wines served with the various dishes, the greater will the host be regarded as a rich and wealthy man of fashion. As much money is spent over there in giving a dinner as would ruin a moderately rich man of our country.

Sitting cross-legged on a wooden seat on the ground, with a similar one to lean his back against, the Arya used to take his food on a single metal plate, placed on a slightly-raised wooden stool. The same custom is still in rogue in the Punjab, Rajputana, Mahârâshtra, and Gujarat. The people of Bengal, Orissa, Telinga, and Malabar, etc., do not use wooden stools to put the plates on, but take their food on a plate or a plantain-leaf placed on the ground. Even the Maharaja of Mysore does the same. The Mussulmans sit on a large, white sheet, when taking their food. The Burmese and the Japanese place their plates on the ground and sit supporting themselves on their knees and feet only, and not flat on their haunches like the Indians. The Chinamen sit on chairs, with their dishes placed on a table, and use spoons and wooden chop-sticks in taking their food. In the olden times, the Romans and Greeks had a table before them and, reclining on a couch, used to eat their food with their fingers. The Europeans also, sitting on chairs, used to take their food with their fingers from the table; now they have spoons and forks. The Chinese mode of eating is really an exercise requiring skill. As our Pân (betel)-vendors make, by dexterity of hand, two separate pieces of thin iron-sheets work like scissors in the trimming of Pan leaves, so the Chinese manipulate two sticks between two fingers and the palm of the right hand, in such a way as to make them act like tongs to carry the vegetables up to their mouths. Again, putting the two together, and holding a bowl of rice near the mouth, they push the rice in with the help of those sticks formed like a little shovel.

The primitive ancestors of every nation used to eat, it is said, whatever they could get. When they killed a big animal, they would make it last for a month and would not reject it even after it got rotten. Then gradually they became civilised and learnt cultivation. Formerly, they could not get their food every day by hunting and would, like the wild animals, gorge themselves one day and then starve four or five days in the week. Later they escaped that, for they could get their food every day by cultivation; but it remained a standing custom to take with food something like rotten meat or other things of the old days.

Primarily, rotten meat was an indispensable article of food; now that or something else in its place became, like the sauce, a favourite relish. The Eskimos live in the snowy regions, where no kind of corn can be produced; their daily food is fish and flesh. Once in a way when they lose their appetite, they take just a piece of rotten flesh to recover their lost appetite. Even now, Europeans do not immediately cook wild birds, game, and venison, while fresh, but they keep them hanging till they begin to smell a little. In Calcutta the rotten meat of a deer is sold out as soon as brought to the market, and people prefer some fish when slightly rotten. In some parts of Europe, the cheese which smells a little is regarded as very tasty. Even the vegetarians like to have a little onion and garlic; the Southern Indian Brahmin must have them in his cooking. But the Hindu Shastras prohibited that too, making it a sin to take onions, garlic, domestic fowl, and pork to one caste (the Brahmin); they that would take them would lose their caste. So the orthodox Hindus gave up onions and garlic, and substituted in their place asafoetida, a thing which is more strikingly offensive in smell than either of the other two! The orthodox Brahmins of the Himalayas similarly took to a kind of dried grass smelling just like garlic! And what harm in that? The scriptures do not say anything against taking these things!

Every religion contains some rules regarding the taking of certain foods, and the avoiding of others; only Christianity is an exception. The Jains and the Bauddhas will by no means take fish or meat. The Jains, again, will not even eat potatoes, radishes, or other vegetable roots, which grow underground, lest in digging them up worms are killed. They will not eat at night lest some insect get into their mouths in the dark. The Jews do not eat fish that have no scales, do not eat pork, nor the animals that are not cloven-hoofed and do not ruminate. Again, if milk or any preparation of milk be brought into the kitchen where fish or flesh is being cooked, the Jews will throw away everything cooked there. For this reason, the orthodox Jews do not eat the food cooked by other nations. Like the Hindus, too, they do not take flesh which is simply slaughtered and not offered to God. In Bengal and the Punjab, another name of flesh that is offered to the Goddess is Mahâprasâda, lit., the "great offering". The Jews do not eat flesh, unless it is Mahaprasada, i.e. unless it is properly offered to God. Hence, they, like the Hindus, are not permitted to buy flesh at any and every shop. The Mussulmans obey many rules similar to the Jews, but do not, like them, go to extremes; they do not take milk and fish or flesh at the same meal, but do not consider it so much harmful if they are in the same kitchen or if one touches another. There is much similarity respecting food between the Hindus and the Jews. The Jews, however, do not take wild boar, which the Hindus do. In the Punjab, on account of the deadly animosity between the Hindus and the Mussulmans, the former do what the latter will not, and the wild boar has come to be one of the very essential articles of food with the Hindus there. With the Rajputs, hunting the wild boar and partaking of its flesh is rather an act of Dharma. The taking of the flesh of even the domesticated pig prey ails to a great extent in the Deccan among all castes except the Brahmins. The Hindus eat the wild fowl (cock or hen), but not domesticated fowls.

The people of India from Bengal to Nepal and in the Himalayas as far as the borders of Kashmir, follow the same usages regarding food. In these parts, the customs of Manu are in force to a large extent even up to this day. But they obtain more especially in the parts from Kumaon to Kashmir than in Bengal, Bihar, Allahabad, or Nepal. For example, the Bengalis do not eat fowl or fowl's eggs, but they eat duck's eggs; so do the Nepalese; but from Kumaon upwards, even that is not allowed. The Kashmiris eat with pleasure eggs of the wild duck, but not of the domesticated bird. Of the people of India, beginning from Allahabad, excepting in the Himalayas, they who take the flesh of goat take fowl as well.

All these rules and prohibitions with respect to food are for the most part meant, no doubt, in the interests of good health; of course, in each and every instance, it is difficult accurately to determine which particular food is conducive to health and which is not. Again, swine and fowls eat anything and everything and are very unclean; so they are forbidden. No one sees what the wild animals eat in the forest; so they are not disallowed. Besides, the wild animals are healthier and less sickly than the domesticated ones. Milk is very difficult of digestion, especially when one is suffering from acidity, and cases have happened when even by gulping down a glass of milk in haste, life has been jeopardised. Milk should be taken as a child does from its mother's breast; if it is sucked or sipped by degrees, it is easily digestible, otherwise not. Being itself hard of digestion, it becomes the more so when taken with flesh; so the Jews are prohibited from taking flesh and milk at the same meal.

The foolish and ignorant mother who forces her baby to swallow too much milk beats her breast in despair within a few months, on seeing that there is little hope of her darling's life! The modern medical authorities prescribe only a pint of milk even for an adult, and that is to be taken as slowly as possible; and for babies a "feeding-bottle" is the best means. Our mothers are too busy with household duties, so the maid-servant puts the crying baby in her lap and not unfrequently holds it down with her knee, and by means of a spoon makes it gulp down as much milk as she can. And the result is that generally it is afflicted with liver complaint and seldom grows up—that milk proves to be its doom; only those that have sufficient vitality to survive this sort of dangerous feeding attain a strong and healthy manhood. And think of our old-fashioned confinement rooms, of the hot fomentations given to the baby, and treatments of like nature. It was indeed a wonder and must have been a matter of special divine grace that the mother and the baby survived these severe trials and could become strong and healthy!

IV. CIVILISATION IN DRESS

In every country the respectability of a person is determined, to a certain extent, by the nature of the dress he wears. As our village-folk in Bengal say in their patois, "How can a gentleman be distinguished from one of low birth unless his income is known?" And not only income, "Unless it is seen how one dresses oneself, how can it be known if one is a gentleman?" This is the same all over the world, more or less. In Bengal, no gentleman can walk in the streets with only a loincloth on; while in other parts of India, no one goes out of doors but with a turban on his head. In the West, the French have all along taken the lead in everything—their food and their dress are imitated by others. Even now, though different parts of Europe have got different modes of clothes and dress of their own, yet when one earns a good deal of money and becomes a "gentleman", he straightaway rejects his former native dress and substitutes the French mode in its place. The Dutch farmer whose native dress somewhat resembles the paijâmâs of the Kabulis, the Greek clothed in full skirts, the Russ dressed somewhat after the Tibetan fashion—as soon as they become "genteel", they wear French coats and pantaloons. Needless to speak of women—no sooner do they get rich than they must by any means have their dresses made in Paris. America, England, France, and Germany are now the rich countries in the West, and the dress of the people of these countries, one and all, is made after the French fashion, which is slowly and surely making its way into every part of Europe. The whole of Europe seems to be an imitation of France. However, men's clothes are better made nowadays in London than Paris, so men have them "London-made", and women in the Parisian style. Those who are very rich have their dresses sent from those two places. America enforces an exorbitant tax upon the importation of foreign dresses; notwithstanding that, the American women must have them from Paris and London. This, only the Americans can afford to do, for America is now the chief home of Kubera, the god of wealth.

The ancient Aryans used to put on the Dhoti and Châdar[1]. The Kshatriyas used to wear trousers and long coats when fighting. At other times they would use only the Dhoti and Chadar; and they wore the turban. The same custom is still in vogue, except in Bengal, among the people in all parts of India; they are not so particular about the dress for the rest of the body, but they must have a turban for the head. In former times, the same was also the custom for both the man and the women. In the sculptured figures of the Buddhistic period, the men and the women are seen to wear only a piece of Kaupin. Even Lord Buddha's father, though a king, is seen in some sculptures, sitting on a throne, dressed in the same way; so also the mother, only has, in addition, ornaments on her feet and arms; but they all have turbans! The Buddhist Emperor, Dharmâshoka, is seen sitting on a drum-shaped seat with only a Dhoti on, and a Chadar round his neck, and looking at damsels performing a dance before him; the dancing girls are very little clothed, having only short pieces of loose material hanging from the waist; but the glory is—that the turban is there, and it makes the principal feature of their dress. The high officials of the State who attended the royal court, are, however, dressed in excellent trousers and Chogas, or long coats. When the King Nala, was disguised as a charioteer in to service of the King Rituparna, he drove the chariot at such a tremendous speed that the Chadar of the king Rituparna was blown away to such a distance that it could not be recovered; and as he had set out to marry, or join a Svayamvara, he had to do so, perchance, without a Chadar. The Dhoti and the Chadar are the time-honored dress of the Aryans. Hence, at the time of the performance of any religious ceremony, the rule among the Hindus even now is to put on the Dhoti and Chadar only.

The dress of the ancient Greeks and Romans was Dhoti and Chadar—one broad piece of cloth and another smaller one made in the form of the toga, from which the word Choga is derived. Sometimes they used also a shirt, and at the time of fighting, trousers and coats. The dress of the women was a long and sufficiently broad, square-shaped garment, similar to

---
1. Dhoti is a piece of cloth about four or five yards long, worn by the Indians round the loins instead of breeches, and Chadar is a piece of cloth three yards long, used as a loose upper garment.

that formed by sewing two sheets lengthwise, which they slipped over the head and tied round, once under the breast and again round the waist. Then they fastened the upper parts which were open, over both the arms by means of large pins, in much the same way as the hill tribes of the northern Himalayas still wear their blankets. There was a Chadar over this long garment. This dress was very simple and elegant.

From the very old days, only the Iranians used shaped dresses. Perhaps they learnt it from the Chinese. The Chinese were the primeval teachers of civilisation in dress and other things pertaining to various comforts and luxuries. From time immemorial, the Chinese took their meals at a table, sitting on chairs, with many elaborate auxiliaries, and wore shaped dresses of many varieties—coat, cap, trousers, and so on.

On conquering Iran, Alexander gave up the old Greek Dhoti and Chadar and began using trousers. At this, his Greek soldiers became so disaffected towards him that they were on the point of mutiny. But Alexander was not the man to yield, and by the sheer force of his authority he introduced trousers and coats as a fashion in dress.

In a hot climate, the necessity of clothes is not so much felt. A mere Kaupin is enough for the purpose of decency; other clothes serve more as embellishments. In cold countries, as a matter of unavoidable necessity, the people, when uncivilised, clothe themselves with the skins of animals, and when they gradually become civilised, they learn the use of blankets, and by degrees, shaped dresses, such as pantaloons, coats, and so on. Of course it is impossible in cold countries to display the beauty of ornaments, which have to be worn on the bare body, for if they did so they would suffer severely from cold. So the fondness for ornaments is transfered to, and is satisfied by, the niceties of dress. As in India the fashions in ornaments change very often, so in the West the fashions in dress change every moment.

In cold countries, therefore, it is the rule that one should not appear before others without covering oneself from head to foot. In London, a gentleman or a lady cannot go out without conforming himself or herself exactly to what society demands. In the West, it is immodest for a woman to show her feet in society, but at a dance it is not improper to expose the face, shoulders, and upper part of the body to view. In our country, on the other hand, for a woman to show her face is a great shame, (hence that rigorous drawing of the veil), but not so the feet. Again, in Rajputana and the Himalayas they cover the whole body except the waist!

In the West, actresses and dancing-girls are very thinly covered, to attract men. Their dancing often means exposing their limbs in harmonious movements accompanied by music. In our country, the women of gentle birth are not so particular in covering themselves thoroughly, but the dancing-girls are entirely covered. In the West, women are always completely clothed in the daytime; so attraction is greater in their being thinly covered. Our women remain in the house most of the time, and much dressing themselves is unusual; so with us, attraction is greater in their fully covering themselves. In Malabar, men and women have only a piece of cloth round their loins. With the Bengalis it is about the same, and before men, the women scrupulously draw their veils, and cover their bodies.

In all countries except China, I notice many queer and mysterious ideas of propriety—in some matters they are carried too far, in others again, what strikes one as being very incorrect is not felt to be so at all.

The Chinese of both sexes are always fully covered from head to foot. The Chinese are the disciples of Confucius, are the disciples of Buddha, and their morality is quite strict and refined. Obscene language, obscene books or pictures, any conduct the least obscene—and the offender is punished then and there. The Christian missionaries translated the Bible into the Chinese tongue. Now, in the Bible there are some passages so obscene as to put to shame some of the Purânas of the Hindus. Reading those indecorous passages, the Chinamen were so exasperated against Christianity that they made a point of never allowing the Bible to be circulated in their country. Over and above that, missionary women wearing evening dress and mixing freely with men invited the Chinese to their parties. The simpleminded Chinese were disgusted, and raised a cry, saying: Oh, horror! This religion is come to us to ruin our young boys, by giving them this Bible to read, and making them fall an easy prey to the charms of these half clothed wily women! This is why the Chinese are so very indignant with the Christians. Otherwise, the Chinese are very tolerant towards other religions. I hear that the missionaries have now printed an edition, leaving out the objectionable parts; but this step has made the Chinese more suspicious than before.

V. ETIQUETTE AND MANNERS

Again, in the West, ideas of decency and etiquette vary in accordance with the different countries. With the English and Americans they are of one type, is with the French of another, with the Germans again different. The Russians and the Tibetans have much in common; and the Turks have their own quite distinct customs, and so on.

In Europe and America, the people are extremely particular in observing privacy, much more than we are. We are vegetarians, and so eat a quantity of vegetables etc., and living in a hot country we frequently drink one or two glasses of water at a time. The peasant of the Upper Provinces eats two pounds of powdered barley, and then sets to drawing and drinking water from the shell every now and again, as he feels so thirsty. In summer we keep open places in our house for distributing water to the thirsty, through a hollowed bamboo stem. These ways make the people not so very particular about privacy; they cannot help it. Compare cowsheds and horses' stables with lions' and tigers' cages. Compare the dog with the goat. The food of the Westerners is chiefly meat, and in cold countries they hardly drink any water. Gentlemen take a little wine in small glasses. The French detest water; only Americans drink it in great quantities, for their country is very warm in summer. New York is even hotter than Calcutta. The Germans drink a good deal of beer, but not with their meals.

In cold countries, men are always susceptible to catching cold, so they cannot help sneezing; in warm countries people have to drink much water at meals, consequently we cannot help eructating. Now note the etiquette: if you do that in a Western society, your sin is unpardonable; but if you bring out your pocket handkerchief and blow your nose vigorously, it will see nothing objectionable in that. With us, the host will not feel satisfied, so to say, unless he sees you doing the former, as that is taken as a sign of a full meal; but what would you think of doing the latter when having a meal in the company of others?

In England and America, no mention of indigestion or any stomach complaints, you may be suffering from, should be made before women; it is a different matter, of course, if your friend is an old woman, or if she is quite well known to you. They are not so sensitive about these things in France. The Germans are even less particular.

English and American men are very guarded in their conversation before women; you cannot even speak of a "leg". The French, like us, are very free in conversation; the Germans and the Russians will use vulgar terms in the presence of anybody.

But conversations on being in love are freely carried on between mother and son, between brothers and sisters, and between them and their fathers. The father asks the daughter many questions about her lover (the future bridegroom) and cuts all sorts of jokes about her engagement. On such occasions, the French maiden modestly laughs down her head, the English maiden is bashful, and the American maiden gives him sharp replies to his face. Kissing and even embrace are not so very objectionable; these things can be talked of in society. But in our country, no talk, nor even all indirect hint of love affairs, is permissible before superior relations.

The Westerners are now rich people. Unless one's dress is very clean and in conformity with strict etiquette, one will not be considered a gentleman and cannot mix in society. A gentleman must change his collar and shirt twice or thrice every day; the poor people, of course, cannot do this. On the outer garment there must not be stains or even a crease. However much you may suffer from heat, you must go out with gloves for fear of getting your hands dirty in the streets, and to shake hands with a lady with hands that are not clean is very ungentlemanlike. In polite society, if the act of spitting or rinsing the mouth or picking the teeth be ever indulged in—the offender will be marked as a Chandâla, a man of low caste, and shunned!

The Dharma of the Westerners is worship of Shakti—the Creative Power regarded as the Female Principle. It is with them somewhat like the Vâmâchâri's worship of woman. As the Tântrika says. "On the left side the women ... on the right, the cup full of wine; in short, warm meat with ingredients ... the Tantrika religion is very mysterious, inscrutable even to the Yogis." It is this worship of Shakti that is openly and universally practised. The idea of motherhood, i.e. the relation of a son to his mother, is also noticed in great measure. Protestantism as a force is not very significant in Europe, where the religion is, in fact, Roman Catholic. In the religion, Jehovah, Jesus, and the Trinity are secondary; there, the worship is for the Mother—She, the Mother, with the Child Jesus in her arms. The emperor cries "Mother", the field-marshal cries "Mother", the soldier with the flag in his hand cries "Mother", the seaman at the helm cries "Mother", the fisherman in his rags cries "Mother", the beggar in the street cries "Mother"! A million voices in a million ways, from a million places—from the palace, from the cottage, from the church, cry "Mother", "Mother", "Mother"! Everywhere is the cry "Ave Maria"; day and night, "Ave Maria", "Ave Maria"!

Next is the worship of the woman. This worship of Shakti is not lust, but is that Shakti-Pujâ, that worship of the Kumâri (virgin) and the Sadhavâ (the married woman whose husband is living), which is done in Varanasi, Kalighat, and other holy places. It is the worship of the Shakti, not in mere thought, not in imagination, but in actual, visible form. Our Shakti-worship is only in the holy places, and at certain times only is it performed; but theirs is in every place and always, for days, weeks, months, and years. Foremost is the woman's state, foremost is her dress, her seat, her food, her wants, and her comforts; the first honours in all respects are accorded to her. Not to speak of the noble-born, not to speak of the young and the fair, it is the worship of any and every woman, be she an acquaintance or a stranger. This Shakti-worship the Moors, the mixed Arab race, Mohammedan in religion, first introduced into Europe when they conquered Spain and ruled her for eight centuries. It was the Moors who first sowed in Europe the seeds of Western civilisation and Shakti-worship. In course of time, the Moors forgot this Shakti-Worship and fell from their position of strength, culture and glory, to live scattered and unrecognised in an unnoticed corner of Africa, and their power and civilisation passed over to Europe. The Mother, leaving the Moors, smiled Her loving blessings on the Christians and illumined their homes.

VI. FRANCE — PARIS

What is this Europe? Why are the black, the bronze, the yellow, the red inhabitants of Asia, Africa, and America bent low at the feet of the Europeans? Why are they the sole rulers in this Kali-Yuga? To understand this Europe one has to understand her through France, the fountain-head of everything that is highest in the West. The supreme power that rules the world is Europe, and of this Europe the great centre is Paris. Paris is the centre of Western civilization. Here, in Paris, matures and ripens every idea of Western ethics, manners and customs, light or darkness, good or evil. This Paris is like a vast ocean, in which there is many a precious gem, coral, and pearl, and in which, again, there are sharks and other rapacious sea-animals as well. Of Europe, the central field of work, the Karmakshetra, is France. A picturesque country, neither very cold nor very warm, very fertile, weather neither excessively wet nor extremely dry, sky clear, sun sweet, elms and oaks in abundance, grass-lands charming, hills and rivers small, springs delightful. Excepting some parts of China, no other country in the world have I seen that is so beautiful as France. That play of beauty in water and fascination in land, that madness in the air, that ecstasy in the sky! Nature so lovely—the men so fond of beauty! The rich and the poor, the young and the old, keep their houses, their rooms, the streets, the fields, the gardens, the walks, so artistically neat and clean—the whole country looks like a picture. Such love of nature and art have I seen nowhere else, except in Japan. The palatial structures, the gardens resembling Indra's paradise, the groves, even the farmer's fields—everywhere and in everything there is an attempt at beauty, an attempt at art, remarkable and effected with success, too.

From ancient times, France has been the scene of conflict among the Gauls, the Romans, the Franks, and other nations. After the destruction of the Roman Empire, the Franks obtained absolute dominion over Europe. Their King, Charlemagne, forced Christianity into Europe, by the power of the sword. Europe was made known in Asia by these Franks. Hence we still call the Europeans Franki, Feringi, Planki or Filinga, and so on.

Ancient Greece, the fountain-head of Western civilisation, sank into oblivion from the pinnacle of her glory, the vast empire of Rome was broken into pieces by the dashing waves of the barbarian invaders—the light of Europe went out; it was at this time that another barbarous race rose out of obscurity in Asia—the Arabs. With extraordinary rapidity, that Arab tide began to spread over the different parts of the world. Powerful Persia had to kiss the ground before the Arabs and adopt the Mohammedan religion, with the result that the Mussulman religion took quite a new shape; the religion of the Arabs and the civilisation of Persia became intermingled.

With the sword of the Arabs, the Persian civilisation began to disseminate in all directions. That Persian civilisation had been borrowed from ancient Greece and India. From the East and from the West, the waves of Mussulman invaders dashed violently on Europe and along them also, the light of wisdom and civilisation began dispersing the darkness of blind and barbarous Europe. The wisdom, learning, and arts of ancient Greece entered into Italy, overpowered the barbarians, and with their quickening impulse, life began to pulsate in the dead body of the world-capital of Rome. The pulsation of this new life took a strong and formidable shape in the city of Florence—old Italy began showing signs of new life. This is called Renaissance, the new birth. But this new birth was for Italy only a rebirth; while for the rest of Europe, it was the first birth. Europe was born in the sixteenth century A.D. i.e. about the time when Akbar, Jehangir, Shahjahan, and other Moghul Emperors firmly established their mighty empire in India.

Italy was an old nation. At the call of the Renaissance, she woke up and gave her response, but only to turn over on her side in bed, as it were, and fall fast asleep again. For various reasons, India also stirred up a little at this time. For three ruling generations from Akbar, learning, wisdom, and arts came to be much esteemed in India. But India was also a very old nation; and for some reason or other, she also did the same as Italy and slept on again.

In Europe, the tide of revival in Italy struck the powerful, young and new nation, the Franks. The torrent of civilisation, flowing from all quarters to Florence and there uniting, assumed a new form; but Italy had not the power within herself to hold that stupendous mass of fresh energy. The revival would have, as in India, ended there, had it not been for the good fortune of Europe that the new nation of the Franks gladly took up that energy, and they in vigour of their youthful blood boldly floated their national ship on the tide; and the current of that progress gradually gathered in volume and strength—from one it swelled into a thousand courses. The other nations of Europe greedily took the water of that tide into their own countries by cutting new channels, and increased its volume and speed by pouring their own lifeblood into it. That tidal wave broke, in the fullness of time, on the shores of India. It reached as far as the coast of Japan, and she became revitalised by bathing in its water. Japan is the new nation of Asia.

Paris is the fountain-head of European civilisation, as Gomukhi is of the Ganga. This huge metropolis is a vision of heaven on earth, the city of constant rejoicing. Such luxury, such enjoyments, such mirthfulness are neither in London nor in Berlin nor anywhere else. True, there is wealth in London and in New York, in Berlin there is learning and wisdom; but nowhere is that French soil, and above all, nowhere is that genius of the French man. Let there be wealth in plenty, let there be learning and wisdom, let there be beauty of nature also, elsewhere—but where is the man? This remarkable French character is the incarnation of the ancient Greek, as it were, that had died to be born again—always joyful, always full of enthusiasm, very light and silly, yet again exceedingly grave, prompt, and resolute to do every work, and again despondent at the least resistance. But that despondency is only for a moment with the Frenchman, his face soon after glowing again with fresh hope and trust.

The Paris University is the model of European universities. All the Academies of Science that are in the world are imitations of the French Academy. Paris is the first teacher of the founding of colonial empires. The terms used in military art in all languages are still mostly French. The style and diction of French writings are copied in all the European languages. Of science, philosophy, and art, this Paris is the mine. Everywhere, in every respect, there is imitation of the French. As if the French were the townspeople, and the other nations only villagers compared with them! What the French initiate, the Germans, the English, and other nations imitate, may be fifty or twenty-five years later, whether it be in learning, or in art, or in social matters. This French civilisation reached Scotland, and when the Scottish king became the king of England, it awoke and roused England; it was during the reign of the Stuart Dynasty of Scotland that the Royal Society and other institutions were established in England.

Again, France is the home of liberty. From here, the city of Paris, travelled with tremendous energy the power of the People, and shook the very foundations of Europe. From that time the face of Europe has completely changed and a new Europe has collie into existence. "Liberté, Equalité, Fraternité" is no more heard in France; she is now pursuing other ideas and other purposes, while the spirit of tile French Revolution is still working among the other nations of Europe.

One distinguished scientist of England told me the other day that Paris was the centre of the world, and that the more a nation would succeed in establishing its connection with the city of Paris, the more would that nation's progress in national life be achieved. Though such assertion is a partial exaggeration of fact, yet it is certainly true that if anyone has to give to the world any new idea, this Paris is the place for its dissemination. If one can gain the approbation of the citizens of Paris, that voice the whole of Europe is sure to echo back. The sculptor, the painter the musician the dancer, or any artist, if he can first obtain celebrate in Paris, acquires very easily the esteem and eulogy of other countries.

We hear only of the darker side of this Paris in our country—that it is a horrible place, a hell on earth. Some of the English hold this view; and the wealthy people of other countries, in whose eyes no other enjoyment is possible in life except the gratification of the senses, naturally see Paris as the home of immorality and enjoyments.

But it is the same in all big cities of the West, such as London, Berlin, Vienna, New York. The only difference is: in other countries the means of enjoyment are commonplace and vulgar, but the very dirt of civilised Paris is coated over with gold leaf. To compare tile refined enjoyments of Paris with the barbarity, in this respect, of other cities is to compare the wild boar's wallowing in the mire with the peacock's dance spreading out its feathers like a fan.

What nation in the world has not the longing to enjoy and live a life of pleasure? Otherwise, why should those who get rich hasten to Paris of all places? Why do kings and emperors, assuming other names come to Paris and live incognito and feel themselves happy by bathing in this whirlpool of sense-enjoyment? The longing is in all countries, and no pains are spared to satisfy it; the only difference is: the French have perfected it as a science, they know how to enjoy, they have risen to the highest rung of the ladder of enjoyment.

Even then, most of the vulgar dances and amusements are for the foreigner; the French people are very cautious, they never waste money for nothing. All those luxuries, those expensive hotels and cafés, at which the cost of a dinner is enough to ruin one, are for the rich foolish foreigner. The French are highly refined, profuse in etiquette, polished and suave in their manners, clever in drawing money from one's pocket; and when they do, they laugh in their sleeve.

Besides, there is another thing to note. Society, as it is among the Americans, Germans, and the English, is open to all nations; so the foreigner can quickly see the ins and outs of it. After an acquaintance of a few days, the American will invite one to live in his house for a while; the Germans also do the same; and the English do so after a longer acquaintance. But it is very different with the French; a Frenchman will never invite one to live with his family unless he is very intimately acquainted with him. But when a foreigner gets such all opportunity and has occasion and time enough to see and know the family, he forms quite a different opinion from what he generally hears. Is it not equally foolish of foreigners to venture an opinion on our national character, as they do, by seeing only the low quarters of Calcutta? So with Paris. The unmarried women in France are as well guarded as in our country, they cannot even mix flatly in society; only after marriage can they do so in company with their husbands. Like us, their negotiations for marriage are carried on by their parents. Being a jolly people, none of their big social functions will be complete without professional dancers, as with us performances of dancing-girls are given on the occasions of marriage and Puja. Living in a dark foggy country, the English are gloomy, make long faces and remark that such dances at one's home are very improper, but at a theatre they are all right. It should lie noted here that their dances may appear improper to our eyes, but not so with them, they being accustomed to them. The girl may, at a dance, appear in a dress showing the to neck and shoulders, and that is not taken as improper; and the English and Americans would not object to attending such dances, but on going hone, might not refrain from condemning tile French customs!

Again, the idea is the same everywhere regarding the chastity; of women, whose deviation from it is fraught with danger, but in the case of men it does not matter so much. The Frenchman is, no doubt, a little freer in this respect, and like the rich men of other countries cares not for criticism. Generally speaking, in Europe, the majority of men do not regard a little lax conduct as so very bad, and in the West, the same is the case with bachelors. The parents of young students consider it rather a drawback if the latter fight shy of women, lest they become effeminate. The one excellence which a man must have, in the West, is courage. Their word "virtue" and our word "Viratva" (heroism) are one and the same. Look to the derivation of the word "virtue" and see what they call goodness in man. For women, they hold chastity as the most important virtue, no doubt. One man marrying more than one wife is not so injurious to society as a woman having more than one husband at the same time, for the latter leads to the gradual decay of the race. Therefore, in all countries good care is taken to preserve the chastity of women. Behind this attempt of every society to preserve the chastity of women is seen the hand of nature. The tendency of nature is to multiply the population, and the chastity of women helps that tendency. Therefore, in being more anxious about the purity of women than of men, every society is only assisting nature in the fulfilment of her purpose.

The object of my speaking of these things is to impress upon you the fact that the life of each nation has a moral purpose of its own, and the manners and customs of a nation must be judged from the standpoint of that purpose. The Westerners should be seen through their eyes; to see them through our eyes, and for them to see us with theirs—both these are mistakes. The purpose of our life is quite the opposite of theirs. The Sanskrit name for a student, Brahmachârin, is synonymous with the Sanskrit word Kâmajit[1]. Our goal of life is Moksha; how can that be ever attained without Brahmacharya or absolute continence? Hence it is imposed upon our boys and youth as an indispensable condition during their studentship. The purpose of life in the West is Bhoga, enjoyment; hence much attention to strict Brahmacharya is not so indispensably necessary with them as it is with us.

Now, to return to Paris. There is no city in the world that can compare with modern Paris. Formerly it was quite different from what it is now—it was somewhat like the Bengali quarters of Varanasi, with zigzag lanes and streets, two houses joined together by an arch over the lane here and there, wells by the side

---

1. One who has full control over his passions.

of walls, and so on. In the last Exhibition they showed a model of old Paris, but that Paris has completely disappeared by gradual changes; the warfare and revolutions through which the city has passed have, each time, caused ravages in one part or another, razing every thing to the ground, and again, new Paris has risen in its place, cleaner and more extensive.

Modern Paris is, to a great extent, the creation of Napoleon III. He completed that material transformation of the city which had already been begun at the fall of the ancient monarchy. The student of the history of France need not be reminded how its people were oppressed by the absolute monarchs of France prior to the French Revolution. Napoleon III caused himself to be proclaimed Emperor by sheer force of arms, wading through blood. Since the first French Revolution, the French people were always fickle and thus a source of alarm to the Empire. Hence the Emperor, in order to keep his subjects contented and to please the ever-unstable masses of Paris by giving them work, went on continually making new and magnificent public roads and embankments and building gateways, theatres, and many other architectural structures, leaving the monuments of old Paris as before. Not only was the city traversed in all directions by new thoroughfares, straight and wide, with sumptuous houses raised or restored, but a line of fortification was built doubling the area of the city. Thus arose the boulevards, and the fine quarters of d'Antin and other neighbourhoods; and the avenue of the Champs Elysées, which is unique in the world was reconstructed. This avenue is so broad that down the middle and on both sides of it run gardens all along, and in one place it has taken a circular shape which comprises the city front, toward the West, called Place de la Concorde. Round this Place de la Concorde are statues in the form of women representing the eight chief towns of France. One of these statues represents the district of Strasburg. This district was wrested from the hands of the French by the Germans after the battle of 1870. The pain of this loss the French have not yet been able to get over, and that statue is still covered with flowers and garlands offered in memory of its dead spirit, as it were. As men place garlands over the tombs of their dead relations, so garlands are placed on that statue, at one time or another.

It seems to me that the Chandni Chauk of Delhi might have been at one time somewhat like this Place de la Concorde. Here and there columns of victory, triumphal arches and sculptural art in the form of huge statues of man and women, lions, etc., adorn the square.

A very big triumphal column in imitation of Trajan's Column, made of gun-metal (procured by melting 1,200 guns), is erected in Place Vendome in memory of the great hero, Napoleon I; on the sides are engraved the victories of his reign, and on the top is the figure of Napoleon Bonaparte. In the Place de la Bastille stands the Column of July (in memory of the Revolution of July 1789) on the side of the old fortress, "The Bastille", afterwards used as a State prison. Here were imprisoned those who incurred the king's displeasure. In those old days, without any trial or anything of the kind, the king would issue a warrant bearing the royal seal, called "Lettre de Cachet". Then, without any inquiry as to what good acts the victim had done for his country, or whether he was really guilty or not, without even any question as to what he actually did to incur the king's wrath, he would be at once thrown into tile Bastille. If the fair favourites of the kings were displeased with anyone, they could obtain by request a "Lettre de Cachet" from the king against that man, and the poor man would at once be sent to the Bastille. Of the unfortunate who were imprisoned there, very few ever came out. When, afterwards, the whole country rose as one man in revolt against such oppression and tyranny and raised the cry of "Individual liberty, All are equal, No one is high or low", the people of Paris in their mad excitement attacked the king and queen. The very first thing the mob did was to pull down the Bastille, the symbol of extreme tyranny of man over man, and passed the night in dancing, singing, and feasting on the spot. The king tried to escape, but the people managed to catch him, and hearing that the father-in-law of the king, the Emperor of Austria, was sending soldiers to aid his son-in-law, became blind with rage and killed the king and the queen. The whole French nation became mad in the name of liberty and equality—France became a republic—they killed all the nobility whom they could get hold of, and many of the nobility gave up their titles and rank and made common cause with the subject people. Not only so, they called all the nations of the world to rise—"Awake, kill the kings who are all tyrants, let all be free and have equal rights." Then all the kings of Europe began to tremble in fear lest this fire might spread into their countries, lest it might burn their thrones; and hence, determined to put it down, they attacked France from all directions. On the other side, the leaders of the French Republic proclaimed, "Our native land is in peril, come one and all", and the proclamation soon spread like the flames of a conflagration throughout the length and breadth of France. The young, the old, the men, the women, the rich, the poor, the high, the low, singing their martial song, La Marseillaise, the inspiring national song of France, came out—crowds of the poor French people, in rags, barefooted, in that severe cold, and half-starved—came out with guns on their shoulders—परित्राणाय ... विनाशाय च दुष्कृताम् for the destruction of the wicked and the salvation of their homes—and boldly faced the vast united force of Europe. The whole of Europe could not stand the onrush of that French army. At the head and front of the French army, stood a hero at the movement of whose finger the whole world trembled. He was Napoleon. With the edge of the sword and at the point of the bayonet, he thrust "Liberty, Equality, and Fraternity" into the very bone and marrow of Europe—and thus the victory of the tri-coloured Cocarde was achieved. Later, Napoleon became the Emperor of France and successfully accomplished the consolidation of the French Empire.

Subsequently, not being favoured with an heir to the throne, he divorced the partner of his life in weal and woe, the guiding angel of his good fortune, the Empress Josephine, and married the daughter of the Emperor of Austria. But the wheel of his luck turned with his desertion of Josephine, his army died in the snow and ice during his expedition against Russia. Europe, getting this opportunity, forced him to abdicate his throne, sent him as an exile to an island, and put on the throne one of the old royal dynasty. The wounded lion escaped from the island and presented himself again in France; the whole of France welcomed him and rallied under his banner, and the reigning king fled. But this luck was broken once for all, and it never returned. Again the whole of Europe united against him and defeated him at the battle of Waterloo. Napoleon boarded an English man-of-war and surrendered himself; the English exiled him and kept him as a lifelong prisoner in the distant island of St. Helena. Again a member of the old royal family of France was reinstated as king. Later on, the French people became restless under the old monarchy, rose in rebellion, drove away the king and his family and re-established the Republic In the course of time a nephew of the great Napoleon became a favourite with the people, and by means of intrigues he proclaimed himself Emperor. He was Napoleon III. For some time his reign was very powerful; but being defeated in conflict with the Germans he lost his throne, and France became once more a republic; and since then down to the present day she has continued to be republican.

VII. PROGRESS OF CIVILISATION

The theory of evolution, which is the foundation of almost all the Indian schools of thought, has now made its way into the physical science of Europe. It has been held by the religions of all other countries except India that the universe in its entirety is composed of parts distinctly separate from each other. God, nature, man—each stands by itself, isolated from one another; likewise, beasts, birds, insects, trees, the earth, stones, metals, etc., are all distinct from one another; God created them separate from the beginning.

Knowledge is to find unity in the midst of diversity—to establish unity among things which appear to us to be different from one another. That particular relation by which man finds this sameness is called Law. This is what is known as Natural Law.

I have said before that our education, intelligence,

and thought are all spiritual, all find expression in religion. In the West, their manifestation is in the external—in the physical and social planes. Thinkers in ancient India gradually came to understand that that idea of separateness was erroneous, that there was a connection among all those distinct objects—there was a unity which pervaded the whole universe—trees, shrubs, animals, men, Devas, even God Himself; the Advaitin reaching the climax in this line of thought declared all to be but the manifestations of the One. In reality, the metaphysical and the physical universe are one, and the name of this One is Brahman; and the perception of separateness is an error—they called it Mâyâ, Avidyâ or nescience. This is the end of knowledge.

If this matter is not comprehended at the present day by anyone outside India—for India we leave out of consideration—how is one to be regarded as a Pandit? However, most of the erudite men in the West are coming to understand this, in their own way—through physical science. But how that One has become the many—neither do we understand, nor do they. We, too, have offered the solution of this question by saying that it is beyond our understanding, which is limited. They, too, have done the same. But the variations that the One has undergone, the different sorts of species and individuality It is assuming—that can be understood, and the enquiry into this is called Science.

So almost all are now evolutionists in the West. As small animals through gradual steps change into bigger ones, and big animals sometimes deteriorate and become smaller and weaker, and in the course of time die out—so also, man is not born into a civilised state all on a sudden; in these days an assertion to the contrary is no longer believed in by anybody among the thoughtful in the West, especially because the evidence that their ancestors were in a savage state only a few centuries ago, and from that state such a great transformation has taken place in so short a time. So they say that all men must have gradually evolved, and are gradually evolving from the uncivilised state.

Primitive men used to mange their work with implements of wood and stone; they wore skins and leaves, and lived in mountain-caves or in huts thatched with leaves made somewhat after the fashion of birds' nests, and thus somehow passed their days. Evidence in proof of this is being obtained in all countries by excavating the earth, and also in some few places, men at that same primitive stage are still living. Gradually men learnt to use metal—soft metals such as tin and copper—and found out how to make tools and weapons by fusing them. The ancient Greeks, the Babylonians, and the Egyptians did not know the use of iron for a long time—even when they became comparatively civilised and wrote books and used gold and silver. At that time, the Mexicans, the Peruvians, the Mayas, and other races among the aborigines of the New World were comparatively civilised and used to build large temples; the use of gold and silver was quite common amongst them (in fact the greed for their gold and silver led the Spaniards to destroy them). But they managed to make all these things, toiling very hard with flint instruments—they did not know iron even by name.

In the primitive stage, man used to kill wild animals and fish by means of bows and arrows, or by the use of a net, and live upon them. Gradually, he learnt to till the ground and tend the cattle. Taming wild animals, he made them work for him or reared them for his own eating when necessary; the cow, horse, hog, elephant, camel, goat, sheep, fowls, birds, and other animals became domesticated; of all these, the dog is the first friend of man.

So, in course of time, the tilling of the soil came into existence. The fruits, roots, herbs, vegetables, and the various cereals eaten by man are quite different now from what they were when they grew in a wild state. Through human exertion and cultivation wild fruits gained in size and acquired toothsomeness, and wild grass was transformed into delicious rice. Constant changes are going on, no doubt, in nature, by its own processes. Few species of trees and plants, birds and beasts are being always created in nature through changes, brought about by time, environment and other causes. Thus before the creation of man, nature was changing the trees, plants, and other animals by slow and gentle degrees, but when man came on the scene, he began to effect changes with rapid strides. He continually transported the native fauna and flora of one country to another, and by crossing them various new species of plants and animals were brought into existence.

In the primitive stage there was no marriage, but gradually matrimonial relations sprang up. At first, the matrimonial relation depended, amongst all communities, on the mother. There was not much fixity about the father, the children were named after the mother: all the wealth was in the hands of the women, for they were to bring up the children. In the course of time, wealth, the women included, passed into the hands of the male members. The male said, "All this wealth and grain are mine; I have grown these in the fields or got them by plunder and other means; and if anyone dispute my claims and want to have a share of them, I will fight him." In the same way he said, "All these women are exclusively mine; if anyone encroach upon my right in them, I will fight him." Thus there originated the modern marriage system. Women became as much the property of man as his slaves and chattels. The ancient marriage custom was that the males of one tribe married the women of another; and even then the women were snatched away by force. In course of time, this business of taking away the bride by violence dropped away, and marriage was contracted with the mutual consent of both parties. But every custom leaves a faint trace of itself behind, and even now we find in every country a mock attack is made on such occasions upon the bridegroom. In Bengal and Europe, handfuls of rice are thrown at the bridegroom, and in Northern India the bride's women friends abuse the bridegroom's party calling them names, anti so on.

Society began to be formed and it varied according to different countries. Those who lived on the seashore mostly earned their livelihood by fishing in the sea, those on the plains by agriculture. The mountaineers kept large flocks of sheep, and the dwellers in the desert tended goats and camels. Others lived in the forests and maintained themselves by hunting. The dwellers on the plain learnt agriculture; their struggle for existence became less keen; they had time for thought and culture, and thus became more and more civilised. But with the advance of civilisation their bodies grew weaker and weaker. The difference in physique between those who always lived in the open air and whose principal article of food was animal diet, and others who dwelt in houses and lived mostly on grains and vegetables, became greater and greater. The hunter, the shepherd, the fisherman turned robbers or pirates whenever food became scarce and plundered the dwellers in the plains. These, in their turn, united themselves in bands of large numbers for the common interest of self-preservation; and thus little kingdoms began to be formed.

The Devas lived on grains and vegetables, were civilised, dwelt in villages, towns, and gardens, and wore woven clothing. The Asuras[1] dwelt in the hills and mountains, deserts or on the sea-shores, lived on wild animals, and the roots and fruits of the forests, and on what cereals they could get from the Devas in exchange for these or for their cows and sheep, and wore the hides of wild animals. The Devas were weak in body and could not endure hardships; the Asuras, on the other hand, were hardy with frequent fasting and were quite capable of suffering all sorts of hardships.

Whenever food was scarce among the Asuras, they set out from their hills and sea-shores to plunder towns and villages. At times they attacked the Devas for wealth and grains and whenever the Devas failed to unite themselves in large numbers against them, they were sure to die at the hands of the Asuras. But the Devas being stronger in intelligence, commenced inventing, all sorts of machines for warfare. The Brahmâstra, Garudâstra Vaishnavâstra, Shaivâstra— all these weapons of miraculous power belonged to the Devas. The Asuras fought with ordinary weapons, but they were enormously strong. They defeated the Devas repeatedly, but they never cared to become civilised, or learn agriculture, or cultivate their intellect. If the victorious Asuras tried to reign over the vanquished Devas in Svarga, they were sure to be outwitted by the Devas' superior intellect and skill, and, before long, turned into their slaves. At other times, the Asuras returned to their own places after plundering. The Devas, whenever they were united, forced them to retire, mark you, either into the hills or forests, or to the sea-shore. Gradually each party gained in num-

1. The terms "Devas" and "Asuras" are used here in the sense in which they occur in the Gitâ (XVI), i.e. races in which the Daivi (divine) or the Âsuri (non-divine) traits preponderate.

bers and became stronger and stronger; millions of Devas were united, and so were millions of Asuras. Violent conflicts and fighting went on, and along with them, the intermingling of these two forces.

From the fusion of these different types and races our modern societies, manners, and customs began to be evolved. New ideas sprang up and new sciences began to be cultivated. One class of men went on manufacturing articles of utility and comfort, either by manual or intellectual labour. A second class took upon themselves the charge of protecting them, and all proceeded to exchange these things. And it so happened that a band of fellows who were very clever undertook to take these things from one place to another and on the plea of remuneration for this, appropriated the major portion of their profit as their due. One tilled the ground, a second guarded the produce from being robbed, a third took it to another place and a fourth bought it. The cultivator got almost nothing; he who guarded the produce took away as much of it as he could by force; the merchant who brought it to the market took the lion's share; and the buyer had to pay out of all proportion for the things, and smarted under the burden! The protector came to be known as the king; he who took the commodities from one place to another was the merchant. These two did not produce anything—but still snatched away the best part of things and made themselves fat by virtually reaping most of the fruits of the cultivator's toil and labour. Tile poor fellows who produced all these things had often to go without his meals and cry to God for help!

Now, with the march of events, all these matters' grew more and more involved, knots upon knots multiplied, and out of this tangled network has evolved our modern complex society. But the marks of a bygone: character persist and do not die out completely. Those who in their former births tended sheep or lived by fishing or the like take to habits of piracy, robbery, and similar occupations in their civilised incarnation also. With no forests to hunt in, no hills or mountains in the neighbourhood on which to tend the flocks—by the accident of birth in a civilised society, he cannot get enough opportunity for either hunting, fishing, or grazing, cattle—he is obliged therefore to rob or steal, impelled by his own nature; what else can he do? And the worthy daughters of those far-famed ladies[1] of the Paurânika age, whose names we are to repeat every morning—they can no longer marry more than one husband at a time, even if they want to, and so they turn unchaste. In these and other ways, men of different types and dispositions, civilised and savage, born with the nature of the Devas and the Asuras have become fused together and form modern society. And that is why we see, in every society, God plating in these various forms—the Sâdhu Nârâyana, the robber Narayana, and so on. Again, the character of any particular society came to be determined as Daivi (divine) or Âsuri (non-divine) quality, in proportion as one or the other of these two different types of persons preponderated within it.

The whole of tile Asian civilization was first evolved on the plains near large rivers and on fertile soils—on the banks of the Ganga, the Yangtse-Kiang, and the Euphrates. The original foundation of all these civilisations is agriculture, and in all of there the Daivi nature predominates. Most of the European civilization, on the other hand, originated either in hilly countries or on the sea coasts—piracy and robbery form the basis of this civilisation; there the Asuri nature is preponderant.

So far as can be inferred in modern times, Central Asia and the deserts of Arabia seem to have been the home of the Asuras. Issuing from their fastnesses, these shepherds and hunters, the descendants of the Asuras, being united in hordes after hordes, chased the civilized Devas and scattered them all over the world.

Of course there was a primitive race of aborigines in the continent of Europe. They lived in mountain-caves, and the more intelligent among them erected platforms by planting sticks in tile comparatively shallow parts of the water and built houses thereon. They used arrows, spearheads, knives, and axes, all made of flint, and managed every kind of work with them.

Gradually the current of the Asian races began to break forth upon Europe, and as its effects, some parts became comparatively civilised; the language of

---
1. Ahalyâ, Târâ, Mandodari, Kunti, and Draupadi.

a certain people in Russia resembles the languages of Southern India.

But for the most part these barbarians remained as barbarous as ever, till a civilised race from Asia Minor conquered the adjacent parts of Europe and founded a high order of new civilization: to us they are known as Yavanas, to the Europeans as Greeks.

Afterwards, in Italy, a barbarous tribe known as the Romans conquered the civilised Etruscans, assimilated their culture and learning, and established a civilization of their own on the ruins of that of the conquered race. Gradually, the Romans carried their victorious arms in all directions; all the barbarous tribes in the southwest of Europe came under the suzerainty of Rome; only the barbarians of the forests living in the northern regions retained independence. In the efflux of time, however, the Romans became enervated by being slaves to wealth and luxury, and at that time Asia again let loose her armies of Asuras on Europe. Driven from their homes by the onslaught of these Asuras, the barbarians of Northern Europe fell upon the Roman Empire, and Rome was destroyed. Encountered by the force of this Asian invasion, a new race sprang up through the fusion of the European barbarians with the remnants of the Romans and Greeks. At that time, the Jews being conquered and driven away from their homes by the Romans, scattered themselves throughout Europe, and with them their new religion, Christianity, also spread all over Europe. All these different races and their creeds and ideas, all these different hordes of Asuras, heated by the fire of constant struggle and warfare, began to melt and fuse in Mahâmâyâ's crucible; and from that fusion the modern European race has sprung up.

Thus a barbarous, very barbarous European race came into existence, with all shades of complexion from the swarthy colour of the Hindus to the milk-white colour of the North, with black, brown, red, or white hair, black, grey, or blue eyes, resembling the fine features of face, the nose and eyes of the Hindus, or the flat faces of the Chinese. For some time they continued to tight among themselves; those of the north leading the life of pirates harassed and killed the comparatively civilised races. In the meantime, however, the two heads of the Christian Churches, the Pope (in French and Italian, Pape[2]) of Italy and the Patriarch of Constantinople, insinuating themselves, began to exercise their authority over these brutal barbarian hordes, over their kings, queens, and peoples.

On the other side, again Mohammedanism arose in the deserts of Arabia. The wild Arabs, inspired by tile teachings of a great sage, bore down upon the earth with all irresistible force and vigour. That torrent, carrying everything before it, entered Europe from both the East and the West, and along with this tide the learning and culture of India and ancient Greece were carried into Europe.

A tribe of Asuras from Central Asia known as the Seljuk Tartars, accepted Mohammedanism and conquered Asia Minor and other countries of Asia. The various attempts of the Arabs to conquer India proved unsuccessful. The wave of Mohammedan conquest, which had swallowed the whole earth, had to fall back before India. They attacked Sindh once, but could not told it: and they did not make any other attempt after that.

But a few centuries afterwards, when the Turks and other Tartar races were converted from Buddhism to Mohammedanism—at that time they conquered the Hindus, Persians, and Arabs, and brought all of them alike under their subjection. Of all the Mohammedan conquerors of India, none was an Arab or a Persian; they were all Turks and Tartars. In Rajputana, all the Mohammedan invaders were called Turks, and that is a true and historical fact. The Chârans of Rajputana sang "turuganko bodhi jor —The Turks are very powerful"—and that was true. From Kutubuddin down to the Mogul Emperors—all of them are Tartars. They are the same race to which the Tibetans belong; only they have become Mohammedans and changed their flat round faces by intermarrying with the Hindus and Persians. They are the same ancient races of Asuras. Even today they are reigning on the thrones of Kabul, Persia, Arabia, and Constantinople, and the Gândhâris (natives of Kandahar) and Persians are still the slaves of the Turks. The vast Empire of China, too, is lying at the feet of the Manchurian Tartars; only these Manchus have not given up their religion, have not become Mohammedans, they are disciples of the

---
2. pronounced as *Pâp*.

Grand Lama. These Asuras never care for learning and cultivation of the intellect; the only thing they understand is fighting. Very little of the warlike spirit is possible without a mixture of that blood; and it is that Tartar blood which is seen in the vigorous, martial spirit of Northern Europe, especially in the Russians, who have three-fourths of Tartar blood in their veins. The fight between the Devas and the Asuras will continue yet for a long time to come. The Devas marry the Asura girls and the Asuras snatch away Deva brides—it is this that leads to the formation of powerful mongrel races.

The Tartars seized and occupied the throne of tile Arabian Caliph, took possession of Jerusalem, the great Christian place of pilgrimage, and other plates, would not allow pilgrims to visit the holy sepulchre, and killed many Christians. The heads of the Christian Churches grew mad with rage and roused their barbarian disciples throughout Europe, who in their turn inflamed the kings and their subjects alike. Hordes of European barbarians rushed towards Asia Minor to deliver Jerusalem from the hands of the infidels. A good portion of them cut one another's throats, others died of disease, while the rest were killed by the Mohammedans. However, the blood was up of the wild barbarians, and no sooner had the Mohammedans killed them than they arrived in fresh numbers—with that clogged obstinacy of a wild savage. They thought nothing even of plundering their own men, and making meals of Mohammedans when they found nothing better. It is well known that the English king Richard had a liking for Mohammedan flesh.

Here the result was the same, as usually happens in a war between barbarians and civilised men. Jerusalem and other places could not be conquered. But Europe began to be civilised. The English, French, German, and other savage nations who dressed themselves in hides and ate raw flesh, came in contact with Asian civilisation. An order of Christian soldiers of Italy and other countries, corresponding to our Nâgâs, began to learn philosophy; and one of their sects, the Knights Templars, became confirmed Advaita Vedantists, and ended by holding Christianity up to ridicule. Moreover, as they had amassed enormous riches, the kings of Europe, at the orders of the Pope, and under the pretext of saving religion, robbed and exterminated them.

On the other side, a tribe of Mohammedans, called the Moors, established a civilised kingdom in Spain, cultivated various branches of knowledge, and founded the first university in Europe. Students flocked from all parts, from Italy, France, and even from far-off England. The sons of royal families came to learn manners, etiquette civilisation, and the art of war. Houses, temples, edifices, and other architectural buildings began to be built after a new style.

But the whole of Europe was gradually transformed into a vast military camp—and this is even now the case. When the Mohammedans conquered any kingdom, their king kept a large part for himself, and the rest he distributed among his generals. These men did not pay any rent but had to supply the king with a certain number of soldiers in time of need. Thus the trouble of keeping a standing army always ready was avoided, and a powerful army was created which served only in time of war. This same idea still exists to a certain extent in Rajputana, and it was brought into the West by the Mohammedans. The Europeans took this system from the Mohammedans. But whereas with the Mohammedans there were the king and his groups of feudatory chiefs and their armies, and the rest—the body of the people—were ordinary subjects who were left unmolested in time of war—in Europe, on the other hand, the king and his groups of feudatory chiefs were on one side, and they turned all the subject people into their slaves. Everyone had to live under the shelter of a military feudatory chief, as his man, and then only was he allowed to live; he had to be always ready to fight at any time, at the word of command.

What is the meaning of the "Progress of Civilisation" which the Europeans boast so much about? The meaning of it is the successful accomplishment of the desired object by the justification of wrong means, i.e. by making the end justify the means. It makes acts of theft, falsehood, and hanging appear proper under certain circumstances; it vindicates Stanley's whipping of the hungry Mohammedan guards who accompanied him, for stealing a few mouthfuls of bread; it guides and justifies the well-known European ethics which says, "Get out from this place, I want to come in and possess it", the truth of which is borne out by the evidence of history, that where-ever the Europeans have gone, there has followed the extinction of the aboriginal races. In London, this "progress of civilisation" regards unfaithfulness in conjugal life, and, in Paris, the running away of a man, leaving his wife and children helpless and committing suicide as a mistake and not a crime.

Now compare the first three centuries of the quick spread of the civilisation of Islam with the corresponding period of Christianity. Christianity, during its first three centuries, was not even successful ill making itself known to the world; and since the day when the sword of Constantine made a place for it in his kingdom, what support has Christianity ever lent to the spread of civilisation, either spiritual or secular? What reward did the Christian religion offer to that European Pandit who sought to prove for the first time that the Earth is a revolving planet? What scientist has ever been hailed with approval and enthusiasm by the Christian Church? Can the literature of the Christian flock consistently meet the requirements of legal jurisprudence, civil or criminal, or of arts and trade policies? Even now the "Church" does not sanction the diffusion of profane literature. Is it possible, still, for a man who has penetrated deep into modern learning and science to be an absolutely sincere Christian? In the New Testament there is no covert or overt praise of any arts and sciences. But there is scarcely any science or branch of art that is not sanctioned and held up for encouragement, directly or indirectly, in the Koran, or in the many passages of the Hadis, the traditional sayings of Mohammed. The greatest thinkers of Europe—Voltaire, Darwin, Büchner, Flammarion, Victor Hugo, anti a host of others like them—are in the present times denounced by Christianity and are victims of the vituperative tongues of its orthodox community. On the other hand, Islam regards such people to be believers in the existence of God, but only wanting in faith in the Prophet. Let there be a searching investigation into the respective merits of the two religions as regards their helpfulness, or the throwing of obstacles in the path of progress, and it will be seen that wherever Islam has gone, there it has preserved the aboriginal inhabitants—there those races still exist, their language and their nationality abide even to the present day.

Where can Christianity show such an achievement? Where are, today, the Arabs of Spain, and the aboriginal races of America? What treatment are the Christians according to the European Jews? With the single exception of charitable organisations no other line of work in Europe is in harmony with the teachings of the Gospel. Whatever heights of progress Europe has attained, every one of them has been gained by its revolt against Christianity—by its rising against the gospel. If Christianity had its old paramount sway in Europe today, it would have lighted the fire of the Inquisition against such modern scientists as Pasteur and Koch, and burnt Darwin and others of his school at the stake. In modern Europe Christianity and civilisation are two different things. Civilisation has now girded up her loins to destroy her old enemy, Christianity, to overthrow the clergy, and to wring educational and charitable institutions from their hands. But for the ignorance-ridden rustic masses, Christianity would never have been able for a moment to support its present despised existence, and would have been pulled out by its roots; for the urban poor are, even now, enemies of the Christian Church! Now compare this with Islam. In the Mohammedan countries, all the ordinances are firmly established upon the Islamic religion, and its own preachers are greatly venerated by all the officials of the State, and teachers of other religions also are respected.

The European civilisation may be likened to a piece of cloth, of which these are the materials: its loom is a vast temperate hilly country on the sea-shore; its cotton, a strong warlike mongrel race formed by the intermixture of various races; its warp is warfare in defence of one's self and one's religion. The one who wields the sword is great, and the one who cannot, gives up his independence and lines under the protection of some warrior's sword. Its woof is commerce. The means to this civilisation is the sword; its auxiliary—courage and strength; its aim enjoyment here and thereafter.

And how is it with us? The Aryans are lovers of

peace, cultivators of the soil, and are quite happy and contented if they can only rear their families undisturbed. In such a life they have ample leisure, and therefore greater opportunity of being thoughtful and civilised. Our King Janaka tilled the soil with his own hands, and he was also the greatest of the knowers of Truth, of his time. With us, Rishis, Munis, and Yogis have been born from the very beginning; they have known from the first that the world is a chimera. Plunder and fight as you may, the enjoyment that you are seeking is only in peace; and peace, in the renunciation of physical pleasures. Enjoyment lies not in physical development, but in the culture of the mind and the intellect.

It was the knowers who reclaimed the jungles for cultivation. Then, over that cleared plot of land was built the Vedic altar; in that pure sky of Bhârata, up rose the sacred smoke of Yajnas; in that air breathing peace, the Vedic Mantras echoed and re-echoed—and cattle and other beasts grazed without any fear of danger. The place of the sword was assigned at the feet of learning and Dharma. Its only work was to protect Dharma and save the lives of men and cattle The hero was the protector of the weak in danger—the Kshatriya. Ruling over the plough and the sword was Dharma, the protector of all. He is the King of kings; he is ever-awake even while the world sleeps. Everyone was free under the protection of Dharma.

And what your European Pundits say about the Aryan's swooping down from some foreign land, snatching away the lands of the aborigines and settling in India by exterminating them, is all pure nonsense, foolish talk! Strange, that our Indian scholars, too, say amen to them; and all these monstrous lies are being taught to our boys! This is very bad indeed.

I am an ignoramus myself; I do not pretend to any scholarship; but with the little that I understand, I strongly protested against these ideas at the Paris Congress. I have been talking with the Indian and European savants on the subject, and hope to raise many objections to this theory in detail, when time permits. And this I say to you—to our Pundits—also, "You are learned men, hunt up your old books and scriptures, please, and draw your own conclusions."

Whenever the Europeans find an opportunity, they exterminate the aborigines and settle down in ease and comfort on their lands; and therefore they think the Aryans must have done the same! The Westerners would be considered wretched vagabonds if they lived in their native homes depending wholly on their own internal resources, and so they have to run wildly about the world seeking how they can feed upon the fat of the land of others by spoliation and slaughter; and therefore they conclude the Aryans must have done the same! But where is your proof? Guess-work? Then keep your fanciful guesses to yourselves!

In what Veda, in what Sukta, do you find that the Aryans came into India from a foreign country? Where do you get the idea that they slaughtered the wild aborigines? What do you gain by talking such nonsense? Vain has been your study of the Râmâyana; why manufacture a big fine story out of it?

Well, what is the Ramayana? The conquest of the savage aborigines of Southern India by the Aryans! Indeed! Râmachandra is a civilised Aryan king, and with whom is he fighting? With King Râvana of Lankâ. Just read the Ramayana, and you will find that Ravana was rather more and not less civilised than Ramachandra. The civilisation of Lanka was rather higher, and surely not lower, than that of Ayodhyâ. And then, when were these Vânaras (monkeys) and other Southern Indians conquered? They were all, on the other hand, Ramachandra's friends and allies. Say which kingdoms of Vâli and Guhaka were annexed by Ramachandra?

It was quiet possible, however, that in a few places there were occasional fights between the Aryans and the aborigines; quite possible, that one or two cunning Munis pretended to meditate with closed eyes before their sacrificial fires in the jungles of the Râkshasas, waiting, however, all the time to see when the Rakshasas would throw stones and pieces of bone at them. No sooner had this been done than they would go whining to the kings. The mail clad kings armed with swords and weapons of steel would come on fiery steeds. But how long could the aborigines fight with their sticks and stones? So they were killed or chased away, and the kings returned to their capital. Well, all this may have been, hut how does this prove that their lands were taken away by the Aryans? Where in the Ramayana do you find that?

The loom of the fabric of Aryan civilisation is a vast, warm, level country, interspersed with broad, navigable rivers. The cotton of this cloth is composed of highly civilised, semi-civilised, and barbarian tribes, mostly Aryan. Its warp is Varnâshramâchâra[1], and its woof, the conquest of strife and competition in nature.

And may I ask you, Europeans, what country you have ever raised to better conditions? Wherever you have found weaker races, you have exterminated them by the roots, as it were. You have settled on their lands, and they are gone for ever. What is the history of your America, your Australia, and New Zealand, your Pacific islands and South Africa? Where are those aboriginal races there today? They are all exterminated, you have killed them outright, as if they were wild beasts. It is only where you have not the power to do so, and there only, that other nations are still alive.

But India has never done that. The Aryans were kind and generous; and in their hearts which were large and unbounded as the ocean, and in their brains, gifted with superhuman genius, all these ephemeral and apparently pleasant but virtually beastly processes never found a place. And I ask you, fools of my own country, would there have been this institution of Varnashrama if the Aryans had exterminated the aborigines in order to settle on their lands?

The object of the peoples of Europe is to exterminate all in order to live themselves. The aim of the Aryans is to raise all up to their own level, nay, even to a higher level than themselves. The means of European civilisation is the sword; of the Aryans, the division into different Varnas. This system of division into different Varnas is the stepping-stone to civilisation, making one rise higher and higher in proportion to one's learning and culture. In Europe, it is everywhere victory to the strong and death to the weak. In the land of Bhârata, every social rule is for the protection of the weak.

---

[1]. The old Aryan institution of the four castes and stages of life. The former comprise the Brâhmin, Kshatriya, Vaishya, and Shudra, and the latter, Brahmacharya (student life), Gârhasthya (house-holder's life), Vânaprastha (hermit life), and Sannyâsa (life of renunciation).

Discovery Publisher is a multimedia publisher whose mission is to inspire and support personal transformation, spiritual growth and awakening. We strive with every title to preserve the essential wisdom of the author, spiritual teacher, thinker, healer, and visionary artist.

www.ingramcontent.com/pod-product-compliance
Lightning Source LLC
Chambersburg PA
CBHW080535170426
43195CB00016B/2572